Rhetoric and Community

Studies in Rhetoric/Communication
Thomas W. Benson, Series Editor

Rhetoric and Community
Studies in Unity and Fragmentation

Edited by J. Michael Hogan

University of South Carolina Press

© 1998 University of South Carolina

Published in Columbia, South Carolina, by the
University of South Carolina Press

Manufactured in the United States of America

02 01 00 99 98 5 4 3 2 1

Library of Congress Cataloging-in-Publication Data

Rhetoric and community : studies in unity and fragmentation /
    edited
by J. Michael Hogan.
      p.   cm. — (Studies in rhetoric/communication)
    Includes bibliographical references (p.) and index.
    ISBN 1-57003-185-1
    1. Rhetoric—Social aspects.   I. Hogan, J. Michael, 1953–.
II. Series.
P301.5.S63R48 1997
808—dc21   97-33888

For Leland M. Griffin

Contents

Contents

Foreword

David Zarefsky

Over coffee during the 1987 convention of the Central States Speech Association, Michael Leff and I reflected on the revival of scholarly interest in studies of public address. Lamenting the fact that there were no existing vehicles for facilitating the kind of dialogue we thought would be helpful, we came up with the idea of an intensive public address conference. It would be small and highly interactive, and the format would consist of sessions in which a single scholar would offer a major paper analyzing one or more texts, another scholar would respond, and then a full hour would be available for discussion. Owing largely to Mike Leff's energy and commitment, our vague idea was brought to fruition in a conference held at the University of Wisconsin in June of 1988.

Participants found the experience so valuable that there soon was demand for a successor conference, and before long it came to be widely understood (I deliberately do not say "institutionalized") that it would be a biennial event hosted on different campuses. Subsequent public address conferences were held in 1990 at Northwestern University, in 1992 at the University of Minnesota, in 1994 at Indiana University, and in 1996 at the University of Illinois.

The papers and responses contained in this volume had their origin as presentations at the Fourth Biennial Public Address Conference, at Indiana University in October of 1994. Every aspect of the Indiana conference, from the selection of presenters to the logistics of the event itself, was in the capable hands of a four-person committee consisting of James R. Andrews, Robert L. Ivie, and John Louis Lucaites, all members of the faculty of the Department of Speech Communication at Indiana, and J. Michael Hogan, now at Pennsylvania State University. They deserve the sincere thanks not only of all who attended the conference but also of the readers of this volume, who will benefit greatly from the fruits of their work.

One of the unwritten traditions of the Public Address Conference is that some time is carved out at each one to honor and celebrate the work of a distinguished scholar in the field. It was my good fortune to be invited to speak at Indiana about the conference honoree, who is my mentor, colleague, and good friend, Leland M. Griffin, professor emeritus of communication studies at Northwestern University.

Leland Griffin came to Northwestern in the fall of 1956 and remained on the faculty for 33 years, until his retirement. He had taught previously at Boston University and Washington University after receiving his doctorate from Cornell in 1950. At Northwestern, Griffin taught a variety of graduate and undergraduate courses in public address, rhetorical theory, and criticism, as well as beginning courses in public speaking. He took a strong interest in his students. Undergraduates often stayed in touch with him long after the class was over and even after they had left the University. And graduate students eagerly sought him out to direct their theses and dissertations. During his years at Northwestern he directed almost forty doctoral dissertations and a large number of master's theses. Among Griffin's doctoral advisees are several who became significant scholars and teachers in the communication discipline. The range of dissertation topics is indicative of the breadth of Griffin's interests. To be sure, a number focused on early-nineteenth-century public address or on contemporary social movements, his own special research interests. But he also directed textual critiques, Burkean readings of rhetorical artifacts, studies of controversy and debate, explorations of fundamental issues in classical and medieval rhetoric, and studies in homiletics. And he made a significant contribution to the work of promising scholars in each of these areas.

On the occasion of Leland Griffin's retirement from Northwestern, a group of his students and colleagues announced plans to publish a festschrift in his honor. Fitting into both categories, I became the editor of the volume titled *Rhetorical Movement* and published in 1993 by Northwestern University Press. Its nine essays, taken together, illustrate the topics and the methods that engage Griffin's attention as well as the scope and reach of his own interests. From classical rhetoric to contemporary culture, he found wisdom and insight in the phenomenon of human communication.

This volume is not yet another *festshrift* in honor of Leland Griffin. The essays presented here reach beyond even Griffin's broad and diverse interests, and none is written by a former student. The volume is, however, dedicated to Griffin—and appropriately so. Community is an important value for Leland M. Griffin, so it is particularly appropriate that the Fourth Biennial Public Address Conference featured the theme of "rhetoric and community." This volume contains revised versions of the major research papers presented there. Taken together, they reveal the fertile nature of contemporary studies of public address. They are varied but rigorous in method, rich in evidence and supporting material, diverse in their subjects and modes of organization, compelling in their argument, provocative in their insight, and productive of further inquiry and speculation. They offer the kind of intellectual feast that can be found in Leland Griffin's own work. It is especially fitting that he was the honoree at the conference where they were first presented.

Preface
Rhetoric and Community

J. Michael Hogan

As a young speechwriter for Richard Nixon, Patrick Buchanan once expounded upon the politics of polarization. "If we tear the country in half," Buchanan assured his boss in a perversely optimistic memo, "we can pick up the bigger half."[1] Two decades later Buchanan still viewed the world in much the same way, as he declared "cultural war" on Bill Clinton and the Democrats in a remarkable speech to the 1992 Republican National Convention. On the one side in a "struggle for the soul of America," Buchanan declared, stood the defenders of Judeo-Christian values and the principles of the Founders. On the other side were the Democrats—the party of the "militant ... homosexual rights movement," "radical feminism," "environmental extremists," "carping critics," and "prophets of doom."[2]

Buchanan, of course, hardly has a monopoly on the rhetoric of polarization. Nor has such rhetoric been the exclusive domain of the radical Right. In a speech at Kean College in 1993 Khalid Abdul Muhammad, an aide to Nation of Islam leader Louis Farrakhan, railed not only against "blood-sucking" Jews and "honkeys" but also against fellow African Americans: those who had "made it" in the white man's world of politics, athletics, and entertainment. In Khalid Muhammad's view these black achievers were not to be celebrated as role models but, rather, condemned as "boot-lickin' . . . pasteurized, homogenized nigger[s]."[3]

No wonder that a growing number of social and political commentators fear that the United States has lost all sense of "community"—that repository of shared purpose, values, and traditions which historically has defined the American character. To many it seems that the United States has turned some crucial corner, that the very fabric of our society has begun to unravel. The signs of stress and fragmentation appear everywhere, not just in our national political and cultural dialogue but in all of the various communities that define our social lives—our families, our neighborhoods, our towns and cities, our professions, and our social and cultural associations.

Social and political fragmentation is hardly unprecedented in the United States. American history is replete with episodes of polarization, intolerance, hatred, and alienation. Wars invariably have led Americans to question their nation's identity and purposes, as have conflicts over immigration, ethnic differences, and religious doctrines. Surely, one might argue, Americans are no more divided today than they were over states' rights or abolitionism in the mid-nineteenth century or over the war in Vietnam or civil rights a hundred years later. The United States survived those cataclysms and, some would argue, emerged with new and even stronger conceptions of national purpose and character.

Still, no less a historian than Arthur Schlesinger Jr. senses something different and especially troubling about new threats to the United States's "bonds of national cohesion." Focusing his critique upon a new "multicultural dogma" that "belittles *unum* and glorifies *pluribus*," Schlesinger fears that rejecting "the idea of a melting pot," or "the concept of one people,'" can only lead to "separate ethnic and racial communities," with "assimilation" replaced "by fragmentation, integration by separatism." Schlesinger concedes that the rise of ethnic consciousness has had some positive effects: Americans have learned about "other races, other cultures, other continents," developing "a more complex and invigorating sense of the world—and of themselves." Pressed too far, however, this dogma "reverses the historic theory of America as one people—the theory that has thus far managed to keep American society whole." If these "separatist tendencies go on unchecked," Schlesinger warns, "the result can only be the fragmentation, resegregation, and tribalization of American life."[4]

For Schlesinger, as well as for those on the other side of the debate over multiculturalism, the problem of community in the United States is rooted in racial and ethnic differences—differences that historically (depending upon one's political viewpoint) have been either transcended or suppressed. Others blame our political and cultural traditions, as in Robert Bellah and his colleagues' critique of an American "individualism" grown "cancerous," an individualism that has overwhelmed larger commitments to family, religion, and the political community.[5] Still others focus upon class and gender differences, the failings of mainstream churches and public education, the mass media and the entertainment industry, or the breakdown of law and order and the family. Whatever the explanation, all seem to agree that the fragmentation of community poses a serious threat to the American democracy, perhaps even a threat to "the survival of freedom itself."[6]

Nowhere is the problem of community more evident than in the changing tenor of contemporary public discourse. As James Davison Hunter has observed in *Culture Wars,* today's political and moral debates are characterized not by civility and respect for the opposition but by a "grammar of hostility," in which dialogue has been replaced by "name calling, denunciation, and even outright intolerance." Hunter concedes that this loss of "civility in public discourse" might serve to unite and rally specific communities: "In the act of opposing an adversary . . . the community expresses a common moral indignation, and asserts its moral authority anew. . . . Thus, not only is the community drawn together, united as a collectivity, but it is reminded of its heritage, its duty, and its mission to the larger world." In the larger cultural context, however, the rhetoric of vilification, this "impulse toward polarization," results in an "eclipse of the middle," with more "quiet" and "reflective" voices—in Hunter's view, the majority of voices in the United States—becoming, "for all practical purposes, *silent* in the broader public discussion." This trend, according to Hunter, poses a "serious threat" to the most basic and essential "traditions of the democratic experience."[7]

In the wake of the Oklahoma City bombing in April 1995 President Clinton added his voice to those concerned about the growing divisiveness of our public talk. Returning again and again to the theme that "inflammatory rhetoric," "incendiary talk," and "words spouting violence" accounted in no small measure for the bombing, Clinton urged those "purveying hate" and "implying . . . with words that violence is alright" to consider "the consequences of what they say and the kind of emotion they are trying to inflame."[8] In an address to the American Association of Community Colleges shortly after the bombing, Clinton reminded us that "bitter words can have consequences," and he argued that freedom of speech came "coupled with an enormous . . . responsibility," not just for speakers but for each and every citizen. Calling upon all Americans to stand up against the "purveyors of hatred and division," Clinton concluded:

In this country we cherish and guard the right of free speech. We know we love it when we put up with people saying things we absolutely deplore. And we must always be willing to defend their right to say things we deplore to the ultimate degree. But we hear so many loud and angry voices in America today whose sole goal seems to be to try to keep some people as paranoid as possible and the rest of us

all torn up and upset with each other. They spread hate. . . . It is time
we all stood up and spoke against that kind of reckless speech.[9]

Whether the "grammar of hostility" in American public discourse
merely symptomizes the problem of community (as Hunter suggests)
or actually causes polarization and violence (as Clinton insists), the
relationship between rhetoric and community warrants scholarly attention. While all seem to recognize that rhetoric shapes the character
and health of communities in countless ways, we have only begun
to map the discursive routes that lead communities either to constructive unity or to fragmentation, even bloodshed. This book contributes
to that effort by exploring, in a variety of contexts, how rhetoric defines, rallies, polarizes, or marginalizes specific communities.
Composed of essays by fifteen leading scholars of language and
public discourse, it is premised upon the truth of President Clinton's
claim: words do indeed have "consequences," not just for individuals
but for whole communities and cultures.

Rhetoric and Community

The contributors to this volume themselves represent a community
of scholars who, despite differing historical and theoretical interests,
share a common bond. Recognizing that communities are largely defined, and rendered healthy or dysfunctional, by the language they use
to characterize both themselves and others, all share an abiding concern
with how communities are constituted and sustained—or, in some cases,
threatened and disrupted—by the words their leaders choose to characterize both themselves and others.

Roderick Hart, the Liddell Professor of Communication and Government at the University of Texas, sounds the keynote of the volume
in an introductory essay, "Community by Negation: An Agenda for
Rhetorical Inquiry." With melancholy eloquence Hart confronts the
sad question at the center of the recent debate over the problem of
community in the United States: Is it "possible to have community
without hate?" In search of the answer Hart reflects widely upon
communities past and present, ultimately focusing upon an American public reveling in the demonization of Saddam Hussein. "Hate,"
Hart concludes, has "long been the handmaiden of community," but
we still have much to learn "about the vocabularies of hate," and
"we need to know if hate has, during our lives and times, finally become a national habit."

The remainder of the book consists of seven major case studies in rhetoric and community, each consisting of an interpretive essay and a response. The case studies examine a variety of communities, both historical and contemporary, and they produce numerous insights about the relationship between rhetoric and community. Three of the case studies take us back to the late nineteenth and early twentieth century in search of the definitive rhetorical characteristics of early African-American and feminist communities. Two others focus upon the rhetoric of war, examining in one case the military culture itself and in the other efforts to rally a nation to war. The two remaining case studies focus upon specialized communities within contemporary culture: in the first case Hollywood filmmakers and in the other biological scientists. United by their common interest in language and community, all of the studies revolve around the same essential questions: How do communities define themselves rhetorically? How do they construct and reflect their distinctive worldviews? How do they position themselves in relation to other communities and society at large? And how does language function to promote unity or fragmentation?

The answers that emerge from the case studies are as varied as the subjects themselves. From these studies we see how, as Hart suggests, communities may be defined by shared prejudices or hatreds. Yet we also see how communities may be understood in terms of shared beliefs, values, or visions, distinctive patterns of metaphor, common experiences or collective memories, technical vocabularies, and a host of other communal bonds manifested in their discourse. All of the case studies illustrate how language not only reflects but also shapes the character of particular communities. However unique their historical context or theoretical approach, each study illustrates how communities are defined and constituted, for good or ill, by rhetorical discourse.

Race, Gender, and Community

Questions of race and gender have been at the heart of many recent discussions of community, and the three case studies in part 1 contribute to that conversation. While one's gender or the color of one's skin obviously distinguishes a person physically, it should be equally obvious, as these studies remind us, that the political and cultural significance of those differences is established through language, by those who speak on behalf of the community as well as by outsiders.

In "Patterns of Metaphor among Early Feminist Orators" Michael Osborn, the pioneering student of archetypal metaphor, explores some intriguing questions about the rhetoric of early feminists: How were gender differences manifested in the metaphors of women's rights advocates in the late nineteenth century? And what is the significance of those differences for understanding their worldview? As always, Osborn treats metaphor not as stylistic ornamentation but as fundamental to thought, and on that basis he teases out the significance of the patterns he discovers in twenty-eight speeches by early American feminists. He encourages our appreciation for the images that mirrored the "powerful constructive impulses" of these feminist pioneers. Being ever the champion of our "fundamental humanity," Osborn does not hesitate to identify "ethical flaws" manifested in the feminists' metaphors, such as their penchant for war metaphors despite their "aversion to war" and their use of metaphors to "dehumanize their adversaries."

Responding to Osborn, Martha Watson, who has written widely about rhetoric and gender, applauds Osborn's "critical perspicuity" and his trademark "human sympathy," but she doubts that all of the metaphors Osborn identifies were consciously crafted or significant to the reception of the speeches. In addition, Watson questions whether some of the gender differences Osborn discerns might, in fact, be better accounted for by the status of these women as political "outsiders." Finally, Watson urges us to not allow our interest in patterns to distract us from important differences among the early feminists. Watson thus reminds us of an important point: while rhetorical patterns may indeed distinguish communities, all communities ultimately are composed of unique individuals.

Karlyn Kohrs Campbell, a pioneer in the study of historical feminism, also takes us back in time to reflect upon questions of language, oppression, and community. Specifically, she looks at a "debate" over the causes and prevention of racially motivated lynchings in the pages of the *North American Review* in 1904—an exchange between Thomas Nelson Page, representing the white South, and Mary Church Terrell, the "voice of African Americans." In a Marxian reading Campbell argues that "this debate did not occur in a free and open marketplace of ideas" but, rather, was constrained by the interests of the Northern capitalists, who owned most major media of the day. Although Terrell was allowed to respond to Page's disingenuous attempt to blame lynchings on the victims themselves, Campbell shows how her response was constrained not only "by the racist logic" of Page's argument but also by a larger milieu of "institutionalized" and "naturalized" racism.

In response, James Aune, a leading authority on Marxism, not surprisingly focuses upon Campbell's interpretive stance. Suggesting that Campbell's reading of Marxist cultural theory might be "too simplistic," he offers a different reading of the debate based upon Gramsci's theory of hegemony, a reading that considers not just the economic interests of the mass media but also their "role . . . in identifying and legitimating advocates for the African-American cause." According to Aune, a more "thoroughgoing study of the interaction among the elite press, intellectuals, and mass audiences would provide us with a more complete view of the texts Campbell presents to us." Nevertheless, Aune recognizes Campbell's essay as an important first step toward understanding the rhetorical dynamics of this historic clash between the powerful and the powerless—between communities differing radically in both worldview and cultural authority.

Also addressing questions of oppression and community is Stephen H. Browne's "Du Bois, Double-Consciousness, and the Modern City," a study of the city as "culture text" in turn-of-the-century America. Comparing and contrasting the city as portrayed in "dominant culture" with the city as "refracted through the lens of race," Browne shows how W. E. B. Du Bois, in "Of the Wings of Atalanta," produced a "stylized distortion" of the city as envisioned by the dominant culture, a distortion arising out of Du Bois's principle of "double-consciousness." While the dominant culture developed a "monocular" view of the problems and glories of urban life, Du Bois produced a "double-telling" of the story, a binocular view of the city in which questions about urban culture were always answered twice, from the perspectives of two communities with very different urban experiences.

In his response James Darsey, whose work often focuses on questions of identity in marginalized communities, wonders whether Du Bois's "sense of diremption" is in fact more complex than the double-consciousness Browne employs to frame his analysis. According to Darsey, Du Bois was not "at home" in either the white or the black community; indeed, while "nominally associated with many communities," he was "squarely a member of none, not on this earth." Throughout his life Du Bois continued to "search for a community in which he could be himself and be at peace," but, as a black intellectual, Darsey concludes, he simply was "unable to trust the promise of home on this earth, not until his death."

These six essays illustrate some of the ways in which marginalized communities define themselves and relate rhetorically to the dominant culture. In each case the distinctiveness of the group—its separate identity, even its alienation—is reflected in its language, yet so too are some of the traditions, experiences, and ambitions that its members shared with all Americans. In short, all spoke as outcasts but also as Americans. In negotiating this tension, none was entirely successful; none lived to see the day of equal rights, equal opportunity, and simple justice for all. Nevertheless, all contributed in subtle yet important ways to a long, slow process of liberation. Highlighting the contradiction between the nation's ideals and the status of women and blacks in the United States, they posed a moral dilemma that the nation could not ignore forever.

War and Community

The rhetoric of war both divides and unifies; it not only separates "us" from "the enemy" but often divides us among ourselves. At the same time, however, the rhetoric of war can be a powerful force of community building. The two historical episodes examined in part 2 show how: by forging special bonds within the military community itself and by rallying whole nations against a common foe. In both cases war—an act of organized hatred and orchestrated destruction—provides the somewhat ironic context for lessons in community building, lessons in how communities *can* be persuaded to come together in common cause.

In his essay "On Rhetoric in Martial Decision Making" Ronald Carpenter demonstrates how military decision making is often *not* characterized by "objective estimates about the enemy and one's own forces" but, rather, is influenced by the rhetorical skills and the ethos of military commanders. With General Douglas MacArthur's plan to land marines at Inchon during the Korean War as his example, Carpenter illustrates how MacArthur overcame a host of "rational" objections to the landing site with a "Churchillian oration" to the Joint Chiefs of Staff on 23 August 1950. Precisely because it seemed so "impossible" to land successfully at Inchon, MacArthur predicted that the operation would take the enemy by complete surprise and thereby ensure victory. According to Carpenter, MacArthur's speech became the "pivotal" factor in the decision to land there, especially in the context of MacArthur's control over other sources of information that might have cast doubt upon his plan.

In his response Martin J. Medhurst, a well-known student of Cold War rhetoric, urges a broader view of the rhetorical dimensions of the Inchon decision by illustrating how not only MacArthur's speech but also a host of interpersonal, attitudinal, and situational factors may have contributed to the outcome of deliberations. Medhurst offers a significantly different interpretation of the Inchon deliberations, but in the process he reinforces Carpenter's central claim that military communities are no less rhetorical than other sorts of communities. Indeed, Medhurst greatly broadens and extends Carpenter's analysis of the rhetorical dimensions of military decision making. He illustrates how not only MacArthur's speech but also a number of other factors, "equally rhetorical in nature," all contributed to the decision to land at Inchon.

Celeste M. Condit and April M. Greer illuminate the literal meaning of "Churchillian" oratory in "The Particular Aesthetics of Winston Churchill's 'War Situation I,'" an analysis of Churchill's address to the House of Commons on 20 August 1940. Striking a balance between those who have viewed Churchill as merely articulating existing community sentiment and those who credit him with radically transforming British attitudes toward the war, Condit and Greer view the relationship between Churchill and his nation as "reciprocal." According to the authors, most Britons supported the war effort and saw the need to eliminate Hitler, but this sentiment was "unfocused and unamplified." Moreover, many remained fearful that British forces were no match for the Nazi war machine, especially in taking the offensive on the European continent with no help from the Americans. Thus, the British people needed a leader who could "articulate their sensitivities, honing them into an effective community" and assuring them of ultimate victory. This Churchill did in "The War Situation I," the authors argue, with a masterful blend of logic and imagery, a blend that both tapped into preexisting sentiments yet turned them into a "cogent, powerful, and effective" appeal for taking the war to Hitler.

In his response James Jasinski argues that "postmodern thought . . . challenges the presumed identity and stability of context that is at the core of Condit and Greer's project." As such, "even an exhaustive account of communal sensitivities"—a standard that he concedes Condit and Greer approach—"remains plagued by the possibility of alternative renderings of a community's sentiments." To illustrate, Jasinski develops one such alternative: an interpretation of Churchill's speech grounded in Pocock's notion of a "Machiavellian moment"—that moment of "anxiety" when a community confronts "its own fragility and mortality." According to Jasinski, this "relatively minor modification in the mode of contextualization" leads to "some fairly significant alterations in the way we analytically reconstruct the Churchill address." By foregrounding "the experience of anxiety," he concludes, we can see how Churchill drew upon the resources of "fortune and providence" to "negotiate the anxieties" of this Machiavellian moment.

War is often viewed as the antithesis of rhetoric, a resort to force signaling the failure of words to resolve disputes among nations. As the two episodes examined in these essays illustrate, however, military action is inevitably the product of rhetorical action. Within the military community strategies and tactics must be deliberated, while in the larger community the political will to fight must be created and sustained, sometimes over extended periods of time. Even within rigidly hierarchical military communities persuasion remains the essential tool of leadership and community building, and no war effort can long be sustained without continuous and effective rhetorical appeals.

Artistic and Scientific Community

The studies in part 3 of this book approach questions of rhetoric and community from yet another angle, exploring how professional communities relate to the larger culture. Focusing upon filmmakers and scientists, two influential yet sometimes suspect communities, these studies illuminate the uneasy relationship that often exists between professional communities—with their own perspectives, values, and even languages—and the larger society. In the process both communities are, in some measure, demystified; they are no less human, and no less rhetorical, than the rest of us. At the same time, however, we also see how these communities do, in fact, live in different symbolic worlds, often separate and distinct from the public they serve.

In "Thinking through Film: Hollywood Remembers the Blacklist" Thomas W. Benson offers a fascinating study in a filmmaker's attempt to address the question of where Hollywood "fits" into the larger political community. Focusing upon the 1990 film *Guilty by Suspicion*, Benson explores how this "retelling" of the story of the Hollywood blacklist both attempted to reshape our memory of political events and, ironically, "depoliticized" those events by "relying on shallow formulas" that rendered "both politics and personal life as Hollywood stereotypes." In one sense, then, Benson argues that *Guilty by Suspicion* is "a bravely political film" in that it condemned the blacklist and the House Un-American Activities Committee. On the other hand, by employing common formulas, it undermines its own political message "by depicting a world in which neither the committee nor its victims were actually doing politics": the hearings are but a "malevolent carnival" staged for the news media, while the major victim, David Merrill (Robert DeNiro) is "a sort of Hollywood Everyman," a "non-political liberal" who finally stands up to the committee to achieve personal redemption, not to make a political point. Thus, a political film turns into a traditional "antipolitical melodrama," pitting "the formula hero against the demonic bad guys." With the politics of Hollywood, and the political activism of the film community, still under scrutiny today, Benson offers an important study in the rhetorical construction of a community "whose politics is no politics."

In his response Bruce Gronbeck, one of our most creative and insightful students of mass media, elaborates upon this very notion: that the film is most "explicitly rhetorical" not in its "reconstruction of the past" but as "an exhortative construction *in* 1990 *for* 1990." Calling the film "a fable about artists in society," Gronbeck senses more contemporary political relevance in the film than Benson elaborates. Indeed, he views the film not as "a historical study" but as "a textualization of collective memory," a film "adaptable to our own time," perhaps more a commentary on the "red scare" of Reagan's America than the blacklist era, and an "articulation of positive, not negative, relationships between the personal and the political." Whatever their differences in reading the text, Benson and Gronbeck together teach us much about an artistic community and its place and purposes in the larger society.

John Lyne, in "Rhetoric and Scientific Communities," likewise reflects upon the rhetoric of a special community in exploring how the discourse of science impacts the "thought, action, and culture" of the larger community. Lyne debunks five "myths" that have insulated science from rhetorical critique—myths that sustain the notion that science is for scientists, not for "the public." Arguing that scientific discourse is, in fact, "going public" at "virtually every minute of its production and dissemination," Lyne advocates critiques of the "discourses in, of, around, and about science" grounded in "moral imagination," or the "capacity to envision how a situation can admit of other descriptions and perspectives." Failing to engage in such critiques, Lyne warns, encourages the abuse of scientific knowledge in politics and society: "Mark a space as being empty of rhetoric—as writers sometimes do with respect to science—and you invite rhetorical abuse. Mark a place as 'not public,' and you discourage scrutiny."

Charles Alan Taylor is part of a new generation of rhetorical critics heeding Lyne's call for critical attention to the rhetoric of science. Like Lyne, Taylor is concerned with the insulation of science from public scrutiny, and, like Lyne, he seeks to demystify and democratize science. At the same time, however, Taylor senses in Lyne's critique an "ironic globalization of science" which, to his mind, leads away from a genuinely democratic critique of science and toward "a sort of postmodern feudalism." By building their own critiques of biorhetorics upon an empirical foundation, Taylor argues, Lyne and his frequent collaborator, Henry Howe, vest certain "right-thinking" scientific subcommunities with "literal 'ownership' of knowledge claims," leaving the rest of us without "opportunity for meaningful critique on this epistemological manor—an intellectual and communal feudalism."

These studies hardly exhaust the possibilities for studying the relationship between professional communities and the larger culture. In many ways filmmakers and scientists may well be unique, but they also share much in common with other communities set apart from the larger society by a special calling, specialized training, and perhaps even languages of their own. Lawyers and medical doctors, musicians and artists, police officers and government officials, academics and clerics—all must negotiate the tension between living in their separate worlds and relating productively to society at large. When they do so successfully, they enjoy privileged social status and seldom want for the resources necessary to sustain their communities. When they fail, however, their professional identities become burdens rather than badges of honor.

Questions about Community

These case studies in rhetoric and community offer no easy answers to problems of community. They do lay bare, however, some of the key issues, some of the crucial questions, which must be addressed if healthy, constructive communities are to prevail over those that divide and destroy. How can communities of racial, ethnic, or other minorities sustain their own identities and still relate productively to the larger culture? How can an undemocratic military culture be tolerated and controlled within a democratic nation, and how are diverse democratic communities inspired to go to war? How can communities of artists or experts—communities set apart by special missions yet beholden to the larger culture—explore new frontiers without leaving behind their public constituencies? These are the basic questions raised by the fifteen essays that follow, and all represent important steps toward a better understanding of how communities function rhetorically.

We shall return in the conclusion of this book to consider some of the implications of these studies and some proposals for solving the problem of community in contemporary culture. The first task, however, is to understand what defines a community, to learn about some of the ways in which communities are constituted and sustained rhetorically, and to ponder why some communities unify people for constructive purposes while others serve to polarize and divide.

Notes

1. Robert Hughes, *Culture of Complaint: The Fraying of America* (New York: Warner Books, 1993), 49.

2. Patrick Buchanan, speech before the Republican National Convention, 17 August 1992.

3. Khalid Abdul Muhammad, speech at Kean College, 29 November 1993.

4. Arthur M. Schlesinger, Jr., *The Disuniting of America: Reflections on a Multicultural Society* (New York: W.W. Norton, 1992), 1518.

5. Robert N. Bellah, Richard Madsen, William M. Sullivan, Ann Swidler, and Steven M. Tipton, *Habits of the Heart: Individualism and Commitment in American Life* (New York: Harper and Row, 1985), vii.

6. Ibid.

7. James Davison Hunter, *Culture Wars: The Struggle to Define America* (New York: Basic Books, 1991), 136, 156, 159, 317.

8. *60 Minutes*, 23 April 1995.

9. "Remarks By the President to the American Association of Community Colleges," Press Release, Office of the Press Secretary, The White House, 24 April 1995.

Introduction
Community by Negation—
An Agenda for Rhetorical Inquiry

Roderick P. Hart

We need to know more about hate. When I say "we" I mean those who study communication, for hate can be a very rhetorical thing indeed. When I say "hate" I mean feelings of antipathy directed toward some person or group that succeeds in making them pariahs. Typically, the rhetoric of hate is reductionistic and overwrought, but not always. Typically, we can detect hate's distinctive hum before it becomes a pronounced whine, but not always. Typically, we know who the haters among us are, where they live and work, how and why they hate. But not always.

In this essay I ask whether it is possible to have community without hate. At first the question seems absurd since community means bondedness, common allegiance, fraternity—the very opposites of hate. But there is also an underside to community, and it is this underside I wish to examine in this essay. For each community in existence, I assert, there is also an "uncommunity," an assembly of the befouled and besotted who have heard the Word and rejected it. Such persons are benighted not because they are ignorant but because they are willful. They have mindfully chosen a course different from our own and pursued it with abandon. The uncommunal are not quiet in their protests; they thoroughly, enduringly, spurn the Elect and the heirs of their heirs as well. Salvation is impossible for such persons, or so argues the rhetoric of hate.

By invoking the uncommunity—graphically, athletically—society's leaders get us to take risks we otherwise would not take. They make us see the Other in his full depravity, and they embolden us as a result. For Jesus it was the moneychangers in the Temple, for Martin Luther an obscene hierarchy in Rome. For Luther's American namesake it was a southern governor whose lips dripped with the words of interposition and nullification. For Andrea Dworkin it is the modern male and his ancient hubris. But there is yet more. Haters need hate as well. For Hitler it was the old Jew, for Khalid Muhammad the new Jew. For the new Jew it is the PLO. All who speak, all who would be rhetorical, are caught in the cycle of hate, or so I shall argue here.

Perhaps the reader objects. Perhaps the reader thinks my definition of hate too broad. Perhaps the reader wishes to reserve the term *hateful* for those the reader does not like—for the unchristian, the unwashed, the uncivil, the uncouth, the unseemly, the unkempt, the unknowing. Here, surely, are uncommunities deserving of the name. You, the reader, understandably take no special pleasure in dispatching them but dispatch them you must. Your ends, after all, are pure, your license for vitriol up-to-date. You use hate only when it *must* be used.

So say us all. In pointing this out, I perhaps offer nothing new. Kenneth Burke tells us that it is the human creature who invented the negative.[1] When the enemy draws near, says Burke, we instinctively take heed. Rhetoric helps by redisplaying the community's values and by spotting the enemy's precise movements near the gates of the city. Thus forewarned and forearmed, we march to the barricades. This is the story of all political motivation, a powerful story indeed.

Hate, I therefore conclude, has long been the handmaiden of community. The virgin sacrifice—a hate crime by any contemporary definition—helped the tribe rally 'round its ancestral beliefs, a function also served when American puritans dispatched the witches among them and when Senator Joseph McCarthy attacked the aesthetes of his day. Burnings in effigy are but transmogrifications of these same practices. Such rituals range from the mundane, torching the quarterback from Columbus East before the big game, for example, to the obscene, torching a church in Birmingham filled with children, for example. These practices were also used by the antiwar protestors of the sixties ("Hey, hey, L.B.J. How many kids did you kill today?"), who thereby produced the exquisitely paradoxical formula: enmity in the service of amity.

Asking the question of how hate serves community requires more than a bit of fortitude. It asks us to look through society's glass darkly and, then, toward the mirror that lies beyond. Do we inevitably find ourselves staring back? Has hatred, finally, become our friend? Does it now give us personal pride, as well as personal pleasure (supermarket tabloids and *Saturday Night Live*, for example, as well as talk radio)? Does vilification of Baseball Incorporated help today's Americans establish common cause with one another, as did the savaging of robber barons in earlier times? Have we, as a result, become addicted to hate's therapies? Do we now require a straw man for each of our arguments?

Indeed, can rhetoric even be called rhetoric anymore unless hate is its attendant?[2] Can a Newt Gingrich rise to power without an eviscerated Tom Foley? Must a Murphy Brown be furnished for each Dan Quayle running for office? Is antipathy toward undocumented workers required for California to keep its economic house in order? Can the residents of Simi Valley really know one another without hosting a Rodney King trial from time to time? Can a right to life (*or* a right to choose) exist without dead abortionists, a Reagan administration without an Ayatollah in Iran? Do all persuaders require a Willie Horton?

Personifications such as these make rhetoric efficient, but hate can also go generic. The hypothetical *they*, for example, is often used to build motivation in those instances when naming names is judged unseemly. "There are those who would have us abandon our course, but I say nay!" thunders the Fourth of July orator. "Let them look me in the eye and call me that," echoes the quadrennial campaigner. These are moments of bravado, to be sure, and they move us forward by making us furtive. But can a furtive people really thrive? When no names are named, are not all persons named by default? If so, what happens to the genuinely innocent, to innocence itself?

Because hate does so much to so many, we need to know its refrains better than we do at present. The human story is the story of love but it is also the story of hate. Because rhetoric is part of both stories, we need to know its story too.

A Gulf of Hate

In trying to introduce that story, I will read hate broadly here, perhaps overly broadly. I err in this direction because hate is not a small matter and because the question I ask—can people come together only by opposing others?—is a large question and a chilling question. I discovered this twin conclusion when speaking to a conservative audience about the rhetoric of hate used during the Gulf War. After the talk I was told by some that my answers were unacceptable because my question was unacceptable. No nation as good as ours, I was told, could be hateful. If we were hateful, I was also told, it was because we deserved to be. The rhetoric of hate thereby seals itself perfectly. It is rhetoric with a husk; it resists inspection so as to maintain itself.

Perversely, perhaps, I will attempt to open up that rhetoric here. And there is no better place to start on such a project than with the discourse surrounding the Gulf War. Here, surely, was a lightning rhetoric. In a matter of weeks, not months, hundreds of thousands of American troops were flown to the Middle East to remove the Iraqi army from Kuwait and then flown home again. The speed with which the war was prosecuted was exceeded only by the efficiency of the nation's war rhetoric.

Recall the strains of that rhetoric. *Newsweek* reported brisk sales of a Saddam Hussein Voodoo doll. The Houston Lighting and Power Company used Saddam images in their "buy America" campaign while the Minneapolis Transit Company used them to increase ridership. Hollywood Toys and Costumes ran out of Saddam Hussein masks for Halloween, while one newsmagazine placed Saddam's picture side-by-side with Joseph Stalin's to show their remarkable facial similarities (and, presumably, their similar leadership styles). Graffiti on one bomb stacked on the USS *Independence* promised, "This is for you, Saddam, baby," while a San Diego advertising executive observed, "Everybody's trying to piggyback on Saddam's notoriety." Perhaps humorist Steve Martin captured the national sentiment best when he observed "If the press would keep talking about [Saddam's] mistress," perhaps "his wife would kill him."[3]

There is nothing new here. These are standard wartime diatribes that have leached into the national mainstream. But equally energetic in this regard was President George Bush, who used the ancient arts of synecdoche and personification to move the war forward. Whenever Bush spoke, he spoke of a naked Saddam:

Saddam Hussein met every overture of peace with open contempt. In the end, despite the world's prayers for peace, Saddam brought war upon himself.[4]

You can't negotiate with a terrorist. If a person kidnaps another, should the kidnapper be given face? Should that person be given some way out so he can have a little face when he gets back into the world? The answer is no, you do not compromise with that.[5]

Prime Minister John Major of the United Kingdom said it wel yesterday, "Saddam," he said, "may yet become a target of his own people.

It is perfectly clear that this man is amoral. He takes hostages, he attacks population centers, he threatens prisoners. He's a man without pity, and whatever his fate may be," said Prime Minister Major, "I, for one, will not weep for him." No one should weep for this tyrant when he is brought to justice—no one, anywhere in the world.[6]

In a recent book I trace the phenomenology of politics produced in the television age.[7] Central to that phenomenology is the heightened sense of the psychological that George Bush evidences here. By featuring the *person* of Saddam, Bush kept our eyes off collective realities. At times he had to use a tortuous logic to do so, as when he argued: "Our quarrel is not with the people of Iraq. We do not wish for them to suffer. The world's quarrel is with the dictator who ordered that invasion."[8] In politics, of course, such a statement is absurd. Politics is nothing if not collective. Individuals may engage in fisticuffs, but entire nations go to war. George Bush may not have felt quarrelsome toward the Iraqi people but he was quarrelsome enough to kill one hundred thousand of them.[9]

Margaret Thatcher was also no fan of Saddam. She once declared: "This man is a loser . . . a person who has taken hostages cruelly, brutally, a person who has hidden behind the skirts of women and children."[10] Notice, again, the psychological motif as the Iron Maiden takes the inner trek toward the inner Saddam. George Bush took the trek also and found an overweening id at the center of Saddam's problem (he observed that Saddam was by nature a bully).[11] *Newsweek*, in contrast, found a weak ego: "the Iraqi president's relative ignorance of the outside world only enhances his sense of building conspiracy."[12] One talk-show guest turned to Jungian archetypes for his analysis: "For the first time in Saddam's career, he is exactly where he wants to be—at the center of power, the focus of attention."[13] The nation's cognitive psychologists were also heard from, with one of them reporting that Saddam blinked 113 times per minute (vs. a normal blink rate of 30–50 BPM), putting Saddam in the "dangerously high" range.[14] Perhaps showing the influence of these pontifications, when asked in a public opinion poll whether Saddam should be allowed to "save face" or "be humiliated," 62 percent of the respondents opted for humiliation.[15]

Because of the deadly efficiency of rhetoric such as this, the Gulf War began quickly and was prosecuted successfully before a hasty retreat was sounded. It was, by most measures, a "popular" war, in part because the American people could unite against a larger-than-life individual who willingly played the fool (witness Saddam's clumsy attempts to manipulate the Western media). Admittedly, that same fool had lowered the illiteracy rate in Iraq to 11 percent (the best in the region), doubled the calorie supply of his people, and dramatically improved the nation's housing and highways.[16] But his aggressiveness in Kuwait cost Pakistan a billion dollars in lost oil-field wages, raised Eastern Europe's oil prices by another half-billion dollars, and imperiled the fifty billion dollars in reserves that Kuwait had stashed with Morgan Stanley in New York.[17] Clearly, something had to be done. It was.

The strategy of hate-by-personification was not George Bush's alone. Even print reporters joined in, traveling down Saddam's mental pathways and inevitably finding them twisted. In doing so they often echoed the president directly, in one case finding an identity between Saddam and Adolph Hitler: "If you dismissed George Bush's comparisons between Saddam Hussein and Adolph Hitler, consider this. Saddam, like Hitler, outlined his vision of the world—and his place in history—in a book whose title in German is 'Unser Kampf,' or 'Our Struggle.' (Hitler did the same in 'Mein Kampf,' or 'My Struggle.')"[18]

Although Saddam was stupefyingly linear throughout the war—releasing hostages for diplomatic reasons, attacking Israel for pan-Arab reasons, burning oil supplies for military reasons, working the media for propagandistic reasons—he was inevitably declared irrational. One newsmagazine became positively lyrical when describing his final depredations: "Saddam's last stand was Wagnerian in its madness. He backlit himself with the flames of Kuwait's oil wells, which he turned into torches. As the air filled with the sulfurous stench of rotten eggs, his troops executed civilians in the streets of Kuwait City. One moment, he swore defiance; the next he tried to get Mikhail Gorbachev to save him. When that failed, he withdrew to his bunker, playing Hitler, who wanted to take everyone with him when he fell."[19]

Such psychologizing often had a scientistic air to it. This was a bit tricky to effect since journalists are journalists and not mental health professionals. But the rhetoric of hate is permissive, and so very little quibbling over credentials was found in the reportage. Said *Newsweek:* "Saddam's insularity and his pride . . . have confounded the Bush administration . . . [B]rute force may be the only aspect of the wider world Saddam truly does not comprehend, and his pride won't let him bend to it."[20] Elsewhere, *Newsweek* presented rumor in articles, no doubt because the rumor it chose was so richly psychodramatic: "There's a story making the rounds among diplomats in Baghdad that one day at a cabinet meeting Saddam Hussein asked if any of his ministers had a contrary view on one of his proposals. One minister spoke up, and Saddam thanked him graciously and invited him to discuss it further in his private office. Inside, he beat him to death with a club. *That story has never been confirmed, but it is widely believed.*"[21]

The Gentrification of Hate

The rhetoric of the Gulf War is a parable for many things. It shows how political abstractions can be concretized, cultural complexities simplified, and evil made familiar. If Hannah Arendt is correct that Nazi rhetoric shows us the banality of evil, the rhetoric of the Gulf War signals its gentrification. This was made possible by television which is, it seems clear, brilliantly stupid. Because it can fit precious little into its fifteen-inch vertical screen, television shows what it can show—faces. Because television's technology preferences faces, its phenomenology prizes personalities. As a result, television becomes monocular, showing us person after person after person, reducing all politics to the social and the social to the psychodynamic.

In so doing, television reveals how a postmodern medium can happily serve modernist ends. George Bush's rhetoric of hate was, after all, thoroughly textual. In the mid-1990s Saddam Hussein still reigned in Iraq while George Bush lived in his new home in Houston. After having ensured that Western oil supplies would not be disrupted and that wealthy Arabs would still have dominion over poor Arabs, Mr. Bush in 1991 did what all postmodern haters do: he changed texts, directing his latter-day loathings at a grid-locked Democratic Congress. No infantry soldiers marched into Baghdad. No CIA hits were ordered. George Bush simply turned to other matters. His rhetoric of the Gulf War, therefore, had no interstitial character to it. It was hate on the margins.

What does it mean that hate can come and go so quickly? Why were so many Americans ready to do battle against a blustering despot but then to look past the sufferings of his people? These are not polemical questions. I make no brief here for Saddam Hussein or for his several henchmen. But I am asking this: If hate can be drummed up so quickly, and drummed up on psychological rather than political grounds, is there a bottom to its reservoir? With hate rhetoric now so entrenched in the media, are we not being taught daily how to speak its refrains? Are we not being taught that hate can be called back easily (the song always ends, the rally inevitably concludes, the show is finally over) when, in fact, hate-experienced always and forever remains hate-experienced?

My point, then, is that hate in our times has become discursive. It is now an engaging, absorbing discourse that can serve as therapy for an uncertain foreign policy, for post-Soviet geopolitics, for feelings of political drift, for a mélange of disenchantments. The rhetoric of hate is thereby compensatory to its core; even in its most exultative moments it signals a kind of defeat, an inability to get beyond its own consummatory satisfactions and the outrages in which it takes delight. For people bereft of imagination hate gives them something to say. It lets them wallow in concretizations—skin color, nationality, gender, food stamps, fetuses, accidents of geography—and to stave off the death of a thousand cuts required by standard political negotiations.

The hater is thus an arch-empiricist who resorts to thingness because the yet-to-be, the possible, is so hard to imagine and even more difficult to describe. The rhetoric of hate is therefore almost always commemorative, savoring old slights and ancient curses. It retraces the savageries of the past and puts them in new contexts. It feeds on examples, not arguments. Even in its (rare) eschatological moments it finds it easier to describe the forthcoming agonies of the damned than the epiphanies of the chosen.

Because the rhetoric of hate has no future, it is a performative, not a philosophic, rhetoric. Its power comes from fitting fresh facts to old paradigms. "See, I told you so" thus becomes its standard locution. The constant disgorging of new incidents, new atrocities, gives it its propulsive force but also betrays its profound ontological uncertainty. That is, hate operates as if old truths are true only when they are constantly refurbished by facts which, curiously enough, always vanish at morning's light. Hate's only intellectual challenge, as a result, becomes that of finding new grist for a mill that has been churning for centuries.

Hate rhetoric is also circumstantial in the extreme. As George Bush showed, its narrowness of focus sanctifies it ("I have no quarrel with the people of Iraq, just Saddam"). Others argue similarly ("I love homosexuals but hate homosexuality"; "save motherhood; eliminate the abortionists"). Particularistic arguments of this sort counteract perceptions of true malevolence on the parts of its users. Except for the nativist (who repudiates all foreigners) or the radical atheist (who attacks religionists of every stripe), most contemporary haters present themselves as *specialists* who want nothing more than to recede into the background once the enemy is dispatched. This gives its spokespersons plausible deniability: "I have no character flaw; the circumstances required my bile. Once Saddam is gone, it's back to the thousand points of light."

Given its particularism, the rhetoric of hate has been especially popular in an over-socialized nation like the United States where, from the beginning, ethnic, regional, class, religious and, more recently, gendered rhetorics have confronted American nationalism at every turn. So, for example, ethnic pride rallies inevitably lead to counter-demonstrations and to greater ethnic antagonism—*différance* as the handmaiden of hate. There is nothing inevitable about this, of course, and some resist its siren call. But with each new wave of immigration, with each new social movement, the seeds of hate are planted once again.

In other words, oversocialization may well be the natural enemy of community. This is because community depends almost completely on abstractions, on faux identifications ("one nation under God," "as American as apple pie"). Because day-to-day experience is so solitary and so heartily empirical, these abstractions inevitably lose their force for many people.

Because life is so unfair to so many, it is probably best to think of hate as natural, not as some sort of bizarre mutation. Hate is not really manufactured (a mechanistic metaphor) as much as it is recovered (an organic metaphor). It is called up from within us to help repudiate the fact that we are, all of us, nested in social complexity and that our ideas, all of them, are socially determined and not eternal. Hate is thus a way of reestablishing *gemeinschaft* even as *gesellschaft* bears down upon us. It gives us a sense of rectitude and is, therefore, what Kenneth Burke might call secular prayer. Perhaps that is why Michel Foucault has observed that "for centuries in Europe the speech of the madman was either not heard at all or else taken for the word of truth."[22]

Making Hate Beautiful

Perhaps the most disturbing thing about hate rhetoric is its beauty, its driving, compulsive quality, its capacity to light up the mind. The Gothic painters, for example, were better at depicting the tortures of Hades than imagining the saved in paradise. Too, images of the Saracen launched the Crusades, and images of the heathen inspired British colonialism. Those of lawless Native Americans helped George Custer inspire his troops; the concept of the perfidious Japanese gave Franklin Roosevelt his rhetorical cudgel, his day of infamy. Out of such acts, such images, wars have been made and, afterwards, truces fashioned. Out of such acts, such images, we are told in this volume's essays, Joseph McCarthy whipped up anti-Communism and "Bull" Halsey inspired military conquest. Out of such acts, such images, Elizabeth Cady Stanton fashioned a "creeping, crawling, debased, [and] selfish monster" that oppressed womankind. Thus has hate been turned into art.

Hate is beautiful because it is uncomplicated or, better, because it can be made to seem so. Like the hangman, hate concentrates the mind. It allows—no, demands—that we think in binaries, and it turns a world of Technicolor into pure black, pure white. The alternative to hate is the postmodern condition, a world of surfaces at best, of *aporia* more often. In such a world we are pushed this way, then that. Who in such a situation can resist the clarities hate provides?

Certainly television cannot. Sam Donaldson serves up a hate object a week on "Prime Time Live." Ross Perot launches broadsides against rapacious Mexicans during the NAFTA debate. Camille Paglia, taking over for an aging Norman Mailer, complains of a "Second Backlash." People such as these are artists of the emotions, their worlds divided in twos. They treat hate as if it were its own hermeneutic, a self-interpreting force. They reason that if a person can feel hate (and who cannot?), he or she can be taught to think hatefully.

Hate is beautiful because it reaches so deeply inside of us. It feeds on childhood slights, on the bully in the schoolyard and the bogeyman who visits us at home when the shadows lengthen. These are primal memories, are they not?—part of Hobbes's war of all against all; they demand resolution. "Geraldo" obliges, giving us bikers who hate transvestites, abused waifs who hate their fathers, Chinese engineers who hate French streetwalkers. David Duke obliges by making hate pictorial—drug-crazed loafers married to aging welfare queens. Oliver Stone obliges, making hate ludenic in *Natural Born Killers*.

Hate is beautiful because it gives us purpose in a purposeless world. As Michael Lacy has shown, hate can be made to sound academic and racism made to seem a logical option rather than an emotional sewer.[23] Such a rhetoric allows us to become accountants rather than racists ("African Americans are a drain on the economy") or historians rather than racists ("the Holocaust is a Jewish fabrication"). More important, however, hate gives us something to feel in an age when feeling comes hard. Hate lets us feel something whole, complete, and to do so without self-consciousness or remorse. Because of this, the rhetoric of hate may have less to do with hate than with emotionality itself, with the need to be reborn as adolescents, with the need to make love as if we had never made love before.

Conclusion

Hate. Who can resist it? Certainly not the human creature. It beckons constantly. We need to know more about it. We need to know if the speed with which George Bush deployed it in the Gulf War was more ominous, or less ominous, than the speed with which he undeployed it. We need to know where hate goes when it is put back on the shelf. Is it text today, chimera tomorrow? Or is it transformed for some new purpose? Did the hatred in the Gulf inspire David Koresh or Tanya Harding or Stacey Koons? Was George Bush their serial coconspirator?

We need to know more about the vocabularies of hate. We need to study its blatant manifestations (the Ku Klux Klan, say) as well as its subtler ones (the Gulf War rhetors, say). We need to learn about the cultural amnesia that attends hate, how the now-enfranchised in Milwaukee can lose sympathy for the unenfranchised in Miami. We need to learn the ground rules of hate, why a George Bush can hate a Saddam Hussein but not a Menachem Begin, why some African Americans can hate Americans but not Africans, why environmentalists can hate polluters but not Poles.

We need to know more about the *how* of hate, but we also need to know its *why*. Hate, it seems clear, is a methodology, a way of talking and doing, a set of learned (and taught) behaviors. As such, it masks two common emotions—fear and anger. Thus, we need to look beyond hate's awful manifestations to its ontology. What has made the racist joker so angry, so dependent on a banal and unyielding rhetorical form? Why has the anti-Semite's imagination become so worn-down that now only paint and swastikas suffice? To stop with hate, that is, is to stop too soon. We must go beyond its curtain of shame to the emotions it hides, call them out in the open, and find new feelings to replace them. Only then can hate become a memory.

Paradoxical as it may seem, perhaps we should also consider if there might be a happy side to hate. Is it possible, for example, that hate rhetoric functions therapeutically by providing consummatory satisfactions for its recipients *and hence arrests their more overtly hateful behaviors*? That is, when a Montel Williams prompts whites to hurl epithets at blacks on his television show, perhaps he is helping to keep such persons off our streetcorners by offering them a safer purgation. Similarly, perhaps Ricki Lake performs an important community service when refereeing hair-pulling matches between mothers and their disaffected daughters. Perhaps this is Freud's theory of displacement gone societal, with television's viewers as its beneficiaries. And then there are these possibilities: Perhaps Williams and Lake are dangerous, Freud daft, and those who watch such stuff cretins.

No matter what we learn about the psychology of hate, however, we still need to understand it philosophically. We need to know, for example, when hate is required. Is not the parade of history, after all, the story of the moral individual who knows when to hate? Do we not take pride in Northern antipathies of Southern slaveholders, of Darrow's denunciations of Bryant, of a defiant Chicago Seven, of Malcolm X's repudiations? Were these hateful moments not also moral moments, at least for some people? Was Luke (6:22) not right to exult "Happy are you when people hate you, drive you out, abuse you, denounce you as criminal, on account of the Son of Man?"

We do not know very much about hate. We do not know, for example, its moral calculus: Is hate a neutral stratagem that must be viewed, like other stratagems, strictly on teleological grounds? That is, if George Bush's demonizations saved ten thousand, or a hundred thousand, American lives, was it not worth it? Might Rush Limbaugh not have been right to denounce Bill Clinton for having failed to "whip us up" sufficiently about the cruelties of the Haitian counterrevolutionaries? Perhaps hatred is, and must be, central to democratic governance. Perhaps the failure to use hate well is now an unacceptable political scruple.

Political theorist Carl Schmitt tells us that the essence of politics is the capacity to "group men according to friend and enemy." When a society "no longer possesses the capacity or the will to make this distinction," says Schmitt, "it ceases to exist politically."[24] What does such a concept mean for rhetoric in a pluralistic democracy? What does it mean for a society with a voracious and diversified mass media? Can the vessel of goodness now be seen only through the mist of hate? Is there a benevolent rhetoric of hate as well as a toxic one? If so, what do they sound like? Who listens to them? Why? It seems to me that we need to know more about these matters, but mostly we need to know if hate has, during our lives and times, finally become a national habit.

Notes

1. A particularly useful discussion of Burke's view of the negative is that by William Rueckert, *Kenneth Burke and the Drama of Human Relations* (Minneapolis: University of Minnesota Press, 1963), 130.

2. This certainly was the view of community organizer Saul Alinsky, who staged "cinch fights" for his followers. Such a move was used early in a campaign, and it involved boycotting a feckless neighborhood store manager (who inevitably relented to the pressure) so the protestors' confidence could be built. Deployments like this are described in Alinsky's *Rules for Radicals: A Practical Primer for Realistic Radicals* (New York: Random House, 1971).

3. For these and other anecdotes about popular culture and the Gulf War, see the following issues of *Newsweek* magazine: 3 September 1990, 18; 24 September 1990, 6; 29 October 1990, 63; 17 December 1990, 16; 21 January 1991, 6.

4. "Remarks to the Reserve Officers Association," 23 January 1991, *Public Papers of the Presidents: George Bush, 1990,* 1:60.

5. "Remarks and an Exchange with Reporters following Discussions with Prime Minister Margaret Thatcher," 19 November 1990, *Public Papers of the Presidents: George Bush, 1990,* 2:1636.

6. "Remarks to the Reserve Officers Association," 23 January 1991, *Public Papers of the Presidents: George Bush, 1991,* 1:60.

7. *Seducing America: How Television Charms the Modern Voter* (New York: Oxford University Press, 1994).

8. "Address before the 45th Session of the United Nations General Assembly," 1 October 1990, *Public Papers of the Presidents: George Bush, 1990,* 2:1330.

9. Truly accurate estimates of Iraqi war dead are hard to come by, but 100,000 is a generally accepted figure. See *Facts on File,* 28 March 1991, 215.

10. "Overheard," *Newsweek,* 17 September 1990, 19.

11. See, for example, "Remarks at a Reception for Gubernatorial Candidate Pete Wilson," 3 November 1990, *Public Papers of the Presidents: George Bush, 1990,* 2:1535.

12. "The Blunderer from Baghdad," *Newsweek,* 25 February 1991, 35.

13. These are the remarks of Professor Jerrold Post of George Washington University. See "Looking the West 'Right in the Eye,'" *Newsweek,* 10 December 1990, 38.

14. "Don't Blink!" *Newsweek,* 18 February 1991, 12.

15. "Face or Disgrace?" *Newsweek,* 4 March 1991, 40.

16. "More than a Madman," *Newsweek,* 7 January 1991, 21.

17. "The High Cost of Giving," *Newsweek,* 17 September 1990, 31.

18. "His 'Kampf,'" *Newsweek,* 4 March 1991, 6.

19. "Saddam's Last Stand," *Newsweek,* 4 March 1991, 18.

20. "The Blunderer from Baghdad," *Newsweek,* 25 February 1991, 35.

21. "Inside Iraq," *Newsweek,* 8 October 1990, 22; my emphasis.

22. Robert Young, ed., *Untying the Text: A Post-Structuralist Reader* (Boston: Routledge and Kegan Paul, 1981), 53.

23. "Toward a Rhetorical Conception of Civil Racism" (Ph.D. diss., University of Texas at Austin, 1992).

24. *The Concept of the Political,* trans. G. Schwab (New Brunswick: Rutgers University Press, 1976), 49.

Rhetoric and Community

Part One

Race, Gender, and Community

CHAPTER ONE

Patterns of Metaphor among Early Feminist Orators

Michael Osborn

I have always been interested in close readings of speech texts, especially in the metaphorical patterns that interweave through the fabric of words.[1] Metaphors can reveal both surface and depth agendas as well as the vulnerability of an audience. They can also illuminate the political and social features of the ages and communities in which they arise. But individual texts, as Professor McGee has recently reminded us, are treacherous.[2] Even if they are valid transcriptions, they remain artifacts of real-life, blood rhetorical events that were as ephemeral as they were once intense. They are often like the pottery shards I sometimes discover in my walks along the Tennessee River, faded fragments of lost eras.

Perhaps because of this fragile, if not fragmentary, nature of the speech text, I have long concentrated on reading patterns of metaphor across many texts—what one might call a "trans-textual" approach. My assumption is that, as unstable and incomplete as the individual text may be, the larger domain of texts is more reliable and predictable. At any given moment, some star in the universe is always imploding or coming into being, but I can depend on seeing the Big Dipper most nights from my deck, and it will always point to Polaris.

This trans-textual program has centered previously on the "archetypal metaphor." Influenced especially by the work of Philip Wheelwright,[3] this concept predicts that, among the many sources available to rhetors at given moments for the formation of metaphors, a few will emerge as especially productive of important figures across different eras, rhetorical situations, and cultural settings. Because of their deep moorings in human sensibility, these special sources will generate more metaphors than others, and the figures they produce should be especially intense and vital to the rhetorical work of the texts in which they appear. This select group of vehicles should be grounded in imposing features of the natural world or in especially significant dimensions of our lives. They should connect in profound ways with human motives, susceptibilities, and needs. Their meaning should resist corrosive change, lending some lasting appeal to the ephemeral texts in which they appear. And for all these reasons they should be especially worthy of study, because they would seem ideal instruments of identification in moments that threaten to divide communities over controversial proposals.[4] Scholars must also understand their potential for abuse, especially when they are exploited to place an appealing mask on madness. For example, metaphors of light and darkness, space, and the life-death-rebirth cycle were prominent in the National Socialist rhetorical program; within such masterpieces as Riefenstahl's *Triumph of the Will* they became—to appropriate Baudelaire's title—*fleurs du mal.*

Most of my claims about such metaphors have been based on an analysis of fifty-six speech texts. These speeches were those most frequently listed in 1960s speech anthologies as so-called great speeches of the Western world. As graduate students have been reminding me for some time, almost all of them were given by "old white men." Utilizing a method I shall describe shortly, I identified in these speeches 340 instances of significant metaphor, representing some 60 types, or vehicles. Among these 60 types 6 emerged as especially productive of powerful figures: these included, in order of *frequency* in the texts, water and the sea, light and darkness, the human body, space, war, and structures. To put the matter simply: 10 percent of the vehicles accounted for 43 percent of the instances. Additionally, three types stood out because of their special *prominence* in the texts: space, disease, and family metaphors. Thus, this early research focused my attention on the following eight sources of rhetorical metaphor: disease, the family, the human body, light and darkness, space, structures, war, and water/sea.

Many of the students who scolded me about the white maleness of this sample speculated on how the results might differ if female orators were included. There is considerable irony in claiming archetypal status for certain metaphors when the evidence represents only half the population (not to mention the other obvious restrictions based on race, class, etc.). My claims to cross-cultural and cross-temporal appeal for certain metaphors must assume that there are no significant gender differences involved. Correcting this imbalance, however, presents immediate problems. Because women have been discouraged for many centuries from assuming the role of public speaker, there is at present no parallel range of orations which would make possible gender comparisons across time and culture.[5] We can develop only a snapshot view of women speaking during the past several centuries in certain Western countries. Moreover, until recently female orators have not received a great deal of scholarly attention, and anthologies of such speaking supervised by scholars of rhetoric are a recent phenomenon. It may go without saying that critical studies of style, which engage texts at the microscopic level of verbal texture, are especially sensitive to considerations of textual accuracy and authenticity.

A recent anthology, however, Karlyn Kohrs Campbell's *Man Cannot Speak for Her: Key Texts of the Early Feminists,* offers some reassurance for these concerns. Compiled by an acknowledged scholar of feminist rhetoric, it offers authoritative texts that represent almost a hundred years of agitation, leading up to the passage of the Nineteenth Amendment to the United States Constitution in 1920. Moreover, it features "key rhetorical works [that] . . . form the core of the persuasive message of early feminism."[6] Therefore, despite the diversity of points of view represented in the anthology, the collection offers the opportunity to study a group of orators who share a time, place, and general purpose. By examining the metaphorical patterns that emerge across the major orations in this community of speakers, we may find revealed the motives, visions, and stresses of the early feminist movement. These strengths of the collection are, for the purpose of this study, also its weakness. Its relatively precise focus in time, space, and purpose limits somewhat its usefulness as a corrective supplement to my earlier work. Even if one should discover striking differences between female orators, observed over one hundred years within the context of a specific movement, and male orators chronicled in diverse rhetorical situations over several millennia, how should one negotiate these differences to construct some transcendent list of major or archetypal metaphors? Despite this obvious problem, I hope to begin generating evidence that might make such a list eventually possible. Specifically, by examining twenty-eight texts recovered in the Campbell collection,[7] I will seek answers to the following questions: Are certain metaphors conspicuously powerful and frequent in these texts? What might these metaphorical patterns reveal about the nature of the movement in which they participated? And how do these patterns compare with those revealed in the previous research?

Feminist orators must surely have intuited the special importance of archetypal metaphors in framing their arguments and appeals. Beyond the usual advantages of vivid, colorful imagery, archetypal metaphors are especially useful when the prevailing cultural vocabulary of symbols seems turned against one's cause. When the culturetypes of a nation form a powerful negative presumption against one's position, archetypal metaphors can offer more favorable symbolic alternatives of enduring appeal. Moreover, given that these speakers were seeking fundamental social change, they needed a vocabulary grounded in depth appeals with leverage sufficient to move and overturn recalcitrant social structures. Furthermore, the early feminists encountered conflict and division within their own community. Since archetypal metaphor, by definition, activates shared experience and emotions, such figuration can be useful for promoting identification within an action group.[8] Finally, we should note the special connection between archetypal metaphor and the fundamental humanity that we share. Such metaphors are rooted in the experience of being human. Just to use them is to stake an implicit claim to one's own humanity, similar to the "I Am a Man" signs worn by striking sanitation workers in Memphis in 1968. If women were humans, then they were endowed with certain natural rights. This was an argument central to early feminist rhetoric, and the self-certifying use of archetypal metaphor would reinforce the "women are human" presumption at a deep symbolic level. For all these reasons we should expect unusual reliance on archetypal metaphor among the early feminists and many powerful examples.

Methodology

My focus on prominent textual metaphors differs somewhat from the approach taken in Lakoff and Johnson's influential *Metaphors We Live By.*[9] Those researchers were interested in metaphor as it passes into ordinary language but continues to structure thought, attitude, and action. They apparently find the idea of "dead metaphor" to be deceptive, if not dangerous: I would characterize their focus as more upon "fugitive metaphor," figuration that disappears into a text. They are especially alert to apparently weak or mundane surface metaphors that are but the visible tips of elaborate conceptual structures.

In contrast, my research emphasizes conspicuous, vivid instances of metaphor which are more self-conscious and more dependent upon artistic development by speakers. To compare such metaphors across an extensive domain of texts, I use a ten-point scale, with "1" representing the least conspicuous and "10" the most prominent metaphors. Metaphors with a rating of 1 would be practically invisible and, like many of Lakoff and Johnson's fugitive figures, would simply blend into the ordinary language of a text. Metaphors rated from 2 to 5 would represent relatively weak, trite, or incidental expressions. As I. A. Richards once noted, it is hard to get through two or three sentences without using them,[10] and any text of sustained length may include hundreds of them. Thus, the scale implies that weaker metaphors are more frequent and that prominent metaphors are more unusual. With my emphasis on conspicuous rhetorical metaphors, only those rated 6 and above are included in the analysis. In brief, these ratings may be explained as follows:

> 6: *Given to any vivid figure that develops briefly within the speech in no more than a sentence or two.* Angelina Grimke, addressing a "promiscuous" audience in Philadelphia with a mob howling outside, provided an example: "If the arm of the North had not caused the Bastille of slavery to totter to its foundation, you would not hear those cries."[11]

> 7: *Indicates such a figure that is extended to paragraph length or a less-developed figure that occurs at some vital moment in the speech, as at the introduction or conclusion.* Anna Howard Shaw provided a rather striking example as she responded to a hypothetical opposing orator: "'The voice of the people is the voice of God,' and the orator forgets that in the people's voice there is a soprano as well as a bass. . . . How are we ever going to know what God's voice is when we are content to listen to a bass solo? . . . We will never know what the Deity's voice in government is until the bass and soprano are mingled together, the result of which will be the divine harmony."[12]

> 8: *Represents a figure of paragraph length that recurs in the text or is used at a critical moment in the speech.* Frances Willard, president of the Women's Christian Temperance Union (WCTU), provided an example that may encourage some to take the White Cross Pledge: "There is no man whom women honor so deeply and sincerely, as the man of chaste life; the man who breasts the buffetings of temptation's swelling waves, like some strong swimmer in his agony, and makes the port of perfect self-control."[13] Willard extended this metaphor into an illustrative tale of life on the Adriatic Sea which, combining also with musical and light and darkness motifs, provided a parable for her times.

9: *Represents a thematic metaphor that may accompany and symbolize the speech proposition. It will usually recur throughout the speech.* An especially interesting example of such prominent metaphors was the Temple of Liberty figure that dominated both Elizabeth Cady Stanton's speech in Kansas in 1867 and Carrie Chapman Catt's rousing "Crisis" speech in 1916.[14] The vision of the Temple of Liberty opened the Stanton speech and provided its anthem as it re-echoed throughout. In the Catt speech the concept of building the Temple allowed the speaker to trace the chronology of significant events in the suffragist movement and helped heighten the drama and build the moral imperative of the moment: the time had come to complete the Temple.

10: *Such rare metaphors are thematic to the text, extend their influence throughout, and supply the basic structure of the thought within the speech.* Elizabeth Cady Stanton's work *A Slave's Appeal*, which interwove elevation, structural, and artistic strands into a powerful composite figure that resonated from the beginning to the end of her speech, may represent such an instance.[15]

This rating system allows comparisons across a broad domain of discourse and can generate conclusions that describe overall tendencies. Its danger is that it may create a facade of objectivity for research that is essentially critical and interpretive. Decisions concerning a metaphor's prominence and type may vary according to the researcher. But, if such work is hardly objective, one should not over-emphasize its subjectivity. My work with graduate student raters suggests that eight out of ten examiners of texts will agree that a given instance is or is not metaphorical. Among these eight at least six will agree on the prominence rating of the figure in question within a magnitude of one variation (the six will agree, e.g., that a given instance merits a 6 or a 7 rating). We are certainly talking about more than mere chimeras of the critical imagination. Perhaps the best description for this method is "systematic subjectivity."

Patterns

Analysis of the 28 speeches considered in this study identified 208 instances of significant metaphor. In contrast, the 56 speeches considered by male orators yielded 340 such instances, but the varying length of the speeches makes any comparison impossible unless, for example, one should consider frequency of significant metaphor per thousand words.

The 208 instances used 63 vehicles, compared to the 60 types identified in the study of male orators. Among the 208 instances, there were 118 "6" ratings, 46 "7" ratings, 29 "8" ratings, 12 "9" ratings, and 3 "10" ratings, thus confirming the expectation of an inverse relationship between prominence and frequency. The average rating for female orators was 6.73, in comparison to the 6.69 average for male orators. I had expected, however, that prominence ratings for women would be higher. William Reynolds has traced a flight into fantasy and symbolism among pre–Civil War Southern orators as the national debate over slavery and other divisive issues reached a stalemate.[16] As the resources of invention were exhausted over the years in the effort to resolve that dispute by words, frustrated orators invested their energies in stylistic innovation as they sought to strengthen fixed positions. I expected that similar frustration might cause feminist orators to rely more and more heavily on vivid metaphor as one discouraging decade followed another without significant change. Another reason for expecting higher prominence ratings for female orators goes to the heart of rhetoric as revealed by Kenneth Burke. When unfavorable perspectives are entrenched in national laws and mores, then rhetoric often turns to *perspective-by-incongruity,* radical, powerful metaphors that challenge, uproot, and reconstruct the prevailing orientation.[17] Since women had to confront unfavorable perspectives, and because powerful metaphors are usually conspicuous in texts, one might expect to find a plenitude of such metaphors at work within the orations under consideration. The actual ratings difference between male and female orators is not that large, however, even though small differences are magnified in importance when they occur across wide domains of discourse. The matter remains for further study.

The most interesting result of the study is the profile of favored metaphor types among feminist orators. Ten among the 63 vehicles used by these orators accounted for 127 of the 208 instances identified. That is, 16 percent of the sources produced 61 percent of the examples. These included: space-related types, 32 instances; water and the sea, 15 instances; chains/bonds, 14 instances; animal metaphors, 13 instances; war, 11 instances; light and darkness, 9 instances; structures, 9 instances; vegetation, 8 instances; personification, 8 instances; and music, 8 instances.

Interpretations

A mere listing of results hides some rather remarkable stories. I want to tell some of them in necessarily brief detail. The most dramatic discovery of this study was the almost obsessive sense of space among feminist orators. Space had also been vital for male orators: recall that the spatial metaphor was third most frequent among men, and their images of space were highest in prominence ratings. But both the magnitude of this importance and the meaning and quality of spatial imagery change when we consider feminist orators. The male speakers had a relatively simple, linear, two-dimensional conception of space. They thought of it along vertical and horizontal lines, in which the contrasts between above and below, forward and back, are most vital. To rise, to lift, to reach above, to climb—and to avoid falling and descending— these are impulses common to the male conception. An important subsidiary image is the mountain vehicle, and vertical space also clusters often with light and darkness, associating above with the sun and darkness with below. Similarly, to press forward and to avoid retreat are central to the male notion of horizontal space. Forward movement often coheres with the Progress culturetype discussed by Richard Weaver, and it also often clusters with martial imagery of marching toward distant horizons where victories and rewards loom.[18] For men, therefore, space becomes typically a preferred vehicle for expressing their aspirations, their sense of power, their triumphant self-esteem.

The female orators, however, have a far more complex, three-dimensional, often exquisitely painful sense of space. Stanton expressed the unique complexity of this feminist spatial conception at the beginning of her first speech: "Woman alone can understand the height, the depth, the length, and the breadth of her own degradation."[19] Women share men's fascination with vertical space, but especially during the early years of the movement they perceive themselves as confined to a low point upon that implied scale. Typical was the observation by Lucretia Coffin Mott which opened her "Discourse on Women": "I have long wished to see woman occupying a more elevated position than that which custom for ages has allotted to her."[20] That theme of stifled elevation interweaves throughout her speech. For the earliest feminist speakers especially, height represented anything but a challenge and an opportunity for climbing and rising. Woman may yearn for a "higher existence," Stanton noted in 1848, but "her sphere is home," and all her aspirations are "buried beneath the weight of these undivided cares."[21]

Thus, these orators expressed the vastness of power that loomed above women and constantly pressed them downward. That power was often exercised in tyrannical marriages, in which, as Ernestine Rose put it, "the husband holds the iron heel of legal oppression on the subjugated neck of the wife until every spark of womanhood is crushed out."[22]

Such contemporary metaphors as "glass ceiling" are obviously lingering fragments of this frustrated consciousness of symbolic vertical space. On the other hand, women—at least during most of the period surveyed in this study—had little interest in forward-backward movement. Rather, they had a spherical point of reference for their lives. Usually, they saw themselves as confined within a circle.[23] Typical was the opening of the 1838 Address of the Convention of Anti-Slavery Women: "We fear not censure from you for going beyond the circle which has been drawn around us by physical force, by mental usurpation, by the usages of ages. . . . We are told that it is not within the 'province of woman,' to discuss the subject of slavery; . . . and we are 'stepping out of our sphere,' when we take part in its discussion."[24] Resolution 8 of the Declaration of Sentiments and Resolutions in 1848 declared: "Resolved, That woman has too long rested satisfied in the circumscribed limits which corrupt customs and a perverted application of the Scriptures have marked out for her, and that it is time she should move in the enlarged sphere which her great Creator has assigned her."[25] Growth for women would require a release from that repressive circle and would entail a radiating outward in many directions. As Clarinda Howard Nichols put the matter in 1851, "It is only since I have met the varied responsibilities of life, that I have comprehended woman's sphere; and I have come to regard it as lying within the whole circumference of humanity."[26] As long as women were confined to the circle predetermined for them, they would be belittled. As Stanton noted in her 1867 Kansas speech, "Our lawmakers have legislated us into a nutshell, technically saying that . . . we have not souls large enough to claim justice and equality." These laws, she said, produced "the dwarfed and crippled creations of your fancies."[27] Thus, "women's sphere" and "women's place" for the feminist orators were most often metaphors of opprobrium.

As the women's movement became fixated upon—and, ironically, largely confined itself to—the suffrage issue, and as hope rose in the early decades of the twentieth century that this goal might actually be achieved, the feminist spatial metaphors became more linear and simple, expressing less a consciousness of depressed life conditions and more an impulse toward achievement and power.[28] Nowhere was this changing consciousness more interesting than in speeches by Carrie Chapman Catt. Catt opened her 1902 Presidential Address to the National American Woman's Suffrage Association by picturing women on an upward and forward trajectory toward the greater political and social power that gaining the ballot represented.[29] She painted a dynamic picture to inspire and activate women during a time, Campbell notes, when the movement was becalmed.[30] In her enthusiasm she almost created a rhetorical problem for herself as she interpreted John Stuart Mill: "For the past five hundred years, man as the dominant power in the world has been going down the ladder and woman has been climbing up. Every decade has brought them nearer together."[31] That depiction, describing a loss of power for men, was not likely to reassure possible male converts, but then she quickly amended the image: "There is but one answer and that is, to lift the subject woman to the throne by the side of the sovereign man."[32] In her 1917 speech to Congress Catt's vivid sense of forward movement allowed her to reconstruct rhetorical Time.[33] For her time had become a moving force, rushing forward. The world was in a race for justice for women, and justice itself required accelerated time. Some states were "behind the time," and time could not wait for them to catch up. Since the movement forward toward the ballot was inevitable, it would be foolish to stand in front of it. On the other hand, time's movement swept all along with it and converged onto moments of moral choice, vital decision: nothing is mightier than "the power of an idea when its time has come to move." But there was a guide for this relentless movement. "Holding her torch aloft, Liberty is pointing the way onward and upward and saying to America, 'Come.'"[34] This fertile metaphor entwining rhetorical time and space dominated much of the speech.

Metaphors that preoccupy a domain of discourse as constantly as this sense of symbolic space often attract powerful satellite figures. The chains and bonds of slavery were a powerful culturetype for nineteenth-century America. Used as metaphor for the fate of woman, this vehicle dramatized and extended the sense of restricted space. Typical was the demand by Ernestine Rose: "We call on the nation to remove the legal shackles from woman . . . . [Under such laws her] mind becomes cramped and stifled, for it cannot expand under bolts and bars; . . . confined within the narrowest possible limits."[35] Others saw the institution of marriage as woman's prison and depicted the church as also imposing chains upon her. The dominant vision was that of woman as slave, and the most hopeful note in the history of this sad image was Carrie Chapman Catt's report in 1916 that, "above the roar of cannon, the scream of shrapnel and the whirr of aeroplanes, one who listens may hear the cracking of the fetters which have long bound the European woman to outworn conventions."[36]

The theme of war in this example calls attention to a rather interesting anomaly among the feminist metaphors. Many of these speeches were peace oriented: war, these speakers implied, was *man's* creation, and they envisioned a day when women, acting from positions of greater influence in public life, would abolish it. It is ironic, therefore, to discover how often the feminists perpetuated the mentality of warfare by frequent and vivid uses of military metaphors. The Address to Anti-Slavery Women, for example, condemned violence but depicted its followers as "battling for the world's freedom."[37] Stanton began her speaking career with a speech that offered a dramatic, concluding portrait of heroic women at war with their adversaries.[38] In her last great speech, more than four decades later, she depicted life itself as war and people as soldiers. "Life," she said, "must ever be a march and a battle." And "in the long, weary march, each one walks [and presumably must fight] alone."[39] Many other examples of vivid metaphors of war could be offered, but the point seems clear: despite their aversion to war, the feminist orators exploited the human fascination for war in the symbols they created. The price they paid for these heroic, dramatic portraits of woman's struggle was to romanticize the very mentality many of them professed to despise.

Another tragic irony of the movement—and to my mind one of its ethical flaws—is that its metaphorical patterns reveal a more prominent role for derogatory animal metaphors than appeared in the rhetoric of male orators. Women who were pleading for the greater humanism of the self, and who painted eloquent pictures of the moral importance of that emergence, did not hesitate to dehumanize their adversaries. Animal metaphors often license demeaning attitudes, if not brutal behaviors. Ida Wells accurately portrayed how whites used such metaphors to condone lynching in the so-called New South: in white-oriented newspapers blacks were depicted as "coons"; they were "fiendish and brutal"; they were "lustful wild beasts . . . who have lost their 'healthy fear' of whites."[40] Yet the feminist orators were hardly more kind to their adversaries: they emphasized portraits of men as monsters and predators. Stanton's portrayals were especially vivid: her stereotypical depiction of the beastly husband in her "Slave's Appeal" speech lingers in memory.[41] In her Seneca Falls speech she absolved God of any responsibility for the creation of man: "Say not that He has had any part in the production of that creeping, cringing, crawling, debased, selfish monster, now extant, claiming for himself the name of man."[42] As for the so-called protection provided by the husband for the wife, it was "such as the wolf gives the lamb—such as the eagle the hare he carries to his eyrie!"[43] Feminist depictions of the women who opposed them were quite contemptuous: these women were "flies in the sunshine," worthless "clams,"[44] or, as Stanton put it more elegantly in the conclusion of her 1854 speech to the New York legislature, "fashionable butterflies who, through the short summer days, seek the sunshine and the flowers; but the cool breezes of autumn and the hoary frosts of winter will soon chase all these away."[45] Such animal metaphors created a grotesque quality in early feminist rhetoric, perhaps in response to the rising frustration felt within the movement, and encouraged a regrettable degree of stereotyping.

As the movement advanced, animal metaphors became less frequent and more healthy when they did occur. The last significant instance I identified was in Catt's 1902 speech, in which she vividly portrayed the condition of women across many centuries as "drones in a hive of bees" with little purpose beyond procreation.[46] These women, she said, were like "the imprisoned bird which sings in its cage in forgetfulness of the freedom which is its birthright." But, she noted, "how quickly these imprisoned ones learn to lift their wings and to fly when the bars are no longer there."[47] Thus, this story of a darker side to the women's movement can end upon a hopeful note.

Feminist orators have a keener awareness of flora as well as fauna, when we compare them to the male speakers. At times vegetation images cohere with the dominant themes of confinement and repression, as when Maria Miller Stewart complained of the effects of low, hard labor: "The ideas become confined, the mind barren, and, like the scorching sands of Arabia, produces nothing; or, like the uncultivated soil, brings forth thorns and thistles."[48] At other times vegetation images formed derogatory comparisons, as when Catt summarized a traditional male attitude toward woman: "He loved to think of her as the tender clinging vine, while he was the strong and sturdy oak."[49] Stanton used such imagery in 1848 to form a realistic prediction of the course of the movement: "We do not expect our path will be strewn with the flowers of popular applause, but over the thorns of bigotry and prejudice will be our way."[50] For the most part, however, these orators felt an affinity with nature, especially interesting in light of Kolodny's argument that the land-as-woman is a metaphor of archetypal proportions in male conceptions of the American landscape.[51] Many of the early feminist orators appear to have accepted an intuitive sense of sisterhood with the land. Their vegetation images expressed a patient, constructive outlook: they seemed willing to wait for the seeds they were planting to sprout, for the buds they were tending to bloom. In her Kansas speech Stanton illustrated this attitude: "The precious seeds of equality garnered from the sufferings of our forefathers under a British yoke, brought in the May Flower [sic] to these western shores, are to find here for the first time, a rich soil and genial atmosphere and with woman to help in the planting you may look for a full fruition and harvests of plenty. On the rock bound coast of New England . . . there was no soil for seed like this."[52] As she concluded "Discourse on Woman," Lucretia Coffin Mott advised women: "I would charge you to water the undying bud, and give it healthy culture, and open its beauty to the sun—and then you may hope, that when your life is bound up with another, you will go on equally, and in a fellowship that shall pervade every earthly interest."[53] As Catt observed in her 1902 speech: "Whenever so little encouragement was given them, these women grew, and unfolded and blossomed, until like the lilies of the field, they filled the air with the fragrance of their well doing."[54]

There are obvious dangers to such images. For one thing they lack urgency: the patience they imply could invite exploitation by opponents and procrastination by supporters. As she created a sense of dynamic Time in her 1917 speech, Catt had to confront this attitude among some supporters of the movement. Such images also lack energy, that impulse to action so dear to the heart of rhetoric. At times they can seem downright enervating, as in the kind of overscented tribute to ideal marriage we see in Frances Willard's speech "A White Life for Two": "It is the fairest, sweetest Rose of Time, whose petals and whose perfume expand so far that we are all inclosed and sheltered in their tenderness and beauty."[55] Of course, this image was designed for the earlier and select sensibilities of Willard's audience, but one wonders about the overall impact of such effeminated metaphors on the fate of a movement.[56]

Other images seem less compromising. The feminist orators excelled in creating powerful artistic metaphors, such as the musical images already mentioned. Especially striking was a sculptural metaphor that developed in Stanton's 1860 address to the Judiciary Committee of the New York State Legislature. The speech began with a mention of the figure of woman at the pinnacle of a structure of rights. The image developed through a concluding narrative that told of a competition in Athens to mold a statue to stand at the crown of the Temple of Minerva. One statue, which wins instant applause, depicts the goddess as soft, appealing, life-size. The other, rejected at first by the public, is a gigantic Amazonian figure whose massive features seem hard and offensive. But, when these figures are placed on the temple, the first seems trivial and the second suddenly appropriate to the majesty of the edifice. Stanton concluded: "If she is to be raised up to adorn a temple, or represent a divinity—if she is to fill the niche of wife and counselor to true and noble men, if she is to be the mother, the educator of a race of heroes or martyrs, of a Napoleon, or a Jesus—then must the type of womanhood be on a larger scale than that yet carved by man."[57]

Stanton's sculpting image connected with the predominant theme of vertical space. But it also introduced another significant cluster of images based upon the structural vehicle. For female as well as male orators structural metaphors usually embody an inherent humanism: they depict the human power to control our environment and to shape a better fate. They are not always constructive—for example, Angelina Grimké described "the Bastille of slavery" that was beginning "to totter to its foundation";[58] Matilda Joslyn Gage described the church as a "bulwark" raised against liberty and new ideas;[59] and Anna Howard Shaw deplored a kind of architectural division of the sexes, concluding: "No government which erects an insurmountable barrier between one half of the citizens and their rights as citizens can call itself a Republic."[60] The most significant structural metaphors in the feminist speeches, however, expressed the powerful constructive impulses of the movement. Following in the spirit of her Temple of Minerva metaphor in the 1860 speech, Stanton developed at the opening of her Kansas speech a vision of a new ideological structure: "I reverently tread this soil as the vestabule [sic] to our Temple of Liberty, the opening vista to the future grandeur of the new republic. . . . It is fitting that the cornerstone of the new republic should be laid here, where the first battles of liberty were fought and won over the monster slavery."[61] Later she predicted that this temple would be erected "on a foundation that will stand forever and ever."[62] And she went on to dream of a day "when the polling booth shall be a beautiful Temple, surrounded by fountains and flowers and triumphal arches through which young men and maidens shall go up in joyful procession to ballot for justice and mercy and when our elections shall be like the holy feasts of the Jews at Jerusalem."[63] We have yet to attain that vision in Tennessee.

Stanton's dream of building the Temple of Liberty was taken up some fifty years later by Carrie Chapman Catt as the dominant vision of her speech, "The Crisis." Here the metaphor dramatized the constructive highlights of the movement's history, paying tribute to those who built the foundation, to those whom she called the "suffrage master-masons" who laid the stones, to the laying of the cornerstones representing the four major demands of the movement, and to the capstones on top which represented the achievement of these demands. For members of her audience there remained the task of completing the roof. Already the planks had been "stretched across the top-most peak of this edifice of woman's liberty," made up of the planks from the platforms of all majority and minority political parties. "Over our heads, up there in the clouds, but tantalizing [sic] near, hangs the roof of our edifice,—the vote. What is our duty? Shall we spend time in admiring the capstones and cornice? Shall we lament the tragedies which accompanied the laying of the cornerstones? Or, shall we, like the builders of old, chant, 'Ho! all hands, all hands, heave to! All hands, heave to!' and while we chant, grasp the overhanging roof and with a long pull, a strong pull and a pull together, fix it in place forevermore?"[64] When they completed their work, of course, they would have built a home worthy of New Woman, whether she chose to stand atop it or to reside within it.

The previous statement reminds us that woman's traditional "home," her usual habitation, did not often resonate positively with feminist orators. Too often, we have noted, home was the site of woman's bondage. That may be the key to a striking discovery when one compares the figurative tendencies of male and female speakers: men are attracted frequently and favorably to images of the family, while the feminist orators prefer other sources. Perhaps the reality of their situations precluded much romanticizing about "the human family."[65] A similar contrast occurs when we consider the relatively reduced emphasis among feminist orators on metaphors of light and darkness. Certainly, the metaphor remains a significant source for them, but for much of the movement's history, as represented here, women pictured themselves as plunged into such utter darkness that any promise of the light would have seemed only cruel illusion. The tone of such imagery was expressed in the "Address to Anti-Slavery Women" in 1838: "The events of the last two years have 'cast their dark shadows before,' overclouding the bright prospects of the future, and shrouding the destinies of our country in more than midnight gloom."[66] Stanton in 1848 could see only an ironic sun: "the sphere of woman gradually becomes wider, but not even under what is thought to be the full blaze of the sun of civilization is it what God designed it to be."[67] Mott spoke of those who "prefer darkness to light" and of "oppression [that] has so long darkened the mind that it cannot appreciate [the blessing of Liberty]."[68] She dreamed in her conclusion of women elevated to the point that they could be cultivated by the sunlight of knowledge. "How long is it," echoed Ernestine Rose, "since any of us have come out of the darkness into the light of day?"[69] Stanton's magnificent speech "The Solitude of Self" continued the preoccupation with darkness when she pictured the lonely soul as launched upon a midnight sea.[70]

So goes the litany of darkness over the light within the earlier decades of the movement. But in the 1890s the emphasis within this metaphor began to change. From her crow's nest Frances Willard announced the bright hope of mutual chastity in the sky of modern life.[71] She forecast "better days dawning" and celebrated "the sunshine of God's love."[72] Though a world apart in orientation, Matilda Joslyn Gage concurred in the same year that "Yes, it is daybreak everywhere; we see its radiance in Europe, in South America, in Africa."[73] But hers would be the dawning of a storm that would eventually destroy church influence over the lives of women. Finally, in "The Crisis" Catt praised Alice Stone Blackwell, daughter of Lucy Stone, as a source of light in the overwhelming darkness: "[She] presides over the *Woman's Journal* and, like a lamp in a lighthouse, the rays of her intelligence, farsightedness and clear-thinking have enlightened the world concerning our cause."[74] Catt went on to celebrate the "rosy tints of the coming day." Clearly, in the last decades of the early movement women finally were able to use the full darkness and light contrast without implicitly mocking the condition of their audiences.

The "lighthouse" reference forms a bridge to metaphors of water and the sea. Stanton's "Solitude of Self" has rightly been celebrated by Campbell as a moving, if somewhat strange, oration.[75] In nothing was the Stanton speech more "strange" than in its preoccupation with the sea metaphor. The speech began by imagining the state of woman as comparable to that of Robinson Crusoe, isolated upon a lonely island in the midst of a vast implicit ocean. Stanton went on to say:

> [Women] . . . must make the voyage of life alone, and for safety in an emergency, they must know something of the laws of naviga-tion. To guide our own craft, we must be captain, pilot, engineer; with chart and compass to stand at the wheel; to watch the winds and waves, and know when to take in the sail, and to read the signs in the firmament over all. It matters not whether the solitary voyager is man or woman; nature, having endowed them equally, leaves them to their own skill and judgment in the hour of danger, and if not equal to the occasion, alike they perish.[76]

She elaborated as she described "the immeasurable solitude of self": "No mortal ever has been, no mortal ever will be like the soul just launched on the sea of life."[77] And she returned to this metaphor until, in her conclusion, she finally described that solitude that each of us must carry within as "more inaccessible than the ice-cold mountains, more profound than the midnight sea."[78]

One reason for the seeming strangeness of this thematic metaphor is the infrequent use of sea images among the female orators considered here. By far they prefer less turbulent, more domestic water metaphors such as pools or the "fountain in the garden." This discovery confirms my earlier speculation that the sea metaphor had long belonged to the rhetorical domain of men, who return to it often for dramatic depictions of personal and social conditions.[79] An ironic illustration of this point occurred during the 1860 debate on the subject of divorce at the Na-tional Woman's Rights Convention. Wendell Phillips—in his brief speech proposing to strike all the resolutions on divorce from the convention journal—launched an extended sea metaphor:

> You know that, when you look at a barometer on a common sun-shiny day, you must furnish yourself with an infinitesimal point of brass, and a machinery of delicate wheels to move it a small atom of space, sufficient to measure the changes of the quicksilver. But when you are in the East India seas, and the monsoon is about to blow, or the tempest is about to sweep the surface of the waters, the barometer will jump an inch, or fall down an inch, according as the change is to be. You need no machinery then, when a storm

is coming that will lift your ship out of the very sea itself. I think, that in the twenty years that have gone by, we have had the little, infinitesimally minute changes of the barometer; but the New York Legislature has risen a full inch in the moral barometer the last twenty months. (Applause.) It is a proof that the monsoon is coming that will lift the old conservative ship, carrying the idea that woman is a drudge and a slave, out of the waters, and dash her into fragments on the surface of our Democratic sea.[80]

While Phillips may have found this an apt metaphor for the progression of women's rights, no feminist orator other than Stanton turned often to the sea for figuration. Even she avoided such romantic views of the ocean as the positive setting for a constructive storm of change. Hers was more the classical sea of risk and danger. Why this general avoidance, if not antipathy, among early feminist orators, for the sea? I believe that these orators, in most rhetorical situations, intuited that their audiences might not respond to images of the ocean. And the reason might be obvious. After all, the image of self at sea implies the lack of confinement, the release from all moorings of obligation—indeed, the condition of freedom. During most of the times represented by these speeches the image of woman at sea on the voyage of life would have seemed a mockery.

Stanton's powerful sea imagery, on one level, represented an intrusion into the sacred preserve of male symbolism. But it also suggested that the cause of women had now evolved to the point that they too might dream of themselves as launched upon symbolic seas in life's great adventure. Therefore, Stanton's usage signified a stylistic revolution, a small rebellion contained within the language of agitation, which might well portend beyond the mere occupation of privileged symbolic forms. Beneath the lyricism of the speech moved a powerful implicit message, what Ishmael might have called a "Looming."

Final Thoughts

This study must end in incompleteness. We have accomplished only a partial telling—and a brief telling at that—of the stories suggested by this analysis. Left untold and unexplained is the strange unpopularity of disease metaphors for feminist orators in contrast with male speakers. Even more fascinating perhaps is a possible gender contrast in the use of anthropomorphic metaphors, those based upon the human form:

the men in the sample appear to prefer more precise synecdochal references to specific anatomical features as representative of some whole (such as "the arm of the empire"), while the women prefer more holistic representation by personification (Kansas pictured as heroine, the church viewed as "digging its own grave," etc.)

As noted at the outset, we require a more complete picture of female orators across time, especially including twentieth-century speakers, before we can begin to assess figurative differences by gender and to reconstruct the theory of archetypal metaphor in rhetoric. It is possible at this point, I think, to advance what I shall call the "little more" hypothesis: in general women appear to be a little more creative than men in their uses of metaphor. They explore a greater variety of metaphor types, they elaborate them further, and they turn to metaphor a little more frequently to express their ideas. Beyond this general hypothesis we can venture certain observations and speculations. The limited range of evidence here surely confirms the archetypal status of spatial figuration as well as the very human preoccupation with war and conflict. The evidence might also suggest that a more complete picture of twentieth-century orators, both male and female, would underscore the enduring symbolic importance of light and darkness. Predicting greater access to sea imagery for later twentieth-century female orators does little to change my earlier prediction of waning overall importance of the ocean as an archetypal setting for the human condition.[81] One disturbing trajectory perhaps foreshadowed in the evidence is the possible rise of dehumanizing animal metaphors as the justification for deadly conflict during our conflicted century. Finally, the greater interest evinced here in cultural and artistic metaphors and in vegetation metaphors may be examined as possibly distinctive gender traits as we construct a more adequate account of rhetoric's figurative resources.

This analysis, it is hoped, suggests the richness of the data discovered in this survey and validates the possible utility of a trans-textual approach to rhetorical criticism. Through the patterns of metaphor established in their speeches these orators revealed the soul of their movement and of their emerging community. In the occasional meanness as well as magnificence of their rhetoric they projected their own complex humanity. Since that, after all, was their primary purpose, to establish their full humanity bounded only by mortal limitations, their rhetoric has a reflexive, self-validating quality.[82] They spoke out of passion and pain, especially as they created spatial metaphors that reflected their terrible sense of confinement and repression. To underscore that point they fashioned metaphors that connected the archetype of space with the culturetype of human slavery. They were innovative in the rhetorical use of artistic metaphors, which helped emphasize the creativity of their political mission. But their images also glorified the spirit of war, even while their arguments often condemned war as a male preoccupation. Too often they dishonored their campaign to achieve greater humanity by their use of dehumanizing animal metaphors. They made muted uses of the archetypes of light and darkness and the sea, understandable in terms of their life conditions. And gradually, out of the darkness and frustration of their cause, they shaped a grand vision of a greater nation that offered to its women undreamed-of chances for fulfillment. Fusing religious with political themes, they envisioned a Temple of Liberty that would nurture women worthy of residing within it or presiding over it. This grand, graphic icon they created for the ideograph they cherished may indicate most conclusively how their long struggle enriched the rhetorical heritage of the nation.

Notes

1. The research and ideas presented in this essay were first explored in my course Seminar in Style held in the fall of 1993 at the University of Memphis. The discussions in that seminar were especially productive for the work presented here. I express fond thanks to all the members of that seminar.

2. Michael Calvin McGee, "Text, Context, and the Fragmentation of Contemporary Culture," *Western Journal of Speech Communication* 54 (Summer 1990): 274–89.

3. Philip Wheelwright, *The Burning Fountain: A Study in the Language of Symbolism* (Bloomington: Indiana University Press, 1954).

4. I discuss these qualities of "archetypal metaphor" in Michael Osborn and Douglas Ehninger, "The Metaphor in Public Address," *Speech Monographs* 29 (August 1962): 223–34; and in "The Archetypal Metaphor in Rhetoric: The Light-Dark Family," *Quarterly Journal of Speech* 53 (April 1967): 115–26.

5. Karlyn Kohrs Campbell, *Man Cannot Speak for Her: A Critical Study of Early Feminist Rhetoric* (New York: Praeger, 1989), 1:1.

6. Karlyn Kohrs Campbell, *Man Cannot Speak for Her: Key Texts of the Early Feminists* (New York: Praeger, 1989), 2:x.

7. I made only two exceptions regarding the speeches included in the Campbell collection. In applying the methods I shortly describe, I first excluded a speech by Wendell Phillips at the National Woman's Rights Convention Debate in 1860, for the obvious reason that this study examines patterns of usage

among women orators. I do cite this speech for contrast later in the study. A second exclusion was the Stanton speech "On Divorce," given before the Judiciary Committee of the New York Senate in 1861. The speech repeats verbatim much of the speech she made during the 1860 debate. Double listing of the same metaphors would have contaminated the study. All textual citations in this study are to the Campbell collection.

8. In a recent study of Mott's "Discourse on Woman" A. Cheree Carlson focuses on the speaker's use of "inner light" as a Burkean "bridging device" to transcend both contemporary social differences and the tensions rising from Mott's personal background and needs ("Defining Womanhood: Lucretia Coffin Mott and the Transformation of Femininity," *Western Journal of Communication* 58 [Spring 1994]: 85). But the Quaker concept of inner light itself taps into the more fundamental archetypal metaphor of light and darkness (Michael P. Graves, "Functions of Key Metaphors in Early Quaker Sermons, 1671–1700," *Quarterly Journal of Speech* 69 [November 1983]: 364–78). It is from the resources of such privileged vehicles that orators often draw transcendent symbolic appeals.

9. George Lakoff and Mark Johnson, *Metaphors We Live By* (Chicago: University of Chicago Press, 1980).

10. *The Philosophy of Rhetoric* (New York: Oxford University Press, 1936), 92.

11. Angelina Grimké [Weld], "'Address at Pennsylvania Hall,' 1838," 30.

12. Anna Howard Shaw, "'The Fundamental Principle of a Republic,' 1915," 442–43.

13. Frances E. Willard, "'A White Life for Two,' 1890," 332.

14. Elizabeth Cady Stanton, "'Kansas State Referendum Campaign Speech at Lawrence, Kansas,' 1867," 260–77; Carrie Chapman Catt, "'The Crisis,' Atlantic City, NJ, 1916," 483–502.

15. Stanton, "'A Slave's Appeal,' Speech to the Judiciary Committee, New York State Legislature, 1860," 168–86.

16. William Martin Reynolds, "Deliberative Speaking in Ante-Bellum South Carolina: The Idiom of a Culture" (Ph. D. diss., University of Florida, 1960).

17. Kenneth Burke, *Permanence and Change: An Anatomy of Purpose* (New York: New Republic, 1935), 118–64.

18. "Ultimate Terms in Contemporary Rhetoric," *The Ethics of Rhetoric* (Chicago: Henry Regnery, 1953), 211–32.

19. Stanton, "'Speech at the Seneca Falls Convention,' 1848," 42.

20. Lucretia Coffin Mott, "'Discourse on Woman,' 1849," 74.

21. Stanton, "Seneca Falls," 46, 47.

22. Ernestine Potowski Rose, "'National Woman's Rights Convention Debate," New York City, 1860," 215.

23. It is interesting that Charles Conrad uses the same metaphor when he describes life conditions during the early feminist era: "Nineteenth-century

women were imprisoned within a narrowly circumscribed sphere by discrimination sanctioned by both custom and law" ("The Transformation of the 'Old Feminist" Movement," *Quarterly Journal of Speech* 67 [August 1981]: 285).

24. "'Address, Convention of Anti-Slavery Women,' 1838," 11, 12.

25. "'Declaration of Sentiments and Resolutions,' 1848," 38.

26. Clarina Howard Nichols, "'The Responsibilities of Woman,' Second National Woman's Rights Convention, Worcester, MA, 1851," 125.

27. Stanton, "Kansas Campaign Speech," 274, 275.

28. There seems an unmistakable connection between the spherical, three-dimensional sense of space and the broad program of human rights espoused by early feminists. As this program became focused on the specific issue of suffrage, the sense of space itself became "masculinized" within the rhetoric of movement orators (see the argument in Conrad's essay).

29. Catt, "Presidential Address,' 1902," 463–82.

30. Campbell, *Key Texts,* 462.

31. Catt, "Presidential Address," 480.

32. Ibid., 481.

33. Catt, "'Address to the United States Congress,' 1917," 503–32.

34. Ibid., 531.

35. Rose, "'Speech at the National Woman's Rights Convention,' Worcester, MA, 1851," 115.

36. Catt, "Crisis," 492.

37. "Anti-Slavery Women," 15.

38. Stanton, "Seneca Falls," 70.

39. Stanton, "Solitude of Self," 376, 381.

40. Ida B. Wells, "'Southern Horrors: Lynch Law in All Its Phases,' 1892," 389–419.

41. Stanton, "Slave's Appeal," 178–79.

42. Stanton, "Seneca Falls," 49.

43. Ibid., 56.

44. Rev. Antoinette Brown [Blackwell], 1860 debate, 212, 214.

45. Stanton, "'Address to the Legislature of New York,' 1854," 166.

46. Catt, "'Presidential Address,' 1902," 471.

47. Ibid., 477.

48. Maria W. Miller Stewart, "'Lecture Delivered at the Franklin Hall,' 1832," 6.

49. Catt, "Presidential Address," 474.

50. Stanton, "Seneca Falls," 70.

51. Annette Kolodny, *The Lay of the Land: Metaphor as Experience and History in American Life and Letters* (Chapel Hill: University of North Carolina Press, 1975).

52. Stanton, "Kansas Campaign Speech," 264.

53. Mott, "Discourse on Woman," 97.

54. Catt, "Presidential Address," 477.

55. Willard, "White Life," 319.

56. For a discussion of Willard's rhetorical legacy, see Bonnie J. Dow, "The 'Womanhood' Rationale in the Woman Suffrage Rhetoric of Frances E. Willard," *Southern Communication Journal* 56 (Summer 1991): 298–307.

57. Stanton, "Slave's Appeal," 185.

58. Grimké, "'Address at Pennsylvania Hall,' 1838," 30.

59. Matilda Joslyn Gage, "'The Dangers of the Hour,' Women's National Liberal Convention, 1890," 343, 352.

60. Shaw, "'The Fundamental Principle of a Republic,' 1915," 442.

61. Stanton, "Kansas Campaign Speech," 260–61.

62. Ibid., 267.

63. Ibid., 270.

64. Catt, "Crisis," 496.

65. This apparently intuitive avoidance of the family metaphor as an unfriendly identity trap has become quite self-conscious in modern feminism. Lynn M. Stearney traces the rise of a consciousness that resists the reduction of women to motherhood— and, hence, by usual association to family role— in her essay "Feminism, Ecofeminism, and the Maternal Archetype: Motherhood as a Feminine Universal," *Communication Quarterly* 42 (Spring 1994): 145–59. We must remember, however, that, during the time of the early feminists, women were hardly a united constituency. The women (and men) who listened to Frances Willard's appeals to "true womanhood" presumably had quite positive associations with home and family, since she used "home protection" as the rationale for her pro-suffrage arguments (Dow, "'Womanhood' Rationale," 302).

66. "Anti-Slavery Women," 14.

67. Stanton, "Seneca Falls," 43.

68. Mott, "Discourse on Woman," 75, 89.

69. Rose, "1851 NWRC Speech," 121.

70. Stanton, "Solitude," 384.

71. Willard, "White Life," 332.

72. Ibid., 336, 337.

73. Gage, "Dangers of the Hour," 369.

74. Catt, "Crisis," 495.

75. Karlyn Kohrs Campbell, "Stanton's 'The Solitude of Self': A Rationale for Feminism," *Quarterly Journal of Speech* 66 (October 1980): 304–12.

76. Stanton, "Solitude," 374.

77. Ibid.

78. Ibid., 384.

79. Michael Osborn, ""The Evolution of the Archetypal Sea in Rhetoric and Poetic," *Quarterly Journal of Speech* 63 (December 1977): 347–63.

80. Wendell Phillips, "'National Woman's Rights Convention Debate,' New York City, 1860," 223–24.

81. This was one of the conclusions of my "Archetypal Sea" essay.

82. Such a proof function, which accumulates in these speeches at an unconscious level of demonstration, has been described elsewhere as "enactment," a rhetorical phenomenon in which the speaker and the speech "incarnate the argument," themselves constituting the proof of what is said (Karlyn Kohrs Campbell and Kathleen Hall Jamieson, "Introduction" in *Form and Genre: Shaping Rhetorical Action,* ed. Karlyn Kohrs Campbell and Kathleen Hall Jamieson [Falls Church, Va.: Speech Communication Association, 1978], 9–11).

CHAPTER TWO

The Perils of Patterning

Martha Watson

No place so sacred from such fops is barred
Nor is Paul's church more safe than Paul's church yard:
Nay, fly to altars; there they'll talk you dead:
Fools rush in where angels fear to tread.
 Alexander Pope, "Essay on Criticism"

Pope's witty observation about "bookful blockheads" has special resonance for me. Often, too often, in my professional life I have rushed in where other wiser heads have hesitated. Unfortunately, I haven't learned much from experience, and I still tend to forge ahead when more careful contemplation might lead me to pause or at least ask questions.

In this essay I have no choice. My task is to respond to Michael Osborn's essay on metaphoric patterns in woman's rights rhetoric. Only when I began to engage the essay did I realize that I had been foolish. Taking on "Mr. Metaphor" (or, alternately, "Metaphor Man"), who is doing a "corrective" to his previous work based entirely on all male rhetors, poses a substantial dilemma for me: I like Mike, I like his work, and I like adding the study of women's rhetoric in almost any way to our discipline. So, I am in the awkward position—foolish, one might say—of critiquing a person and a project for which I have the keenest sympathy.

In reading his essay, one cannot help but be struck by the sensitivity with which Mike approaches these texts. His sensitivity is clear not only in his deft textual analysis but also in his interpretations of the works. When he speaks of women orators' "complex, three-dimensional, often exquisitely painful sense of space" or explores Cady Stanton's use of the sea metaphor, his critical perspicuity and his human sympathy cannot be missed. Thus, as I broach my "questions" about this essay, I hope these can be seen in the context of my admiration for his work, here and elsewhere.

For my critique I want to take as a point of departure one passage from Kenneth Burke which has been repeatedly useful to me as a scholar. The excerpt is from "Terministic Screens" in *Language as Symbolic Action*. As you probably recall, in this section Burke is working toward a distinction between a "scientistic" and a "dramatistic" approach to the nature of language. "A 'scientistic' approach," he avers, "begins with questions of *naming,* or *definition.*"[1] Arguing that even the most objective-seeming language is still suasive, he notes: "Even if any given terminology is a *reflection* of reality, by its very nature as a terminology it must be a *selection* of reality; and to this extent it must function also as a *deflection* of reality. . . . Also, *many of the "observations" are but implications of the particular terminology in which the observation was made.*"[2] With this as background I want to examine Mike's essay with a degree of skepticism which does not reflect my appreciation of what he has done.

The first question I want to address is about the source of metaphors and about "metaphorness" as a textual feature. In particular, I want to consider where metaphors "are" in rhetoric. To many the answer is transparent: metaphors are in texts, put there by rhetors. Mike writes, for example, that feminist orators must surely have intuited the special importance of archetypal metaphors in framing their arguments and appeals." My first objection to Mike's approach is to challenge his notion of the rhetor's awareness of metaphors. Certainly, some skillful, astute rhetors may craft metaphors with care and precision. Some may even be aware of recurrent patterns, what Mike terms archetypal metaphors. But I am skeptical that we can assume that these women were aware of the power of the patterns they chose. Indeed, I am wary of assuming that they realized that they were crafting metaphors. If metaphors are cognitive devices, as Lakoff and Johnson suggest, some of their power comes from our obliviousness to them. While I obviously cannot disprove Mike's assumption, I think we must be careful to attribute the creation of metaphors so quickly to the ingenuity of rhetors.

My second objection to Mike's approach to metaphor is a bit easier to address concretely. Just as I am convinced that metaphors work differently in "literary" texts and "rhetorical" texts, as I think Mike's work implicitly argues, I am troubled that we as critics tend to see metaphors as lying about in texts ready to be seized and analyzed. If we regard texts as primarily written documents that we can explore and peruse at our leisure, this may be the case. But, if we consider speech texts from the perspective of the audience, then the matter is more complicated.

An audience member's exposure to a spoken text is transitory; many, if not most, listeners never actually peruse a text; metaphors that we perceive with careful attention may escape the listener altogether.

Let me cite an example from the materials Mike quotes. He mentions a passage from Lucretia Coffin Mott's 1849 "Discourse on Woman": "I have long wished to see woman occupying a more elevated position than that which custom for ages has allotted to her."[3] As a trained critic, I can label that as metaphor and proceed throughout the speech picking up mentions of "sphere" and "position" to buttress a claim for the power of that metaphor in this text. But I remain unconvinced that an audience member would perceive the metaphorness of "elevated position" and that somehow that metaphorness would be significant to the rhetorical impact of the speech. A bit later he cites Cady Stanton's 1848 speech in which she avers:

A little music, that she may while an hour away pleasantly, a little French, a smattering of the sciences, and in rare instances, some slight classical knowledge, and woman is considered highly educated. She leaves her books and studies just as a young man is entering thoroughly into his. Then comes the gay routine of fashionable life, courtship and marriage, the perplexities of house and children, and she knows nothing besides. And whatever yearning her spirit may have felt for a higher existence, whatever may have been the capacity she well knew she possessed for more elevated enjoyments, enjoyments which would not conflict with those holy duties, but add new lustre to them, all, all is buried beneath the weight of these undivided cares.[4]

I have quoted more of the passage than Mike does in his essay to a purpose. To my mind the final image, "buried beneath the weight of these undivided cares," and the "yearning" that introduces the final sentence reverberate far more dramatically with Cady Stanton's immediately preceding observations than the metaphorical "*higher* existence" and "*elevated* enjoyments" to which Mike's comments draw attention. Further, I would suggest that the space metaphors that Mike cites in these passages are what Lakoff and Johnson might term "dead," or "fugitive," metaphors. Thus, to label these "clearly evident, vivid instances of metaphor," as Mike does, is, I think, at least questionable, if not inaccurate.

Another example from Mike's discussion strikes me as equally, if not more, problematic. He classes women's use of *sphere* to refer to their socially approved roles as a metaphor. I, for one, am skeptical of this classification on two grounds. First, since this term was quite common at the time to refer to the differences between women's and men's lives, one must wonder whether the women themselves had any notion of the metaphorness that Mike perceives. Second, current usage today includes the sense in which these women used the term as one part of the definition of *sphere*. How, then, can anyone determine whether this term is metaphorical to anyone except the alert critic?

I am not simply quibbling about whether metaphors are "dead" or "live"; rather, I am trying to suggest that any critically useful concept of rhetorical metaphor must approach the figure from an audience perspective. What critics can ferret out as metaphors may risk, I think, over-reading speech texts, assuming our careful scrutiny reflects the same perceptions that naive audience members would bring to hearing or casually reading the text. Put another way, with a glance back at Burke, we are finding "metaphors" both because we have set out to find them and because we have inherited an approach toward metaphor that derives from literary critics. In short, I would question some of Mike's work because it privileges the critic's perception of what is metaphorical rather than considering what an audience member might consciously or unconsciously perceive as metaphorical. Is a metaphor rhetorically significant if it might easily escape the notice of the listener?

A second issue that arises in my mind involves Mike's assumptions about the "gendering" of metaphorical patterns. Let me be clear. I would be second in line, behind Karlyn Kohrs Campbell, to insist that we need to consider texts that have been excluded from our canon. And I would be enthusiastic about any effort to study the impact of gender, class, or ethnicity on rhetorical practice. But I am wary of efforts to read gendering into patterns or practices that might reflect other factors. Let me give some examples of how this issue emerges in Mike's analysis and, I think, confounds his observations.

Mike expresses surprise that the average intensity rating for women was only slightly higher than that for men: 6.74 versus 6.69. He explains his conjecture on two fronts. Another study has indicated that pre–Civil War rhetors in the South moved into "a flight into fantasy and symbolism" as the debate over slavery reached a stalemate. Further, because women were engaged in challenging "unfavorable perspectives . . .

deeply entrenched and embodied in national laws and mores," Mike expected that they would turn to more vivid images and radical metaphors. These are certainly plausible bases for his expectation. In the interpretations that follow, however, Mike does not return to these possibilities to explain his findings. Rather, he focuses on the patterns he perceives as having to do with the gender of the rhetors. Thus, he expresses surprise that women resort to negative animalistic metaphors and that they use military images when they were largely pacifists.

In essence, Mike connects the patterns he perceives to the "womanness" of the rhetors rather than to larger cultural patterns or influences. I would suggest that at least some of the recurrent patterns that Mike perceives stem from the political and, hence, rhetorical position of the rhetors rather than their gender. Many of the patterns he notes—the particular structural metaphors, the animalistic metaphors, as well as others—are commonplace in the rhetoric of abolitionists, whether male or female, African-American or Caucasian. Thus, the patterns Mike perceives may reflect the political realities this group, like others, confronted. And this essay may, in fact, tell us more about rhetors from oppressed groups than rhetors who are female.

Mike's eagerness to provide a corrective to his earlier male-based analysis and to introduce gender as a rhetorical variable creates other problems. He develops a set of expectations which seem to me to reflect some sexual stereotypes. I make this observation with some trepidation, knowing Mike's strong commitment to feminist perspectives. So, let me try to extricate myself from the controversy this point might arouse by being a bit more explicit. Let me return to the pacifism issue first to illustrate my point.

Mike begins his analysis in the hope of showing how attention to a collection of speeches by a group of women orators "who share a time, place, and general purpose" might reveal "the motives, visions, and stresses of the early feminist movement." While I appreciate his eagerness to explore the woman's rights discourse, I am a bit uncomfortable with two methodological problems here. First, these women do not, except in the loosest sense, share a time or a place. Carrie Chapman Catt in 1902 is far removed in time as well as stance from Lucretia Mott; Ernestine Potowski Rose in 1851 has little in common with Frances Willard, particularly in terms of rhetorical stance and persona. What these women do share, to some extent, is a commitment to advancing the cause of women. The discourse anthologized by Kohrs Campbell coheres around a theme of woman's rights. But the concerns and views of these women differed dramatically. What Mike has explored is a group of somewhat thematically related speeches; what he has not shed much light on is these women as a group of speakers. Moreover, in focusing only on woman's rights advocates, Mike has left unexamined the discourse of female opponents as well as women who focused on other issues. Thus, his study does pertain only to persons who shared, to some extent, a political position. Whatever we learn from this study helps us understand the rhetorical practices of its advocates only; we can draw few, if any, conclusions about the gendering of rhetorical practice.

In this section Mike candidly admits the limitations of his study. But, in acknowledging that he is only exploring the rhetoric of the early feminist movement, Mike confronts another, unacknowledged difficulty. Equally problematic is his equating of these speeches with the rhetoric of the early feminist movement. A good number of men who supported woman's rights spoke and wrote eloquently about the relevant issues. If Mike wishes to learn about "the motives, visions, and stresses of the early feminist movement," he should broaden his scope to include works by the male spokespersons. But then, of course, he would lose the value of this study as a corrective to his earlier work.

Both of these methodological issues—treating these women as a group and overlooking the male contributors to the cause of woman's rights—reveal a deeper problem with Mike's reliance on Kohrs Campbell's anthology, which is a fine, useful work in many ways. Kohrs Campbell's agenda is to begin construction of women's rhetorical history; she sets out to "restore one segment of the history of women."[5] Kohrs Campbell quite explicitly delineates how this goal constrained and shaped her project. In relying on this group of speeches for his study, Mike inherits the self-imposed limitations of Kohrs Campbell's work. These limitations, particularly as they determine editorial selection of speeches to include, to my mind, make them somewhat inappropriate for either of Mike's projects: to correct his former focus on male orators or to offer insights into rhetoric of the early feminist movement.

Let me return to my larger point—Mike's focus on the gendering of rhetoric. Mike suggests that women's use of images of war is anomalous, since most of the feminist speakers were pacifists. Many woman's rights advocates were pacifists; Lucretia Mott and Anna Howard Shaw are particularly notable. Others, however, do not address this topic in the texts under consideration, and the subject does not dominate this discourse. Moreover, the attitudes of these women toward war was complex: many became ardent supporters of the Union during the Civil War, and later others supported the United States after it entered World War I. In short, it is misleading to label these women as a group as pacifists and to conclude that, "despite their professed hatred of actual war, the feminist orators exploited the very human fascination in their audiences for symbolic warfare. The price they paid for these heroic, dramatic portraits of woman's struggle was to reinforce the very mentality they professed to despise." My sense is that Mike's enthusiasm for particularly "womanly" features of metaphors led him to an overly broad, simplistic, and, I think, unwarranted critical leap.

My third question about this essay moves away from questions of gender to larger issues of method. Obviously, Mike here is after *patterns* of metaphor, and he seeks those patterns in the *vehicles* that recur. Thus, he looks for references to flora, fauna, space, and other elements. And he amasses some interesting examples. However, this focus on vehicles, I think, obscures points that are perhaps more interesting than those they reveal. Let me turn to the group of animal and floral metaphors discussed in the essay to explain my point.

Mike notes that animal metaphors are, unfortunately, more common in women's rhetoric than in men's; this is, he believes, an ethical failure of the movement. His first example, however, is problematic. He notes that Ida Wells Barnett mentions the animalistic depictions of blacks in Southern newspapers. Clearly, she does refer to these citations, but she is quoting their depictions, not creating her own. And my reading of those materials in Wells Barnett's speech indicates that these were not used as metaphors but as literal depictions of African Americans. In contrast, Cady Stanton's 1848 disparagement of men as a "creeping, cringing, crawling, debased, selfish monster" is strong language indeed and may deserve the disapproval Mike expresses toward this strain in the discourse. However, it seems inappropriate to lump that sort of opprobrium together with Cady Stanton's description of some women as "fashionable butterflies who, through the short summer days, seek the sunshine and flowers." While both are disapproving in context, the two particular vehicles—monster and butterfly—seem to have little in common. Treating them together as examples of a single metaphoric pattern seems to obscure more than it reveals.

Similarly, in focusing on the vehicle, Mike is led to sort together the disparate figures that refer to any sort of plant life. Miller Stewart's view of the spirit-numbing effects of hard physical labor—"scorching sands of Arabia. . . .uncultivated soil [that] brings forth thorns and thistles"— is seen as similar to Chapman Catt's reference to men's view of women as "tender clinging vine" while they themselves are "strong and sturdy oak." Added to that are a reference by Cady Stanton to the "precious seeds of equality " that came over on the *Mayflower* and another by Coffin Mott urging the watering of and caring for women's "undying bud" to produce what Chapman Catt described much later as a blossoming "lily of the field." While I understand the temptation of grouping together these disparate figures under a convenient heading— "flora"—such a classification, to my mind, does great injustice to the ideas behind the metaphor.

I could educe other examples to illustrate my belief that this metaphoric classification deflects as much of the reality of the texts as it discloses. Treating chains and bonds metaphors as well as images of the progress of time under the rubric of space may produce some insight. But in the former case, at least, it obscures an important and persistent image in women's rhetoric which probably deserves consideration in its own right.

I have other quibbles with this analysis. I am not at all convinced that Stanton's use of the sea metaphor in "Solitude" marks some kind of advance in the women's cause. The image of a new woman seems to merit more consideration than simply being grouped with structural metaphors. But these are minor matters.

The major questions I have raised will, I hope, stimulate further investigation. Where and what are rhetorical metaphors, and how do they differ from literary ones? How can we separate the impact of gender on rhetorical patterns from the influence of other factors? Does the search for metaphoric patterns lead us to overlook significant differences and to class together disparate images under convenient headings? In short, I hope I have done at least partial justice to Burke's admonition that our observations often reflect our methodology more than they do reality, whatever that may be. Mike's search for metaphoric patterns has led him to intriguing shards of discourse, but those shards need not all be part of the same pot. Sitting on his deck he may usually see the Big Dipper, but it is only because he searches for a pattern that others have imposed and he has learned.

Notes

1. Kenneth Burke, "Terministic Screens," *Language as Symbolic Action* (Los Angeles: University of California Press, 1966), 44.

2. Ibid., 45–46.

3. Lucretia Coffin Mott, "Discourse on Woman," 1849, *Man Cannot Speak for Her,* 2 vols., ed. Karlyn Kohrs Campbell (New York: Praeger, 1989), 2:74. All subsequent references to speeches will be from this volume, unless otherwise noted.

4. Elizabeth Cady Stanton, "Speech at the Seneca Falls Convention," 1848, 46–47.

5. Kohrs Campbell, *Man Cannot Speak for Her,* 1:1.

CHAPTER THREE

The Power of Hegemony
Capitalism and Racism
in the "Nadir of Negro History"

Karlyn Kohrs Campbell

The media construct for us a definition of what *race* is, what meaning the imagery of race carries, and what the "problem of race" is
understood to be.

Stuart Hall,
"The Whites of Their Eyes: Racist Ideologies and the Media"

The relationship between text and context has been an issue argued
as if it were a contest between rhetorical criticism and rhetorical history
or as if an emphasis on one inevitably leads to a deemphasis on the
other. In addition, studies of public address and studies of the rhetoric
of the mass media often have taken separate paths. In what follows I
hope to give text and context equal emphasis and to treat a public debate from a perspective that stresses the ideological role of the mass
media. The time is the post-Reconstruction era that historian Rayford
Logan called the "nadir of Negro history."[1] Accordingly, the media are
major newspapers and magazines of opinion. The debaters are Thomas
Nelson Page, spokesman for the white South, and Mary Church Terrell,
the voice of African Americans. The issue? Ostensibly, the causes and
prevention of lynching, but the debate is part of a much larger ideological struggle. In my analysis I hope to show in a small way how the
ownership and practices of the print media shaped the debate over
post-Reconstruction public policy which institutionalized and "naturalized" white racism in the United States.

Whatever else a community may be, it is a group of persons unified
by shared values and beliefs. The Civil War was dramatic evidence of
the fragility of the consensus forged by the founders in the Constitution.
Following Appomattox, passage of the Thirteenth Amendment made

slavery illegal, but in subsequent years a struggle ensued over the enforcement of the Fourteenth and Fifteenth Amendments and over the constitutionality of laws passed to protect the civil rights of former slaves, of laws passed to segregate public facilities, and of state constitutions that disenfranchised former slaves.

White racism has a long history in the United States, but it is illuminating to consider just how it came to be absorbed into the national ideology. The concept of hegemony might have been invented to describe these processes. As developed by Antonio Gramsci, hegemony describes the processes by which a social class with economic and political power dominates through rhetorical efforts that are designed to attract allies with similar economic and political interests and to obtain the assent of other classes or groups. In other words, economic power alone cannot ensure the interests of a dominant class; rhetorical efforts are required to enlist allies and obtain the consent of others.[2]

First, some history. In 1877 the last federal troops were withdrawn from the South. By 1882 lynchings of African Americans were occurring at a rate of over two per week, a rate maintained or exceeded into the new century.[3] In the 1883 *Civil Rights Cases* the Supreme Court ruled unconstitutional congressional efforts to guarantee the rights promised under the Fourteenth Amendment.[4] In 1890 Mississippi began revising its state constitution, a process emulated throughout the South, to disenfranchise African Americans,[5] and, with the 1896 *Plessy v. Ferguson* decision, segregation became the law of the land.[6] By the turn of the century the courts as well as the Republican Party had all but abandoned the 90 percent of African Americans who lived in the South.

The 1877 compromise removing federal troops from the South was largely the work of leaders in finance and industry who were eager to exploit commercial opportunities in the "New South." They, in turn, strongly influenced the reporting and editorializing in newspapers. Historian Ellis B. Oberholzer wrote, "never before had newspaper owners been such creatures of the corporation financiers and the politicians who were being fed from the rich men's hands."[7] Twelve major Northern newspapers unanimously supported the removal of federal troops; only two were sympathetic to Justice John Marshall Harlan's dissent in the 1883 *Civil Rights Cases*. As a group, they exaggerated African-American crime, usually accepting accusations as proof of guilt in lynchings, and generally printed articles, anecdotes, cartoons, and jokes reinforcing stereotypes of "the Comic Negro."[8]

The leading magazines of culture and opinion were *Harper's, Scribners' (Century* after 1881), *Atlantic Monthly, North American Review,* and *Forum,* and analyses of them present a similar picture.[9] Except for Walter Hines Page, editor of *Forum* from 1886 to 1895 and of *Atlantic* after 1897, all the editors were Northerners; similarly, their readership was predominantly Northern.[10] In general, their style was genteel; they made "few concessions to the contemporary scene and none to vulgar taste."[11] The exception was their treatment of African Americans; historian Logan was moved to "wonder why Northern devotees of the Genteel Tradition found such evident delight in the lampooning of Negroes."[12] In their fiction and poetry, reinforced by cartoons, as in their coverage of crime, they ridiculed, derided, and stereotyped, consistently reinforcing ideas of white superiority.

No competing images appeared in their pages. Only the *Forum* was available to African Americans, and those published invariably were accommodationist Bookerites; even Frederick Douglass appeared only once.[13] On subjects as extreme as lynching these magazines attempted to avoid controversy and to maintain "balance."[14] Accordingly, they routinely published white Southerners supporting a "hands-off" governmental policy and singing the siren song of the New South.

This was the milieu in 1904, when Mary Church Terrell engaged in a public debate with Thomas Nelson Page over the causes and prevention of lynching. Page was a white Southerner, born in 1853 on a Virginia plantation, son of a Confederate army officer. His fiction derided and stereotyped African Americans, and his essays propounded the most extreme forms of white racism. Page had been trained as a lawyer, was a best-selling author, and gave readings and lectured throughout the country after 1898. As a descendant of the founders, Page was prominent and respected; Woodrow Wilson named him ambassador to Italy.[15]

Mary Church Terrell was born in Memphis in 1863, the daughter of the first African-American millionaire.[16] She was educated in the North, earned a B.A. and M.A. degree from Oberlin, studied languages in Europe, and taught at Wilberforce University then at M Street High School in the District of Columbia. In 1891 she married Harvard and Howard Law School graduate Robert Heberton Terrell, whom President Theodore Roosevelt appointed to a municipal judgeship, the first African American to be so honored.

Sexism ended her teaching career when she married, but she pursued a second career as a lecturer and public reformer, with her husband's active support. She served on the Washington, D.C., school board (1895–1901, 1906–11) and was the first president of the National Association of Colored Women. Her journey toward greater militancy is reflected in her decision to become a charter member of the National Association for the Advancement of Colored People (NAACP).[17] She was an activist to the end, spearheading a campaign that combined a lawsuit with lobbying, boycotts, and sit-ins to desegregate public accommodations in the District of Columbia in 1953. She died in her ninety-first year as the Supreme Court was preparing to issue its historic *Brown v. Board of Education of Topeka* decision. As a public reformer, her rhetorical philosophy was an unshakable belief that, if whites knew about and understood the plight of African Americans, they would act to reaffirm national values and to create conditions offering equality of opportunity to all.

The ideological processes at work in the magazine industry are evident in Thomas Nelson Page's ability to urge white racist views in articles in prominent magazines. He published his first essays in 1892 and 1904 in the *North American Review,* with a circulation of about twenty-five thousand.[18] He published a three-part series in 1904 and a single essay in 1907 in *McClure's,* the magazine in which journalistic muckraking was invented.[19] The context for Page's three-part series in 1904 was Ida Tarbell's history of Standard Oil, Lincoln Steffens's investigative reports on corruption in state and local government, and Ray Stannard Baker's exposés of labor union racketeering.

There were great advantages to publishing in *McClure's.* In response to the articles by Tarbell, Steffens, and Baker, *McClure's* gained even greater preeminence as its circulation rose to a half-million and its advertising revenues grew to be the largest of any periodical at this time.[20]

In June 1904 the *North American Review* agreed to publish Church Terrell's "Lynching from a Negro's Point of View" to balance Page's essay "The Lynching of Negroes—Its Causes and Its Prevention," which had appeared in January.[21] Her work never again appeared in the *North American Review,* and, although she met with a *McClure's* representative in 1905 about writing for the magazine about her experiences in the South, no article was ever published. She wryly commented in her daybook: "They want nothing controversial."[22] Her response to Page's 1907 essay on white superiority in *McClure's* languished among her papers.

From a Marxian perspective all conflicts are fundamentally economic. In order for a capitalist minority to gain the assent of the less advantaged minority—that is, to persuade them that the interests of the capitalists are in their best interests—economic conflicts must be displaced, projected onto other conflicts, usually between ethnic or other groups. Such displacement obfuscates economic competition and shifts the locus of argument. In that way conflicts of interest are mystified, and class struggles are muted or suppressed because they are reframed in other terms. In other words, class conflicts are redefined in ways that identify the interests of capitalists with those of the lower classes who share their ethnic or gender identity. That has obvious benefits. Deflecting economic issues onto questions of ethnicity or gender allows economically advantaged whites to bond with other whites against non-whites and males to bond together against women. It also prevents regroupings based on class that would pit the economically disadvantaged majority against the (usually) white male capitalist minority.

Historians have long argued the causes of the Civil War, debating the relative importance of economic and moral issues. Interpretations of the post-Reconstruction era are less controversial. The works of historians Henry K. Beale and Eric Foner, among others, document the economic forces that worked to remove federal troops from the South in 1877 and which shaped public opinion and governmental policy.[23] These forces enabled the South to reestablish the economic relationships that had existed before the war—that is, to place freed slaves in a position of peonage based on the system of sharecropping, a system that mimicked the economic relationships of slavery. A critical part of this was the denial of citizenship rights to freed slaves, which excluded them from any legal and civil recourse. Terrorism and mob violence were essential instruments in that process.[24]

From the end of Reconstruction into the early years of the twentieth century, however, a rhetorical struggle ensued which was aimed at shaping Northern public opinion regarding federal interference to deal with the increasing problem of mob violence and vigilante justice. The rhetoric of that period systematically deflected attention from economic conflicts. Southern spokesmen, led by Thomas Nelson Page, worked diligently to frame the problem of vigilante justice in racial and moral (usually sexual) terms. African Americans, led by two remarkable women, Ida B. Wells Barnett and Mary Church Terrell, resisted. Later white women, led by Jessie Daniel Ames in the Association of Southern Women for the Prevention of Lynching, followed in their footsteps to identify the sexism that undergirded the views of Page and others.

As noted, this debate did not occur in a free and open marketplace of ideas; rather, Northern capitalists who owned and controlled the major newspapers and journals ensured that only those voices would be heard who supported their interests. Ida B. Wells Barnett was able to present her cogent and well-documented economic and social analyses only in black-owned outlets or in pamphlets, and her lectures were almost exclusively to African-American audiences. Indeed, it was only because of reports in British newspapers about her lecture tours there that U.S. newspapers were finally forced to take note of her activities.

The 1904 exchange between Page and Church Terrell is a lens through which to understand "the production and transformation of ideology" which Stuart Hall identifies as "the media's main sphere of operations"[25] Equally, it reveals the obstacles that those such as Church Terrell faced in responding to the racial redefinition of relationships between capitalists and former slaves and explores more generally the ideological processes that guaranteed the outcome of the rhetorical struggle.

Media practices were reinforced by historical events. Following the economic dislocations of the 1890s and in the aftermath of the Spanish-American and Philippine Wars, Americans were eager for a period of calm. The icon of the Union in Lincoln's rhetoric was featured, as the lives and rights of African Americans were sacrificed to reintegration of the Confederate states into the nation. The South's coal and cotton beckoned entrepreneurs; the Republicans were riding high— African-American votes did not seem vital to electoral politics, and European immigration could satisfy the need for unskilled labor.

Page's essay "The Lynching of Negroes—Its Cause and Its Prevention," in the January *North American Review,* was followed by a three-part series in March, April, and May in *McClure's* which analyzed the Reconstruction and post-Reconstruction periods.[26] Then, in 1907 he published another essay in *McClure's* propounding what is best described as the "black peril," a nearly classic expression of white racism.[27]

Page's 1904 essay on lynching is notable for its narrow compass, an important element in the logic that framed the issues. Although he included substantial amounts of statistical data (in tables) collected by the *Chicago Tribune,* which documented that less than one-quarter of lynchings involved charges of rape, "while over three-fourths of them are for murder, attempts at murder, or some less heinous offense," and although he acknowledged that these data "may be accounted for, in part, by the fact that the murders in the South partake somewhat of the nature of race-conflicts," the arguments that followed developed as if those data did not exist or did not matter. Instead, Page proceeded on the assumption that the rape of white women by African-American men was the primary, if not the sole, occasion of lynching and that this cause could be blamed entirely on Northern reformers and African Americans.

That reframing is vital to his purpose. First, it unifies all whites against a common scourge that threatens "their women," a threat he dramatizes in extreme terms and with detailed examples. It obscures the economic and social dimensions of the struggle in which lynching played such a key part, and it forestalled an economic realignment that would have sparked coalitions between freed slaves and poor whites. Moreover, revulsion at the charge of rape overpowered Northern impulses to protect the economic, legal, or political rights of freed slaves. Finally, of course, the redefinition divides women—African Americans who protest against lynching may be cast as heartless abettors of assaults on white women—and it obscures a larger problem, that of white men raping African-American women.

Page offered a dramatic scenario to engage his readers, a scenario that obscured and overwhelmed those boring *Chicago Tribune* statistics. Northerners poisoned race relations in this Southern Eden, because, he argued, social equality "to the ignorant and brutal young negro . . . signifies but one thing: the opportunity to enjoy, equally with white men, the privilege of cohabiting with white women" (45). Obviously, he assumes the stereotype of "negroes" as primitives which pervaded newspapers and magazines.

In a depiction that would be recreated in D. W. Griffith's *Birth of a Nation*, Page vividly described the dire state of Southern white women:

> To-day, no white woman, or girl, or female child, goes alone out of sight of the house except on necessity; and no man leaves his wife alone in his house, if he can help it. The white population is sparse, the forests are extensive, the officers of the law distant and difficult to reach; but, above all, the negro population has appeared inclined to condone the fact of mere assault. (37)

Although he admitted that ravishers were invariably caught and executed, belying the need for vigilante justice, he declared judicial processes inadequate. Despite the evidence, he claimed that assaults had increased. Continuing his scenario, he described convicted rapists as having "got religion" and from the gallows urging others to join them in glory, with the result "that the punishment lost to these emotional people much of its deterrent force." Moreover, the law required "the innocent victim . . . to relate in public the story of the assault—an ordeal which was worse than death" (38). These pale, fragile victims had to be protected by Southern white chivalry.[28]

One historian describes the elaboration of that scenario, such that the fear of rape, like the practice of lynching, was embedded far beyond the reach of factual refutation—in the heart not only of U.S. racism but of U.S. attitudes toward women as well. Rape and rumors of rape became a kind of acceptable folk pornography in the Bible Belt. As stories spread, the attacker became not just a black man but a ravenous brute, the victim a beautiful, frail, young virgin. The experience and condition of the woman (who could not be put on the witness stand to suffer the "glare and stare of public curiosity") were described in minute and progressively embellished detail: a public fantasy that implies a kind of group participation in the rape of the woman almost as cathartic as the subsequent lynching of the alleged attacker.[29] Under the power of that scenario fiction became fact.

Page carefully assigned the blame not to the mobs but to African Americans; in his words, lynchings "will not greatly diminish until the negroes themselves take it in hand and stamp it out" (44), and he issued a sweeping condemnation: "At bottom, their sympathy is generally with the 'victim' of the mob, and not with his victim" (46).

Page's scenario led to two conclusions, one overt and one implied: that lynching cannot be ended until African Americans stop assaulting white women, that is, stop seeking equality, because white Southerners will always fight rape, that is, any efforts to achieve equality, with their only truly effective weapon, the lynch mob.

In replying, Mary Church Terrell faced numerous constraints. First and foremost, she had to avoid offending editors and Northern, much less Southern, readers, which meant that the highly confrontational but perceptive arguments about the economic bases for mob violence and the sexual relationships that lynchings were used to hide, which had been articulated by Ida B. Wells Barnett, were off limits.[30] Second, because she was responding to Page, her basic strategy had to be refutational, which meant that he had defined the terms of argument. In addition, of course, she was constrained by her own history and experience both as an African American and as a woman.[31] As an African American, her views were suspect as "biased," and issues of credibility would loom large. As a woman, discussion of intimate and controversial sexual topics would be difficult and delicate.

Church Terrell adapted to her audiences by structuring her refutation as responses to areas of ignorance or misinformation. The strategy reflected her rhetorical philosophy; at the same time, it was tolerant of readers who might have overlooked the incompatibility between the *Chicago Tribune* statistics and Page's dramatic scenario, which ignored them. She wisely reiterated those data, "that, out of every hundred negroes who are lynched, from seventy-five to eighty-five are not even accused of this crime, and many who are accused of it are innocent," in responding to Page's claim that the rape of white women was the cause of lynching and made the telling point that "men who admit the accuracy of these figures gravely tell the country that lynching can never be suppressed, until negroes cease to commit the crime with which less than one-fourth of those murdered by mobs are charged" (854).

She also responded to his charge that increasingly brutal lynchings were occasioned by increasingly brutal rapes. Emulating a technique honed by Ida B. Wells Barnett, she used white sources, in this case the *Vicksburg Evening Post* (Miss.), for grisly details of the lynching of a man and wife for alleged murder and buttressed it with authoritative statements from credible white Southerners who reiterated that only a small number of those lynched were accused of assaulting white women and admitted that "most of our Southern lynchings are carried through in *sheer, unqualified and increasing brutality.*" Refuting these charges, however, did not provide an alternative explanation for the lynchings, and citing statistics, even from the most credible and reluctant sources, was unlikely to scuttle Page's dramatic scenario.

Church Terrell also challenged a central premise, "that the negro's desire for social equality sustains any relation whatsoever to the crime of rape" (855). She never denied that African Americans desired equality,[32] but she attacked the conclusion Page had drawn from it through a comparison: "In the North, which is the only section that accords the negro the only scrap of social equality enjoyed by him in the United States, he is rarely accused of rape" (875). Her usually moderate tone here became more biting as she introduced the great but ignored problem, the rapes of black women; in effect, she reversed Page's argument: "The only form of social equality ever attempted between the two races, and practised to any considerable extent, is that which was originated by the white masters of slave women, and which has been perpetuated by them and their descendants even unto the present day" (857).[33] At this point, however, Church Terrell was struggling against the powerful stereotype of the oversexed African-American female, whose seductiveness and immorality were used as the rationale for interracial sex. That stereotype was also used against Ida B. Wells Barnett.[34]

She responded to Page's claim that even "the best negroes" are so morally stunted that they "do not appreciate the enormity and heinousness of rape" (857) by claiming that pity for the victims of lynch mobs was appropriate because most were innocent. A series of detailed examples documenting their innocence followed. She concluded by praising African-American commitment to community values and adherence to the rule of law: "It is to the credit and not to the shame of the negro that he tries to uphold the sacred majesty of the law, which is so often trailed in the dust and trampled under foot by white mobs."

Finally, she addressed the problem of the mass media, the error of drawing one's "facts from the accounts in the newspapers" (859). Her critique of press coverage buttressed her claim that most victims were innocent. She discussed the lynching of Sam Hose in April 1899 in detail, which, although the facts did not support his claim, was an instance Page had used as evidence of increased and bolder ravishing.[35] Church Terrell never denied that Hose murdered the plantation owner for whom he had worked, although she implied what was widely known, that Hose was reacting to the man's attempt to cheat him; she merely discussed how the case was reported. In Hose's case, "a well-known, influential newspaper immediately offered a reward of $500" for his capture, "predicted a lynching, and stated that . . . it was the consensus of opinion that the negro should be burned at the stake and tortured before being burned." Subsequently, a rumor started, circulated by the press, that after the murder Hose assaulted the wife of his victim. Again, Church Terrell turned to credible evidence, a white Chicago detective hired to examine the case, who "declared it would have been a physical impossibility, . . . and expressed it as his opinion that the charge of assault was an invention to make the burning a certainty" (859).

Detailing Church Terrell's refutation of these interrelated charges clearly reveals how she was constrained by the racist logic in which the debate was framed. The issue was lynching, not the disenfranchisement of freed slaves and the laws and policies adopted by Southern states to reduce them to peonage as sharecroppers. The issue was how to stop lynching, not what actions were needed to guarantee the civil and political rights of freed slaves. The issue was whether or not lynching was caused by the rape of white women by black men, not how mob violence could be eliminated. The issue was whether or not freed slaves understood equality to mean miscegenation, not what protection and support they would need for self-improvement. The issue was racial, not economic, conflict. She had impugned the sources of misinformation, but she could point to few, if any, alternative sources. She had attacked the dramatic "rape of the white virgin scenario," but she offered no alternative scenario.

Church Terrell recognized the limitations of refutation and now moved to the offensive. She redefined the cause of lynching as the "race hatred . . . of a stronger people for a weaker once held as slaves" (860), an analysis that hinted at economic issues. Page blamed African-American lawlessness; she pointed to widespread Southern lawlessness. Whereas Page had placed all responsibility for lynching on African Americans, she said simply that it would be "impossible for the negroes of this country to prevent mob violence by any attitude of mind which they may assume, or any course of conduct which they may pursue," reflecting actual power relationships between the groups. Church Terrell attributed white race hatred to attitudes nurtured in a slaveholding culture, which implied attitudes shaped by oppressive economic relationships. She noted the role of the most advantaged in racial conflict, using reluctant evidence to point out that Southern newspapers routinely described lynch mobs as "generally composed of the 'best citizens' of a place," and remarked that these were likely to be descendants of slaveholders. Implicitly, she challenged the view that lynching was the work of "white trash." She indicated that the newspaper that played a key role in the Sam Hose case, for instance, "was neither owned nor edited by the poor whites," but she commented that the ancestors of poor whites also "were brutalized by their slaveholding environment" (861). Briefly developed instances of actual re-enslavement and descriptions of the near-slavery conditions of sharecroppers attested to efforts to reestablish the conditions that had previously existed prior to emancipation. As evidence of whites' many exertions to retain their dominant position, she stepped outside Page's framework to call attention to attempts "to curtail the educational opportunities of colored children" (863), including a recently enacted state law prohibiting colored children from receiving instruction above the sixth grade.[36] These data suggested extensive efforts to oppress freed slaves, contextualizing lynching as one among many measures designed to oppress African Americans and eliminate any structures that might lead to self-improvement.

The slave environment that nurtured white race hatred was linked to white lawlessness, and the extent of lawlessness was dramatized by a startling, apt comparison drawn from the white *Nashville American* "that, if the killings in the other states had been in the same ratio to population as in South Carolina, a larger number of people would have been murdered in the United States during 1902 than fell on the American side in the Spanish and Philippine wars" (864).[37] General white lawlessness was linked to sexual assault. The low moral climate that existed during slavery persisted, she argued: "From the day they were liberated to the present time, prepossessing young colored girls have been considered the rightful prey of white gentlemen in the South, and they have been protected neither by public sentiment nor by law." Once again she buttressed her claim with the words of a white Methodist Episcopal minister (865). She also offered some startling statistics that broadened the issue. These data showed that "only one colored male in 100,000 over five years of age was accused of assault upon a white woman in the South in 1902, whereas one male out of every 20,000 over five years of age in Chicago [then virtually all white][38] was charged with rape during the same year" (863). She had dared to hint that white male lawlessness, in particular, sexual assault, was also a problem in the North.

In her final arguments the power of Page's racist logic overwhelmed her efforts to broaden the issue. Although she had hinted at economic issues and at the critical role of the media and of the "best white citizens," she now asserted that "lynching can never be suppressed in the South, until the masses of ignorant white people in that section are educated and lifted to a higher moral plane." Perhaps a need to praise the progress of her own people, a staple of her rhetoric,[39] led her to emphasize a point that strengthened Page's redefinition of the conflict as wholly racial and moral. She cited the *Atlanta Constitution,* which contrasted the level of illiteracy among whites, unchanged for fifty years, to the progress of the African American, "who has reduced his illiteracy 44.5 percent in forty years."[40] She added that more advantaged whites also had to change, because "lynching cannot be suppressed in the South until all classes of white people who dwell there . . . respect the rights of other human beings, no matter what may be the color of their skin" (867). At the end she attributed the terrible ills of lynching, segregation, disenfranchisement, and even peonage to a decline in Americans' commitment to the principles of liberty and equality which presumably bound the nation together. As the United States was to demonstrate for over a half-century, however, the so-called liberal consensus is compatible with white racism. As concepts, liberty, freedom, and equality of opportunity can be incorporated into widely divergent ideologies. At this point in her argument economic issues have been forgotten.

As I have noted, the institutionalization of white racism through the courts and the state government was well under way. The rationalization and justification of these processes was still incomplete. If ideology refers "to those images, concepts, and premises which provide the frameworks through which we represent, interpret, understand, and 'make sense' of some aspect of social existence,"[41] this debate was part of the process by which overt racism, the explicit articulation and defense of racist policies and views, moved toward inferential racism, "those apparently naturalized representations of events and situations relating to race, whether 'factual' or 'fictional,' which have racist premises and propositions inscribed in them as a set of *unquestioned assumptions.*"[42]

Page's essay and Church Terrell's response capture the historical process through which a fictional scenario comes to be accepted as truth, becomes part of "common sense," and is virtually impervious to evidence and argument. As essayist and fiction writer, Page worked assiduously to develop, elaborate, and justify the scenario. Equally energetically, Ida B. Wells Barnett and Church Terrell worked to deny it. They labored under severe disadvantages, however. Chief among them was their inability to find outlets that would allow them to compete against the Southern apologists. The economic interests that found it advantageous to use cheap African-American wage labor in the South owned and controlled the print media. They rejected the rhetoric of those who opposed their interests, they routinely published the stories and essays of the Southern apologists, and they allowed only those African Americans who were accommodationists to express their views.

Page was no more eloquent than Church Terrell; he was surely far less eloquent and cogent that Ida B. Wells Barnett. But he had two powerful advantages: he worked from premises and stereotypes that were echoed consistently in the mass media, and he spoke without fear of contradiction. Until U.S. audiences saw alternative scenarios and characters on television during the civil rights protests of the 1960s, the plantation and rape fantasies created by Southern apologists, realized on film in *Birth of a Nation* and *Gone with the Wind,* dominated the mass media.[43]

In discussing mediated constructions of race Stuart Hall writes:

Three characteristics provided the discursive and power-coordinates of the discourses in which these relations were historically constructed. (1) Their imagery and themes were polarized around fixed relations of subordination and domination. (2) Their stereotypes were grouped around the poles of "superior" and "inferior" natural species. (3) Both were displaced from the "language" of history into the language of Nature.[44]

The exchange between Page and Church Terrell, particularly when viewed in relation to Page's other published works of this period, reinforces Hall's analysis. Page polarizes and insists on fixed relationships of subordination and domination, with whites as superior and nonwhites as an inferior species. Church Terrell is constantly at work to deny fixed relationships, insisting on data that show progress and which document variation. Equally, she rejects relationships of subordination and domination as natural, calling attention to defects in the moral character of whites—for example, illiteracy and sexual assault—and the progress made by members of her race. She insists on the history of slavery as the crucial backdrop for understanding contemporary efforts as economic repression. But in this milieu her subject matter and her arguments were sharply constrained, and in a single essay she was no match for the much published Page and his chorus of supporters.[45]

Hall's analysis omits at least two other factors that loom large in this period. One is the power of a dramatic scenario that has the capacity to overwhelm facts; the other is the significance of overtly racist messages that go unchallenged. The very fact that overtly racist statements appear in prestigious, reputable outlets makes such views "respectable." When they go unchallenged, it becomes far easier for them to be absorbed and naturalized as unexamined assumptions, as an accepted part of national ideology. In other words, in the rhetorical struggle that was part of the "nadir of Negro history," the editorial practices of the print media played a central and decisive role.

The Thirteenth, Fourteenth, and Fifteenth Amendments were ratified in the aftermath of the Civil War, creating a constitutional opportunity to extend full citizenship rights to African Americans. Powerful forces were at work to repeal in fact what the words of these amendments promised. The exchange between Page and Church Terrell is a case study that illustrates the rhetorical processes by which the nation came to define itself not as a community united around the values of equality of rights and opportunity but, rather, as a nation divided by beliefs and policies committed to maintaining white superiority.

Notes

1. Stuart Hall, "The Whites of Their Eyes: Racist Ideologies and the Media," in *Silver Linings,* ed. George Bridges and Rosalind Brunt (London: Lawrence and Wishart, 1981), 35.

2. Rayford W. Logan, *The Negro in American Life and Thought: The Nadir, 1877–1901* (New York: Dial Press, 1954).

3. Antonio Gramsci, *Selections from the Prison Notebooks.* Ed. and trans. Q. Hoare and G. N. Smith (New York: International Publishers, 1987).

4. "Perhaps the most reliable statistics show the following numbers of persons lynched in the United States. Beginning with 1882 the annual number was 114, 134, 184, 211, 138, 122, 142, 176, 128, 195 in 1891. Most of them were Negroes living in the South" (Logan, *Negro in American Life,* 76). In 1899, "109 persons, of whom 87 were Negroes, were lynched" (91). From 1889 through 1899 approximately 83 percent of all lynchings occurred in the South—the eleven former Confederate states plus Missouri, Kentucky, and what became Oklahoma in 1907. During the first decade of the new century 91.1 percent of lynchings were in these states (Rayford Logan, *The Betrayal of the Negro: From Rutherford B. Hayes to Woodrow Wilson,* new, enlarged ed. of *The Negro in American Life and Thought: The Nadir, 1877–1901* [New York: Collier Books, 1965], 348).

5. 109 U.S. 1 (1883). "The decisions of the Court were largely the handiwork of Northerners and Republicans. . . . There were . . . only two Southerners, both of them Republicans [one was John Marshall Harlan of Kentucky, who had fought in the Union army], and one Democrat, from California, on the bench when it handed down the devastating Civil Rights decision in 1883. In 1896 when the Court wrote the more controversial decision, *Plessy v. Ferguson,* there was only one Southerner, Edward Douglass White of Louisiana. There were only two Democrats" (Logan, *Betrayal,* 105).

6. "By 1910, all eleven of the former Confederate states and the new state of Oklahoma had accomplished, by various devices, discriminatory disenfranchisement" (Logan, *Negro in American Life,* 346).

7. Segregation was also becoming institutionalized in the workplace. "By the 1890s the A.F. of L. craft unions and the railroad brotherhoods were setting the pace with exclusionist policies and segregated locals, though a few unions, like the United Mine Workers (with almost two-thirds of its membership Ne-

gro) were racially democratic" (August Meier, *Negro Thought in America, 1880–1915: Racial Ideologies in the Age of Booker T. Washington* [Ann Arbor: University of Michigan Press, 1963], 21). Meier also points out that the first big surge of Jim Crow laws took place in the years 1887 to 1891 (23).

8. *A History of the United States since the Civil War*, 5 vols. (New York: Macmillan, 1917–37), 2:541.

9. Logan, *Negro in American Life*, 173–75, 217–25. The newspapers were the *Boston Evening Transcript, New Haven Evening Register, New York Times, Philadelphia North American, Washington Star, Cincinnati Inquirer, Pittsburgh Dispatch, Indianapolis Journal, Detroit Tribune* (*Post and Tribune*, October 1877–July 1884), *Chicago Tribune, St. Louis Globe-Democrat,* and *San Francisco Examiner.*

10. "They developed, according to Professor Sterling Brown, the authoritative literary and historical critic, seven stereotypes: The Contented Slave, The Wretched Freedman, The Comic Negro, The Brute Negro, The Tragic Mulatto, The Local Color Negro, and the Exotic Primitive. . . . 'All of these stereotypes are marked either by exaggeration or omission; they all agree in stressing the Negro's divergence from an Anglo-Saxon norm to the flattery of the latter.' . . . [P]lays written during this period were cast in the same molds. . . . Thomas Nelson Page, the personification of the Plantation Tradition, . . called Moses in [the novel] *Red Rock* (1898) 'a hyena in a cage,' 'a reptile,' 'a species of worm,' 'a wild beast'" (Logan, *Negro in American Life*, 162). Stereotyping persisted after the turn of the century: "Thomas Dixon's *The Leopard's Spots* (1902) surpassed in bigotry and vituperation his *The Clansman* (1905) and Thomas Nelson Page's *Bred in the Bone* (1904)" (Logan, *Betrayal*, 354; see also chap. 18, "The Negro as Portrayed in Representative Northern Magazines and Newspapers," 371–92, for results of analyses from 1901 to 1918).

11. "The composite picture of the Negro that emerges from this chapter [which analyzes *Harper's, New Monthly Magazine, Scribner's* (*Century* after 1881), *Atlantic Monthly, North American Review,* and *Forum*] is, therefore, that which appealed to editors who were overwhelmingly Northern, to writers who were largely Northern except in the case of fiction and poetry, and to readers who were predominantly Northern" (Logan, *Negro in American Life*, 240). Logan describes the derisive terms, the exaggerated dialect, the ridicule and the stereotyping of African Americans in their pages (240–41). Thomas Page's fictional contributions to *Harper's* are used as illustrations ("All the Geography a Nigger Needs to Know"; cited on 240; "The Story of Charlie Harris," *Harper's* 86 [April 1893]: 804–5; cited on 243; "The True Story of the Surrender of the Marquis Cornwallis," ibid. 65 [November 1892]: 968–69; "Plaski's Tunaments," ibid. 82 [December 1890]: 111–18; see also Merland M. Turner, "The Negro as Portrayed in *Harper's New Monthly Magazine*, 1877–1901" [Master's thesis, Howard University]). Logan concludes that "Page glorified the plantation tradition in *Harper's* more effusively than did any other writer" (252). Drawings and cartoons reinforced the ridiculing stereotypes.

12. In 1950 Frederick Lewis Allen, editor of *Harper's* from 1941 to 1952, characterized its style in 1891 as "academic and timorous genteelism"; Henry Steele Commager used those words to describe *Atlantic* and *Century* of that period (cited in Logan, *Negro in American Life*, 239).

13. Ibid., 240.

14. Of these magazines only the *Forum* regularly published work by African Americans such as Booker T. Washington and others who held his views. "It is significant that [Frederick] Douglass was not a contributor. . . . the points of view expressed [in its pages] were similar to those already presented. Suffice it to say that the balance was, on the whole, firmly kept even in articles dealing with lynching" (ibid., 262). Logan comments: "What was needed to offset the hardening attitudes was a magazine whose editor would have proclaimed as Garrison had done in the first issue of the *Liberator:* 'I am in earnest—I will not equivocate—I will not excuse—will not retreat a single inch—AND I WILL BE HEARD.' No such magazine, or newspaper, is conceivable in the last years of the century. The nation was attuned to the soft strains of the 'New South'" (263).

Booker T. Washington's views also were published in the *Atlantic Monthly* 78 (September 1896): 322–28. Frederick Douglass's single essay, "The Color Line" (*North American Review*, 132 [June 1881]: 568, 575–76), strongly criticized economic and judicial discrimination, segregation, and disenfranchisement and noted the contradiction between segregation and the use of colored people as servants.

15. Logan, *Negro in American Life*, 262. "Even the erudite *North American Review* helped to perpetuate the stereotype of the faithful plantation Negro" (255). "A symposium conducted by the *North American Review (NAR)* resulted in almost unanimous approval of the withdrawal of troops [in 1877]" (257). In 1892 *NAR* published an article by Page that "not only insisted that the South be left alone but added: 'We have educated him [the Negro]; we have aided him; we have sustained him in all right directions. We are ready to continue our aid; but we will not be dominated by him" ("A Southerner on the Negro Question," *NAR* 159 [April 1892]: 402–13).

White Northern journalist Ray Stannard Baker received warnings from the editor of the *American* when, in 1906, he proposed the series that became "Following the Color Line." Editor J. S. Phillips "was primarily concerned with the circulation value of the proposed series, and even when it was under way cautioned Baker that 'For the sake of effect, we must keep the interest and friendliness of Southern readers'" (cited in Robert C. Bannister, *Ray Stannard Baker: The Mind and Thought of a Progressive* [New Haven: Yale University Press, 1966], 127). Baker's essays were collected in *Following the Color Line: American Negro Citizenship in the Progressive Era* (1908; rpt., New York: Harper and Row, 1964).

16. He was described as a "romancer who, perhaps more than any single man of his generation, exploited the conception of the antebellum South as a region of feudalistic splendor" (*Dictionary of American Biography*, 22 vols., ed.

Dumas Malone [New York: Charles Scribner's Sons, 1934], 7:142). Page authored popular works, including a volume of tales in Negro dialect; a novel *Red Rock* (1898); two volumes for children, *Two Little Confederates* (1888) and *Among the Camp* (1891); and a biography of Robert E. Lee (1911). He served as ambassador to Italy from 1913 to 1919. He died in 1922.

17. "Last Will and Testament of Robert Reed Church, Senior (1839–1912)" (with notes by M. Sammye Miller, *Journal of Negro History* 65 [Spring 1980]: 156–63) documents the extent of his holdings.

18. She began the twentieth century as a "Bookerite," supporting Booker T. Washington's more accommodationist views, but by 1909, when she became a charter member of the National Association for the Advancement of Colored People (NAACP), an organization that represented W. E. B. Du Bois's more radical demands for full equality, her views had changed. An editorial by F. H. Murray in the November 1907 *Horizon,* the organ of the Niagara movement, published by Murray, Du Bois, and L. M. Hershaw, out of which the NAACP emerged, described her shift of opinion:

> Mrs. Mary Church Terrell, who has been until very lately the right very high priestess, the veritable "She" of the Bookerites, has been "named" for excommunication. . . . Why? Because the very kernel of the cult is: "Everything is going on all right, and whatever trifling troubles trail after our race are of our own making." But Mistress Mary, quite contrary, at the opening of her tour in Cleveland, addressing the American Missionary Association, was guilty of the heresy of asserting; and that too in the present tense, indicative mood, active voice; that in the South where our best friends swarm, we Black Folks do not get justice and fair play and that even now under the present reign things go from bad to worse. (Cited in a letter from August Meier to MCT, dated 9 July 1952, MCT Papers, Library of Congress, reel 12; see also Meier, *Negro Thought,* 239–40)

19. Frank Luther Mott, *A History of American Magazines,* 5 vols. (Cambridge, Mass: Belknap Press of Harvard University, 1957–68), 2:258.

20. "The Lynching of Negroes—Its Cause and Its Prevention," *North American Review* 178, no. 566 (January 1904): 33–48. "The Negro: The Southerner's Problem: First Paper: Slavery and the Old Relation between the Southern Whites and Blacks," *McClure's* 22, no. 5 (March 1904): 548–54; "Second Paper: Some of Its Difficulties and Fallacies," *McClure's* 22, no. 6 (April 1904): 619–26; "Third Paper: Its Present Condition and Aspect, as Shown by Statistics," *McClure's* 23, no. 1 (May 1904): 96–102; "The Great American Question: The Special Plea of a Southerner," *McClure's* 28, no. 1 (May 1907): 565–72. The 1904 article in the *North American Review* and the articles that appeared in *McClure's* in 1904, plus some other essays on the race problem, were published together as *The Negro: The Southerner's Problem* (New York: Charles Scribner's Sons, 1904). Hereafter the

1904 NAR essay is cited only by page; the three-part 1904 series is cited by month and page.

21. Mott, *History of American Magazines*, 4:599. Earlier in 1900 *McClure's* had a circulation of 370,000, larger than all but one general magazine, two women's magazines, and the *Farm Journal* and *Youth's Companion*. *Printer's Ink* declared that, in the years 1895–99, *McClure's* "carried the greatest quantity of advertising of any magazine in the world" (28 [30 August 1899]:13; in Mott, *History of American Magazines*, 4:597), a pattern that continued into 1907. *McClure's* was founded in 1893.

22. "Lynching from a Negro's Point of View," by Mary Church Terrell, honorary president of the National Association of Colored Women, *North American Review* 178, no. 570 (June 1904): 853–68.

23. MCT Papers, 14 February 1905, Library of Congress, reel 1. Just what would have been acceptable is unclear. Church Terrell was no rabble rouser. For example, her diary of 19 January 1909 refers to a letter from Tampa, Florida, stating that some local politicians did not want her to deliver an address there, in her words, "for fear I would stir up race strife and they would have to leave Tampa that night." In her diary on 20 January 1909 she reports that she wrote back to say that, given such fears, under no circumstances would she speak, because "my mission is to promote peace and harmony in the race not to stir up strife in it nor to create friction between the races." Her unpublished response to Page's 1907 essay is in her papers, Library of Congress, reel 23, container 32, nos. 283–97.

As noted in note 14, when premier white Northern journalist Ray Stannard Baker decided to write a series of articles on lynching, *McClure's* editors warned him against offending their Southern readers.

24. In *Reconstruction: America's Unfinished Revolution, 1863–1877* (New York: Harper and Row, 1988) Eric Foner views the failure to achieve a land redistribution program as a deliberate attempt to force a Northern concept of free labor on the South. By arguing for this ideological imperialism, Foner echoes Howard K. Beale's concept of Reconstruction as a period of Northern capitalistic exploitation of the South (see *The Critical Year: A Study of Andrew Johnson and Reconstruction* [New York: F. Ungar, 1958]). Officials of the Freedmen's Bureau ordered former slaves to sign labor contracts either with former masters or with new landowners, who often were even less eager to foster black independence than were the old slaveholders. Faced with this demand, blacks became defiant. Strikes increased the determination of white landowners to force workers back into the fields. Their successful counterattack, Foner writes, "began the forging of a new class structure to replace the shattered world of slavery—an economic transformation that would culminate, long after the end of Reconstruction, in the consolidation of a rural proletariat composed of the descendants of former slaves and white yeomen, and a new owning class of planters and merchants, itself subordinate to Northern financiers and industrialists" (qtd. by William S.

McFeely, review, *New York Times Book Review* [22 May 1988]: 11). Through the systematic use of terror black voters were intimidated, and white supremacist rule in the South was restored. Ignoring these processes, Northern reformers believed that, because blacks had been given the vote, they should be able to protect themselves.

25. Although major advances have been made in voting and other civil rights, economic relationships in the South have remained unchanged to this day. These institutionalized economic and class relationships preclude the development that would improve the real conditions of most African Americans in the Southern states. See Peter Applebome, "The New South and the Old," *New York Times*, 3 August 1994, A11. This is the last in a series of four articles on this topic.

26. Hall, "Whites of Their Eyes," 31.

27. In the three-part 1904 series in *McClure's* which followed Page's defense of lynching in the *North American Review,* which appeared prior to Church Terrell's reply in June, Page argued that disenfranchising freed slaves was necessary, pleaded for unity of opinion, and claimed that "the best-informed, the most clear-sighted and straight-thinking men of the North, admit sadly that the experiment of Negro suffrage . . . has proved a failure" (March, 550).

He appealed to the implied threat of a growing, impoverished, and crime-prone African-American population, writing that "in large sections they outnumber the whites 2 and 3 to 1, and in some parishes 10 and 20 to 1, with this population owning less than 4 percent of the property and furnishing 85 to 93 percent of the total number of criminals" (March, 549). This threat became the rationale for economic oppression: "The South . . . further held that, suddenly released from slavery, he must be controlled and compelled to work" (April, 620).

He consistently asserted white superiority and argued that a "policy [based on equality] would destroy not only the White race of the South, but even the civilization which the race has helped to establish, and for which it stands, and so, in time, would inevitably debase and destroy the nation itself" (April, 620).

He argued that economic development became possible only after Reconstruction and the disenfranchisement of freed slaves. "With the overthrow of the carpet-bag governments, and the destruction of Negro domination of the South, the South began to shoot up into the light of a new prosperity. . . . Mills have been started and manufactories established, and this not only by Southern investors, but, to a considerable extent, by Northern capital, until the South has become one of the recognized fields for investment." (April, 626)

Page blamed African Americans for their lack of economic progress and contrasted the "good slaves" of the past and the "new issue": "Universally, they [Southern whites] will tell you that while the old-time Negroes were industrious, saving, and, when not misled, well-behaved, kindly, respectful, and self-respecting, and while the remnant of them who remain still retain generally these characteristics, the 'new issue,' for the most part, are lazy, thriftless, intemperate, insolent, dishonest, and without the most rudimental [*sic*] elements of morality.... Unhappily, the fountain is tainted at the source. The great body of the race have scarcely any notion of the foundation principles of pure family life" (May, 101).

28. Page's 1907 essay makes explicit tacit arguments of 1904. It began: "There are some things so well understood by those who know the negroes, as to appear to them almost truisms" (565). These included:

> That the white race is superior to the negro race . . . inherently and fundamentally.... That negroes under subjection are, for the most part, docile, amiable, tractable, and pleasant to deal with. That negroes in power are, for the most part, arrogant, swaggering, dangerous, and intolerable.... That negroes understand by "social equality," for the most part, one thing only: the right to stand with white women on precisely the same ground as that on which white men stand with them. That the salvation of the white race depends upon preventing this; and further, depends on the white race's remaining dominant. That so long as the white race remains dominant, the white race and the negro race can live together amicably; otherwise not. (565)

Page exploited scientific ignorance and anthropological misinformation: "Ordinary science informs us that the negro's physical structure is in many manifest particulars essentially different from that of the Caucasian race.... We are informed equally that his other nature—which, for convenience, we may call his mental nature—also differs in important particulars from the Caucasian's" (567), identified as "their liability to be inflamed by passions, . . . which renders them so dangerous" (566). Population data magnified this threat: "There are in these United States at the present time not less than 10 million negroes.... This people has doubled every 4 decades since the Revolution, and unless some unforeseen conditions occur to prevent the continuance of this rate of increase, it is likely to amount within the next 3 or 4 generations to the appalling number of 80 millions of negroes in this country.... the negro is the specter that stands ever at the door" (567).

Assimilation was unthinkable—it would be "debasement and degradation" (568). "The only barrier" to mongrelization "is the white race of the South" (569). His words reveal the fundamental irrationality of these views: "But if the entire negro race on this continent were men as highly educated as Booker Washington, ... there would still be a race question to reckon with.... If it should be said, let superior intelligence and character win—.... Are the American people prepared to accept that practically? Not in exceptional cases, but all the way through? ... Negroes in power—political, commercial social! In the legislature; on the supreme bench; at the bar; in the medical faculty;—in all hotels! All parlors full of negroes! . . . It means miscegenation" (571). He asked, "How is this race question to be solved?" and replied, "first and foremost, this superiority [of the great white race over all others] should be maintained by every means in our power" (572). "Natural" superiority required vigilant protection.

In her unpublished response Church Terrell acknowledged her disadvantageous position: "Bold and brave indeed is the man [*sic*] who dares suggest to the average white Southerner that his views must be biased and partisan from the very nature of the case, since it is difficult for any human being to overcome his environment and defy traditions, no matter how hard he may try" (1). She also noted the constraints created by the editorial practices of the media: "The columns of nearly every large daily and magazine in the North are open to the Southerner who wishes to give the public the benefit of his opinion upon the vices and defects of the Negro and the only way in which the race problem can be wisely solved, while it is almost impossible for the victims of prejudice and oppression to induce the press of the North to publish their side of the story" (7).

She crafted two appeals targeted at Northerners. First, she recalled the Civil War: "At the close of the War, if an abolitionist or union soldier had been told that in less than forty years much of the work which it cost millions of treasure and rivers of blood to accomplish would be practically undone in every state of the South without an earnest protest from the North, he would have dismissed such a prediction as too wild and idiotic to discuss." She added a political appeal: "It is an indisputable fact that through the disfranchisement of colored men in the South, the vote of one white man in that section counts as much in national affairs as the votes of five men in some northern states, of 7 men in others, and as much as 10 men in some" (3).

She responded to Page's alarm over miscegenation:

"Are we ready to make this a negroid nation?" excitedly asks Mr. Page. If this question had come from a Northerner, as he beheld for the first time the hundreds of mulattoes, quadroons, and octoroons he met in the South, who are sons and daughters of some of the best citizens of that section, it would seem a very pertinent and natural query indeed. But being propounded by a gentleman living in that section in which for nearly 300 years efforts were continually made by white masters of slave women to mingle the blood of the two races, it seems strange and remarkable indeed. (15)

Later she added:

The moment Mr. Page claims that it is possible for 10 million people belonging to a race which was held for nearly 300 years in this country in the most degrading, dehumanizing bondage the world has ever seen, and but 40 years out of slavery at that, to mongrelize and destroy 70 million people who alone hold the reins of power, control the government, possess fabulous wealth, and who have had the advantages of centuries of education and culture over the impudent intruders besides, he postulates in the race numerically, financially, and educationally weak a strength which is as miraculous as it must be considered admirable to the race itself and its friends. At the same time, . . . Mr. Page attributes to his race a weakness did it really exist which would be fatal to the maintenance of that superiority upon which he insists. (21)

She also stated directly the central inference of Page's 1904 essay: "There is only one way the Negro himself can prevent the growth of 'this fierce race feeling' [Page's words] among many of his white neighbors in the South, and that is to remain ignorant and shiftless and poverty-stricken and allow himself to be used as a floor mat by all who wish to trample upon his prostrate form" (23–24).

29. See Barbara Welter, "The Cult of True Womanhood," *American Quarterly* 18 (1966):151–74. Anne Firor Scott, *The Southern Lady: From Pedestal to Politics, 1830–1930* (Chicago: University of Chicago Press, 1970), shows how the cult was adapted to the South and became part of the antebellum justification for slavery. For a demonstration of the falsity of that claim, see Jacqueline Dowd Hall's *Revolt against Chivalry: Jessie Daniel Ames and the Woman's Campaign against Lynching* (New York: Columbia University Press, 1979), a study of the Association of Southern Women for the Prevention of Lynching.

30. Jacqueline Dowd Hall, "'A Truly Subversive Affair': Women against Lynching in the Twentieth Century South," in *Women of America: A History* ed. Carol Ruth Berkin and Mary Beth Norton (Boston: Houghton Mifflin, 1978), 370–71.

31. See Ida B. Wells, *Southern Horrors: Lynch Law in All Its Phases* (1892; rpt. [as *On Lynchings*] New York: Arno and the New York Times, 1969), 24 pp. Wells first made these arguments in a 21 May 1892 editorial in her paper, *Free Speech.* The white Memphis community destroyed the newspaper office and threatened the lives of the owners, one of whom was Wells. Wells Barnett's difficulties in reaching white U.S. audiences is documented in Mary M. Boone Hutton, "Ida B. Wells Barnett," in *Women Public Speakers in the United States, 1800–1925*, ed. K. K. Campbell (Westport, Conn.: Greenwood Press, 1993), 462–75.

32. She never referred to Page directly. Elsewhere I have noted Church Terrell's ability to speak in a "feminine style" adapted to an audience of white females. In avoiding any appearance of debating Page, Church Terrell may have been adapting to constraints on women's public discourse. See "Style and Content in Early Afro-American Feminist Rhetoric," *Quarterly Journal of Speech* 72 (1986): 434–45; and *Man Cannot Speak for Her*, vol. 1: *A Critical Study of Early*

Feminist Rhetoric (New York: Greenwood Press, 1989), 12–14; 150–54. Conversely, *North American Review* may have required her to omit such references to avoid controversy. This was a significant omission, which distinguished her views from those propounded by Booker T. Washington, especially in the 1895 Atlanta Exposition Address.

33. The success of Washington's accommodationist policies suggests that only a denial of the desire for equality could assuage the fears of whites. According to V. P. Franklin, *Black Self-Determination: A Cultural History of the Faith of the Fathers* (Westport, Conn.: Lawrence Hill, 1984), 182–83, African-American newspaper editors did not support such policies, educators were divided, and the masses disagreed with them.

34. The attack on Ida B. Wells Barnett by the head of the Missouri Press Association was a precipitating cause of the formation of the National Association of Colored Women in 1896. See Paula Giddings, *When and Where I Enter:The Impact of Black Women on Race and Sex in America* (New York: William Morrow, 1984), 92–93.

35. Page's use of this case in 1904 smacks of willful deception if tested by the comments of W. E. B. Du Bois. The Hose lynching was a turning point in Du Bois's life. After reading about the murder in the newspaper, Du Bois said: "I wrote out a careful and reasoned statement concerning the evident facts and started down to the Atlanta *Constitution,* carrying in my pocket a letter of introduction to Joel Chandler Harris. I did not get there. On the way news met me: Sam Hose had been lynched, and they said his knuckles were on exhibition at a grocery store farther down on Mitchell Street, along which I was walking. I turned back to the University. I began to turn aside from my work. I did not meet Joel Chandler Harris nor the editor of the *Constitution.* . . . One could not be a calm, cool, and detached scientist while Negroes were lynched, murdered, and starved" (*Dusk of Dawn* [New York: Schocken Books, 1968], 67; cited in Herbert Shapiro, *White Violence and Black Response: From Reconstruction to Montgomery* [Amherst: University of Massachusetts Press, 1988], 63). Much later, in an interview, Du Bois added: "What had happened was that a black plantation laborer wasn't paid at the—it might have been at the end of the year, but at any rate his plantation owner didn't settle with him, and Sam Hose made a fuss about it, and they got into a fight, and the plantation owner was killed. They started then to find Sam Hose and they couldn't find him. And then, suddenly there was the accusation that Sam Hose had raped the wife. Now, everybody that read the facts of the case knew perfectly well what had happened. The man wouldn't pay him, so they got into a fight, and the man got killed—and then, in order to arouse the neighborhood to find this man, they brought in the charge of rape. Even from the newspapers you could see there was no foundation to it" (Oral History Project, Columbia University, 1960, 147; cited in Shapiro, *White Violence,* 481 n. 42).

36. "As late as 1920, 85 percent of all Negro pupils in the South were enrolled in the first four grades. In 1916, there were only sixty-seven Negro public high schools with fewer than twenty thousand students" (Virgil A. Clift, "Educating the American Negro," *The American Negro Reference Book* [Englewood Cliffs, N.J.: Prentice-Hall, 1966], 369).

37. The analogy was designed to penetrate the apathy of Northern whites, some of whom were outraged by the loss of U.S. and Filipino life in these military actions. The "battle to capture San Juan Hill and the other outlying fortifications around Santiago [in Cuba] was bloody enough; it decimated the American force. Illness followed. . . . [The Philippine Insurrection] dragged on for three years, . . cost more American lives than the Spanish American War and perhaps as many as two hundred thousand Filipino lives" (Frederick Merk, "Dissent in the Spanish-American War and the Philippine Insurrection," *Dissent in Three American Wars* [Cambridge, MA: Harvard University Press, 1970], 75, 93). Merk also notes that imperialistic efforts were fueled by racist beliefs, that there was, "in that quite racist era, a general willingness to regard smaller, brown-skinned people as inferiors, scarcely entitled to the privileges of self-government" (77).

38. The U.S. Bureau of the Census, *Negro Population, 1790–1915* (Washington, D.C.: GPO, 1918), 93, reports that in 1910 only 2 percent of Chicago's population was Negro (cited in Karl E. Taeuber and Alma F. Taeuber, "The Negro Population in the United States," *American Negro Reference Book,* 119).

39. "The Progress of Colored Women" was a speech delivered first in 1904 and updated and repeated numerous times, for example.

40. "Census statistics indicate an almost phenomenal rise in the literacy rate of Negroes between 1870 and 1890. It rose from 18.6 in 1870 to 30 percent in 1880, to 42.9 percent in 1890" (Logan, *Negro in American Life,* 58).

41. Hall, "Whites of Their Eyes," 31.

42. Ibid., 36.

43. In *The Sponsor: Notes of a Modern Potentate* (New York: Oxford University Press, 1978), 49–50, Erik Barnouw points to pressures from advertisers which affected the editorial policies of television networks from their beginnings, specifically, a policy of keeping series free of all race relations stories, which were regarded by many, including the FBI, as signs of communist leanings.

44. Hall, "Whites of Their Eyes," 38.

45. There are many items in Church Terrell's papers which address these wider issues. For instance, "Difficulties of Negroes in the United States: A Word about Lynching," dated 2 November 1905, bemoans "the revulsion of feeling toward Colored people all over the United States." In what follows, however, she documents the economic barriers they face, that there are only a few trades they are allowed to practice, that they are denied entry to labor unions, and that, when they can work, they are ill paid. She describes the credit system that transformed sharecropping into peonage, the disincentives to education when professional positions are denied, and the impact of Southern scorn and contempt

on their sense of self-esteem. She also details the many efforts to prevent colored people from obtaining education, the systematic disenfranchisement of former slaves, and the humiliating segregation in public transportation. In other words, without the constraints I have identified, she articulated the economic conflicts and understood the dynamics that were at work.

CHAPTER FOUR

"The Power of Hegemony" and Marxist Cultural Theory

James Arnt Aune

The late E. P. Thompson remarked at the beginning of *The Making of the English Working Class* that his goal was to "rescue the poor stockinger, the Luddite cropper, the 'obsolete' hand-loom weaver, the 'utopian' artisan, and even the deluded follower of Joanna Southcott, from the enormous condescension of posterity."[1] Professor Campbell's work in this essay, like all of her work in the recovery of women's public address, represents the liberatory moment of historical research at its best. Thomas Nelson Page, of course, *deserves* the enormous condescension of posterity, but a reading of Mary Church Terrell's side of this debate on lynching, reconstructed through artful rhetorical criticism, gives us a moment in which, as Herbert Marcuse wrote, "the terror is called up, called by its name, and made to testify, to denounce itself."[2]

In a time when those of us who teach both the history and methods of public address are assailed for "fetishizing the autonomous speaking subject," it is important to remember what enormous labor and, indeed, courage, it has required for Professor Campbell to rescue the texts of those who, against all odds, asserted their autonomy and their right to speak.[3]

Marginality, hegemony, subjectivity, and the cultural Left's holy trinity of race, class, and gender are very much in the mind of any late-twentieth-century audience approaching these texts. The very theme of this volume—rhetoric and community—may be viewed with suspicion by radical critics, because the community-building function of rhetoric often works as much by exclusion as by inclusion.

None of the documents in the Page-Terrell debate are in any meaningful sense part of a "canon" of American public address.[4] But they and Campbell's reading of them do raise important questions about the nature, scope, and function of rhetorical studies in a time of widespread confusion and even hostility about issues such as the relationship of text to context, the uses of the concept of hegemony, and the proper understanding of the interrelationships of race, class, and gender in social analysis. I want to discuss each of these methodological issues in turn, arguing that Campbell relies on a too simplistic reading of Marxist cultural theory and defending a somewhat different interpretation of these texts in terms of the original purpose of Gramsci's theory of hegemony: the development of a rhetoric of intellectuals.

Text and Context

My first reaction upon reading this essay, and the accompanying texts by Page and Terrell, was how few critical models we have for the analysis of debates as a rhetorical form. Many of us came to the field of communication through early participation in intercollegiate debate, but when we come to the practice of rhetorical criticism we tend to focus on the single text rather than the context of an entire debate. We experience the notorious difficulty of moving from text to context, or from close reading to generalization about the role of rhetoric in the development and maintenance of ideology. Despite the immensely increased sophistication of our methods for close reading of texts, it has proven difficult to come to any larger consensus in rhetorical studies about ways of understanding rhetorical effects or "effectiveness."

In cultural studies the line is often drawn between those who, to use Todd Gitlin's phrase, seem to view hegemony as "a sort of immutable fog that has settled over the whole public life of capitalist societies" and those who view all texts as "open," if one simply decodes strenuously enough.[5] To use the very word *rhetoric* would seem to take a stance in opposition to a "dominant ideology thesis," supplanting it, as Condit and Lucaites write, with "the rhetorical process of public argumentation in which various organized and articulate interest groups negotiate the problems of resource distribution" and with "a shared rhetorical culture out of which they all draw as they strive to express their particular interests."[6]

Over the long haul the liberal-pluralist reading that Condit and Lucaites provide of the American quest for equality may be an accurate one, but, as they themselves recognize, a focus on rhetorical processes may neglect the role of violence and coercive manipulation of information in blocking and creating social change. Public opinion, even in liberal democracies, is often formed as much by force and by cash as by persuasion.

Campbell gives us a useful way in toward resolving such methodological problems with her focus on the way in which "ownership and
practices of the print media shaped the debate over post-Reconstruction
public policy that institutionalized and 'naturalized' white racism in the
United States." Campbell urges us to focus on "the ideological processes
at work in the magazine industry" and, by a strategy of critical reduction, helps us to see operating in Page's rhetoric, as well as the selection
of his rhetoric by these journals of opinion, a way of mystifying conflicts
of interest and muting or suppressing class struggle. Campbell argues
that, "from a Marxian perspective, all conflicts are fundamentally economic" and that "deflecting economic issues onto questions of ethnicity
or gender allows economically advantaged whites to bond with other
whites against non-whites and males to bond together against women."

Campbell invokes Stuart Hall to explain the relationship between
such rhetorical strategy and the ideological processes of the mass media
themselves. Campbell persuasively shows how Page's rhetoric employed
imagery and themes polarized around fixed relations of subordination
and domination, how poles of superior and inferior natural species are
created, and how both are displaced from the language of history into
the language of Nature.

Campbell also illustrates how a rhetorical perspective on ideology
enables us to see things that critics such as Hall, with their semiotic
vocabulary, sometimes miss, namely the importance of dramatic scenarios or rhetorical visions in overwhelming simple facts and the
importance of simple repetition of unchallenged messages in forming
public opinion.

Campbell also provides a tantalizing, brief description and criticism
of Mary Church Terrell's "rhetorical philosophy" as a belief in the importance of providing information about the plight of African Americans.
I was reminded here of the distinction Christine Oravec draws between
the implicit rhetorical theories of the Whigs and Democrats in the nineteenth century as well as of Michael Schudson's discussion of the
distinction between "story" and "information" journalism in the late
nineteenth century.[7] I am convinced that it is in the interaction of text,
implicit rhetorical theory, ideology, and context that a full reading of
rhetorical documents can be found, and I would have liked to see
Campbell do more to discuss the sources and limitations of Terrell's rhetorical philosophy. A mystical faith in the power of information, as
opposed to persuasion, is a key characteristic of a certain type of radical

discourse, from Karl Marx to Noam Chomsky. The discourse of the right, in turn, seems to be better at spinning yarns, from Page down to Rush Limbaugh.

Hegemony, Ideology, and Rhetoric

It is, however, Campbell's use of Hall that reveals some problems with her analysis. I consider myself to be a Marxist (a term that now seems more pathetic than transgressive in applying it to oneself), but I recognize more of Adam Smith or Alexander Hamilton or Milton Friedman than Marx in the statement that all conflicts are fundamentally economic. I think we need to get clear about the nature of the Marxist concept of ideology if we are to create constructive dialogue between rhetorical studies and cultural studies. As I have argued elsewhere, the following are the key elements of the Marxist paradigm.[8]

First, Marxists share a fundamental "representative anecdote." As Kenneth Burke writes, a conceptual vocabulary—representative anecdote—must do two things: it must reduce human action and select a set of terms that justify such a reduction.[9] The various Marxisms share a common representative anecdote: human beings are laboring animals. They must work in order to live and in order to fulfill themselves. The error of economists before Marx was their assumption that enjoyment of the fruits of material labor is sufficient for human beings.

A second assumption does seem to make a form of economic determinism central to historical analysis. The mode of production in a given social totality—that is, the level of development of productive forces in addition to the type of work relations that accompany those forces—is a determining factor in establishing that totality's social being. Exactly how and how much a mode of production determines social being is a subject of considerable debate. A minimal version of this assumption would mean that a capitalist economic system based chiefly on industrial production tends to have consequences for a host of seemingly independent things such as individual psychology, artistic expression, religion, and politics. As Fredric Jameson has argued, it may be most useful to think of capitalism as largely affecting form rather than content per se; the oration, the pamphlet, the partisan debate, the magazine or newspaper editorial, and the television campaign commercial represent forms of public address as they are altered by changing forces and relations of production.[10] It is in the contradictory relationships among communication technology, capitalist development, and class struggle that a Marxist perspective on public address must be found, not in the simple reduction of argument to economic issues.

Third, all hitherto existing societies have been characterized by a struggle between classes over the control or allocation of the surplus from production. Workers, at least under capitalism, produce more than is needed to sustain themselves. This surplus, under capitalism, is expropriated by capitalists. Marxists will differ about the notion of "surplus value." Because of formal problems in the theory of price, it seems to make more sense to talk of the *exploitation* of workers than of the extraction of surplus value.[11] A focus on exploitation and struggle over exploitation has important political consequences.

As Erik Olin Wright points out, it is possible to be oppressed without being exploited. Exploitation implies a mutual relationship between exploiter and exploited. The capitalist needs the worker, at least until the worker is replaced by a machine, but even then the crisis of capitalism is created by the capitalist's forgetting that the worker is also a consumer.[12] The capitalist may very well discover that slavery, racial segregation, sexism, and homophobia represent a limitation on the possibilities of capitalist production or may prevent groups with tremendous purchasing power from being opened up as markets. There is no linear relationship between capitalism and oppression on the basis of race and gender; class struggle and the development of the productive forces will affect race and gender politics, because the symbols of race and gender can serve as powerful unifying or alienating devices, depending on the conventions and exigencies of the rhetorical situation in which advocates find themselves. A focus on the language of oppression also has the tendency of emphasizing the victim status of particular groups and thus runs the risk both of patronizing them and of de-emphasizing the role of human agency in social change.

Fourth, the level of development of the productive forces determines—in the sense of setting boundary conditions for—the sort of class structure and class struggle a given social system will have. A combination of increased exploitation of labor, for instance, with a centralization of economic power may make clashes between labor and capital inevitable over matters such as wages, work rules, and the length of the working day. A Marxist feminist might point to developments in reproductive technology (abortion, artificial contraception) as providing the material basis for the revolt of women against male domination. Marxists generally may be distinguished from other radicals by their conviction that a successful movement for social change must acknowledge material prerequisites for such a change.

Fifth, because the productive forces tend to develop over time, "history" is generally predictable in terms of the succession of modes of production. Capitalism has outlived its usefulness as a mode of production. That is, it helped develop productive forces to their currently high level, but its chronic crises and its wastefulness of natural resources and human talent mean that it will (or at least can) pass away. The precise mode of its passing away will vary, both in terms of what sort of Marxist politics one subscribes to and in terms of what sort of resistance is offered by the contending classes. Capitalism appears to be patterned into "long swings" of growth and decline, culminating in a period of economic crisis in which instability requires major institutional reconstruction for renewed stability and growth. The previous crisis, that of 1929, resulted in the moderately statist solution of the New Deal and the social-democratic welfare state of almost all Western democracies. The current crisis, reflecting changes in information technology and the concomitant globalizing of capitalism, represents an opportunity for restructuring which has thus far been dominated exclusively by the Right.[13]

Sixth, the class that controls the mode of production in a given society tends to repress, either through the threat of violence or through persuasion (or through a combination of both), radical alterations in the control of the productive forces. Marxists will differ in the extent to which they assess the relative power of such repression. Whether ideology is conceived in a narrow way as "false consciousness" or as a class-based "structure of feeling" or as "common sense" implicated in structures of power and domination, the critique of ideology as disseminated in communicative texts and in institutions is an important goal of Marxist practice.

Although Stuart Hall has been one of the primary forces in overturning simplistic economic determinism in Marxist media studies, he is used by Campbell to defend the least defensible part of Marxist theorizing about the relationship between culture and class struggle.

Ideology is the single most unstable term in Marxism. Its instability makes it similar to the way *rhetoric* itself functions in Western culture. One could construct a narrative in which the rhetorical tradition somehow goes "underground" in the Marxist notion of ideology. A simpler argument would be to point out that the notion of ideology functions much like a notion of rhetoric would work in previous Western political philosophy.

Ideology is false or deluded speech about the world and the human beings who inhabit it. Marx's great contribution to the social sciences is that he is not content to show that mistaken speech is false logically or referentially. He also wishes to *explain how* that mistaken speech came about. There seem to be two conditions for the emergence of mistaken speech.

As Jon Elster writes, false speech can be explained in terms either of a speaker's position or interest. A *position-explanation* locates false speech in terms of the cognitive errors a speaker makes because of an inability to see the whole of a phenomenon.[14] If I falsely state that the sun moves around the earth, it is because I have not been educated to move out of my limited position of observation. The role of the mass media in restricting access to information may perhaps be more usefully described as a position-explanation than an *interest-explanation*. Ideology emerges generally from faulty seeing in historical time. It also occurs from faulty placement in social space: "Everyone believes his craft to be the true one. Illusions regarding the connection between their craft and reality are the more likely to be cherished by them because of the very nature of the craft."[15] In this case of false speech the speaker's "occupational psychosis" is a cognitive failure caused by self-interest, wishful thinking, and one-sided training. According to Elster, it is a case of the *fallacy of composition,* assuming that what is characteristic of the part is also characteristic of the whole.

There is another form of position-explanation in which cognitive failure is traceable to needs to compensate for a miserable reality. Marx and Engels' indictment of religion as the "opium of the people" falls into this category. False religious speech occurs as the result of cognitive failure reinforced by the internal need for solace in a "heartless world."[16] It is unlikely that Thomas Nelson Page knowingly misrepresented the "facts" about lynching, because he was himself so caught up in a mythic evasion of reality.

Unfortunately, Marx and Engels' real contribution to social theory—position-explanation—has been obscured and confused with interest-explanation. In an interest-explanation ideology, and by extension rhetorical action, becomes the transparent expression of a person's economic or occupational interests. The classic passage is this one:

The ideas of the ruling class are in every epoch the ruling ideas, i.e. the class which is the ruling *material* force of society is at the same time its ruling *intellectual* force. The class which has the means of material production at its disposal, consequently also controls the means of mental production, so that the ideas of those who lack the means of mental production are on the whole subject to it. The ruling ideas are nothing more than the ideal expression of the dominant material relations, the dominant material relations grasped as ideas; hence of the relations which make the one class the ruling one, therefore, the ideas of its dominance.[17]

This passage is a major source of problems for Marxism. First, as Elster argues, it does not explain how the ideas of the ruling class get to be the ruling ideas. [18] Second, it fails to explain how nonruling class or oppositional ideas get heard at all. Third, it makes "ideas" simply straightforward "communications" (almost in the sense of transportation) of interests and not themselves complex sites of struggle for meaning. Fourth, it contributes to the vicious tendency of the Left to represent differing political beliefs as produced solely by an intention to oppress another. This is not to deny that interest-explanations are at times valid—the cynical use of religion by Southern mill owners comes to mind—but to universalize them is also a form of cognitive failure. Much of the conceptual confusion of contemporary "cultural studies" and the attempt to import it into rhetorical studies stems from the muddling of interest- and position-explanations.

A solution to the tendency of position-explanations to slide into interest-explanations is to focus on ideology as practical rhetoric, liable to all the distortions and rationalizations that any political discourse possesses in the heat of conflict. One can thus avoid name-calling and the scientifically murky problem of intention by seeing how ideological choices are dictated by practical rhetorical goals.

Mass Media and Legitimation Processes

A different approach to the relationship between these arguments about lynching and the mass media is to discuss the role of the mass media in identifying and legitimating advocates for the African-American cause. As Adolph Reed Jr. has written, "Afro-American politics has been structured persistently around a client relation that binds black elites individually and primarily to external sources of patronage while they simultaneously require legitimation internally among blacks."[19] From Booker T. Washington until the passage of the 1965 Voting Rights Act, "verifiable mechanisms for validating leadership claims were practically nonexistent in the black community."[20]

In the absence of voting rights blacks had to rely on the press and the church to legitimate black leadership: "In the Afro-American context the antidemocratic character of the organic leadership style has been obscured by the primacy of external linkages to white elites. Protest leadership is beset by the contradiction that certification of its authenticity is attained outside the black community," thus creating "a model of political authority that is antidiscursive and deemphasizes popular accountability."[21]

Just as the press legitimated Booker T. Washington more than W. E. B. Du Bois in an earlier period, the media have tended to overemphasize the power of Christian religious authority in the black community. Reed draws our attention to the negative effects of religious rhetoric. The "antiparticipatory and antiintellectual" nature of religion "deauthorizes the principle of individual autonomy, which is the basis of citizenship."[22] "The projection of the church as a source of leadership authenticity assigns responsibility for political legitimation to an intrinsically apolitical agency."[23]

If Reed's analysis of media legitimation and Elster's critique of the Marxist notion of ideology are correct, it is an exaggeration to tie Page too directly to the interests of northern manufacturers. The problem, then as now, is the way in which the mass media do not serve as truly democratic organs but are deformed, instead, by the need to make a profit. Such capitalist deformation, however, may better be attributed to a position-explanation than an interest-explanation, at least in the absence of direct evidence about the intentions of the publishers of these magazines.

A more useful strategy for analyzing the rhetoric of Page and Terrell might be to use Gramsci's distinction between "organic" and "traditional" intellectuals.[24] According to Gramsci, organic intellectuals are needed by a new class seeking to develop a new social order and are contrasted to traditional intellectuals, who are tied to earlier historical periods. The job of intellectuals is to forge cultural-social unity ("hegemony") which can serve as the basis of a "historic bloc." History, for Gramsci, is a succession of historic blocs created by political praxis and not merely a succession of modes of production. The distinction is crucial, for it enables Campbell's analysis to allow for the shifting alliances of capitalism with racist and antiracist forces over the course of the twentieth century. A thoroughgoing study of the interaction among the elite press, intellectuals, and mass audiences would provide us with a more complete view of the texts Campbell presents to us.

General Implications

If it is the case that adding Hall's concept of ideology to this instance of public address criticism is not necessarily progress, I want to end by pointing to some other roads not taken in Campbell's analysis.

First, we simply do not have enough studies of racist rhetoric itself; understandably, the recovery of the heroic voices of subjects on the margins has been a priority activity, but in order to write a full history we need to understand the rhetoric of Page as much as that of Terrell, if not more so. The figure of the sexually voracious black man, from Page to Richard Wright's Bigger Thomas to George Bush and (lest we forget who first played the card) Al Gore's Willie Horton, remains a central character in the American rhetorical vision.

Second, it may be useful to examine Page's fiction in tandem with his journalism. The production and distribution of Southern fiction may have served an even greater ideological role than journalism in promoting racist rhetorical visions. Campbell rightly points out that Page is by far the better storyteller than Terrell and that Terrell fails to provide an alternative to the dramatic "rape of the white virgin scenario." Further support for Campbell's argument comes from the fact that Page and Terrell both tell the same tale of Negro virtue during the Civil War: "During the War, the men were away in the army, and the negroes were the loyal guardians of the women and children"; and "While the men of the South were off fighting to keep the negro in bondage, their mothers, wives and daughters were entrusted to the black man's care. How faithfully and loyally he kept his sacred trust the records of history attest!"[25]

This vision of the women and children of the plantation cared for by trusted slaves is at the heart of a particular ideological image of Southern community which has been exploited by a host of Southern writers and ideologues as diverse as Margaret Mitchell and Richard Weaver. It is also a vision, as Eugene Genovese, the foremost Marxist historian of slavery reminds us, which has a deeply anticapitalist strain.[26]

Finally, the fact that only Terrell is able to remind us of the invisible black rape victims in Page's rhetorical vision returns us to the problem of rhetorical philosophy again. As bell hooks writes, "black women's bodies were the discursive terrain, the playing fields where racism and sexuality converged."[27] Just as the black woman often became invisible in the lynching debate, the excessive masculinism of black protest rhetoric would in turn later marginalize black women. As hooks writes, accepting "sexual metaphors forged a bond between oppressed black men and their white male oppressors. They shared the patriarchal belief that revolutionary struggle was really about the erect phallus."[28]

Finally, Campbell is right in concluding that Terrell does not attain the eloquence of Ida Wells and that this failure stems partly from Terrell's rhetorical philosophy and partly from the constraining effects of ideology upon media practice. As I was reading Terrell, I was reminded of a line by the late Audre Lorde: "The master's tools will never dismantle the master's house."[29] Lorde's observation (made more mainstream and, perhaps, misrepresented by Naomi Wolf in *Fire with Fire*)[30] leads us back to the larger theoretical problem posed by the intersection of race, class, and gender in rhetorical studies. In this case, do the tools of debate and careful refutation serve as a fitting tool to undermine the rhetoric of Thomas Nelson Page? How we answer that question says much about how we understand the nature of rhetoric and its tradition.

Notes

1. E. P. Thompson, *The Making of the English Working Class* (New York: Alfred A. Knopf, 1963), 12.

2. Herbert Marcuse, *The Aesthetic Dimension* (Boston: Beacon Press, 1978), 63–64.

3. See Barbara Biesecker, "Negotiating with Our Tradition: Reflecting Again (without Apologies) on the Feminization of Rhetoric," *Philosophy and Rhetoric* 26 (1993): 238. The full exchange between Biesecker and Campbell begins with Biesecker, "Coming to Terms with Recent Attempts to Write Women into the History of Rhetoric," *Philosophy and Rhetoric* 25 (1992): 140–61, and continues with Campbell's response, "Biesecker Cannot Speak for Her Either," *Philosophy and Rhetoric* 26 (1993): 153–59.

4. I want to add here, in passing, a point that exchanges about "the canon" are bound to occur only if we adopt a position that public address studies should be more like literary studies than like history or political science. The salutary move toward greater coherence in graduate education about public address and the defense of close readings of rhetorical documents do not, it seems to me, entail an acceptance of "canon" language in describing our field of study. One could note, unkindly perhaps, that new wave critics such as Biesecker are "al-

ways already" committed to a canon of their own, in this case the poststructuralist canon of those noted feminist theorists Michel Foucault, Jacques Derrida, and Michel de Certeau.

5. Todd Gitlin, "Prime Time Ideology: The Hegemonic Process in Television Entertainment," in *Television: The Critical View*, ed. Horace Newcomb, 3d ed. (New York: Oxford University Press, 1982), 428.

6. Celeste Michelle Condit and John Louis Lucaites, *Crafting Equality* (Chicago: University of Chicago Press, 1993), xiv–xv.

7. Christine Oravec, "The Democratic Critics: An Alternative American Rhetorical Tradition of the Nineteenth Century," *Rhetorica* 4 (1986): 395–421; and "The Sublimation of Mass Consciousness in the Rhetorical Criticism of Jacksonian America," *Communication* 11 (1990): 291–314. Michael Schudson, *Discovering the News* (New York: Basic Books, 1978), especially chap. 3.

8. James Arnt Aune, *Rhetoric and Marxism* (Boulder, Colo.: Westview Press, 1994), 9–13.

9. Kenneth Burke, *A Grammar of Motives* (Berkeley: University of California Press, 1969), 59–61.

10. Fredric Jameson, *Marxism and Form* (Princeton: Princeton University Press, 1971).

11. This crucial point is developed by John Roemer, *A General Theory of Exploitation and Class* (Cambridge: Harvard University Press, 1982); and *Free to Lose: An Introduction to Marxist Economic Philosophy* (Cambridge: Harvard University Press, 1988).

12. See Erik Olin Wright, *Classes* (London: Verso, 1985), 64–104.

13. See David M. Gordon, Richard Edwards, and Michael Reich, *Segmented Work, Divided Workers: The Historical Transformation of Labor in the United States* (Cambridge: Cambridge University Press, 1982).

14. Jon Elster, *Making Sense of Marx* (Cambridge: Cambridge University Press, 1983), 465.

15. Marx and Engels, "The German Ideology," *The Collected Works*, vol. 5 (New York: International Publishers, 1975), 92.

16. Karl Marx, "Contribution to the Critique of Hegel's Philosophy of Law: Introduction," *Collected Works*, 3:174.

17. Marx and Engels, "German Ideology," 59.

18. See Elster, *Making Sense of Marx*, 27–37.

19. Adolph L. Reed Jr., *The Jesse Jackson Phenomenon* (New Haven: Yale University Press, 1986), 9.

20. Ibid., 32.

21. Ibid., 34–35.

22. Ibid, 57.

23. Ibid., 60. See also Adolph Reed Jr., "W. E. B. Du Bois: A Perspective on the Bases of His Political Thought," *Political Theory* 13 (August 1985): 431–56.

24. See Aune, *Rhetoric and Marxism*, 70–71.

25. Thomas Nelson Page, "The Lynching of Negros—Its Cause and Its Prevention," *North American Review* 178 (January 1904): 36; Mary Church Terrell, "Lynching from a Negro's Point of View," *North American Review* 178 (June 1904): 862.

26. See Eugene D. Genovese, *The World the Slaveholders Made: Two Essays in Interpretation*, 2d ed. (Middletown, Conn.: Wesleyan University Press, 1988).

27. bell hooks, "Reflections on Race and Sex," *Yearning* (Boston: South End Press, 1990), 57.

28. Ibid., 58.

29. Audre Lorde, *Sister Outsider: Essays and Speeches by Audre Lorde* (Freedom, Calif.: The Crossing Press, 1984), 112.

30. See Naomi Wolf, *Fire with Fire* (New York: Random House, 1993), 54.

CHAPTER FIVE

Du Bois, Double-Consciousness, and the Modern City

Stephen H. Browne

The rise of the modern city is now a fixture in our national mythology, a fact of life made irresistible to the moral, political, and literary imagination of this country. From municipal planning documents to hard-boiled detective novels, from muckraking to the urban idyll, from neon to jazz, new ways of talking about the city have emerged and have ever since shaped our understanding of it. These modes of representation are, of course, as diverse and unpredictable as the city itself and, like it, may be read through the inscriptions of power by which they are defined.[1]

This essay takes as its theme two quite general but distinct traditions of reading the city in fin de siècle America. One such tradition I associate with dominant culture, the preoccupation of which was the organization and control of urban life. It is a complex discourse, to be sure, but we have reason to believe that certain ends gave it coherence and identity. In the words of Dana White, "although late-century urbanists advocated a variety of social philosophies, institutional innovations, and organizational schemes, they all shared the same goal—the achievement of an urban social equilibrium."[2] We know, of course, that the work of restoration has never come easy for Americans, not least of all because it presumes a state that never existed and the appeal to which is almost always self-interested. Such a view may be said to characterize a second tradition of reading the modern city. It represents itself as a counterdiscourse, aiming rather to expose and upset the strategies by which the city-text may be so ordered. This tradition has not figured so prominently in histories of the subject. That it ought to be reckoned with; that we have a rich literature available to us; and that critics of public discourse have a stake in its exploration are the working premises of this essay.

We have before us then two rich and competing discourses, amply in evidence at the turn of the century and influential, I believe, for the ways in which we continue to talk about the city in our time. As a basis for specifying the argument, I want to introduce the issue of race—not so much to locate a theme as to examine the rhetorical and textual dynamics of these two discourses. To this end I point to a literature, for the most part essays from well-known periodicals, which offer vivid accounts of the city as it might be viewed from the vantage points of dominant culture. Alongside this discourse I pose the remarkable collection of essays contained in William E. B. Du Bois's *Souls of Black Folk*. In particular, I examine "Of the Wings of Atalanta," as forceful a reading as one is likely to find within this tradition. My reading in turn relies on Du Bois's principle of "double-consciousness," surely one of his most lasting and disturbing commentaries on the state of being black in America. *Double-consciousness*, I hope to suggest, describes not only a condition of being but also a means to imagine, structure, and express a certain view of the world. It thus projects itself from a state of mind to a practice of reading. In this context "Of the Wings of Atalanta" works by showing us what the city looks like when seeing double. Its rhetoric is to effect a stylized distortion of the city as the city is envisioned by dominant culture.[3]

The City in Dominant Culture

The rise of the modern city had become by century's end a familiar subject to readers of popular and learned periodicals. From about 1895 and for the next decade *Harper's New Monthly, Atlantic Monthly, Cosmopolitan,* and other major magazines routinely featured such essays, while journals of a scholarly cast, ranging from the *North American Review* to the *South Atlantic Quarterly,* addressed more technical issues of city government and municipal reform.[4] It is thus a heterogeneous discourse, differing in aim, tone, source, and stance. At the same time, I believe certain limited generalizations are possible. In the following I group its various expressions with reference to what I call the urban picturesque. The work of such portrayal is to establish a vocabulary of images with which to arrange the chaotic elements of life in the modern city. I wish here to stress the term *perspective*, because this category is meant to suggest modes of comprehending the city, of visualizing and reading it, rather than to designate any generic or fixed attributes. If nothing else, it may serve as a context within which Du Bois's *Souls of Black Folk* may be productively read.

Urban panegyrics ran from gentle satires to loving odes, but the cities of choice were predictable. Aside from the odd Indianapolis or equally unlikely outpost, readers could expect Washington, Atlanta, Baltimore, and Boston to receive the lion's share of praise. The general tone of these essays is familiar, the *topoi* unsurprising. But certain patterns of depiction, never very far from the surface, are instructive for the ways in which they structure our perception of the city and its virtues. Here is Julian Ralph from an 1895 *Harper's* essay on Washington and its citizens:

> They walk as no other cityfolk walk in this country—always with a parade step. There is no bolting along as in New York, or slouching along as in the South. There are no strained faces of men who plunge ahead muttering to themselves as in Chicago. The paraders of Washington all wear their best clothes, and move in stately measure—right foot, 1, 2, 3; left foot, 1, 2, 3; right foot—from the Capitol to the Treasury, and back again, keeping to the right as the law directs.[5]

The urban walk is a familiar conceit in many of these essays, serving at once as an organizing device and as a signifying act. Thus, it is used here to identify, contrast, and stigmatize. We see too that it is also used as a way of keeping the citizen out in the open: hence, the walk, the promenade, the stroll—these are conspicuously public activities suggesting the virtues of civic order. Indeed, it is this capacity for purposeful and collective action which normatively defines urban identity. And that must be why, the author notes, "Washington is the Afro-American's earthly paradise." As evidence, Ralph continues, we can go into any church during services; there we "see nothing to laugh at, no darky peculiarities, in that edifice. The people dress, look, and behave precisely like nice white people, only some are black, and others shaded off from white."[6]

This synthesis of public space, ordered behavior, and civic identity helps illustrate the most prominent features of the urban picturesque. Above all this perspective presumes and requires a vantage point, a place from which those features of the city worth seeing can in fact be seen. The reader is accordingly positioned, as in this example from Stephen Bonsals's 1896 encomium to Baltimore, at once in but above the city:

Coming from the station, the highest point of vantage is reached at the corner of Charles and Chase streets, from where the city can be seen stretching out fan-shaped and interminable to the south along the banks of the Patapsco, and to the east and to the west. From here we also catch a nearer view of Mount Vernon Place, which with its monuments and public edifices, the stately private dwellings, the green open squares, and in its ensemble, certainly presents to the astonished tourist the most imposing site to be found in any American city.[7]

If urban picturesque allowed its reader to see the citizen in his and her proper place, it could also ask what that citizen was doing. Here it offered not so much a portrait of city life as a call to action, and, while it retained a strong appeal to virtue, it insisted that such virtue was the result of duties properly conceived and exercised. Given the magnitude of the circumstances, the *Atlantic Monthly* announced in 1895, "it behooves every American interested in public life and public affairs to study as carefully as he can the phenomena of the life in these cities, and the administration of them."[8] By the end of the century this civic language helped articulate a pervasive cultural logic that required collective and voluntary response to the dangers of urban growth. From the City Beautiful Movement to Chicago's Upward Movement citizens were to devote themselves, reasoned Henry Fuller in 1897, to "the extirpation of the moral and civic evil that has reared itself," a task to be prosecuted, he hoped, "in that spirit of civic regeneration whose signs are just now so encouraging and so abundant."[9]

The language of civic virtue, as I have suggested, is more clearly propositional than imagistic. But it too relies on a perspective that allows the problems of the city to be seen with utter clarity and, consequently, their solutions arrived at with equal assurance. In this case the rise of the modern city was to be a challenge met by reasserting traditional civic values. The solution to whatever ailed the city lay in a return to individual commitment and national pride. Thus, in "The Problem of the Twentieth Century" Strong urged that the

problem of the twentieth century . . . demands for its resolution a higher type of citizenship . . . our public schools must give to the children and youth of today such instruction in the duties and principles of good citizenship as earlier generations did not have. Literature dealing with American citizenship, adapted to all ages, from the high school down to kindergarten, should be absorbed by the scholars until an intelligent civic patriotism becomes a matter of course.[10]

These brief depictions are meant only to suggest something of the tone and character of a more general discourse. Among its more pervasive features is the easy movement from considerations of physical space to ordered action to standards of civic identity and responsibility. This much, I would like to stress, is evident as well in African-American writing, at least at a certain level of thematic abstraction. The distinction rests in the complexity with which these stories of the modern city get told. I refer not so much to artistic density or conceptual rigor or subtly poised ironies but something more basic. It has, rather, to do with a kind of narrative assurance that typifies the language of dominant culture, a habitual recourse to traditions of thinking about urban life—its problems and its glories—which have been drained of their historical permutations. The result is what might be called a monocular city, a world that, however large, can be confidently viewed from a single vantage point. My reading of Du Bois, by contrast, is meant to indicate what the city looks like when refracted through the lens of race, where questions of space, order, and identity remain but must always be answered twice.

Du Bois and the Modern City

Du Bois, of course, was neither the first nor last African American to read the city, in our words, as a culture text. He was part of a tradition dating at least to the antebellum years and which remains clearly in evidence today. With certain important exceptions this discourse sets itself in dramatic relief against the ceremonial, bureaucratic, and civic strains noted earlier. This is not to say that African-American writers were not concerned about each of these modes of comprehension. Clearly, they were, if only because they were so often subject to the terms and strategies of such discourses. And the larger patterns and images that have long fed the city story can be found across cases: the proverbial journey from pastoral innocence to urban experience; the city as both opportunity and danger; the blurred lines between reality and appearance. In this sense the city historically has functioned, in the words of Leo Marx, as "a kind of semantic or ideological field in which a range of attitudes, some of them diametrically opposed, is generated."[11]

But fields, semantic, ideological, or otherwise, are seldom unified. In this case the clearest lines of demarcation are drawn, rather, by perspective and accented by voice. Among the most prominent strains in this tradition is the stress on radical self-consciousness; the disparity between national symbols and lived experience; and the sense of living out the terms of a paradox. Thus, Frederick Douglass exulted that "Baltimore laid the foundations, and opened the gateway, to all my subsequent prosperity." Still, Douglass later recalls:

> It was this everlasting thinking of my condition that tormented me. There was no getting rid of it. It pressed upon me by every object within site or hearing, animate or inanimate . . . I saw nothing without seeing it, I heard nothing without hearing it, and felt nothing without feeling it.[12]

More than a half-century later Mary Church Terrell takes her readers through the streets of nearby Washington, a city fated from the start to live between itself and its symbolic pretensions. What she found there is hardly the stuff of panegyric, for

> surely nowhere in the world do oppression and persecution based solely on the color of the skin appear more hateful and hideous than in the capital of the United States, because the chasm between the principle upon which the government was founded, and which it still professes to believe, and those which are daily practiced under the protection of the flag, yawns so wide and deep.[13]

In our own time James Baldwin wrapped these themes and their legacy into much of *Notes from a Native Son*. In "The Harlem Ghetto" Baldwin reflects that the "terrible thing about being a Negro leader lies in the term itself": "I do not mean," Baldwin writes, "merely the somewhat condescending differentiation the term implies, but the nicely refined torture a man can experience from having been created and defeated by the same circumstances."[14]

Du Bois's place within this tradition is at once clear and complex. Like Douglass before him and Baldwin later, he was able to range across multiple conventions and symbolic fields: thus, autobiography, polemic, poetry, myth, song, and social analysis might all converge in a single rhetorical act, as indeed they do in the *Souls of Black Folk*. At the same time, the text stands in a complicated relationship to the tradition from which it grew and to which it so obviously contributed. First, *Souls of Black Folk* is not only or even primarily about white culture and its ways; it was designed as well to challenge the current leadership within the African-American community at the time—a challenge, demonstrably, that did not go unheeded. Any fully realized account of the text would then need to consider the intricately constructed audiences being addressed. Second, we need to recall that four years prior to the appearance of *Souls of Black Folk* Du Bois had published the highly regarded book *The Philadelphia Negro*. The work was written, White notes, when "almost every metropolis-on-the-make produced a massive social survey à la Booth to accompany its comprehensive park-parkway scheme à la Olmstead and its monumental city-beautiful master plan à la Burchen." Du Bois, White concludes, "would carry the method of the social survey to its scientific limits."[15]

I wish therefore not to imply that *Souls of Black Folk* represents some or even all of the young Du Bois's reading practices. At a minimum, however, we can say that here are two conspicuously different approaches separated by an emerging consciousness of the intellectual as social critic. Thus, what Du Bois writes in *The Philadelphia Negro*—that "above all" the scholar "must ever tremble lest some personal bias, some moral conviction or some unconscious trend of thought due to previous training, has to a degree distorted the picture in his view"—is soon displaced by the overtly rhetorical aims of *Souls of Black Folk*.[16]

The text is composed of fourteen essays, nine of which had been previously published. On the occasion of its fiftieth anniversary Du Bois recollected that his publishers "sought a more popular work along literary lines and inquired if I could not get together a sufficient number of essays to make a book." He now thought the work immature, informed neither by Freud nor Marx, but allowed that the essays in one way or another "outline a phase of my spiritual development."[17] Historians and other readers were to prove less restrained. Arnold Rampersad believed that, "if all a nation's literature may stem from one book, as Hemingway implied about Huck Finn, then it can accurately be said that all of Afro-American literature of a creative nature has proceeded from Du Bois' comprehensive statement on the nature of the people in *Souls*."[18] One reader from St. Louis scribbled a note to Du Bois announcing that she had just finished the book: "across the color line I extend to you a hand of sympathy and profound appreciation," wrote Pauline Schneider. "It must be that hundreds of white people have been moved by this book even as I am, and feel the same heavy, despairing pain over individual inability to contribute even a mite toward the removal of a mountain of ignorance, injustice, and folly."[19] Whatever Du Bois's later sentiments, it continued to speak to generations of audiences from all parts of the country; thus, in 1956 Langston Hughes wrote, "I have just read again your *The Souls of Black Folk*—for perhaps the tenth time—the first time having been some forty years ago when I was a child in Kansas. Its beauty and passion and power are as moving and meaningful as ever."[20]

Today we most likely know of the work for its essay on Booker Washington. It would be difficult to conceive of a more pointed counterstatement on the principles and aspirations of African-American leadership, and, as timely, as eloquent and aggressive, as that piece is, it is perhaps not surprising that "Of Mr. Booker T. Washington and Others" should come to stand as a part for the whole. I think such exclusive attention a mistake, and so one of the aims of this essay is to suggest other, productive ways of reading the work. We approach it first by examining the principle of double-consciousness and on its basis proceed to "Of the Wings of Atalanta." There we will find Du Bois performing an exposition of his own, a stylized reading of the city as seen through his eyes and judged by his own lights.

Du Bois introduces the concept in the first pages of the first essay; less explicitly, it continues to inform and underscore the remaining thirteen. Here is the text from "Of Our Spiritual Strivings":

> After the Egyptian and Indian, the Greek and Roman, the Teuton and Mongolian, the Negro is a sort of seventh son, born with a veil, and gifted with second-sight in this American world,—a world which yields him no true self-consciousness, but only lets him see himself through the revelation of the other world. It is a peculiar sensation, this double-consciousness, this sense of always looking at oneself through the eyes of others, of measuring one's soul by the tape of a world that looks on in amused contempt and pity. One always feels this two-ness,—an American, a Negro; two souls, two thoughts, two unreconciled strivings; two warring ideals in one dark body, whose dogged strength alone keeps it from being torn asunder.[21]

It does nothing to the force of Du Bois's conception to note that versions of it had been circulating for some time. Du Bois scholars have identified his Harvard mentor William James as perhaps the most immediate source; it is featured in James' *Principles of Psychology* as a medical condition akin to schizophrenia. The figurative genealogy of double-consciousness may be traced at the very least to the 1840s, when Emerson gave it classic expression in "The Transcendentalist."[22] We have reason to believe, then, that Du Bois could use the idea to public effect and that, if it was not exactly a commonplace, it could claim some cultural currency. In general, we may say of Du Bois, in the words of Dickson Bruce, that he "was using a term that set up a variety of connotations for the educated reader, thus making an effort to give his readers a reference point on the basis of which to understand the tragedy of racism, especially for the self-conscious individual, and to appreciate his own program for a new definition of what it meant to be black in America."[23]

As a description of consciousness Du Bois's statement is, for all its mythic aura, fairly explicable. At a minimum it designates a sustained and collective condition of mind; that condition is defined by its simultaneity, with an attendant sense of being poised in two realities at once. It is not obvious, however, that this "two-ness" is an inherent liability; in fact, it grants a kind of "second-sight in this American world." If there is anything inherent here, it is struggle—struggle not for total assimilation, à la Washington, nor for separatism, à la Garvey, but for a world irreducible to those terms. "The history of the American Negro," Du Bois writes, "is the history of this strife,—this longing to attain self-conscious manhood, to merge his double self into a better and truer self."[24]

In one regard, then, we have a restatement on the age-old paradox that alienation is a precondition to privileged insight. It is in this sense, for example, that Thomas Holt writes of Du Bois that his stance "may be taken as somehow emblematic of the African American experience generally. By that I mean, African Americans live a kind of paradox embodied in their very lives, which are shaped profoundly by conflicts of ideals and purposes."[25] I do not know how one might go about confirming— or denying—Holt's point, but in any case it is too universal to be of much use. I would propose, rather, that Du Bois's conception of double-consciousness gives us not so much a psychology of race as a hermeneutics of experience. It is about being in the world, to be sure, but especially about how such being may be represented, expressed, and given rhetorical force in contexts of public life. It can, in short, be given texture: double-consciousness offers us a way of reading because it is a way of seeing. "Of the Wings of Atalanta" may be said to work as a kind of lesson in making sense of the modern city. More specifically, we will see the author position himself as he would have the reader positioned: simultaneously within and without the cultural narratives with which the modern city was explained. From this vantage point Du Bois will effect what amounts to a double telling: not a displacement but, rather, a rehearsal and reordering of those myths and the lessons they bear.

Analysis of the Text

Narrative I: The New South

Three interlocking narratives give to the text its discernible form. Each of these narratives—the New South, the Gospel of Wealth, and its utopian tomorrow—is highly stylized but internally coherent. The nineteen paragraphs are in turn held together through a certain lyrical quality, pervasive but not overwhelming, and which imparts to the text the tone of an urban idyll. This much is consistent with the other essays collected in *Souls of Black Folk*, though not perhaps what we would expect from a practicing sociologist. The stance in any case is one of engaged reflection, and the perspective it affords not only frames the text but is its very subject.It is an orientation, moreover, that allows Du Bois to enter into, dwell among, and depart from the narratives in a conspicuous way; to be simultaneously in the story—indeed, telling it according to form— but also commenting upon it and ultimately extracting from it more than the narrative on its own terms will allow. Here are the opening lines:

> South of the North, yet north of the South, lies the City of a Hundred Hills, peering out from the shadows of the past into the promise of the future. I have seen her in the morning, when the first flush of day had half-aroused her; she lay gray and still on the crimson soil of Georgia; then the blue smoke began to curl from her chimneys, the tinkle of bell and scream of whistle broke the silence, the rattle and roar of busy life slowly gathered and swelled, until the seething whirl of the city seemed a strange thing in a sleepy land.

Thus begins Du Bois's story of the New South, and, while it refracts the city of Atlanta—South of the North, yet north of the South—the myth was as familiar then as now. Given what we know of the author, we might well ask just what he was doing in giving such rehearsals. Certainly, all the themes are there: North and South; past and future; soil and smoke; animal and machine; sloth and industry. This story of Atlanta's rise since the war—or Du Bois's telling of it—is, however, not anomalous but basic to the general work of the text. It exemplifies Du Bois's more general claim that cultural identity is a production of such histories; identity cannot therefore be transformed through the simple act of selecting from available alternatives. The challenge, rather, was not to forget the story but to double it—and there to find real possibilities for change.

Du Bois's early restatement of the story of Atlanta is accordingly a kind of setup—not for a fall but for a retelling. We are thus led to see that suspended within any given narrative is a corresponding truth:

It is a hard thing to live haunted by the ghost of an untrue dream; to see the wide vision of empire fade into real ashes and dirt; to feel the pang of the conquered, and yet know that with all the Bad that fell on one black day, something was vanquished that deserved to live, something killed that in justice had not dared to die; to know that with the Right that triumphed, triumphed something of Wrong, something mean and sordid, something less than the broadest and best. All this is bitter hard.

Now this is a surprising passage only as it is isolated from its place and function within the text. True, the lament contrasts sharply with previous lines, and certain readers might be hard-pressed to figure just what in the Old South "was vanquished that deserved to live." But for all that, we find here no radical displacement of one narrative with another; if anything, we have the singular image of this civil rights leader serving reminders that so great a victory comes with a cost. We will see it again: later Du Bois remarks on the passing of "the old ideal of the Southern gentleman" and "the steady disappearance of a certain type of Negro—the faithful, courteous slave of other days, with his incorruptible honesty and dignified humility." Du Bois is, of course, not personally lamenting that passage; he is, I believe, putting on display the working of his own double-consciousness, and he insists as he does throughout that things are never as simple—as monocular—as they may seem. In this regard the gain to be had from second sight is not seeing things in their separateness; it consists in seeing how distorted such distinctions can be. And that is why it remains to Du Bois to point out the real ashes in false dreams, the defeat in victory, and wrong in right.

Narrative II: Gospel of Wealth

I suggested earlier that Du Bois's conception of double-consciousness gives to his reasoning what might be called a "yes, and yet" quality. In the first narrative phase of the text we saw it take the form "Yes, Atlanta has been reborn, and yet something good died along with its passing." Here Du Bois introduces the second narrative with a myth that serves the same purpose—only it works the other way around. The future ex-Marxist poses against his newly industrialized city—cunning, watchful, proud—a blended morality story that mixes pagan eros with Christian guilt.

It is in fact not Du Bois who would displace one myth wholesale with another; this new Atlanta seemed bent on out-northing the North and befouling, in his words, "the Gospel of Work with the Gospel of Pay." Into this prospect and for this reason Du Bois asserts a cautionary tale in the form of ancient myth: "you know the tale," he writes,

> how swarthy Atalanta, tall and wild, would marry only him who out-raced her; and how the wily Hippomedes laid three apples of gold in the way. She fled like a shadow, paused, startled over the first apple, but even as he stretched his hand, fled again; hovered over the second, then, slipping from his hot grasp, flew over river, vale, and hill; but as she lingered over the third, his arms fell around her, and looking on each other, the blazing passion of their love profaned the sanctuary of Love, and they were cursed. If Atlanta be not named for Atalanta, she ought to have been.

Thus, Du Bois inaugurates the second phase of his representation. The story of Atalanta, transparent and moralistic even by his standards, is used as a governing image for much of the text. It is, however, not much more than a conceit, a means to lay one story alongside another as a means to illuminate both. The New South, he has shown, in fact consisted of two pasts, apposite but mutually regarding. Here, too, Du Bois will in effect split our field of vision and thus cause us to resist once more any easy rendering of the city into a single narrative. In this telling we first see Atlanta through the severe New England eyes of the young intellectual: this is the Du Bois of the North, of Harvard and Berlin and the Talented Tenth, posing culture against capital and betraying the Brahmin's fear of a newly industrialized people.

We have every reason to believe that Du Bois's fears for Atlanta's chastity were genuine; he was, in fact, to spend the better part of his life warning away such "wily Hippomedes.'" But, for all the intensity of that fear, Du Bois could still see and appreciate Atlanta's temptations. Indeed, not to see the corresponding story, not to see the reason why, was to make the city doubly vulnerable. Atlanta's race for gold, Du Bois acknowledges, began when "a fearful wilderness lay about the feet of that city after the War,—feudalism, poverty, the rise of the Third Estate, serfdom, the re-birth of Law and Order, and above and between all, the Veil of Race . . . what wings must Atalanta have to flit over this hollow and hill, through sour wood and sullen water, and by the red waste of sun-baked clay!"

The lines recall, by contrast, the opening images of verdant mornings and crimson soil and offer again a kind of sustained double-take on the fortunes of this city. Atlanta's pasts, however, appear now not so much in direct contest as folded into one another—so closely, indeed, that Du Bois cannot separate the two as warring opposites, nor can he wholly extricate himself from their terms. "Golden apples are beautiful," he admits, "I remember the lawless days of boyhood, when orchards in crimson and gold tempted me over fence and field—and too," Du Bois continues, "the merchant who has dethroned the planter is no despicable parvenu. Work and wealth are the mighty levers to lift this old new land; thrift and toil and saving are the highways to new hopes and new possibilities."

Thus, Atlanta stood, poised between and represented by two gospels. The question was not ultimately how to displace one with the other, since that was an impossibility in any case. The real issue, I would stress, was how we are to go about, to use Du Bois's words, "interpreting the world." As general as it sounds, that problem was to take on considerable specificity in "the Black World beyond the Veil." Hence, the story of Atlanta is again refracted, its double histories bent now and for the first time through the lens of race. So far into the text Atlanta has been read as a synechdoche for the modern city in a brave white world, and, for all of Du Bois's work to complicate that image, it has yet to be seen in its full aspect. From his newly assumed vantage point Du Bois sees that the terms are familiar, that "the ferment of his striving toward self-realization is to the strife of the white world like a wheel within a wheel: beyond the Veil are smaller but like problems of ideals, of leaders and the led, of serfdom, of poverty, of order and subordination, and, through all, the Veil of Race."

This story is, as Du Bois puts it, "curiously parallel to that of the Other-world." The difference, of course, is that this world beyond the veil goes largely unseen by whites. Its converse, however, is not true, and this I take to be a crucial feature of Du Bois's case. To see behind the veil, to "feel the two-ness of being at once an American and a Negro," was to see in advance the unfolding narratives of identity through which one's culture was constituted. One had only to train this "second-sight" on "America," in other words, to see what temptations lay before the "Negro." Du Bois speaks with such confidence, we might then say, because he has seen it all before, and he can see it coming again. "In the Black World," he warns,

the Preacher and Teacher embodied once the ideals of this people,— the strife for another and a juster world, the vague dream of righteousness, the mystery of knowing; but today the danger is that these ideals, with their simple beauty and weird inspiration, will suddenly sink to a question of cash and a lust for gold.

If the legacy of such second sight was to be anything other than tragic, it would seem to rest in this capacity to anticipate and act upon a world not of one's making. Such a capacity, the display of which represents the rhetorical action of this text, is most fully realized when engaging both worlds at once, making sense of their comportment as much as their differences. The end was not so much racial harmony as an enhanced ability to interpret the bitter tales of history. It is because Du Bois has read those stories, in their complicity and their complexity, that he is led to ask the questions that he does:

What if the Negro people be wooed from a strife for righteousness, from a love of knowing, to regard dollars as the be-all and end-all of life? What if to the Mammonism of America be added the Mammonism of the re-born South, and the Mammonism of this South be reinforced by the budding Mammonism of its half-awakened black millions?

Narrative III: Utopian Atlanta

Du Bois, as we might expect, has an answer to these questions. It takes the form of a final account, a utopian vision of the city that does not so much contrast with as extend upon the narratives so far rendered. To the question asked—which way?—Du Bois answers: education. Like the Atalanta myth itself, it is a deceptively simple recourse, unsatisfying perhaps, until we again notice how Du Bois subjects it to alternative readings. And if by this point we begin to experience a certain dejà vu, a feeling of having read these accounts before, then that is perhaps evidence of the author's art. The didactic purposes of this text will have been met, on its own terms, when the reader learns to see as its author sees, in twos and relentlessly.

The Atlanta of Du Bois's dream is close at hand--indeed, just outside the window. As the following depiction suggests, he is at once in and above it, part of its sweep yet able to hold it in reflection. The beauty of his surroundings, Du Bois explains,

lies in its simple unity:—a broad lawn of green rising from the red street with mingled roses and peaches; north and south, two plain and stately halls; and in the midst, half hidden in ivy, a larger building, boldly graceful, sparingly decorated, and with one low spire. It is a restful group,—one never looks for more; it is all here, all intelligible.

This is, of course, reminiscent of earlier descriptions of the city, typical, I claimed, of the panegyric found in *Harper's* and *Atlantic Monthly*. And, in fact, Du Bois does not stop here: the portrayal of Atlanta and its people, especially its youngsters, is conspicuously benign. The children pass by, "all dark and heavy haired," to "follow the love song of Dido"; they "listen to the tale of Troy divine"; they "wander among the stars, there to wander among men and nations." "Nothing new," writes Du Bois,

no time-saving devices,—simply old time-glorified methods for delving the Truth, and searching out the hidden beauties of life, and learning the good of living. The riddle of existence is the college curriculum that was laid before the Pharaohs, that was taught in the groves by Plato, that formed the trivium and quadrivium, and is today laid before the freedmen's sons by Atlanta University.

A generation made intelligible by yielding to something greater than itself; this, at least in principle, was the basis for a new story with which to write the future of Atlanta. Du Bois called it the Gospel of Sacrifice, a commitment generated out of the past and from reflection on it. Within the text it represents the final and consummatory narrative; taking the others up and into itself, the Gospel of Sacrifice was literally to create a new city of the future. In this city Du Bois writes, "amid a wide desert of caste and proscription, amid the heart-hurtling slights and jars and vagaries of a deep race-dislike, lies this green oasis, where hot anger cools, and the bitterness of disappointment is sweetened by the springs and breezes of Parnassus." These children, listening now to their Virgil and reckoning the nominative case, Du Bois reasoned, were best suited to build this city, for they were learning "not to earn meat, but to know the end and aim of that life which meat nourishes."

Here, of course, was provocation enough for leaders across the cultural and educational spectrum. The very image, as Du Bois well knew, of a sharecropper's child being trained in the mysteries of heroic pentameter was an incitement. But to those, like Washington and his followers, who would scorn such a prospect, Du Bois appeals again and for a final time to the lessons of the white world. There he could read a history of education debased by its inability to abide the Gospel of Sacrifice. The universities of the Old South, he reminds his readers,

> dwindled and withered under the foul breath of slavery; and ever since the war they have fought a failing fight for life in the tainted air of social unrest and commercial selfishness, stunted by the death of criticism, and starving for lack of broadly cultured men. And if this is true of the white south's need and danger, how much heavier the danger and need of the freedmen's sons! how pressing here the need of broad ideals and true culture, the conservation of soul from sordid aims and petty passions!

Du Bois's essay thus concludes by offering a kind of pedagogy of the spirit, the development of which was to create a more organic, more unified and coherent culture. In a fairly obvious sense the text presents itself as an exemplar of that possibility, as indeed the author was so inclined to present himself. The utopian city was to be brought about by people very much like Du Bois, "of broad culture, catholic tolerance, and trained ability, joining their hands to other hands, and giving to this squabble of the Races a decent and dignified peace."

Conclusion

Du Bois's was not a vision without its critics. Marcus Garvey scorned Du Bois for belonging "to the school of artistic imitation": "He likes to copy the white man in every detail. He is never original."[26] That vision could, moreover, be willfully unmindful of pressing realities; it had no patience for Booker Washington, whom Du Bois bullies here as elsewhere. His was a utopia predicated on alleged distinctions in aptitude and class—a "rule of inequality"—which demarcated scholars from blacksmiths, those who know from those who dig. Looking back on its general argument, Du Bois himself admitted that the "social and economic philosophy was then as I now see it immature, and my outlook on race presocial."[27]

There is, then, much to blame and praise in the essay and in *Souls of Black Folk* as a whole; I have sought in this essay to do neither, wishing instead to ask what the modern city might look like from the perspective it promotes. I cannot pretend to have represented that perspective fully; I do not know what double-consciousness describes as a state of mind; nor are most of the texts in *Souls of Black Folk* in any obvious sense about the city. But, if there is an excuse for reassembling these statements as I have, it lies in the fact that Du Bois was deeply engaged by urban culture; that its problems and prospects disciplined his art generally; and that he understood his art to be an instrument of social transformation. Like many others, Du Bois realized that the modern city was nothing if not a spectacle. His distinction was to have insisted that we never look at it the same way again.

Notes

1. Excellent background sources on the rise of the city in the nineteenth century include Thomas Bender, *Toward an Urban Vision: Ideas and Institutions in Nineteenth-Century America* (Lexington: University Press of Kentucky, 1975); Paul Boyer, *Urban Masses and Moral Order in America, 1820–1920* (Cambridge: Harvard University Press, 1978); and David Ward and Oliver Zunz, eds., *The Landscape of Modernity: Essays on New York City, 1900–1940* (New York: Russell Sage, 1992).

2. Dana White, *The Urbanists, 1865–1915* (Westport: Greenwood, 1989), 206.

3. W. E. Burghardt Du Bois, "Of the Wings of Atalanta," *The Souls of Black Folk* (Chicago: A. C. McClurg, 1903): 75–87. All citations are to this edition.

4. White, *Urbanists*, 195.

5. Julian Ralph, "Our Nation's Capital," *Harper's New Monthly Magazine* 90 (April 1895): 657.

6. Ibid., 673.

7. Stephen Bonsal, "The New Baltimore," *Harper's New Monthly Magazine* 92 (February 1896): 334.

8. *Atlantic Monthly* 75 (April 1895): 553.

9. Henry B. Fuller, "The Upward Movement in Chicago," *Atlantic Monthly* 8 (October 1897): 547.

10. Josiah Strong, "The Problem of the Twentieth Century City," *North American Review* 165 (September 1897): 348–49.

11. Leo Marx, "The Puzzle of Antiurbanism in Classic American Literature," in *Cities of the Mind: Images and Themes of the City in the Social Sciences,* ed. Lloyd Rodwin and Robert Hollister (New York: Plenum Press, 1989), 179.

12. Frederick Douglass, *Narrative of the Life of Frederick Douglass,* ed. Michael Meyer (New York: Modern Library, 1987), 54.

13. Mary Church-Terrell, "What It Means to be Colored in the Capital of the United States," in *Man Cannot Speak for Her: Key Texts of the Early Feminists,* ed. Karlyn Kohrs Campbell (Westport: Praeger, 1989), 432.

14. James Baldwin, "The Harlem Ghetto," *Notes of a Native Son* (Boston: Beacon Press, 1984), 59.

15. W. E. B. Du Bois, *The Philadelphia Negro* (1899; rpt., New York: Schocken Books, 1967); White, Urbanists, 195.

16. Ibid., 3.

17. Du Bois, Papers of W. E. B. Du Bois, reel 85, frame 1470.

18. Arnold Rampersad, *The Art and Imagination of W. E. B. Du Bois* (Cambridge: Harvard University Press, 1976), 89.

19. Pauline Schneider to Du Bois, 23 May 1914. In Papers, reel 4, frame 932.

20. Langston Hughes to Du Bois, 22 May 1956. In ibid., reel 71, frame 1229.

21. Du Bois, "Of Our Spiritual Strivings," *Souls,* 3.

22. Recent work on Du Bois and double-consciousness includes Dickson D. Bruce Jr., "W. E. B. Du Bois and the Idea of Double Consciousness," *American Literature* 64 (1992): 299–309; Thomas C. Holt, "The Political Uses of Alienation: W. E. B. Du Bois on Politics, Race, and Culture, 1903–1940," *American Quarterly* 42 (1990): 301–23; and Lucius Outlaw, "Language and Consciousness: Toward a Hermeneutics of Black Culture," *Cultural Hermeneutics* 1 (1974): 403–13.

23. Bruce, "Idea," 307.

24. Du Bois, "Spiritual Strivings," 4.

25. Holt, "Political Uses of Alienation," 305.

26. Marcus Garvey, in *The Marcus Garvey and Universal Improvement Association Papers,* ed. Robert Hill, vol. 7 (Berkeley and Los Angeles: University of California Press, 1990), 627.

27. Du Bois, Papers, reel 85, frame 1470.

CHAPTER SIX

"The Voice of Exile"
W. E. B. Du Bois and the Quest for Culture

James Darsey

"Displaced persons," he said. "Well now. I declare. What do
that mean?"

"It means they ain't where they were born at and there's
nowhere for them to go—like if you was run out of here and
wouldn't nobody have you."
Flannery O'Connor, *The Displaced Person*

In January 1993 Pico Iyer gave a talk at Yale entitled "Living in the
Transit Lounge." In it he described the life of the "intercontinental wanderer," the "Transit Lounger," "forever heading to the departure gate,
forever orbiting the world":[1] "We pass through countries as through re-
volving doors, resident aliens of the world, permanent residents of
nowhere. Nothing is strange to us, and nowhere is foreign. We are visi-
tors even in our homes."[2]

The modern airport is the vehicle for a groundlessness, a rootless-
ness, which in turn produces the humility, and the arrogance, born of an
epistemological relativism. As Iyer describes it: "For us in the transit
lounge, affiliation is as alien as disorientation. We become professional
observers, able to see the merits and deficiencies of anywhere, to balance our parents' viewpoints with their enemies' positions."[3] Iyer
transcends community, "a seasoned expert at the aerial perspective,"
both literally and metaphorically. In his "floating skepticism" he is beyond the reach of any parochial commitment.[4]

I am reminded of Socrates, to whom Plutarch attributes the statement "I am not an Athenian nor a Greek, but a citizen of the world,"
whose contemporary Aristophanes portrayed him partially in the clouds,
babbling philosophical nonsense, and whose fellow citizens condemned

him to death for his failure to pay homage to the local deities and for inculcating in the minds of young Athenians a restless and subversive curiosity. Like Iyer, Socrates is acutely aware of the difference between local custom and true knowledge; his view is broader than his provincial circumstance.

Though Socrates is geographically rooted in Athens, he, like Iyer, is a visitor in his own community. Socrates' account of his lack of political service stands in striking correspondence to Iyer's confession that he has never voted. Both exemplify what Novalis means when he writes: "Philosophy is really homesickness, it is the urge to be at home everywhere." Lofty and noble such a pursuit may be, but the denial of citizenship in the here and now exacts a terrible price. John Berger notes that, "in traditional societies, everything that made sense of the world was real; the surrounding chaos existed and was threatening, but it was threatening because it was *unreal*. Without a home at the center of the real, one was not only shelterless, but also lost in non-being, in unreality. Without a home, everything was fragmentation."[5]

W. E. B. Du Bois faced just such a threat at the turn of the last century. The most obvious of refractive elements in Du Bois's world, that element that splits a single vision into multiple perspectives, the element that Professor Browne has selected as the basis for reading Du Bois as oppositional discourse, is race, "the color line." I wish to suggest, however, that Du Bois's sense of diremption is, in fact, much more complex than that and that his multiple identities are often in conflict with themselves, too unstable to create a simple antithesis to the dominant discourse. Unlike Socrates and Iyer, Du Bois, the author of *The Souls of Black Folk*, is not able ultimately to make a choice among communities—he cannot consign himself to the world as it is, but he cannot divorce himself from his sense of political obligation—and "Of the Wings of Atalanta" is the preeminent example of his vacillation.

The Souls of Black Folk and Cosmopolitan Angst

At the turn of the century no American was, properly speaking, at home. The profound economic and social dislocations that characterized fin de siècle America prevented this. According to Robert Wiebe: "As the network of relations affecting men's lives each year became more tangled and more distended, Americans in a basic sense no longer knew who or where they were. The setting had altered beyond their power to understand it, and within an alien context they had lost themselves. In a democratic society who was master and who servant? In a land of opportunity what was success? The apparent leaders were as much adrift as their followers."[6] The emerging industrial cities stood as a metonym for an inchoate culture, the transition from rural agrarianism to urban factory production. Not one in Du Bois's day was from the city; all had emigrated there from elsewhere, in so doing, sundering the ties of community and, in John Berger's words, "undoing the very meaning of the world and—at its most extreme—abandoning oneself to the unreal that is absurd."[7]

For African Americans caught up in the Great Migration, the consequences of leaving home were compounded by race. It is in the "Forethought" to The Souls of Black Folk that Du Bois introduces the idea of "two worlds," white and black, and "the Veil" that separates them, and in the first essay he describes the event by which he first personally experienced that division. A newcomer to his school "peremptorily" refuses his visiting card: "Then it dawned upon me with a certain suddenness that I was different from the other, or like, mayhap, in heart and life and longing, but shut out from their world by a vast veil."[8]

Nor are the worlds merely different; they are unequal, and blacks in America are forced to lived in the more circumscribed of the two. A tiny community in Tennessee where Du Bois, early on, taught school, serves as a synecdoche for the black world: "I have called my tiny community a world, and so its isolation made it; and yet there was among us but a half-awakened common consciousness, sprung from common joy and grief, at burial, birth, or wedding; from a common hardship in poverty, poor land, and low wages; and, above all, from the sight of the Veil that hung between us and Opportunity."[9] Du Bois most hauntingly relates his awareness of the place of blacks in these two worlds in his account of the death of his first son.[10] The sense of estrangement is excruciating, and it is compounded pages later when Du Bois confesses to an "awful gladness" at his son's death, the infant's escape to freedom. "Fool that I was to think or wish that this little soul should grow choked and deformed within the Veil."[11]

Though Du Bois laments on this occasion that he will not live to see that "mighty morning" that will "lift the Veil and set the prisoned free"—"I shall die in my bonds"[12]—he, for the larger part of Souls, exhibits a curious mobility between and beyond the two worlds. Almost from his awareness of it, Du Bois claims "no desire to tear down that veil, to creep through; I held all beyond it in common contempt, and lived above it in a region of blue sky and great wandering shadows."[13] Like Iyer and

Socrates, Du Bois is an aerialist; he sees more broadly than residents of either world, having access to both.

Indeed, in terms of authorial viewpoint *Souls* is almost perfectly divided between the two worlds. Du Bois signals this when, following an overview of the first seven of the book's fourteen essays, he writes: "Leaving, then, the white world, I have stepped within the Veil, raising it that you may view faintly its deeper recesses."[14] The near perfect division of the book, the dynamic equilibrium Du Bois achieves, helps to provide the impression of a balanced perspective, but it is the perspective of no one, not that of either world. It is the perspective of the cosmopolitan, the homeless, one whose identity is not fixed or certain. In order to escape the bonds of the black world, Du Bois denies full membership in the black community.

This indeterminacy is reflected throughout *Souls*. Though in the "Forethought" Du Bois informs the reader that he is "bone of the bone and flesh of the flesh of them that live within the Veil," even this announcement betrays a tension in the juxtaposition of ancestral bonds and the third-person narrative voice. The tension is maintained in the first essay, which is titled "Of Our Spiritual Strivings," and which contains a direct appeal to blacks uncharacteristic of the rest of the essays. By the use of the first-person plural Du Bois affirms his identification with the black race.[15] Yet early in the essay, when describing the history of "the American Negro" as a history of strife, Du Bois speaks from somewhere else and employs the second-person voice in asserting the integrity of black identity: "He would not Africanize America, for America has too much to teach the world and Africa. He would not bleach his Negro soul in a flood of white Americanism, for he knows that Negro blood has a message for the world. He simply wishes to make it possible for a man to be both a Negro and an American, without being cursed and spit upon by his fellows, without having the doors of Opportunity closed roughly in his face."[16] The same detached voice appears in "Of Mr. Booker T. Washington and Others," in which Du Bois writes of "the Negro's tendency to self-assertion,"[17] of slavery and race prejudice as "potent if not sufficient causes of the Negro's position,"[18] and the duty of "black men" toward the work of "their greatest leader."[19]

The obvious source of Du Bois's vacillation is the "double-consciousness" experienced by blacks in America. Professor Browne provides Du Bois's most succinct statement of the notion, quoting one of the most critical and most quoted passages from *The Souls of Black Folk,* wherein Du Bois describes the American Negro as "a sort of

seventh son" struggling to keep from being "torn asunder" by the conflicts of the culture.[20] Here is the glamour of the cosmopolitan
consciousness stripped away and all of its pain and alienation revealed.
"Why," Du Bois laments, "did God make me an outcast and a stranger
in mine own house?"[21]

Double-consciousness, though it implies a complexity of vision, the
necessity for members of subordinate subcultures always to know the
rules of the dominant culture as well as of their subculture, seems an
inadequate account of the profound sense of Du Bois's disaffection.
Double-consciousness does not entail homelessness, lack of community;
it entails a community required to see itself, at least part of the time, as
an outsider would see it.

If Du Bois were firmly at home in black America, his estrangement would not seem so overwhelming. Du Bois, however, at the
time of the publication of *Souls,* signals his marginalization with respect to African-American culture by his opposition to the greatest
and most visible black leader of the day, Booker T. Washington. As
Professor Browne points out, *The Souls of Black Folk* is known today
primarily for a single essay, "Of Mr. Booker T. Washington and Others," and Donald Gibson makes this essay the focal point of his
introduction to the Penguin Classics edition of the book.[22] In mounting
his criticism of Washington, Du Bois highlights the fissiparousness of
such an act and reveals an understanding of the consequences of division for himself. He acknowledges Washington's almost synecdochal
relationship to the black race and the stifling by public opinion of other
attempts at criticism,[23] and he castigates other black leaders for their
failure to speak up.[24]

His opposition to Washington along with his occasional identification with the white majority combine to make Du Bois's home in the
black community insecure. It is not that Du Bois ever sought to deny
his morphological characteristics,[25] but his notion of race was more
complex than that, holding sociohistorical elements, based on "common history, traditions, and impulses," in a tension with biological,
or "scientific," criteria.[26] From this perspective the evidence suggests
that Du Bois's experience of his blackness, at least at the time that he
wrote *Souls,* was so atypical that it provided scant ground for the
creation of a solid social identity with most other black Americans of
his day. As Paul Gilroy has put it, "The problems of racialised ontology
and identity—the tension between being and becoming black—are therefore deeply inscribed in Du Bois's own life."[27] By his own report it was

not until his college days at Fisk that Du Bois "replaced" his identity as an American and became "a Negro."[28] In two autobiographies written at different times in his life and reflecting "substantial changes in his thinking,"[29] and in a number of autobiographical writings, Du Bois continued to struggle with the phenomenon of race. Anthony Appiah notes, "Throughout his life, Du Bois was concerned not just with the meaning of race but with the truth about it."[30]

Central to Du Bois's disagreement with Washington was the issue of education—specifically, what sort of education was appropriate for the black man at the turn of the century. As the holder of a doctoral degree, Du Bois was exceptional in his culture; as a black man with a doctorate, remarkably so. It is noteworthy that Du Bois uses the same terminology to refer to the refractory quality of race, *double-consciousness,* which Emerson had earlier used to describe the estrangement of the intellectual.

Du Bois, who argues in passionate opposition to Booker T. Washington's narrow vocational model and for broad liberal arts educational opportunities for blacks,[31] nevertheless reveals most brutally the shattering effect it can have, especially for a black man, in the only fictional work in *Souls,* the short story "Of the Coming of John," a Dickensian fable. Commencement from college is, for John, a kind of second birth, an expulsion from the womb: "He had left his queer thought-world and come back to a world of motion and of men. He looked now for the first time sharply about him, and wondered he had seen so little before."[32] John's emigration has been both metaphorical and literal, but he discovers the alienation that befalls all emigrants: "somehow he found it so hard and strange to fit his old surroundings again, to find his place in the world about him."[33] As Berger notes: "Every migrant knows in his heart of hearts that it is impossible to return. Even if he is physically able to return, he does not truly return, because he himself has been so deeply changed by his emigration."[34] John returns home only to realize, as he appears at the front door of the judge's house, that he has forgotten his place.[35] So profound is John's change that he is lost even to himself. As he sits waiting for the lynch mob to find him, he reflects: "The night deepened; he thought of the boys at Johnstown. He wondered how Brown had turned out, and Carey? and Jones,—Jones? Why, *he* was Jones, and he wondered what they would all say when they knew."[36]

The effect of education is to rend the pleasant and anodyne integration of appearance and reality and to awaken the soul to the possible. It is an emigration from the small, provincial world of the known: "Happy?" Du Bois asks Sears of Dougherty County. "—Well, yes, he laughed and flipped pebbles, and thought the world was as it was."[37] Compare Sears's carefree state to that of John on returning home from college. When John's sister asks him, "Does it make every one—unhappy when they study and learn lots of things?" he responds, "I am afraid it does."[38] Du Bois's profound comprehension of the near-fatal attraction of education reflects his own experience as he universalizes John's: "education among all kinds of men always has had, and always will have, an element of danger and revolution, of dissatisfaction and discontent. Nevertheless, men strive to know."[39]

A culture in chaos, race, education, all may be sources of alienation, but implied in all of them is a change of venue, a geographical displacement: the farmer to the city, the European to America, the African to America, the young man or woman away to school. Du Bois, the author of *The Souls of Black Folk,* is an immigrant as a New Englander living in the South. Black culture, in Du Bois's day even more than in our own, is rooted in the South, where Du Bois locates the Negro's "birthright."[40] Du Bois, though, is a product of Great Barrington, Massachusetts, where, according to Donald Gibson, he was "from the age of six to sixteen," notwithstanding some notable exceptions, "very much a part of the life of the Great Barrington mainstream."[41] Coming to know the South, then, was for Du Bois a paradox, a coming home by leaving home.[42] His description of his acquaintance with the "sorrow songs" is exemplary: "They came out of the South unknown to me, one by one, and yet at once I knew them as of me and of mine."[43] He describes the "Negro church of to-day," with its sources in Southern black culture, as "the social centre of Negro life in the United States, and the most characteristic expression of African character."[44] Its centrality notwithstanding, Du Bois notes that he had "never seen a Southern Negro revival" until, as an adult, he found himself teaching school in the South.[45]

The South may be closer to Africa, but it is New England that is closer to Plato's world of forms. As long as Du Bois spent in the South, it is always the criteria of New England by which he judged it. "Dark Carter's neat barns would do credit to New England," he writes of a farm in Dougherty County.[46] Du Bois's time in the South might be fairly compared to the British raj in terms of its cultural assumptions and direction of influence. The campus of Atlanta University was, in Du Bois's vision, along with the campuses of "Fisk, and Howard, Wilberforce and Claflin, Shaw, and the rest," really an outpost of New England, her "gift . . . to the freed Negro."[47] The "boulder of New England granite" that Du Bois glimpses from his office window, marking the grave site of one of Atlanta University's founding faculty, is likely "New England" only metonymically, but it illustrates vividly Du Bois living simultaneously in two worlds.

Finally, Du Bois is displaced temporally; he is "out of step with his time." Gilroy writes of how *Souls* "unravels the assumptions of progress and develops a critique of the place it has in the strategy for racial amelioration."[48] In an era almost uncritically wedded to Darwinian notions of inexorable improvement, Du Bois's declaration that "progress . . . is necessarily ugly" was heresy.[49] Du Bois talks of the past, even of the Old South and of certain aspects of slavery, eulogistically,[50] and he celebrates, as Professor Browne notes, an educational method based not on innovation but, rather, on the tried-and-true curriculum of the classical liberal arts characterized by a study of classical literature.[51]

Du Bois is nominally associated with many communities, but he is squarely a member of none, not on this earth. There is always a sense of ironic detachment, a pervasive self-consciousness that is absent when one is thoroughly part of the group, as when, for example, Du Bois explains how the various families with whom he spent Friday nights while teaching in Tennessee allowed him some privacy at bedtime[52] or his sly comment at the end of a meditation on progress that he "rode to Nashville in the Jim Crow car."[53] It is the irony that Wayne Booth speaks of as "an elitist protection from reality or commitment."[54] Du Bois, the author of *The Souls of Black Folk* was not at home in the world. His later autobiographical writings, his ultimate renunciation of his U.S. citizenship, and his death at the age of ninety-five in Ghana allow us to see *Souls* as the overture to a journey, Du Bois's search for a community in which he could be himself and be at peace.

"Above the Veil": Du Bois and Universal Culture

Donald Gibson finds Du Bois's claim to a life above the veil unclear but concludes that it "doubtless implies escape from the confines of the veil through the capacity to compete successfully with whites, with those who live outside it."[55] Gibson's explanation is earthbound and ignores the true extent of the hierarchy implied in Du Bois's use of the preposition *above*. There are three places in *Souls* in which Du Bois uses the locution "above the Veil." In each case the suggestion is not of a choice between two human worlds but of something empyrean, something sacred and eternal. One of these cases has already been quoted—Du Bois's reaction to discovering the veil: "I held all beyond it in common contempt, and lived above it in a region of blue sky and great wandering shadows."[56] The association is with heaven, a reading supported by the final sentences of the essay "Of the Passing of the First-Born": "Perhaps now he knows the All-love, and needs not to be wise. Sleep, then, child,—sleep till I sleep and waken to a baby voice and the ceaseless patter of little feet—above the Veil."[57] "Above the Veil" is the home of God, the "All-love"; it represents perfection, unending and universal; it represents what is true as opposed to the meager appearance of the everyday world. These themes come together in the most significant passage describing Du Bois's situation: "I sit with Shakespeare and he winces not. Across the color line I move arm in arm with Balzac and Dumas, where smiling men and welcoming women glide in gilded halls. From out the caves of evening that swing between the strong-limbed earth and the tracery of the stars, I summon Aristotle and Aurelius and what souls I will, and they come all graciously with no scorn nor condescension. So, wed with Truth I dwell above the Veil."[58]

Du Bois's vision has a distinctly Arnoldian penumbra. Matthew Arnold's term for this sacred place, this platonic world of forms, was *culture*, "being a pursuit of our total perfection by means of getting to know, on all the matters which most concern us, the best which has been thought and said in the world."[59] Among the salient aspects of Arnold's idea of culture were a striving toward perfection, a free play of ideas, and an attempt to separate appearance from reality, to "see things as they really are."[60] Arnold feared the lapse of the England of his day into a spiritual miasma obsessed with what he called "machinery," the external. To rectify this obsession with illusion and ephemera, he championed an education based on the classics, "the best that has been thought and said." It is, again, a cosmopolitan voice, one that contains a significant measure of detachment, or what Arnold calls "disinterest."[61] All worldly knowledge has a limited and contingent quality subject to the vagaries of time and locality. "But whether at this or that time, and to this or that set of persons," Arnold writes, "one ought to insist most on the praises of fire and strength, or on the praises of sweetness and light, must depend, one would think, on the circumstances and needs of that particular time and those particular persons."[62] "There is," he assures us a page later, "no *unum necessarium*, or one thing needful, which can free human nature from the obligation of trying to come to its best at all these points."[63] Arnold pulls all of these themes together in the final paragraphs of *Culture and Anarchy*, especially in his brief paean to Socrates: "Socrates has drunk his hemlock and is dead; but in his own breast does not every man carry about with him a possible Socrates, in that power of a disinterested play of consciousness upon his stock notions and habits, of which this wise and admirable man gave all through his lifetime the great example, and which was the secret of his incomparable influence?"[64]

The parallels between Arnold's situation and Du Bois's are almost too easy. Each felt a time of moral desuetude, the siren song of industrial wealth, and a neglect of true values. For everytime Arnold decries a "reliance on machinery," Du Bois is there to condemn "the spirit of the age . . . triumphant commercialism . . . the ideals of material prosperity,"[65] the "gospel of Work and Money . . . overshadow[ing] the higher aims of life,"[66] "the money makers,"[67] "the deification of Bread,"[68] "systematic modern land-grabbing and money-getting,"[69] in short, all that is low, local, transient, and illusory. Arnold more explicitly than Du Bois, though no more insistently, provides a "true North" for our moral compass, the summum bonum, the sempiternal good, true, and beautiful, and the path to this perfection is culture. Du Bois, in his turn, charges "all honorable men of the twentieth century" with the strife of ensuring "that in the future competition of races the survival of the fittest shall mean the triumph of the good, the beautiful, and the true; that we may be able to preserve for future civilization all that is really fine and noble and strong, and not continue to put a premium on greed and impudence."[70] For both men the only true guide is education—as Du Bois puts it, "an education that encourages aspiration, that sets the loftiest of ideals and seeks as an end culture and character rather than bread-winning."[71]

Here, then, at last we have found Du Bois's home, above the Veil, "wed with Truth"; a home beyond time, where it is possible to "sit with Shakespeare," "walk arm in arm with Dumas and Balzac," and "summon Aristotle and Aurelius"—a home beyond the color line, indeed beyond any provinciality. Culture is universal, evident in Du Bois's acceptance as an *idée reçu* of a single standard by which various peoples of the world may be placed on the hierarchy of civilization. This insight, though, does not relieve the anxiety ever present in *Souls*. The universal lacks the exclusionary element necessary to definition. Arnold describes culture as a "striving," signaling with the progressive form the lack of resolution; it is a dialectic ending only in perfection. In similar terms Du Bois describes the "longing" of the "American Negro," "to attain self-conscious manhood, to merge his double self into a better and truer self": "This, then, is the end of his striving: to be a co-worker in the kingdom of culture, to escape both death and isolation, to husband and use his best powers and his latent genius."[72] Du Bois recognizes, as does Arnold, that the end of the journey is not to be found in this life, thus his repeated equation of true freedom with death.[73] The only element that stands outside culture in Du Bois's universe is the world as it is. The real battle is not the color line but, rather, the contest over the soul of humankind.

"Of the Wings of Atalanta"

"Of the Wings of Atalanta" is unusual in the context of *The Souls of Black Folk*. It stands out among the essays, along with "Of Mr. Booker T. Washington and Others," for its direct polemicism, for its concern with the particulars of policy, for its deliberative quality. "Of the Wings of Atalanta" is a morality tale in both its original version and in Du Bois's retelling. Du Bois, resident alien, habitué of the world of ideas, denizen of the cosmos, fin de siècle airport lounger, speaks to Atlanta and, through her, to the South. His descent is signaled in the title and controlling metaphor of the essay: even as Du Bois mounts his minatory fable to the American South of 1903, he employs an ancient myth as the vehicle of the eternal truth he represents. He cannot wholeheartedly commit himself to the specifics of time and place.

Though unusual in its form, "Of the Wings of Atalanta" is marvelously representative of the central themes and tensions in *Souls*, particularly that tension that marks Du Bois's own life at this period, that between the ideal and mundane appearances and the need of education, a university education, as the means of resolution: "Atlanta must not lead the South to dream of material prosperity as the touchstone of all success"; Du Bois admonishes, "already the fatal might of this idea is beginning to spread; it is replacing the finer type of Southerner with vulgar money-getters; it is burying the sweeter beauties of Southern life beneath pretence and ostentation."[74] Du Bois finds in the culture of the Old South something genuine, something "vanquished that deserved to live, something killed that in justice had not dared to die."[75] The Old South, for all of its sins, knew, however imperfectly, of virtue, all lost, all forgotten, in the New South, which threatens to succumb to the degraded ethic of the time, the "Mammonism" to which the rest of the country has already succumbed.[76]

Because Atlanta is merely a synecdoche, DuBois is comparatively uninterested in the specifics of her condition. He signals this when he writes of "the world which Atlanta typifies" and uses "the South" as an appositive for the city.[77] It is almost cliché in 1903, created in large part by two speeches that hover like spirits, one named and one unnamed, over *Souls*, Booker T. Washington's "Atlanta Exposition Address" and Henry W. Grady's "The New South." Atlanta's hundred hills crowned with factories[78] represent no peculiarity of the urban condition but, rather, the "gaunt red buildings, bare and homely, and yet so busy and noisy withal that they scarce seem to belong to the slow and sleepy land."[79] Of the twenty paragraphs in the essay the first eleven are devoted to a chronicling of the status of Atlanta, the South, and portents based on her current course.

It is in these paragraphs that the myth of Atalanta is related. In a self-conscious stretch of nominal resemblance—"If Atlanta be not named for Atalanta, she ought to have been"[80]—Du Bois makes the winged maiden a symbol of the city, subsuming the legend to Du Bois's narrative of the "Queen of the cotton kingdom,"[81] an allegorical casting of the future. In the fable Atalanta spurns all suitors by challenging them to a race and is finally won by Hippomenes and his three golden apples, a gift from Venus. Unfortunately, the new lovers fail to pay proper homage to the goddess of love, and she, in retribution, provokes Cybele to turn them both into lions, beasts that, in ancient culture, were believed unable to mate.

Du Bois is curiously literal in his reading of this tale; he focuses on the golden quality of the apples as though it were their essence rather than an appurtenance commonly associated in fable with enchanted objects, including the Rhinegold to which he alludes in another essay.[82] There is nothing in the Atalanta myth to suggest that the gold is negotiable or desired for that purpose. Indeed, Venus must prod a hesitant Atalanta to stoop for the third apple. The power of the apples, like the power of the Rhinegold, lies not in their pecuniary measure but in their magic.

It is impossible to misread Du Bois misreading Atalanta on this point. He is repeatedly explicit that it was "greed of gold" that led to her downfall,[83] an interpretation reinforced in "The Litany of Atlanta," published after the 1906 Atlanta race riots:

From lust of body and lust of blood, *Great God, deliver us!*

From lust of power and lust of gold, *Great God, deliver us!*

From the leagued lying of despot and of brute, *Great God, deliver us!*

And all this was to sate the greed of greedy men who hide behind the veil of injustice![84]

The consequent moral for Atlanta, thus the South, is clear: she must not forget "the old ideal of the Southern gentleman,—that new-world heir of the grace and courtliness of patrician, knight, and noble";[85] she must stem "the sudden transformation of a fair far-off ideal of Freedom into the hard reality of bread-winning and the consequent deification of bread."[86]

At the twelfth paragraph Du Bois turns away from the city to the source of its possible redemption. "The hundred hills of Atlanta are not all crowned with factories," he writes, underscoring the stasis almost perfectly centered in the essay. Then, in sentences quoted by Professor Browne and taken to be "the Atlanta of DuBois's dreams," Du Bois describes the campus of Atlanta University in its "beauty" and "simple unity." The separation from the city is emphasized in the final sentence of the paragraph: "There I live, and there I hear from day to day the low hum of restful life."[87]

Atlanta University is the antithesis of the city, of the values of commerce, of greed and transitory gain, of relentless noise, excitement, and agitation; it stands "in bold relief," "a restful group," "half hidden" in its almost bucolic landscape above the street. Furthermore, it is sufficient unto itself: "one never looks for more." As Atlanta stands as synecdoche for the New South, Atlanta University stands for all universities but for black universities in particular. The description is archetypal and reflects the etymological tradition of "campus," originally an arena of battle but later a place removed from everyday life.

The theme of retreat, of cloistering, is developed by Du Bois in the rest of this paragraph. In a passage quoted by Professor Browne, Du Bois describes the morning convocation of students on the campus and the life they pursue there.[88] The description conveys a sense of peregrination as the students withdraw "from the busy city below," a sense that stands in sharp contrast to the decidedly purposeful "parade step" Browne finds associated with the city. The scene painted by Du Bois is idyllic and without care: students "wander"; the "here" and "there" suggest something irresponsibly desultory. There is no need of hurry on the campus; the values pursued in that setting are timeless; they will be there when we arrive.

We recognize this life; it is the life of culture, the rejection of the world's false promises for higher and truer ideals; it is the life above the Veil. This is the happy side of cosmopolitanism, unbound in time and space; it is freedom in a profound sense. Du Bois gives no hint of the weariness of the perpetual traveler, no sense of John's unhappiness, not a trace of Du Bois's own conflict-ridden soul, only "a green oasis where hot anger cools, and the bitterness of disappointment is sweetened by the springs and breezes of Parnassus."[89]

Having left the city, the essay never returns. Du Bois renounces "sordid money-getting," "apples of gold" for "ideals, broad, pure, and inspiring ends of living."[90] It is his promise to reveal the university as the vehicle of redemption for modern society, but he is overwhelmed by the sacredness of the hallowed halls. "The true college," he solemnly avers, "will ever have one goal,—not to earn meat, but to know the end and aim of that life which meat nourishes."[91] Themes of purity, an obsession with nineteenth-century Americans, are ubiquitous in the essay, becoming so rapturous at one point as to intimate complete sterility: "The Wings of Atalanta are the coming universities of the South. They alone can bear the maiden past the temptation of golden fruit. They will not guide her flying feet away from the cotton and gold; for—ah, thoughtful Hippomenes!—do not the apples lie in the very Way of Life? But they will guide her over and beyond them and leave her kneeling in the Sanctuary of Truth and Freedom and broad Humanity, virgin and undefiled."[92] Here is the purification complete. Redemption has been achieved, not by means of reform but by removal. Du Bois certainly did not intend as a plan that everyone should seek perpetual residence in the university, but at this time in his life, "This is where I live," and he could not complete the cycle of reaching from one world to instruct the other.[93]

Du Bois steps into the mundane world, impelled perhaps by an Emersonian charge to live in both worlds, to resolve a conflict between the real and the ideal, but the effort ends irresolutely, Du Bois retreating again to the world of the idea. Like the Flying Dutchman, whom he would have known through Wagner's opera, Du Bois is condemned to travel and is unable to trust the promise of home on this earth, not until death. His utopia, his ideal community, lies beyond Atlanta, beyond Ghana even, beyond the Veil.

Notes

1. Pico Iyer, "The Soul of an Intercontinental Wanderer," *Harper's* (April 1993): 13.

2. Ibid.

3. Ibid., 16.

4. Ibid.

5. John Berger, *And Our Faces, My Heart, Brief as Photos* (New York: Pantheon Books, 1984), 56.

6. Robert H. Wiebe, *The Search for Order, 1877–1920* (New York: Hill and Wang, 1967), 42–43.

7. Berger, *And Our Faces,* 56.

8. W. E. B. Du Bois, *The Souls of Black Folk* (New York: Bantam, 1989), 2.

9. Ibid., 48.

10. Ibid., 147.

11. Ibid., 150.

12. Ibid.

13. Ibid., 2. Gibson, too, notes Du Bois's "movement back and forth, inside and outside the veil" (intro., *The Souls of Black Folk,* by W. E. B. Du Bois [New York: Penguin, 1989], xiii).

14. Ibid., xxxi.

15. Not only in the title but also in the body of the essay Du Bois adopts this usage. See for, example, page 8 of the essay, in which he discusses what "we [the American Negro] need."

16. Ibid., 3.

17. Ibid., 36.

18. Ibid., 41.

19. Ibid., 42.

20. Ibid., 3.

21. Ibid., 2.

22. Gibson, intro., *Souls,* xvii–xxiv.

23. *Souls,* 32, 33.

24. Ibid., 38.

25. Some might argue that, to the extent Du Bois capitalized on his relative whiteness and sometimes limited his connection with darker blacks, he did seek to deny his morphological characteristics, but no one I know of argues that Du Bois ever tried to pass for white.

26. W. E. B. Du Bois, "The Conservation of the Races" (paper presented to the American Negro Academy, 1897); qtd. in Anthony Appiah, "The Uncompleted Argument: Du Bois and the Illusion of Race," in *"Race," Writing, and Difference,* ed. Henry Louis Gates Jr. (Chicago: University of Chicago Press, 1986), 23; see 23–29, for Appiah's discussion of Du Bois's idea of race.

27. *The Black Atlantic: Modernity and Double Consciousness* (London: Verso, 1993), 116.

28. W. E. B. Du Bois, *The Autobiography of W. E. B. Du Bois;* qtd. in Gibson, intro., *Souls,* xxix.

29. James M. McPherson, Laurence B. Holland, James M. Banner Jr., Nancy J. Weiss, and Michael D. Bell, *Blacks in America: Bibliographical Essays* (Garden City, N.Y.: Anchor/Doubleday, 1972), 153. Titles of the two works are: *Dusk of Dawn: An Essay toward an Autobiogrpahy of a Race Concept* (New York: Harcourt, Brace, and World, 1940); and *The Autobiography of W. E. B. Du Bois: A Soliloquy on Viewing My Life from the Last Decade of Its First Century* (New York: International Publishers, 1968).

30. Appiah, "Uncompleted Argument," 22.

31. See especially "Of Mr. Booker T. Washington and Others" and "Of the Training of Black Men."

32. *Souls,* 165.

33. Ibid., 171.

34. Berger, *And Our Faces,* 67.

35. *Souls,* 171.

36. Ibid., 175.

37. Ibid., 90.

38. Ibid., 171.

39. Ibid., 23.

40. Ibid., 144.

41. Gibson, intro., *Souls,* xxviii.

42. See ibid., xxx–xvi.

43. *Souls,* 177.

44. Ibid., 136.

45. Ibid., 138. According to Gibson, though Du Bois's family was Episcopalian and though he and his mother sometimes attended the Negro Methodist Zion Church, they joined the congregation of the Congregational Church, as it was the most prominent and best attended, especially by professional people, in their community (intro., *Souls,* xviii).

46. *Souls,* 88.

47. Ibid., 70.

48. Gilroy, *Black Atlantic,* 137.

49. *Souls,* 50.

50. For example, see ibid., 81; in "Of the Dawn of Freedom" Du Bois describes chattel slavery in America as having been "—not the worst slavery in the

world, not a slavery that made all life unbearable, rather a slavery that had here and there something of kindliness, fidelity, and happiness" (21).

51. Ibid., 58.

52. Ibid., 47.

53. Ibid., 52.

54. "The Pleasures and Pitfalls of Irony," in *Rhetoric, Philosophy, and Literature: An Exploration,* ed. Don M. Burks (W. Lafayette, Ind.: Purdue University Press, 1978), 13.

55. Gibson, intro., *Souls,* xiii.

56. *Souls,* 2.

57. Ibid., 151.

58. Ibid., 76.

59. Matthew Arnold, *Culture and Anarchy,* ed. J. Dover Wilson (Cambridge: Cambridge University Press, 1932), 6.

60. For some examples, see ibid., 10, 11, 30, 44, 179, 193, 202.

61. For example, ibid., 178.

62. Ibid., 149.

63. Ibid., 150.

64. Ibid., 211.

65. *Souls,* 31.

66. Ibid., 36.

67. Ibid., 41.

68. Ibid., 57.

69. Ibid., 92.

70. Ibid., 115.

71. Ibid., 66.

72. Ibid., 3.

73. Ibid., 150.

74. Ibid., 55–56.

75. Ibid., 54.

76. Ibid., 57, 56.

77. Ibid., 56.

78. Ibid., 54.

79. Ibid., 95. This usage of "slow and sleepy land" refers to the entire South— "All through the Carolinas and Georgia, away down to Mexico." The use of almost the same imagery and phrasing in the first paragraph of "Of the Wings of Atalanta" reinforces this synecdochal role.

80. Ibid., 54. The tenuousness of Du Bois's connection is underscored by the lack of historical evidence for any relationship between the myth and the name of the city, except similar spellings. Sources at the Atlanta Historical Society, though they provide no definitive pronouncement regarding competing versions of the origin of the name Atlanta, tend to give the greatest credence to the account in Ken K. Krakow, *Georgia Place Names* (Macon: Winship Press, 1975), 8–

9. According to Mr. Krakow, the name was proposed in 1845 by J. Edgar Thompson, chief engineer of the Western and Atlantic Railroad, *Atlanta* being the feminine form of *Atlantic*.

81. *Souls*, 54.

82. Ibid., 76.

83. For example, ibid., 54, 55.

84. In James Weldon Johnson, ed., *The Book of Negro Poetry*, rev. ed. (San Diego, Calif.: Harcourt Brace Jovanovich, 1931), 91.

85. *Souls*, 55.

86. Ibid., 57.

87. Ibid.

88. Ibid., 58.

89. Ibid.

90. Ibid., 61.

91. Ibid., 58.

92. Ibid., 60.

93. Du Bois seems to reach a more balanced and integrated vision of college education in essays such as "The Talented Tenth," written at the same time as *Souls*. In "The Talented Tenth," preoccupied entirely with the question of education for blacks, Du Bois notes, "All men cannot go to college, but some men must," and he outlines three objectives for a college education: "It must strengthen the Negro's character, increase his knowledge and teach him to earn a living" (reprinted in August Meier, Elliott Rudwick, and Francis L. Broderick, eds., *Black Protest Thought in the Twentieth Century*, 2d ed. [Indianapolis: Bobbs-Merrill, 1971], 49, 51).

Part Two:

War and Community

CHAPTER SEVEN

On Rhetoric in Martial Decision Making

Ronald H. Carpenter

On 19 August 1942 six thousand British troops, supported by four thousand men at sea and in the air, crossed the English Channel and attempted an amphibious landing on the coast of German-occupied France. They would seize the port of Dieppe, destroy its military facilities and airfields nearby inland, and then re-embark. Anticipated objectives were not attained. Only thirty percent of the troops who got ashore returned alive; twenty-seven hundred of four thousand men who actually reached Dieppe were killed or captured; from one unit of five hundred men, for example, only six returned unwounded. In 1982 British military historian John Keegan concluded that Dieppe, "in retrospect, looks so recklessly hair-brained an enterprise that it is difficult to reconstruct the official state of mind which gave it birth and drove it forward."[1] In the community of naval and military leadership at high levels, decision-making often entails deliberations about appropriate responses to courses of events. Being ostensibly objective estimates about the enemy and one's own forces, those deliberations assess numbers of personnel, their movements, capabilities of their equipment, support of allies (or lacks thereof), and projected outcomes—both tactical and strategic. But rhetoric *also* can influence participants in martial deliberations.

While investigating the Dieppe disaster, Brian Villa ascertained that some participants in the decision-making process admitted that "even in the best of times it was difficult . . . for a soldier to advise against a bold offensive plan. One lays himself open to charges of defeatism, of inertia, or even of 'cold feet.' Human nature being what it is, there is a natural tendency to acquiesce in an offensive plan of doubtful merit rather than to face such charges."[2] That martial "human nature" has a rhetorical corollary identified by Aristotle: persuaders can evoke "shame" for behaviors that "bring disgrace to ourselves or those we care for," such as "throwing down one's shield, or running away—an act proceeding from cowardice"; for "we feel shame with respect to those who have never known us to fail, since hitherto they have been in a position to admire us" but now "they do not think well of us" (1383b–84b).[3]

Another perspective on martial human nature was articulated by General Douglas MacArthur during the Korean War. When confronted with persuading the Joint Chiefs of Staff to approve his plan for an amphibious landing of the First Marine Division at Inchon, MacArthur recalled that he "could almost hear my father's voice telling me as he had so many years ago, 'Doug, councils of war breed timidity and defeatism.'"[4] So, martial human nature has a contrapuntal rhetorical corollary; for, as Aristotle also observed about "elderly men" (likely participants in "councils of war" at higher levels), "the old have lived long, have often been deceived, have made many mistakes of their own; they see that more often than not the affairs of men turn out badly. And so they are positive about nothing; in all things they err by an extreme moderation. . . . they are slow to hope; partly from experience—since things generally go wrong, or at all events seldom turn out well" (1389b–90a). Whether courage or caution prevails in martial decision making may be attributed to rhetoric operative therein.

Admittedly, many martial actions are mandated by treaty obligations or events dictating only one response. The Japanese attack on Pearl Harbor warranted war, just as radar detection later of Russian bombers and missiles over the horizon would trigger retaliation by the Strategic Air Command. Although the Cold War ended, the United States still deliberates martial endeavors—or their likelihood—as far away as Somalia and as close as Haiti. Moreover, martial leaders' recommendations must mesh with policies of their constitutional commanders. The resultant dilemma can be as perplexing as that about what to do in response to "ethnic cleansing" in Bosnia. While determining appropriate responses, martial leaders persuade within their own unique community and then influence civilian leaders, but now, when communication capabilities of commanders such as Generals Colin Powell and Norman Schwarzkopf are televised for wider audiences, their impress may affect still wider communities. That rhetoric merits analysis for this essential reason: martial endeavors invariably place lives at risk.

Rhetoric in martial decision making is explicated herein with General Douglas MacArthur's pivotal discourse in crucial deliberations in Tokyo on 23 August 1950 during the Korean War, when Joint Chiefs of Staff General Lawton Collins and Admiral Forrest Sherman flew out from Washington for a confrontational meeting. MacArthur's superiors entered that meeting steadfastly opposed to his proposed landing at Inchon; they listened to eighty minutes of briefing by navy experts, who amassed compelling arguments about why the site was unsuitable. But after MacArthur spoke, for approximately forty minutes, Collins and Sherman changed their minds, endorsed Inchon to President Truman, and altered the course of the Korean War—and history thereafter.[5] My explication herein reflects constituents of a rhetorical situation: exigence and constraints upon MacArthur to produce a fitting response for differing audiences of a navy admiral and an army general.[6] I also explicate MacArthur's credibility for that situation as well as "gatekeeping" to preordain the ultimate decision. Although the Inchon deliberations may be unique, rhetoric identified therein may clarify how other martial decisions—for good or ill—are reached for impact upon wider communities.

The Inchon Plan

This rhetorical exigency originated in an impending military disaster. On 25 June 1950 the North Korean People's Army (NKPA) crossed the Thirty-eighth Parallel and invaded South Korea. Although equipped and trained by the United States, the Republic of Korea (ROK) Army "was a corrupt, demoralized body entirely devoid of the motivation that was so quickly apparent in the Communist formations."[7] Resistance to invasion evaporated, Seoul soon fell, and South Korea was being overrun. On 27 June, after the United Nations Security Council requested members' aid in repelling the invasion, President Truman authorized U.S. air and naval forces to support South Korea; by 4 July U.S. ground troops were in action near Osan, where they were overwhelmed by North Korean forces.[8] On 7 July MacArthur, then overseeing occupation of Japan, became supreme commander for UN forces in Korea.

The next several weeks of ground warfare constituted a debacle for the U.S. Army. Despite increasing numbers (and air superiority), "soft" undermanned units from occupation duty in Japan were ill equipped to fight North Koreans with Russian T-34 tanks.[9] Retreats often turned into routs; *bug out* entered GI jargon to signify fleeing in disorder before enemy envelopment; and Marguerite Higgins wrote for the *New York Herald Tribune*, "I saw young Americans turn and bolt in battle, or throw down their arms."[10] Successive defense lines disintegrated as Americans were pushed down the Korean peninsula into a small perimeter around the port city of Pusan for a desperate "Custer's Last Stand"; their grave position was stated on 29 July by Eighth Army General Walton Walker: "There will be no more retreating, withdrawal, or readjustment of the lines or any other term you choose. There is no line behind us to which we can retreat. . . . There will be no Dunkirk, there will be no Bataan; a retreat to Pusan would be one of the greatest butcheries in history. We must fight until the end. Capture by these people is worse than death itself."[11]

As supreme commander, MacArthur planned an audacious counterattack: an amphibious landing by marines at Inchon, on the west coast of Korea near Seoul. That assault, about 150 miles behind the rear of Communist troops surrounding Pusan, would cut their supply lines constricted in routes through and around Seoul, gain political advantage by liberating Seoul, and threaten the North Korean capital, Pyongyang.[12] As army chief of staff General Lawton Collins later averred, Inchon "was the masterpiece" of MacArthur; indeed, the U.S. Army official history of the Korean War states that he "conceived these 'planned operations' a few days after the North Koreans struck"; or, as the navy concedes, "credit for the conception of making an amphibious assault at Inchon can only be given to one man: General Douglas MacArthur."[13] In other circumstances amphibious landings constituted "standard Army doctrine for peninsular warfare, wherein an overextended enemy force, lacking air and sea power, becomes ever more vulnerable on its flanks. It was doctrine that in World War II led to Allied landings first at Salerno, then at Anzio during the peninsular campaign in Italy."[14] But for the extraordinary plight of U.S. arms in Korea, Inchon was anathema—both in Washington, D.C., and among several knowledgeable officers in the Far East.

During a fact-finding mission Generals Lawton Collins (army chief of staff) and Hoyt Vandenberg (air force chief of staff) met with MacArthur on 13 July and learned about "Operation Chromite," Inchon.[15] They found MacArthur "displaying his typical coolness, poise, and élan. The situation was serious, but not desperate," for the general assured them that he "would soon stabilize the battlefront, and the reinforcements on route would be used for an amphibious counterstroke that was already forming in his mind. He did not wish merely to repulse the invaders, but to destroy them. The ultimate goal of his enveloping movement would be 'to compose and unite Korea.'"[16] The next day, before returning to Washington, Collins sought further information about Inchon from the Far East expert on amphibious techniques, Rear Admiral James H. Doyle, commanding Amphibious Group One, attached to Admiral C. Turner Joy's Naval Forces, Far East.[17] Doyle's assessment was disheartening.

The official history of Marine Corps operations in Korea only claims that "Inchon was probably the least desirable" of possible landing sites because "time and tide seemed to have combined forces to protect Inchon from seaborne foes."[18] The tidal range of nearly thirty-two feet was among the highest in the world, racing in and out via narrow channels to yield wide mud flats. Approach channel currents ran as high as seven to eight knots (close to landing craft speed) and left little if any room for maneuver around a sunken or disabled vessel in waters also mineable and commanded by heights or islands suited for artillery. And "of beaches, in the common usage of the word, Inchon has none."[19] Landing Ship, Tanks (LSTs) required twenty-nine feet of water, but high tide lasted only two to three hours. After unloading tanks and heavy equipment, LSTs could be stranded on mud flats until the next high tide, and, with insufficient numbers available in the U.S. Navy, thirty-seven LSTs (some smelling "vividly of fish") were leased from the Japanese merchant service for Inchon, their officers and crews supplemented by Americans flown from the United States.[20] Smaller landing craft needed engines to keep bows against seawalls twelve to fourteen feet high while Marines scaled them on makeshift wooden ladders.[21] Moreover, with evening high tide at 7:20 P.M., Marines had twenty-seven minutes of daylight left to secure a city the size of Omaha—with no reinforcements until the next high tide.[22] Commander Arlie G. Capps of Doyle's staff said, "We drew up a list of every natural and geographic handicap—and Inchon had 'em all"; Commander Monroe Kelly said, "Make up a list of amphibious 'don'ts,' and you have an exact description of the Inchon operation."[23]

After Collins reported back in Washington, the Joint Chiefs of Staff were pessimistic. Although a theater commander nominally "had authority to dispose and employ his forces as he saw fit," the JCS "grew increasingly worried" that MacArthur might "bite off more than the United States could chew."[24] Collins summarized their concerns:

The JCS had received no details of the plan for the landing at Inchon since my oral report in July. In considering the pros and cons of a landing there, the JCS had to weigh our responsibilities to the President as well as to the commander of the United Nations Command.

We could have asked no questions of MacArthur, raised no challenge to the plans as we knew them, and allowed the General to
assume full responsibility for the outcome, which he was perfectly
willing to do. But we could not have washed our hands of any
responsibility for Inchon as long as we had real doubts about its
success. We were not prepared to do this. Furthermore, since
Truman had not asked Congress to approve his actions in entering
the war, he was deeply committed personally and wished to be
kept fully informed as to military operations.[25]

Truman recalled that Collins, upon returning from Tokyo, had "serious
misgivings" about Inchon, and the JCS wanted to "scrutinize" the proposal before endorsing it to a president with reservations about
MacArthur's "mental stability."[26] But in repeated requests for a marine
division to spearhead the landing MacArthur refused to specify *where*
the assault would take place; so, in a White House meeting with Truman
on 10 August chief of naval operations Admiral Forrest Sherman insisted "the Joint Chiefs of staff would have to pass on his plans for
amphibious landings."[27] Ostensibly "to determine more precisely what
was taking place in Tokyo," Collins and Sherman nevertheless went to
dissuade MacArthur from Inchon. On 21 August Sherman told navy and
marine commanders in Yokosuka that he "would support Doyle in his
opposition to Inchon and his proposal to land in a more practical area
farther south," and Secretary of Defense Louis Johnson testified before
Congress that Collins "did not favor Inchon and went over to try to
argue General MacArthur out of it."[28] MacArthur himself recalls that "it
was evident immediately upon their arrival that the actual purpose of
their trip was not so much to discuss as to dissuade" in "a strategic
conference to debate the problem."[29]

The conference began at 5:30 P.M. in the conference room of
MacArthur's Tokyo headquarters in the Dai Ichi Building. In addition
to several members of MacArthur's staff, Admiral Doyle came to avert
seeming disaster. After studying Inchon and alternative sites, Doyle,
shortly before 23 August, confronted General Edward Almond
(MacArthur's chief of staff) and insisted the supreme commander was
"oblivious of the enormous technical hazards" and should be "briefed
on exactly what the Inchon landing involved." Although treated in a
"most dictatorial manner" by Almond, Doyle pleaded successfully that
MacArthur "must be made aware of the details" and had his briefing

included on the meeting agenda for 23 August.[30] So, after MacArthur's G-3 staff officer, General Edwin Wright, "sketched the 'big picture' detailing the forces and scheme of maneuver" for Collins and Sherman, Doyle had his turn.[31] In Doyle's recollection "General Almond asked me not to linger over the details. 'The General's not interested in details,' he told me, 'just the broad picture.' However, since this was such a highly important decision which General MacArthur alone must make, I felt it was our duty to ensure that he had all the facts, including the details. That's why I opened the briefing with the statement that any amphibious landing is an operation of many details—interlocking and interdependent—each of which has to be performed successfully or risk jeopardizing the entire operation."[32] For eighty minutes, while MacArthur calmly smoked his pipe, Doyle brought in eight staff members one by one from Almond's adjoining office (the conference room was too small for everyone), and for ten minutes each they detailed numerous obstacles in a briefing that Collins dispassionately described as "frankly pessimistic."[33] Instead of Inchon, Doyle proposed the "Posung-Myon area, about 30 miles south of Inchon on the west coast where better approach channels and beaches were believed to be available. . . . A landing at this point . . . would not be attended by the risks and restrictions of Inchon, yet after securing a beachhead the troops would be in a position to strike inland at the enemy's main line of rail and highway communications."[34] Then Doyle concluded, "General, I have not been asked nor have I volunteered my opinion about this landing. If I were asked, however, the best I can say is that Inchon is not impossible."[35]

Collins reacted immediately: "I suggested, as an alternative to Inchon, that consideration be given to a landing at Kunsan, which had few of Inchon's drawbacks, was close to the enemy's main supply routes through Nonsan and Taejon, and should ensure more prompt union with the Eighth Army in the vicinity of Taejon. Admiral Sherman seconded my suggestion."[36] MacArthur had his cue. As Almond remembered this "famous show-down conference," MacArthur first said: "Gentlemen your viewpoints have been magnificent and I respect them highly. However, I am the responsible commander and will take the responsibility. INCHON it will be."[37] Oratory ensued. Collins recalled that "MacArthur had listened quietly to the discussion. He continued silently for a few moments to puff on his corncob pipe while we waited for his concluding remarks. He then spoke in a matter-of-fact tone at first, gradually building up emphasis with consummate skill. . . . He closed with a dramatic peroration in which he staked his reputation that Inchon would not fail."[38] Another participant remembered that "he spoke with that slow, deep resonance of an accomplished actor"; Doyle said, "If MacArthur had gone on the stage, you never would have heard of John Barrymore"; and others perceived a "Churchillian oration," a "soliloquy which no one present would ever forget," or "oratory such as the world seldom sees save from the orchestra seats of a theater."[39] The conference room had no tape recorder, so, as Heinl observes, "we shall never know exactly what the General said. . . . The several versions (including his own, in his *Reminiscences*) are at odds. But everyone who heard him that evening . . . agrees that his 45-minute reply, extemporaneous, without a note, was one of the compelling declarations of his career."[40] MacArthur's rhetoric can be reconstructed, however, from counterpoint between what he recalled saying—albeit edited for posterity—and what listeners remember he said, as recounted in their memoirs, correspondence, or interviews with historians.

MacArthur's Speech

MacArthur's response was constrained by his perceptions of how a navy admiral might react in a way different from an army general. He began by expressing petulance toward the navy: "Admiral, in all my years of military service, that is the finest briefing I have ever received. Commander [*sic*], you have taught me all I had ever dreamed of knowing about tides. Do you know, in World War I they got our divisions to Europe through submarine-infested seas? I have a deep admiration for the Navy. From the humiliation of Bataan, the Navy brought us back. I never thought the day would come, that the Navy would be unable to support the Army in its operations."[41] Although its PT boats enabled MacArthur to escape from doomed Corregidor during World War II, the navy "failed" him during the fall of the Philippines, when his forces were "backed into another peninsular perimeter—Bataan—much like the Pusan Perimeter"; for "help . . . had failed to arrive, in part, MacArthur believed, because . . . the 1942 Navy did not have sufficient courage. The upshot had been a disgrace—the largest surrender of American forces in history."[42] For his *Reminiscences* (rhetorically cast for posterity) MacArthur is less petulant: "The Navy's objections as to tides, hydrography, terrain, and physical handicaps are indeed substantial and pertinent. But they are not insuperable. My confidence in the Navy is complete, and in fact I seem to have more confidence in the Navy than the Navy has in itself. The Navy's rich experience in staging numerous amphibious landings under my command in the Pacific during the late war, frequently under somewhat similar difficulties, leaves me with little doubt on that score."[43] In either "text," however, MacArthur appealed to navy pride.

Admiral Sherman rose to the bait. During Doyle's briefing a point was made that "enemy shore batteries could completely command the dead-end channel" into Inchon, whereupon Sherman interrupted boldly, "I wouldn't hesitate to take a ship up there," prompting MacArthur's exclamation, "Spoken like a Farragut!" Likely resenting Sherman's reversal about Inchon, Doyle muttered, "Spoken like a John Wayne."[44] Although gunfire from ships would "soften up" enemy defenses, the navy primarily was transporting and landing troops with their supplies. Some ships might be sunk, but major risks were largely navigational ones to test seamanship. General Almond's view of "Jimmy Doyle's fondness for a landing at Posung-myon" is understatement about intricacies of amphibious landings: "In spite of the Navy's fondness for the ease of the beach to be approached you must always remember that when the Navy lands the troops its task is finished except for their resupply. The Navy is always interested, and understandably so, at delivering the troops at the water's edge. What goes on thereafter is no concern of theirs. Never forget that the ultimate battle is fought on land. The movement to the beach is only the first step."[45] Navy prestige was a factor in Sherman's emerging assent.

Despite petulance about the navy during the fall of the Philippines, MacArthur praised its "rich experience in staging the numerous amphibious landings under my command in the Pacific during the late war" (as he recalled); or, as other accounts indicate, "the amphibious landing is the most powerful tool we have."[46] However the reference was stated, its many familiar referents would "ring true" with narrative fidelity for Admiral Sherman.[47] From Guadalcanal to Iwo Jima, and many islands in between, the navy in the Pacific conducted successful amphibious operations. In Tokyo during August 1950 "no more experienced senior officers in the field of amphibious warfare could have been found," for, in addition to Doyle, the "fortuitous" combination included Admiral Arthur Struble, who "participated in or had supervised twenty-two amphibious operations, including Normandy," and General Oliver P. Smith, who would lead assault forces as "one of the Marines' top amphibious experts."[48] MacArthur need not prove *to Sherman* what the navy could do, but Sherman could prove *to Washington* what the navy and its marines could do.

Under President Truman and Defense Secretary Louis Johnson the navy and marines suffered a "succession of meat-ax blows" after Joint Chiefs of Staff chairman General Omar Bradley testified in 1949 before the House Armed Services Committee, "I predict that large-scale amphibious operations . . . will never occur again."[49] Johnson in 1949 determinedly began trimming "fat out of the Armed Forces," and with "tacit White House support" he did "most of his trimming on the Navy and Marines" because "General Bradley tells me that amphibious operations are a thing of the past. We'll never have any more amphibious operations. That does away with the Marine Corps. And the Air Force can do anything the Navy can nowadays, so that does away with the Navy."[50] The Fleet Marine Force was cut drastically in its strength, and its amphibious craft in commission were drastically slashed. The Fleet Marine Forces commander at that time, General Lemuel Shepherd, said "we were at a very low ebb. . . . We were fighting for our existence [as a service]. . . . Everybody was against the Marine Corps at that time."[51] Although the navy "had thoroughly mastered its own element and had just won the greatest naval war in history," the next war presumably would be waged by air force bombers with nuclear weapons, so the navy had "its back to the wall, while the Marine Corps was literally fighting for existence."[52] As chief of naval operations, Sherman knew Truman's "long and petty distrust of the Navy and its admirals," derided by Bradley as "Fancy Dans" (and he likely knew Truman's belief that "the Marine Corps is the Navy's police force and as long as I am President that is what it will remain. They have a propaganda machine that is almost equal to Stalin's").[53] At MacArthur's conclusion Sherman rose and said: "Thank you. A great voice in a great cause."[54]

Sherman was susceptible to MacArthur's "great voice" for several reasons. He was assigned to Admiral Chester Nimitz's staff in World War II to implement a "more aggressive" Central Pacific campaign, including "island leapfrog tactics" like MacArthur's in the Southwest Pacific.[55] In January 1944 Sherman drafted the "Campaign Plan" for the remaining war against Japan, specifying "close coordination" between MacArthur in the Southwest Pacific theater of war and Nimitz in the Central Pacific.[56] Indeed, Sherman met with MacArthur several times to coordinate operations in that bifurcated command structure, and, although Sherman once lamented MacArthur's "moments of forensic oratory" in those conferences, their relationship was one of mutual professional respect.[57] Moreover, during interservice debates about whether attacking Formosa or Luzon in the Philippines would be next in defeating Japan, Sherman sided with MacArthur and wrote a cogent staff study that "recommended abandoning the plan to seize Formosa," and Admiral Raymond Spruance responded to Sherman's initial draft by saying, "I wouldn't change a word of it."[58] Sherman also was sanguine about sending marines to Korea. After the JCS met in Washington on 11 July 1950 "to consider the employment of Marines in the Far East Command," General Almond in Tokyo was "reliably informed that the matter was about to be brushed off as infeasible, when Admiral Sherman interposed and made the point that it was not infeasible and that in his opinion these troops could be supplied"; although that "staunch statement" in July only advocated their employment generally, the stage thereby was partly set ultimately for their landing at Inchon.[59]

Another factor likely fostered Sherman's appreciation for a great voice. Sherman wrote battle reports for Nimitz. Attributing authorship erroneously, the *New York Times* proclaimed "no finer . . . description of a complicated action has come out of this war than Admiral Nimitz' summary of the Second Battle of the Philippine Sea—Pacific Fleet Communiqué 168 . . . it throbs with the stimulating pace of direct statement; it leaves room for the imagination to picture the exciting events." Nimitz wrote to Sherman, "Several copies of this editorial have now reached me, and I would indeed be guilty if I did not make due acknowledgment to you who wrote it."[60] Sherman appreciated eloquence. But the great cause (along with defeating North Korea) was the future of the navy. For Sherman remained uneasy about Inchon. As Admiral C. Turner Joy recalled MacArthur's "eloquent and passionate" statement: "my own personal misgivings about Inchon were erased. I believe that the General had persuaded me, and all others in the room—with the possible exception of Admiral Sherman—that Inchon could be successful. . . . he retained some slight misgivings," for Sherman the next day confided to Joy about MacArthur, "I wish I had that man's confidence."[61] Those misgivings were not about a landing but, rather, its place: "No naval or Marine officer who had studied the military problem had any quarrel with the need for an amphibious assault. Nor did any naval or Marine officer question the strategic logic, the psychological wisdom, or the political promise of . . . Inchon. Most of the naval and Marine

experts who examined the problem . . . held that *all* of General
MacArthur's objectives could be achieved by landing at *other* places
which offered *fewer* natural hazards than Inchon."[62] But Sherman yielded
to MacArthur's "confidence" and endorsed Inchon back to Washington, for, as Blair concludes, "a successful amphibious landing in Korea,
leading to a Korea-wide victory, would do much to restore the prestige
of the Navy and Marine Corps and ensure those services a far stronger
position in America's post-Korea military establishment."[63] Sherman's
caution about Inchon was counterbalanced effectively by dynamics of
interservice rivalry to influence his decision.

To overcome army objections to Inchon, MacArthur used other arguments. After "being landbound for centuries," some generals feared
as "suicidal" the inherent "folly of attempting to storm a defended beach
in daylight."[64] Being more objective, however, Collins deemed Inchon
too far from Pusan for link-up with Walker and thus believed those
marines might be used better defending Pusan.[65] Admitting that Kunsan
"would eliminate many of the hazards of Inchon," MacArthur explained
why landing there "would be largely ineffective and indecisive." Collins's
choice of Kunsan "would be an attempted envelopment which would
not envelop. It would not sever or destroy the enemy's supply lines or
distribution center, and therefore would serve little purpose. It would
be a 'short envelopment,' and nothing in war is more futile. . . . The only
result would be a hook-up with Walker's troops on his left. . . . In other
words, this would simply be sending more troops to help Walker 'hang
on.' . . . To fight frontally in a breakthrough from Pusan will be bloody
and indecisive."[66] For a professional soldier that appeal would resonate
favorably with what military historian Russell F. Weigley calls "The Quest
for Decisive Warfare":

> War between 1631 and 1815 revolved around grand-scale battles
> because, in that age more than any other, the economic, social, and
> technological circumstances of war permitted the massing of tens
> of thousands of soldiers on a single field for the test of battle, while
> at the same time military strategists hoped by means of battle to
> secure decisions in war, and thereby to secure the objects for which
> men went to war, with a quickness and dispatch that would keep
> the cost of war reasonably proportionate to the purposes attained.
> . . . As long as the grand-scale battle could readily occur . . . strate-
> gists focused on it to achieve decision in war. If in a successful

battle the enemy army could be substantially destroyed—then the whole course of a war might be resolved in a single day, and wars thereby might be won at relatively low costs, by avoiding the prolonged expenditure of resources and lives.[67]

Thus, Napoleonic "victories of Austerlitz and Jena-Auerstädt are regarded as the classic fulfillment of a strategy of annihilation through decisive battle." More significantly, such endeavor "was a rational response to the difficulties of achieving the objects of policy through war. . . . it united the strategy of the era to the rise of officer professionalism. The quest for decisive battle was the educated soldier's rationalist effort to make war cost-effective, the promptness of the decision through battle promising to prevent an inordinate drain upon the resources of the state."[68]

MacArthur understood this imperative for maximal victory at minimal cost. Admittedly, "the quest for rapid strategic decision through the climactic battle" sometimes gave way to strategy "to wear down the enemy and outlast him in a prolonged contest of attrition. The age of battles gave way to exchanges of casualties and resources in sustained combat on the pattern of the late campaigns of the American Civil War and, preeminently, the First World War."[69] But these two conflicts taught lessons of monumental import: in the former more Americans were killed than all their other wars combined, and prolonged stalemates of trench warfare during the latter, when combined with modern armaments, caused horrendous losses of life to achieve miniscule gains in ground, often measured in mere meters or yards. Frontal assault to break out of the Pusan Perimeter only would repeat past attritions—too often for limited, if any, gain. So, MacArthur advocated a mode of operations he delineated earlier to General Edwin F. Harding, at the onset of the campaign to regain the Philippines in World War II: "Here and now I begin a campaign of movement—where speed and tactical surprise and superior strategy will demonstrate again how generalship can win with lighting strategic strokes against potentially overwhelming forces. . . . We shall hit them where they ain't. . . . When I commanded the Forty-Second Division in World War I, I saw both sides fling millions of men to their slaughter in the stupidity of trench warfare. I made up my mind then that when I commanded in the next war, as I knew I would, that I would use my brains instead of the blood and guts of my men."[70]

At the Pusan Perimeter the American army was suffering. The

Twenty-fourth Division had lost half of its men as casualties or missing, and aggregate UN forces were "sustaining a thousand casualties a day."[71] At home Americans were distraught by North Korean "human wave" charges and pictures of American soldiers taken prisoner, bound with barbed wire, and shot by the roadside.[72] MacArthur appropriately emphasized casualties: "The only alternative to a stroke such as I propose will be the continuation of the savage sacrifice we are making at Pusan. . . . Are you content to let our troops stay in that bloody perimeter like beef cattle in the slaughterhouse? Who will take the responsibility for such a tragedy? Certainly, I will not."[73] MacArthur thereby "rhetorically put the monkey on Washington's back."[74] As he concluded, "I can almost hear the ticking of the second hand of destiny. We must act now or we will die." Over the years MacArthur had left "no doubt in the minds of media observers" that "to minimize casualties" was "always one of his chief goals."[75] Resonating with MacArthur, Collins's memoirs quote his saying that Inchon "will save 100,000 lives."[76] So, Inchon was less a present plan likely to elicit caution from an army superior and more the rehearsal of martial lore from the past.

In *Reminiscences* MacArthur implied that his Southwest Pacific tactics reduced casualties with "a triphibious concept" that was new: "It was the practical application of this system of warfare—to avoid the frontal attack with its terrible loss of life; to by-pass Japanese strongpoints and neutralize them by cutting their lines of supply; to thus isolate their armies and starve them on the battlefield; to, as Willie Keeler used to say, 'hit 'em where they ain't'—that from this time forward guided my movements and operations. . . . The system was popularly called 'leap-frogging,' and hailed as something new in warfare." Yet the *Reminiscences* also disclaims that those tactics were innovative: "But it was actually the adaptation of modern instrumentalities of war to a concept as ancient as war itself. Derived from the classic strategy of envelopment, it was given a new name, imposed by modern conditions. Never before had a field of battle embraced land and water in such relative proportions. Earlier campaigns had been decided on either land or sea. However, the process of transferring troops by sea as well as by land appeared to conceal the fact that the system was merely that of envelopment applied to a new type of battle area. It has always proved the ideal method for success by inferior but faster-moving forces."[77] Whether in *Reminiscences* or in Tokyo on 23 August 1950, MacArthur's was not a voice in the wilderness.

Ways to achieve decisive victory were studied assiduously by martial leaders, and Collins's nickname, "Lightning Joe," suggested his own predilections for swift, telling attack. While tracing "the quest for decisive warfare," Weigley identifies what emerged as the salient "means" to achieve that goal:

> In the age of battles, the possibility of tactical decisiveness usually hinged upon the effective use of the most mobile combat arm, the cavalry. The mobile arm could most readily maneuver and strike against the enemy's relatively vulnerable flanks and rear. . . . Whenever an army developed an effective cavalry, that army became capable of winning the tactical decision of the battlefield by margins in favorable casualty rates and psychological advantage wide enough to create at least a possibility that strategic decisiveness might follow as well. . . . Wars fought predominantly by infantry tend to be cursed even more devastatingly by the plague of indecision than do other wars. World War I offers an appalling example. . . . The contrast between World War I and the impact of the new mobile arm, mechanized forces, upon World War II illustrates the point. The military commander in quest of decisiveness needs an effective arm of mobile war.[78]

For Inchon, MacArthur would not use the mobility of men mounted on horseback but, instead, carried quickly by ship to the enemy's rear—a tactic forced upon him in the Southwest Pacific. The appropriateness of such action for army minds was indicated in the Inchon diary of MacArthur's chief of staff, General Almond: "General MacArthur was a master of Strategic military operations. He constantly studied the methods whereby he might take the enemy in reverse as he had done on 10 previous occasions, using amphibious forces against the Japanese locations from Australia to the Philippines in World War II," and that time-honored method was stated to Almond with a directive from his superior to formulate an operational plan to "exploit our air and sea control and, by amphibious maneuver, to strike behind the enemy's mass of ground forces."[79] As D. Clayton James concludes, MacArthur's "mindset about the Pacific war heavily influenced . . . the first year of fighting in Korea" to the point whereby his "grand obsession: Inchon" constitutes "the supreme act of refighting the last war."[80]

For Collins, MacArthur also asserted that "the bulk of the Reds are committed around Walker's defense perimeter. The enemy, I am convinced, has failed to prepare Inchon properly for defense. The very arguments you have made as to the impracticabilities involved will tend to ensure for me the element of surprise. For the enemy commander will reason that no one would be so brash as to make such an attempt."[81] The assertion was founded upon intelligence estimates summarized in the official "Operation Chromite" war diary about the likelihood of an enemy force "incapable" of effective resistance.

> Enemy forces in the Inchon-Seoul area consisted principally of major headquarters, a replacement center, anti-aircraft defenses, operating personnel for an airfield, minor port, coastal defenses, and an army garrison force. In addition, in this area the North Koreans drafted replacements for North Korean forces; however, the state of training and mental attitude of these hastily mobilized "recruits" did little to increase the enemy potential in the objective area.... The total enemy strength in SEOUL was estimated to consist of approximately 5,000 troops; enemy strength at INCHON was reported on 25 July as 1,000.... Estimates of enemy strength proved to be very accurate as the operation progressed.[82]

North Koreans taken prisoner at Inchon and Seoul confirmed those estimates. Enlisted personnel for whom the landing was a "surprise" indicated they had received but "15 days to 2 months of military training," and a captured lieutenant colonel who commanded men having "about 20 days of military training" could admit only that, "during the early part of September 1950, it was rumored among high ranking officers of the brigade that U.S. Forces would make a landing at Wonson, Inchon, or Mokpo in the very near future."[83] MacArthur had reason to be categorical when asserting that "the enemy, I am convinced, has failed to prepare Inchon properly for defense."

But landing at Inchon should *not* have surprised North Korea. Security was "sadly lacking"; Tokyo press club reporters briefed in advance nicknamed the forthcoming landing "Operation Common Knowledge"; and a North Korean spy who infiltrated dock areas was captured with "top secret plans of the Inchon operation in his possession only one week before the landing."[84] Moreover, Marines newly arriving in Japan for reloading on assault transports—but not yet briefed about their destination—"returned from bordellos to report that the news was all over town: Inchon."[85] Perhaps "common knowledge" of the landing location might constitute disinformation intended to mislead. Yet, if "surprise is the most vital element for success in war," MacArthur supported his assertion *not* with intelligence data available to him but with a historical analogue:

> As an example, the Marquis de Montcalm believed in 1759 that it was impossible for an armed force to scale the precipitous river banks south of the then walled city of Quebec, and therefore concentrated his formidable defenses along the more vulnerable banks north of the city. But General James Wolfe and a small force did indeed come up the St. Lawrence River and scale those heights. On the Plains of Abraham, Wolfe won a stunning victory that was made possible almost entirely by surprise. Thus he captured Quebec and in effect ended the French and Indian War. Like Montcalm, the North Koreans would regard an Inchon landing as impossible. Like Wolfe, I could take them by surprise.[86]

Military histories about Inchon often quote or paraphrase this example, including the official marine history, which acknowledges the "precept" of Wolfe's victory at Quebec, "made possible by audacity in overcoming natural obstacles that the enemy regarded as insurmountable."[87] And, in his account of the "brilliant exposition" holding him "spellbound," Collins quoted MacArthur: "The very reasons we cited for not landing at Inchon would tend to ensure surprise. 'For the enemy commander will reason that no one would be so brash as to make such an attempt.' As Wolfe did at Quebec, he would land where the enemy would think it impossible and, with the consequent surprise, gain a decisive victory."[88] With the example of Quebec, MacArthur found that "representative anecdote" that Kenneth Burke perceives as embodying "implicitly what the system that is developed from it contains explicitly," thereby being *"summational* in character."[89]

Collins agreed to an assault predicated upon audacity because of another issue of which he was made vitally aware. MacArthur maintained that "the prestige of the Western world hangs in the balance."

> Oriental millions are watching the outcome. It is plainly apparent that here in Asia is where the Communist conspirators have elected

to make their play for global conquest. The test is not in Berlin or
Vienna, in London, Paris or Washington. It is here and now—it is
along the Naktong River in South Korea. We have joined the issue
on the battlefield. Actually, we here fight Europe's war . . . with
arms, while there it is still confined to words. If we lose the war to
Communism in Asia, the fate of Europe will be gravely jeopar-
dized. Win it and Europe will probably be saved from war and
stay free. Make the wrong decision here—the fatal decision of inertia—and we will be done.[90]

Inertia of indecision is anathema to military leaders, and Weigley avers
that, "the larger the objectives of war, the more acute the frustration of
indecision."

When sometimes in the late seventeenth and the eighteenth centuries wars were in fact as limited in their objectives as the stereotyped
version of the period would suggest, disappointment spawned by
indecision could be contained, and the rigors imposed upon the
soldiers might also be limited and moderate enough to prevent
their inclination toward brutality from rising up in demoniac fury.
But when the chronic indecisiveness of war disappointed the fulfillment of expectations as large as those of hegemony in Europe
or national liberation from hated oppressors, then frustration almost inevitably generated both the calculated and the spontaneous
resort to deeper and baser cruelties, to the sack of cities and the
ravishing of countrysides both in search of revenge and in the usually vain hope that larger cruelties will break the enemy's spirit.[91]

What was written about Europe in earlier centuries applied to Korea (or
Vietnam). So Collins yielded to MacArthur: "upon our return to Washington Sherman and I briefed the other Chiefs, the Secretary of Defense,
and the President. After reviewing our reports, the JCS on August 28
sent MacArthur a conditional approval of his plans."[92]

MacArthur's Persuasiveness

MacArthur spoke in Tokyo with credibility. Yes, his ethos originated
in part from dramatic posturing to project an aura of leadership arête.
The director of Marine Corps Museums and Archives, General Edwin
Simmons (USMC, Ret.), was present on 17 September 1950, when

MacArthur came ashore at Inchon to visit the battlefield (accompanied by inevitable newspaper correspondents, including Marguerite Higgins and Carl Mydans). Then serving as a major commanding a weapons company, he was "at the 1st Marines CP [command post] that day on the occasion of the meeting of the two finest actors in the Far Eastern Theater: General MacArthur and Chesty Puller [Col., USMC, commanding the First Marines Regiment]."[93] Reminiscing further for the MacArthur Archives, Simmons said "both of these persons were consummate actors and they were both playing the role to the hilt." But "General MacArthur so dominated that scene although there were many other notables and dignitaries in the party. . . . my impression always was that the man was a magnificent actor, he always was centre stage."[94] Heroic stances usually were accompanied by heroic words as "one-liners," which reporters in his inevitable entourage quoted for readers back home. Preceding "I have returned" after striding ashore at Leyte in the Philippines, an impressed newsman coming ashore in MacArthur's landing barge recalled how the general ordered the coxswain to approach another landing craft returning from the beach. MacArthur shouted, "where is the hardest fighting going on?" The other helmsman pointed to Red Beach; MacArthur thanked him, pointed to the same spot, and ordered his coxswain, "Head for that beach, son."[95] Earlier, soon after U.S. troops landed on Los Negros in the Admiralty Islands, he walked within range of Japanese riflemen. When an uneasy officer said, "Excuse me, sir, but we killed a Jap sniper in there just a few minutes ago," MacArthur continued to walk in that direction and responded: "Fine. That's the best thing to do with them."[96] Or, during that visit to the front lines after Inchon, a young marine officer said: "General, you can't come up here. . . . We just knocked out six Red tanks over the top of this hill." From his arsenal of appropriate lines for the likes of Marguerite Higgins and Carl Mydans, MacArthur drew "That was the proper thing to do."[97] MacArthur persistently posed for public consumption.

For his martial community, however, MacArthur's credibility had more legitimate sources. When recounting *The American Way of War: A History of United States Military Strategy and Policy*, Weigley is sympathetic to the Southwest Pacific theater commander during World War II. Starting in 1942 from Australia with "his first counteroffensive against the Japanese in New Guinea, MacArthur had made a speciality of the amphibious end run"; to other military leaders he was "the past master of the amphibious operation" to envelop enemy forces.[98] Admitting that "the paucity of the resources at my command made me adopt this method of campaign as the only hope of accomplishing my task," he oversaw the buildup by which his forces "developed proficiency and flexibility in remarkably short order."[99] For, to regain the Philippines, Japanese bases along twelve hundred miles of New Guinea's north coast first had to be neutralized; and "in line with MacArthur's philosophy of waging war at the least possible cost of lives, he intended to bypass as many of the enemy's bases as he could, seizing every opportunity that arose as his operations proceeded" (avoiding well-defended Wewak or Hansa Bay and jumping ahead five hundred miles to Hollandia, e.g.). Indeed, Japan's strongest base in the Southwest Pacific, Rabaul (on New Britain), simply was isolated to "wither on the vine," and for these operations "MacArthur's stock as a master strategist skyrocketed."[100] In the final analysis MacArthur was credible for Collins and Sherman in Tokyo.

MacArthur nevertheless doubted his powers of persuasion on behalf of Inchon. After the 23 August conference he finally sent the requested full details about the operation back to Washington by personal courier, Lieutenant Colonel Lynn D. Smith, who left Tokyo on 10 September with MacArthur's injunction, "Don't get there too soon"; thus, the JCS did not receive their request for complete plans about Inchon until 14 September, when "it was too late to cancel the assault" in the event of a change of heart in Washington.[101] MacArthur "did nothing to make Smith's journey comfortable or fast. Instead of being put on a courier aircraft, Smith waited around Tokyo all night and then boarded a weather-beaten old DC-4 for the long flight across the Pacific, satchels of the documents at his feet. Wake Island: a stopover for fuel, food, and minor repairs. Then on across more ocean to Oahu and another stop. Then on to Travis Air Force Base in California."[102] But another index of MacArthur's uncertainty about the outcome of his oratory is the manipulation of audience for the 23 August conference as well as information made available to participants.

Although a potent representative anecdote for General Collins, "Quebec" might not have been so persuasive had deliberations followed a different format. While "spellbound" by MacArthur's oratory, Collins admitted that "the main point that was missing in this briefing—though neither Admiral Sherman nor I focused on it at the time—had to do with the strength of the enemy in the Inchon area and his ability to concentrate there quickly."[103] That lapse in judgmental faculties also may be attributed to MacArthur and his chief of staff, General Almond, acting as "gatekeepers" to exclude crucial information from the deliberations, for what is effective as argument also may achieve impress because of what is excluded as counterargument.[104] For instance, the navy sent Admiral Arleigh Burke to Tokyo to keep the Pentagon informed about landing plans. Because a typhoon headed toward Japan could hamper the loading of assault ships—and veer to impact the landing area adversely—Burke went to Almond and demanded to see MacArthur about "a tactical problem that's a serious one." Almond's immediate response was defensive: "General MacArthur is very busy . . . you can't see him right now."[105] Similarly, Admiral C. Turner Joy was unsuccessful in voicing concerns about the typhoon because of Almond's admitted gatekeeper actions: "Admiral Joy had asked for a conference with him. . . . I asked Joy his business, so I could inform the Commander-in-Chief. He said, 'Well, it's about the typhoon threat.' Whereupon I took to MacArthur my staff study on typhoons of the past twenty-five years, and I said in no uncertain terms, 'General, this conference is for the purpose of persuading you against Inchon as a landing point. I strongly urge you that you do not let them counter persuade you.'"[106] Accounts of the 23 August deliberations indicate that bad weather was not a factor for consideration.

More significant gatekeeping on 23 August excluded the ranking marine officers in Tokyo: Generals Lemuel Shepherd Jr. (commander, Fleet Marine Forces, Pacific) and Oliver Smith (commanding the newly arriving First Marine Division for Inchon). Although he helped MacArthur obtain JCS authorization for bringing the division to Korea, Shepherd opposed its use at Inchon, "where a landing would be the most difficult you can imagine."[107] Smith, upon arrival in Tokyo on 22 August, first learned about Inchon during a twenty-minute meeting with Doyle and "wasn't very happy with it." Within two hours Smith met General Almond and voiced "objections to Inchon as a landing site." Calling him "son," Almond "annoyed" Smith by saying that "this amphibious stuff is just a mechanical option," causing the marine's conclusion that there was "a complete lack of understanding at GHQ concerning the manner in which amphibious operations were mounted out." Almond then "briefed" MacArthur in private before leading Smith into the supreme commander's office. MacArthur tried unsuccessfully to convert Smith by saying: "The landing of the Marines at Inchon will be decisive. It will win the war and the status of the Marine Corps should never again be in doubt."[108] Both Smith and Shepherd were excluded from the meeting with Collins and Sherman.[109] For, if there, either marine might provide *the* representative anecdote to counteract MacArthur's about Quebec: Tarawa.

"Mechanical difficulties" at Tarawa during World War II contributed to one of the "bloodiest battles" whose "high cost in American lives was . . . a profound shock not only to the people back home but also to the planners of the invasion; every subsequent move in the drive across the central Pacific was to be made with the mistakes of Tarawa in mind." The American public was outraged by newspaper pictures of dead marines "floating in the tide, or piled on the beach" at "Terrible Tarawa," and "angry editorials demanded a Congressional inquiry into 'the Tarawa fiasco.'"[110] Major landing problems were the *same* as those at Inchon: tide and seawalls. From landing craft stranded on coral reefs, marines waded ashore chest deep, as far as four hundred yards, against gunfire making the water bloody from bodies awash in the lagoon. In the seventy-six-hour fight to take an island less than half the size of Central Park in New York, 1,027 marines were killed and 2,292 wounded. Smith and Shepherd could invoke that example if asked or simply through their presence, so patent were the parallels. Although neither man landed at Tarawa, their professional peers did, and in "the ritual of military memory" carnage there had "special vividness" impelling a "moral obligation" to tell others of what they experienced to avoid the same mistakes in "subsequent military policy."[111]

Indeed, "Tarawa" remained rhetorically potent for years thereafter. In a Pentagon briefing for the pivotal decision makers during the Cuban Missile Crisis, the commandant of the Marine Corps, General David M. Shoup, vividly made his point during deliberations about what to do in response to Russian missiles being placed on launch pads in Cuba:

When talk about invading Cuba was becoming fashionable, General Shoup did a remarkable display with maps. First he took an overlay of Cuba and placed it over the map of the United States. To everybody's surprise, Cuba was not a small island along the lines of, say, Long Island at best. It was about 800 miles long and seemed to stretch from New York to Chicago. Then he took another overlay, with a red dot, and placed it over the map of Cuba. "What's that?" someone asked him. "That, gentlemen, represents the size of the island of Tarawa," said Shoup, who had won a Medal of Honor there, "and it took us three days and eighteen thousand Marines to take." He eventually became Kennedy's favorite general.[112]

The example complemented Kennedy's favorable impression about Shoup's "lucid and incisive" statements and how, "as usual, your views went to the heart of the issue involved, and were praiseworthy for their direct and unequivocal manner of expression."[113] With marine generals excluded on 23 August 1950, "Terrible Tarawa" could not counteract "Quebec."

On 15 September 1950 the First Marine Division landed at Inchon. Despite bad weather, the assault "proceeded more or less as designed" to be "one of the easiest landings" in modern warfare.[114] MacArthur's Inchon summary report truthfully said: "Events of the past two weeks have been decisive. . . . The backbone of the North Korean army has been broken and their scattered forces are being liquidated."[115] By Thanksgiving MacArthur's forces had swept through North Korea and were at the Yalu River border with Communist China. All this happened, however, because MacArthur's rhetoric on 23 August 1950 counteracted professional estimates of Doyle, his staff, and previous convictions of Collins and Sherman. So, Inchon now is a "twentieth-century Cannae, ever to be studied" as "a daring and brave conception, brilliantly executed and worthy of study as a precedent of amphibious excellence."[116] And in its way "Inchon" encompasses as much a representative anecdote as "Valley Forge" for sacrifice, "Waterloo" for total defeat, "Maginot Line" for outmoded military planning, or "Pearl Harbor" for sneak attack.

Conclusion

Martial decision making is not simply a matter of objective estimates of the capabilities of both one's own forces and those of the enemy, including assessments of numbers of personnel, ease of their movements, sophistication and reliability of their equipment, support of allies (or lacks thereof), and predictions about outcomes—both tactical and strategic. To affect outcomes of those deliberations, for good or ill, commanders inevitably engage in rhetoric as the process of "*adjusting ideas to people and people to ideas.*"[117] Rhetorical acumen exercised therein can be a significant variable as it motivates others to courage or caution, particularly when compounded by commanders' credibility (or its lack) as well as their willingness to suppress information that might influence outcomes of deliberations. But an inescapable result of martial endeavors can be widespread suffering and death. With increasing television coverage of commanders in various statements before and during martial endeavors, their communication capabilities acquire increasing importance for rhetorical critics.

Notes

1. John Keegan, *Six Armies in Normandy* (London: Viking Press, 1982), 120–21.

2. Brian Loring Villa, *Unauthorized Action: Montbatten and the Dieppe Raid* (Toronto: Oxford University Press, 1989), 93. See also 1–14.

3. The translation I use is that of Lane Cooper, *The Rhetoric of Aristotle* (New York: Appleton-Century-Crofts, 1932).

4. Douglas MacArthur, *Reminiscences* (New York: McGraw-Hill, 1964), 349.

5. My earlier attempt to explicate this speech appeared as "General Douglas MacArthur's Oratory on Behalf of Inchon: Discourse that Altered the Course of History," *Southern Communication Journal* 58 (Fall 1992): 1–12.

6. After Lloyd Bitzer, "The Rhetorical Situation," *Philosophy and Rhetoric* 1 (January 1968): 1–16.

7. Max Hastings, *The Korean War* (New York: Simon and Schuster, 1987), 53. Although it was an independent nation for centuries, Korea between 1876 and 1897 was pressured by Japan for open ports and extraterritorial rights. Finally, from a position of strength in the Russo-Japanese War, Japan invaded Korea and made it a protectorate in 1904. During World War II the Allies' 1943 meeting in Cairo decreed that "Korea should become free and independent 'in due course.'" Anticipating overwhelming difficulties invading Japan, the United States at the Potsdam Conference in July 1945 urged Russia to enter the Pacific war (the USSR and Japan had not declared war on each other)—for American military leaders "regarded the Japanese armies still deployed in Korea and Manchuria as a tough nut for the Red Army to crack and were only too happy to leave the problem, and the expected casualties, to the Russians." After two atomic bombs dropped on 6 and 9 August brought Japan "to the brink of surrender," the Red Army swept through Manchuria and into Korea. Only then did the United States participate by occupying Korea. Russia stopped at the 38th Parallel, and American troops landed hurriedly to occupy Korea's southern half. By 1949 U.S. and Russian armies withdrew from Korea leaving, respectively, the Republic of Korea under Syngman Rhee, with modest but overrated armed forces—and a communist government under Kim Il Sung, with a well-trained and equipped North Korean Peoples Army. See Hastings, *Korean War*, 23–45; and Clay Blair, *The Forgotten War: America in Korea, 195–1953* (New York: Times Books and Random House, 1987), 30–61.

8. Drawn from occupation forces in Japan, these first U.S. combat troops in Korea were 403 men of the 1st Battalion, 21st Regiment, of the 24th Infantry Division. Flown to Pusan from Japan, the unit went by train and truck up to Osan; only 185 men of the battalion met muster five days later. See Hastings, *Korean War*, 15–22; and Blair, *Forgotten War*, 91–103.

9. See Blair, *Forgotten War*, 89–93; and Lynn Montross and Captain Nicholas A. Canzona, USMC, *U.S. Marine Operations in Korea, 1950–1953*, vol. 2: *The*

Inchon-Seoul Operation (Washington, D.C.: Headquarters U.S. Marine Corps, 1955), 8.

10. For a brief, authoritative overview of the early, disastrous stages of the Korean War, see Russell F. Weigley, *The American Way of War: A History of United States Military Strategy and Policy* (New York: Macmillan, 1973), 382–86. As Hastings observes, "fear of being outflanked and cut off became an obsession in many units. 'Bugout fever,' the urge to withdraw precipitately in the face of the slightest threat from the flank, was . . . a serious problem." See Hastings, *Korean War*, 81.

11. See ibid., 80; and Blair, *Forgotten War*, 141, 172–73 (Walker's statement is reprinted on 168); Bevin Alexander, *Korea: The First War We Lost* (New York: Hippocrene Books, 1986), 120; Michael Langley, *Inchon Landing: MacArthur's Last Triumph* (New York: Times Books, 1979), 11; or Roy E. Appleman, *South to the Naktong, North to the Yalu: The United States Army in the Korean War* (Washington, D.C.: Office of the Chief of Military History, 1961), 207. In addition to the 24th Division, the Pusan Perimeter soon was defended as well by the 25th Infantry Division, the 1st Cavalry Division, Marines of the First Provisional Brigade, and two British battalions from Hong Kong. "Dunkirk" refers to the epic evacuation in 1940 of over 300,000 British troops off an open beach, during four days of constant bombing, strafing, and shelling by German forces. Hindsight says another Dunkirk would not have occurred at Pusan. The UN buildup of forces and massed firepower, coupled with air supremacy, would have precluded that possibility, particularly when North Korean supply lines were increasingly longer and susceptible to interdiction by air. UN forces soon were receiving supplies at "the rate of about 1,000 tons a day," whereas the NKPA "was running out of tanks, artillery, trucks, ammo, gasoline, and medical supplies." Conventional military wisdom holds that any attacking force must have significant numerical superiority over entrenched defenders, and the NKPA had suffered "perhaps 20,000 to 30,000 casualties in the August fighting." See Blair, *Forgotten War*, 223; and Langley, *Inchon Landing*, 19–20.

12. Army Chief of Staff General J. Lawton Collins admitted these advantages in retrospect. See his book *War in Peacetime: The Lessons of Korea* (Boston: Houghton Mifflin, 1969), 120.

13. Collins, *War in Peacetime*, 115. See also James F. Schnabel, *The United States Army in the Korean War: Policy and Direction: The First Year* (Washington, D.C.: Office of the Chief of Military History, 1972), 139; as well as Malcolm W. Cagle and Frank A. Manson, *The Sea War in Korea* (Annapolis: United States Naval Institute, 1957), 75.

14. Blair, *Forgotten War*, 87.

15. Schnabel, *United States Army*, 140. Their mission was prompted initially by JCS needs to assess firsthand conditions in Korea, gather information about Communist China's possibly entering the conflict, and ascertain validity of MacArthur's urgent pleas on 7 and 9 July for more troops. See Collins, *War in Peacetime*, 77–85.

16. In Phillip S. Meilinger, *Hoyt S. Vandenberg: The Life of a General* (Bloomington: Indiana University Press, 1989), 165.

17. Schnabel, *United States Army*, 141. After being involved with marine landings "at Guadalcanal and Tulagi in 1942, Doyle had taken part in several ship-to-shore assaults of World War II. Afterward, as commander of Amphibious Shipping for the Pacific Fleet, he had made a career of it." See Montross and Canzona, *U.S. Marine Operations*, 3–5, 38.

18. Ibid., 41–42.

19. Robert Debs Heinl Jr., *Victory at High Tide: The Inchon-Seoul Campaign* (New York: J. B. Lippincott, 1968), 25–26.

20. Schnabel, *United States Army*, 146–47; Hasting, *Korean War*, 105. See also photographs of LSTs stranded on mud flats (176); or in Heinl, *Victory at High Tide*, 108–9; and Lt. General Victor H. Krulak, *First to Fight: An Inside View of the U.S. Marine Corps* (Annapolis: Naval Institute Press, 1984), 138–39.

21. See U. S. Navy photographs of the 5th Marines at Red Beach, in Heinl, *Victory at High Tide*, 108–9; photographs of landing craft bows on the seawalls also appear in Hastings, *Korean War*, 146–47.

22. Montross and Canzona, *U.S. Marine Operations*, 42. See also Andrew Geer, *The New Breed: The Story of the U.S. Marines in Korea* (New York: Harper, 1952), 112.

23. In Heinl, *Victory at High Tide*, 24; as well as Cagle and Manson, *Sea War*, 81.

24. Schnabel, *United States Army*, 148–49.

25. Gen. Lawton J. Collins, *Lightning Joe: An Autobiography* (Baton Rouge: Louisiana State University Press, 1979), 365.

26. Harry S. Truman, *Years of Trial and Hope* (Garden City, N.Y.: Doubleday, 1956), 348. In retrospect, Truman bluntly called MacArthur "a dumb son of a bitch." See Merle Miller, *Plain Speaking: An Oral Biography of Harry S. Truman* (New York: Berkley Publishing, 1973), 287. See also Blair, *Forgotten War*, 230.

27. Heinl, *Victory at High Tide*, 23–24; Sherman is quoted in Collins, *War in Peacetime*, 121.

28. Krulak, *First to Fight*, 131; and Schnabel, *United States Army*, 149.

29. MacArthur, *Reminiscences*, 347. In correspondence to naval historians in 1956, MacArthur expressed the same view that Collins and Sherman came to Tokyo to convince him not to land at Inchon. See Cagle and Manson, *Sea War*, 75–76.

30. See Blair, *Forgotten War*, 230; and Heinl, *Victory at High Tide*, 40.

31. Blair, *Forgotten War*, 231.

32. As described by Doyle to Capt. Walter Karig, USNR, Cmdr. Malcolm W. Cagle, USN, and Lt. Cmdr. Frank A. Manson, USN, for *Battle Report* (New York: Rinehart and Company, 1952), 167.

33. Montross and Canzona, *U.S. Marine Operations*, 45; Heinl, *Victory at High Tide*, 40; and Collins, *Autobiography*, 366.

34. See Montross and Canzona, *U.S. Marine Operations*, 44.

35. Doyle recalled his words for Karig, Cagle, and Manson. This account of the meeting's opening also is reconstructed from Blair, *Forgotten War*, 230–31; Collins, *War in Peacetime*, 121–22; Heinl, *Victory at High Tide*, 40; Montross and Canzona, *U.S. Marine Operations*, 44–46; and Schnabel, *United States Army*, 149–50.

36. In Collins, *War in Peacetime*, 124–25. See also Blair, *Forgotten War*, 231; MacArthur, *Reminiscences*, 349; Schnabel, *United States Army*, 150; and Alexander, *Korea*, 172.

37. Lt. Gen. Edward M. Almond, "How Inchon Korea was Chosen for the X Corps Amphibious Landing there on 15 September 1950," Korean War Diaries and Personal Notes, Record Group-38, box 3, Douglas MacArthur Archives, Norfolk, Va.; hereafter cited as RG, DMA.

38. Collins, *Autobiography*, 366–67.

39. Quoted in Krulak, *First to Fight*, 131; Blair, *Forgotten War*, 231; Heinl, *Victory at High Tide*, 41; and Hastings, *Korean War*, 101–2.

40. Heinl, *Victory at High Tide*, 41. In his *Reminiscences* MacArthur's version of the speech is on 349–50.

41. A participant offered that recollection during interviews in 1985 with Hastings, for *The Korean War*, 13, 101. The sentence addressed to "Commander" probably was directed either to Cmdr. Edmund Marshall, who talked about "navigation" or Lt. Cmdr. Jack L. Lowentrout, who presented "Beach Study" aspects of the briefing. See Montross and Canzona, *U.S. Marine Operations*, 45. See also MacArthur's *Reminiscences*, 349.

42. Blair, *Forgotten War*, 228.

43. MacArthur, *Reminiscences*, 349.

44. Heinl, *Victory at High Tide*, 41; cited correspondence between Heinl and Doyle about the meeting took place in 1966 (see 273 n. 41). The "John Wayne" remark is quoted in Krulak, *First to Fight*, 131. Although Krulak himself did not attend the meeting, he was on Doyle's staff then and heard reports of the event the next day.

45. Edward M. Almond to Walt Sheldon, 10 April 1967, Almond Papers, RG-38, box 4, DMA.

46. MacArthur, *Reminiscences*, 349; and Heinl, *Victory at High Tide*, 41.

47. After Walter R. Fisher, "Narration as a Human Communication Paradigm: The Case of Public Moral Argument," *Communication Monographs* 51 (March 1984): 1–22.

48. Cagle and Manson, *Sea War*, 82–83. Struble himself was not opposed to Inchon: "After a personal study of the problem, I could appreciate why General MacArthur had chosen Inchon: it was the prize gem if we could take it. After careful study, and after the plans had been completed, I was convinced we could take it. I also formed the impression that our chances for a fair amount of surprise at Inchon were good."

49. Quoted in Heinl, *Victory at High Tide*, 3. See also Blair, *Forgotten War*, 227; and General of the Army Omar N. Bradley and Clay Blair, *A General's Life* (New York: Simon and Schuster, 1983), 510.

50. See Heinl, *Victory at High Tide*, 6–7; and Langley, *Inchon Landing*, 10. For overviews of America's changing defense posture after World War II, see Heinl, *Victory at High Tide*, 3–13; and Blair, *Forgotten War*, 3–61.

51. Gen. Lemuel Shepherd, *Oral History Transcript*, 147–48, in the U.S. Marines Corps Historical Museum, Washington, D.C., Navy Yard.

52. Heinl, *Victory at High Tide*, 7–9.

53. Blair, *Forgotten War*, 227, 253. In another view Sherman may have been far more concerned about the navy per se than its marines, for Heinl suggests that Sherman was "never a Marine Corps enthusiast" (*Victory at High Tide*, 22).

54. MacArthur, *Reminiscences*, 350; Blair, *Forgotten War*, 232; and Heinl, *Victory at High Tide*, 42.

55. Adm. George W. Anderson Jr., *Oral History Typescript Reminiscences*, 124; and "Remarks by Captain John E. Sherman, USN, at the USS FORREST SHERMAN (DD 931) Decommissioning Ceremony," 5 November 1982, in the Forrest Sherman Papers, MS Collection no. 70, box 1, "Correspondence, 1942–1951; Miscellany, including clippings," Naval War College Archives, Newport, R.I.

56. "Campaign Plan for Operations of the Pacific Ocean Areas, 1944," Naval War College Archives.

57. In D. Clayton James, *The Years of MacArthur*, vol. 2: *1941–1945* (Boston: Houghton Mifflin, 1975), 402. For other discussion of Sherman's meetings with MacArthur during World War II, see 399, 569, 588, 604.

58. Thomas B. Buell, *The Quiet Warrior: A Biography of Admiral Raymond A. Spruance* (Boston: Little, Brown, 1974), 308–10.

59. Almond, Korean War Diaries and Personal Notes.

60. In the Sherman Papers, box 1, includes both Nimitz's memorandum to Sherman as well as the clipping "A Model Communiqué," *New York Times*, 1 November 1944.

61. In correspondence of 19 March 1956 to Cagle and Manson, *Sea War*, 76.

62. Cagle and Manson, *Sea War*, 81.

63. Blair, *Forgotten War*, 227.

64. See discussions in Montross and Canzona, *U.S. Marine Operations*, 48; Krulak, *First to Fight*, 79, 100; and Geer, *New Breed*, 111.

65. See Collins, *Autobiography*, 366; and *War in Peacetime*, 123–24. See also Blair, *Forgotten War*, 223–24; and Langley, *Inchon Landing*, 51.

66. MacArthur, *Reminiscences*, 349–50.

67. Russell F. Weigley, *The Age of Battles: The Quest for Decisive Warfare from Breitenfeld to Waterloo* (Bloomington: Indiana University Press, 1991), xii.

68. Ibid., 536–37.

69. Ibid., 538.

70. Quoted in Philip L. Follette, *Adventure in Politics* (New York: Holt, Rinehart, and Winston, 1970), 269–70.

71. See Hastings, *Korean War*, 80; Blair, *Forgotten War*, 141, 172–73, 223; and Langley, *Inchon Landing*, 19–20.

72. See Hastings, *Korean War*, 81.

73. MacArthur, *Reminiscences*, 350.

74. Blair, *Forgotten War*, 232.

75. William J. Dunn, *Pacific Microphone* (College Station: Texas A&M University Press, 1988), 218; see also 203.

76. Collins, *War in Peacetime*, 126. Although this book appears five years later, Collins may not have taken the quote from MacArthur's *Reminiscences* because it is not cited in his bibliography.

77. MacArthur, *Reminiscences*, 165–66.

78. Weigley, *Age of Battles*, xiv–xv.

79. Almond, "How Inchon Korea Was Chosen for the X Corps Amphibious Landing." Almond suggests that "at first General MacArthur favored the landing of the amphibious force in the vicinity of WONSON on the east coast of Korea and the best port in the area on either side of the Peninsula, but be recognized that it was some 135 miles by road from SEOUL. Finally, the landing area of INCHON HARBOR was chosen because of its nearness (18 miles) to the objective, SEOUL, and in spite of the known difficulties of the tidal range (31 feet) and its limited harbor facilities."

80. D. Clayton James, *Refighting the Last War: Command and Crisis in Korea, 1950–1953* (New York: Free Press, 1993), 4, 157.

81. MacArthur, *Reminiscences*, 349.

82. Edward M. Almond, Lt. Gen., USA, "Headquarters X Corps War Diary Summary for Operation Chromite, 15 August to 30 September 1950," 5–6, Almond Papers, RG-38, box 3, DMA.

83. Transcripts of prisoner of war interrogations appended to Almond's "War Diary."

84. Heinl, *Victory at High Tide*, 79; Blair, *Forgotten War*, 238; Langley, *Inchon Landing*, 61; as well as Cagle and Manson, *Sea War*, 80.

85. Burke Davis, *Marine! The Life of Lt. General Lewis B. (Chesty) Puller, USMC* (Boston: Little, Brown, 1962), 248.

86. MacArthur, *Reminiscences*, 349.

87. Montross and Canzona, *U.S. Marine Operations*, 46; Blair, *Forgotten War*, 231; Hastings, *Korean War*, 102; Heinl, *Victory at High Tide*, 41; and Langley, *Inchon Landing*, 47. Cagle and Manson paraphrase MacArthur's rationale that North Koreans "would consider a landing at Inchon impossible and insane, and would be taken by surprise" (*Sea War*, 78). In *American Caesar: Douglas MacArthur 1880–1964* (Boston: Little, Brown, 1978) William Manchester quotes the entire example (575).

88. Collins, *War in Peacetime*, 125–26.

89. Kenneth Burke, *A Grammar of Motives* (New York: Prentice-Hall, 1954), 60, 324.

90. MacArthur, *Reminiscences*, 350.

91. Weigley, *Age of Battles*, 543.

92. Collins, *War in Peacetime*, 127. In briefing Truman upon returning, Collins and Sherman endorsed Inchon in such a way that the president said, "I had the greatest confidence that it would succeed" (see Truman, *Memoirs*, 2:358; as well as Schnabel, *United States Army*, 151; and Blair, *Forgotten War*, 264). The JCS still hedged its bet, however, for the message authorizing Inchon also acknowledged another possible landing site: "We concur in making preparations for executing a turning movement by amphibious forces on the west coast of Korea, either at Inchon in the event the enemy defenses in the vicinity of Inchon prove ineffective, or at a favorable beach south of Inchon if one can be located. We further concur in preparations, if desired by CINCFE [Commander in Chief, Far East] for an envelopment by amphibious forces in the vicinity of Kunsan. We understand that alternative plans are being prepared in order to best exploit the situation as it develops." From his imperious perspective MacArthur read the JCS endorsement differently: "On August 29th I received a wire from the Joint Chiefs of Staff: 'We concur after reviewing the information brought back by General Collins and Admiral Sherman, in making preparations for executing a turning movement by amphibious forces on the west coast of Korea— at Inchon'" (see MacArthur, *Reminiscences*, 351).

93. Brig. Gen. Edwin H. Simmons, USMC (Ret.), "Address to the Association of Survivors Luncheon, Officers Club, Washington Navy Yard, 10 November 1987, in the Simmons Papers, PC no. 957 870 863, Marine Corps Archives and Museum, Washington, D.C., Navy Yard.

94. Brig. Gen. Edwin Simmons, USMC (Ret.), *Oral History*, no. 43, RG-32, DMA.

95. Dunn, *Pacific Microphone*, 6.

96. In D. Clayton James, *The Years of MacArthur*, vol. 2: *1941–1945* (Boston: Houghton Mifflin, 1975), 384–85.

97. In Heinl, *Victory at High Tide*, 130–32.

98. Weigley, *American Way of War*, 385. See also Cagle and Manson (*Sea War*, 78) on MacArthur's "hit 'em where they ain't" philosophy in World War II.

99. MacArthur, *Reminiscences*, 165–66; and Weigley, *American Way of War*, 280–81.

100. Rafael Steinberg, *Island Fighting* (Alexandria, Va.: Time-Life Books, 1978), 134–41.

101. James F. Schnabel and Robert J. Watson, *The Joint Chiefs of Staff and National Policy*, vol. 3: *The Korean War* (Washington, D.C.: Joint Chiefs of Staff Historical Study, 1978), 215; see also Meilinger, 165–66.

102. See the account in Joseph C. Goulden, *Korea: The Untold Story of the War* (New York: McGraw-Hill, 1982), 199, 207, 209.

103. Collins, *War in Peacetime*, 125–26.

104. Deliberate omission of information is not unknown by military commanders. In briefings for the British 6th Airborne Division, which would land in France on D-Day, General Montgomery's headquarters "decided to keep the information from the troops" that the German 21st Panzer Division was deployed in their area of assault—"for fear of dampening their morale" (and, to accompany withholding that information, the 6th Airborne was not provided "adequate antitank weapons"). A similar withholding of such information occurred in September 1944 for the British airborne landings at Arnhem in Operation Market Garden (with disastrous results then for the "Red Devils"). See Stephen E. Ambrose, *D-Day June 6, 1944: The Climactic Battle of World War II* (New York: Simon and Schuster, 1994), 516–17.

105. Adm. Arleigh Burke, *Oral History #21*, 5–6, RG-3, DMA.

106. Lt. Gen. Edward M. Almond, *Oral Reminiscences*, Almond Papers, RG-38, box 4, DMA.

107. Shepherd, *Oral History Transcript*, 170.

108. Gen. Oliver P. Smith, *Oral History Transcript*, 199, in the U.S. Marine Corps Historical Museum, Washington, D.C. See also Smith's *Aide Memoire* entry for 22 August 1950; as well as Geer, *New Breed*, 110–13; Montross and Canzona, *U.S. Marine Operations*, 37–40; Hastings, *Korean War*, 104; and Cagle and Manson, *Sea War*, 78.

109. As Almond explained, "If General Shepherd was not present . . . on 23 August it was not through any design on the part of General MacArthur or anybody else. . . . As far as General Smith's being present is concerned, General Smith had many duties. . . . The fact that he was not at the conference on 23 August may have been a matter of his availability. After all, General Smith was not required at this conference. . . . [His] function as landing force commander was that of carrying out the decision of the overall commander" (see Heinl, *Victory at High Tide*, 40, 272–73 n. 40). Some accounts have Shepherd or Smith or both attending the meeting (e.g., Montross and Canzona, *U.S. Marine Operations*, 44; as well as Hastings, *Korean War*, 101). These are in error, as demonstrated in the Heinl-Almond correspondence.

110. Steinberg, *Island Fighting*, 104–31; see in particular 106, 118. See also Ronald Spector, *Eagle against the Sun: The American War with Japan* (New York: Free Press, 1985), 266; and C. L. Sulzberger, *The American Heritage Picture History of World War II* ([New York]: American Heritage Publishing Company, 1966), 364.

111. Paul Fussell, *The Great War and Modern Memory* (New York: Oxford University Press, 1975), 326 ff., 317.

112. In David Halberstam, *The Best and the Brightest* (New York: Random House, 1969), 66–67. This event was verified for me, personally, by the current director, Marine Corps Museums and Archives, Brig Gen. Edwin H. Simmons, USMC (Ret.). On Shoup's staff, then, Simmons prepared the map display that Shoup used.

113. John F. Kennedy to Gen. David M. Shoup, 3 February 1962, box 31, Shoup Papers, Hoover Institution on War, Revolution, and Peace, Stanford University.

114. Blair, *Forgotten War*, 270–71.

115. For an overview of the Inchon campaign see Blair, *Forgotten War*, 267–94; Heinl's is the comprehensive account. To Cagle and Manson "the Inchon landing can be credited with ending the North Korean aggression, for in a matter of days the entire half of the peninsula below the 38th parallel had been recaptured by the UN forces, and the North Korean Army was a beaten and broken army" (*Sea War*, 102).

116. Langley, *Inchon Landing*, 21; and David Rees, *Korea: The Limited War* (New York: St. Martin's Press and Macmillan, 1964), 96.

117. Donald C. Bryant, *Rhetorical Dimensions in Criticism* (Baton Rouge: Louisiana State University Press, 1973), 11, 19. Bryant's earlier expression of this definition was in "Rhetoric: Its Functions and Its Scope," *Quarterly Journal of Speech* 39 (December 1953): 401–24.

CHAPTER EIGHT

Martial Decision Making
MacArthur, Inchon,
and the Dimensions of Rhetoric

Martin J. Medhurst

Professor Carpenter has presented a compelling analysis of the role of rhetoric in military decision making. It is an Aristotelian analysis that focuses on the ethical mode of proof, the power of example, and the recourse to common topics such as courage and caution. Like many Aristotelian readings, Carpenter's is insightful and persuasive—as far as it goes. It does not, however, go far enough and, consequently, affords a highly circumscribed view both of rhetorical art in general and deliberative rhetoric in military settings specifically.

In the effort to broaden the scope of analysis I propose to examine Carpenter's central example—MacArthur's decision to launch a counteroffensive at Inchon—through the lens of Brockriede's essay "Dimensions of the Concept of Rhetoric," first introduced in 1968 as "a framework for theoretical development, practical decision-making, and critical analysis."[1] Central to Brockriede's framework is his conception of rhetoric as "the study of how interpersonal relationships and attitudes are influenced within a situational context."[2] Hence, interpersonal, attitudinal, and situational dimensions form the superstructure of what, for me, will be an instrument of critical analysis and theoretical probing.

Carpenter's central contention is that "MacArthur's oratory was *the* pivotal factor in crucial deliberations in Tokyo on 23 August 1950." He writes of MacArthur's "grandiloquence," his "Churchillian oration," his "brilliant exposition," and how MacArthur left his hearers "spellbound." Although he does not explicitly say so, Carpenter leaves the distinct impression that MacArthur's speech succeeded because of its power to enchant and beguile the audience. Like the Gorgianic discourses of the First Sophistic, MacArthur is pictured as working magic on his listeners, his rhetoric a powerful drug that banished, bypassed, and ultimately overcame the reasoning powers of his listeners. Adding to the mythopoesis is the fact that the speech is lost to history. It was delivered extemporaneously, without notes, and no recording or transcription exists. It lives on only in the memories of the person who gave it, the handful of military officers who heard it, and the slightly larger group who heard about it in the days or weeks immediately following. In ceasing to exist, the speech became eternal, immortal, and, like all sacred texts, overlaid with multiple layers of "tellings," each slightly grander than the one preceding.

While I have no doubt about MacArthur's ability to produce a speech such as the one attributed to him on 23 August 1950, I do have serious reservations about singling the speech out as *the* factor in the approval of the Inchon invasion plan. Other factors, equally rhetorical in nature, operating both through and in concert with but apart from the speech, were of equal—and, I would argue, even greater—significance. The nature and import of these other factors can be recognized by systematically applying Brockriede's three dimensions of interpersonal, attitudinal, and situational factors to this rhetorical act.

The Interpersonal Dimension

The three main components of the interpersonal dimension are liking, power, and distance. Each played a central role in the decision on behalf of Inchon.

MacArthur was not well liked—not by President Truman, not by Secretary of State Acheson, and not by many of his colleagues of general and flag rank in the military, including, most particularly, the officer who had served as MacArthur's right hand for more than seven consecutive years, Dwight D. Eisenhower.[3] One need not search long for the reasons. As MacArthur biographer William Manchester notes: "He was, among other things, extremely devious."[4] Toward no one was this deviousness practiced more openly, more systematically, and with greater negative consequences than Harry S. Truman. Even during the planning and execution of Inchon, MacArthur could not bring himself to conform to American policy—one in a long line of indiscretions that nearly cost him his command even before the invasion was launched. Even those colleagues who did like MacArthur, such as General Matthew Ridgway, testified to his essentially dishonest character. In his book *The Korean War* Ridgway writes:

I came to understand some traits of his complex character not generally recognized: the hunger for praise that led him on some occasions to claim or accept credit for deeds he had not performed, or to disclaim responsibility for mistakes that were clearly his own; the love of the limelight that continually prompted him to pose before the public as the actual commander on the spot at every landing and at the launching of every major attack in which his ground troops took part; his tendency to cultivate isolation that genius seems to require, until it became a sort of insulation . . . that deprived him of the critical comment and objective appraisals a commander needs from his principal subordinates; the headstrong quality . . . that sometimes led him to persist in a course in defiance of all seeming logic; a faith in his own judgment that created an aura of infallibility and that finally led him close to insubordination.[5]

It is not hard to see why MacArthur was not well liked by those with whom he had the closest contact. MacArthur clearly understood that he was not the president's favorite general and that the Joint Chiefs of Staff, led by General Omar Bradley, were an obstacle to be overcome, not an ally to embrace. This self-realization notably affected MacArthur's argumentative strategy on the afternoon of 23 August 1950. Unable to draw on any degree of interpersonal liking to win over his inquisitors, MacArthur chose to build his case on the self-interests of his listeners— especially those representing the navy—and the impeccable logic of his plan. No one had to like MacArthur to recognize in the logos of his plan not just a daring and dangerous mission but also a well-conceived and strategically brilliant blueprint. Contra Carpenter, it was not MacArthur's ethos or eloquence that sold the Inchon landing to the Joint Chiefs but his logos—the ideas, reasoning, and creative use of all the universally recognized lines of argument, the special topoi—concerning tactical warfare.

The second part of Brockriede's interpersonal dimension is power, defined as "the capacity to exert interpersonal influence."[6] Clearly, it is this element that Carpenter sees as central to MacArthur's success, as the general wielded influence through the agency of his oratory. Yet this is only one facet of the power dimension. Moreover, if one were to grant MacArthur's charismatic hold over his listeners, a hold characterized by such descriptors as *mesmerized,*[7] *hypnotized,*[8] *compelling,*[9] and *spell-*

bound,[10] that element does not erase the other sources of power at work in the situation.

First, MacArthur possessed positional power. As the commander in chief, Far East (CINCFE), MacArthur was in charge of all U.S. forces in Asia. As the supreme commander for the Allied Powers (SCAP), he would eventually lead forces from seventeen different countries under the authority of the United Nations. Carpenter has noted how MacArthur used his positional power to include or exclude particular officers from his meeting with General Collins and Admiral Sherman on 23 August. By virtue of occupying the highest position in a very hierarchical bureaucracy, MacArthur could control all aspects of his environment. Even Collins and Sherman, though legally MacArthur's superiors by virtue of their positions on the Joint Chiefs of Staff, did not outrank MacArthur, who, as a five-star general, was one of only five generals of the army in 1950. Of the Joint Chiefs only Omar Bradley held equivalent rank. Clearly, MacArthur enjoyed a position of almost unlimited power.

A second source of this power was MacArthur's control over the channels of communication. From 29 June, when he first conceived the idea of an amphibious envelopment, until the attack commenced on 15 September, MacArthur repeatedly used both his positional power and his control of the channels of information to press his cause. He intentionally withheld information from the State Department, acted as though the time and place of the invasion were still open questions, scheduled private talks with decision makers known to oppose his point of view, and engaged in delaying tactics to ensure that the Inchon invasion would take place as he envisioned. If, as Carpenter contends, it was the extemporaneous oration of 23 August which secured the invasion plan, then why was MacArthur still being questioned by the Joint Chiefs of Staff five days later, on 28 August? On that date the chiefs cabled to MacArthur:

> After reviewing the information brought back by General Collins and Admiral Sherman we concur in making preparations and executing a turning movement by amphibious forces on the west coast of Korea, either at Inchon . . . or at a favorable beach south of Inchon if one can be located. We further concur in preparation, if desired . . . for envelopment by amphibious forces in the vicinity of Kunsan. We understand that alternative plans are being prepared in order to best exploit the situation as it develops. We desire

such information as it becomes available with respect to conditions in the possible objective areas and timely information as to your intentions and plans for offensive operations.[11]

Clearly, the Joint Chiefs felt as though they were being kept in the dark—and they were. While they had given tentative approval to land at Inchon, they had also approved Kunsan and were apparently under the impression that they would have some further input in the decision-making process. This was not to be. As Clay Blair notes: "Perhaps fearing that the JCS would ultimately order a cancellation of Inchon, MacArthur embarked on an astounding course of deceit and deception designed to thwart such an order. He did not reply at all to the JCS August 28 cable. On August 30, Tokyo time, he issued operational orders for Inchon to proceed in accordance with his plan. However, he deliberately delayed sending copies of his operational order to the Pentagon. They would not arrive in Washington until September 8, one week before the Inchon D Day."[12] For someone whose oratory had supposedly carried the day less than a week before, MacArthur's use and abuse of his positional and gatekeeping powers seems to point to a certain lack of confidence in the permanence of those persuasive efforts. The notion that MacArthur, through the power of personal charisma and incantatory oratory, swept the Joint Chiefs off their collective feet and compelled their assent may have romantic appeal, but the whole story of Inchon would seem to point to a more realist, perhaps even Machiavellian, interpretation. MacArthur possessed various types of power and used each to the fullest degree.

Interpersonal distance also played a role in MacArthur's advocacy on behalf of Inchon. Because he was not particularly well liked and because he was far older, far more experienced, and of much higher rank than the men about him, MacArthur occupied a space—geographically, physically, and psychologically—all to himself. By 1950 he had been in the Far East for almost fourteen years. He had been away from the United States for so long that his geographical separation became part of the myth of MacArthur. The general and the East were one: distant, remote, mysterious, and unfathomable. MacArthur used this geographical separation and identity to his rhetorical advantage. He was always too far away and too busy to return to the United States. Hence, a long line of official emissaries were forced to travel to his abode, to meet on his turf, if they wished to communicate with him. On 13 July it was General

Collins and Air Force Chief Hoyt Vandenberg; on 6 August, Averell Harriman; on 12 August, Admiral Sherman; on 23 August, Collins and Sherman; and, finally, on 15 October, Harry Truman, who only had to go as far as Wake Island, still well within MacArthur's sphere of influence.

The geographical separation was paralleled by a physical separation at the Tokyo headquarters. Access to MacArthur was severely restricted. A palace guard, led by MacArthur's chief of staff, General Ned Almond, kept MacArthur from being bothered by interlopers—or people bringing messages that MacArthur did not wish to hear. As Carpenter reports, during the planning for Inchon both Admiral Burke and Admiral Joy tried to talk with MacArthur about the weather conditions, only to be turned away by General Almond. This physical isolation could not have improved the interpersonal distance between MacArthur and his colleagues. What Ridgway described as MacArthur's "insulation" led directly to what Marine General O. P. Smith labeled "an indignation meeting,"[13] following MacArthur's refusal at the 23 August meeting to credit navy objections to Inchon as a landing site.

But no distance was greater—or, ultimately, more harmful—than that created psychologically between MacArthur and his subordinates. The general had a profound belief that he alone among military or civilian leaders truly understood the Orient. This self-conception was the basis for repeated attempts to silence his critics, especially those in Washington, "by chiding them because they simply 'did not understand the oriental mind.'"[14] This psychological perception of distance—both MacArthur's closeness to the thinking patterns of the Far East and Washington's supposed remoteness from and failure to understand those patterns—ultimately had tragic consequences, as subsequent events proved MacArthur to be "completely misguided in his own attempts to read enemy intentions."[15] The connection between psychological distance and ethos was underscored by General Ridgway when he asked:

But how could any man, not obsessed with his own reputation, have persisted in misinterpreting detailed intelligence reports and actual events on the battlefield—not merely the taking of large numbers of Chinese prisoners, clearly belonging to units known to be in the CCF [Chinese Communist Forces] order of battle, but the brutal mauling of a U.S. Regimental Combat Team, and the near-annihilation of an ROK [Republic of Korea] Division? And how could the Commander in Chief not have realized that his forces were too meager, and too thinly supplied, to have held the line of the Yalu and the Tumen—even had he reached it—against an enemy known to be concentrated there in great numbers?[16]

Tragically, MacArthur allowed his previously established ethos, his faith in himself, and his psychic intimacy with the oriental mind to cloud his military judgment. The result was another two and a half years of war and another twenty-five thousand American dead. The immediate precursor to the tragedy was Inchon.

The Attitudinal Dimension

If there were one central attitude that linked the brilliant victory at Inchon with the devastating defeat two months later, as Chinese Communist forces crossed the Yalu River into North Korea, it was the attitude of infallibility evinced by General MacArthur. This attitude manifested itself in many ways: predicting victory even before sizing up a situation; announcing the capture of targets days before they had, in fact, been secured; lecturing colleagues on the "right" course of action, even in the face of overwhelming evidence to the contrary. Although Inchon was a great military victory, it carried with it the unfortunate side effect of validating MacArthur's self-image, which led, in Ridgway's words, to "the development of an almost superstitious regard for General MacArthur's infallibility. Even his superiors, it seemed, began to doubt if they should question *any* of MacArthur's decisions."[17] One of those superiors, Army Chief of Staff J. Lawton Collins, affirmed Ridgway's judgment. "The success of Inchon was so great," wrote Collins, "and the subsequent prestige of General MacArthur was so overpowering, that the Chiefs hesitated thereafter to question later plans and decisions of the general, which should have been challenged."[18]

Central Idea

From the outset of his Korean command MacArthur's central idea was to launch a surprise, rearguard amphibious action at Inchon. He conceived the general idea for such an action on 29 June, only four days after the North Korean invasion commenced, and by 3 July had settled on Inchon as the one and only "right" place to land. Originally scheduled to take place under the code name Operation Bluehearts on 22 July, the counteroffensive had to be postponed because of a lack of men and matériel. It was this delay that gave the JCS time to inquire into the feasibility of MacArthur's daring plan and which ultimately led to the meeting of 23 August. But one should not consider the oratorical performance of that date as though it were isolated from or substantively different than the messages that preceded it or those that followed. As Manchester notes: "In message after message the UN commander bombarded the Pentagon with reasons for an amphibious assault: it would present the PA [People's Army] with a two-front war, starve their troops, cut their communications, seize a large port, and deal the enemy a devastating psychological blow by recapturing Seoul."[19] It is important to note that all of these are *logoi*—reasons—for undertaking the assault. By 25 July MacArthur had convinced the JCS of the soundness of an amphibious operation. The only remaining question was where to strike. For MacArthur, however, the location was never in doubt. The landing, he believed, must be made at Inchon. This became the central idea and motivating force for all of MacArthur's actions from 25 July to 15 September. The fact that "every flag and general officer in Tokyo, including [General] Walker, whose Eighth Army would be freed by a successful drive against the North Korean rear, tried to talk him out of it,"[20] mattered not in the least. It had to be Inchon, not Heiju or Chinnampo further north nor Kunsan or Posung-Myon to the south, even though none of these other locales posed anywhere near the dangers of Inchon. MacArthur was so ego involved in the formulation of the assault plan that no other location, no matter the reasons or rationales, would do. It must be Inchon. MacArthur's recalcitrant attitude on this point was dictated by a complex amalgam of pride, strategic intuition, historical precedent, and realist appraisal.

MacArthur's pride needs little comment. Suffice it to say that, since the New Guinea campaign of 1943, MacArthur was universally recognized as the master of the amphibious end run. He had done it before and was supremely confident of his ability to do it again. MacArthur had a strategic intuition that a landing at Inchon would take the enemy by complete surprise. Using a form of argument from probabilities first perfected by the early Sophists, MacArthur noted that the very reasons why such a landing was considered to be highly dangerous (and therefore improbable) were the same reasons why the enemy would not be expecting an attack at that point, thus allowing U.S. forces to be (probably) victorious. But MacArthur also knew that sea landings at Inchon had historical precedents. In both 1894 and 1904 the Japanese had mounted successful seaborne attacks on Inchon and thereby "seized all Korea."[21] Most important, MacArthur had appraised the plan, now code named Operation Chromite, from both a tactical and strategic viewpoint. He realized that the Pusan Perimeter could not be held indefinitely and that the high casualty rates of June, July, and August could not be sustained for long. It was not mere bombast that led MacArthur to ask his interlocutors on 23 August: "Are you content to let our troops stay in that bloody perimeter like beef cattle in the slaughterhouse? Who will take the responsibility for such a tragedy? Certainly, I will not."[22] MacArthur's point was clear—something had to be done and done quickly. A frontal assault such as those soon to be waged by the Chinese Communists would result in even greater casualties than the effort to hold the perimeter. Clearly, a rearguard action was the preferable tactical solution. But why Inchon? Again, it was not only MacArthur's pride of authorship which suggested the west coast port city but his historical knowledge that such a landing was possible and, even more important, his realization that only Inchon out of all the possible landing sites afforded long-range strategic advantages. As General Collins later wrote:

> Inchon offered rewards that were certainly tempting. A successful landing there, if followed by a quick seizure of nearby Seoul, would sever the enemy's principal supply routes, which radiated into and out of Seoul. Kimpo airfield, the best in South Korea, would fall as part of the drive on Seoul, providing both a good air logistical terminal and an excellent operating base for fighter bombers. The psychological impact of recapturing the traditional political capital of Korea would be enormous and, if the Eighth Army could strike the hammer blow on the anvil of Inchon in time, the North Korean Army might be destroyed.[23]

So MacArthur had ample reasons—all based on a realist appraisal of both the tactical and strategic situations—for his uncompromising attitude toward Inchon as the only proper landing site. This attitude was grounded in a comprehensive appraisal of the military situation. Consequently, counterarguments that focused on only one set of problems—the tides, the seawalls, the mud flats, the weather conditions, the need to pacify Wolmi-do Island before the landing—could not stand against MacArthur's more comprehensive view. In short, MacArthur was able to defend his plan to land at Inchon *not* because he was a great orator per se but because he offered reasoned, irrefutable arguments in a comprehensive format.

A dangerous plan offering possible success was better than the alternatives: continued stalemate with high losses, a frontal attack with even higher losses, a landing at some other coastal city which, while less dangerous, could not yield the strategic objectives of Inchon, or total withdrawal from the peninsula with the resulting damage to U.S. credibility, including the dismantling of the Truman Doctrine and the tacit invitation to the USSR to support aggression elsewhere. When all of the ramifications were considered, MacArthur's plan was adopted not so much because he was oratorically persuasive but because it was the best plan from a strictly military cost-benefit analysis. MacArthur's grandiloquence often masked the fact that his logos—not his ethos and pathos—was the driving force behind his oratory. As Ridgway observed, MacArthur had "an actor's instinct for the dramatic—in tone and gesture. Yet so lucid and so penetrating were his explanations and his analyses that it was his mind rather than his manner or his bodily presence that dominated his listeners."[24] Inchon was finally approved, two weeks after the meeting of 23 August, not because MacArthur's oratory cast a spell over his listeners but because it offered the best chance of success.

Ideology

Closely linked to MacArthur's attitude about Inchon as the proper landing site was the commanding general's overall ideological stance. Put simply, MacArthur was a rigid anticommunist. Less simply, he was a man of high ideals, universal principles, and unflagging devotion to duty—at least as he understood that term. It was at the higher level of ideological abstraction that MacArthur would eventually founder and fall, for not only was his ideological vision narrow and inflexible; it was also in conflict with the vision of the president of the United States.

To MacArthur the task was straightforward: to find the enemy and kill him; to bring victory out of seeming defeat, just as he had done during World War II. What MacArthur never realized, however, was that Korea was not like World War II. The United States was not in Korea to kill as many Communists as possible or to reunify a divided country or to press U.S. hegemony into Manchuria and beyond. Unlike World War II, which, had it not been for the atomic bomb, would have been pressed all the way to Tokyo with a massive invasion of the Japanese mainland, there was no plan and no desire to allow the Korean conflict to escalate into World War III. Truman said as much to MacArthur on several occasions and later noted in his *Memoirs* that "every decision I made in connection with the Korean conflict had this one aim in mind: to prevent a third world war and the terrible destruction it would bring to the civilized world."[25] What MacArthur failed to realize was that both warfare and diplomacy had changed in the five years since the end of the previous war. MacArthur never understood that "American intervention in Korea was primarily symbolic in intention; it was meant to demonstrate to the world America's willingness and ability to aid friends and allies in their struggle to resist Soviet domination. It was a matter of credibility and prestige. It was a matter of timing in relation to events elsewhere. And it was a matter of Truman's demonstrating to the nation and to the world that he was as determined to halt the spread of Communism as was any Republican."[26]

Korea was the first limited war, the first postatomic war, the first shooting war in what was already a Cold War era. It was also the United States' first land war in Asia, fought on the doorstep of the most populous nation on earth, recently turned Communist, and against an enemy who enjoyed the technical and logistical support of the Soviet Union. It was a situation that could easily have led to World War III had Harry Truman held the same attitudinal complex or been operating from the same ideological stance as Douglas MacArthur. In the end there could be only one Asian policy, and it would be formulated by the president and his advisors, not General MacArthur. If MacArthur ever understood the Truman policy, it soon became clear that he was in fundamental disagreement with it and could not, therefore, because of his deeply held ideological beliefs, faithfully execute that policy in the field. Matthew Ridgway accurately reflected MacArthur's ideology, noting that,

> when MacArthur spoke of victory, he did not mean merely victory in Korea—the destruction of all hostile forces on the peninsula and the unification of the country under a democratic government. What he envisaged was no less than the global defeat of Communism, dealing Communism "a blow from which it would never recover" and which would mark the historical turning back of the Red Tide. His "program" included not merely driving to the Yalu, but destroying the air bases and industrial complex in Manchuria;

blockading Communist China's seacoast; demolishing its industrial centers; providing all necessary support to Chiang's invasion
of the mainland; and the transportation of Nationalist Chinese
troops to Korea to beef up our ground forces there. He sincerely
believed that these moves would break the Communist hold on
the mainland.[27]

This was the ideology that motivated all of MacArthur's plans, including the amphibious assault at Inchon, for only an Inchon landing could
lead to the complete destruction of the North Korean Army and open
the way to the Manchurian border. From the outset MacArthur planned
to defeat communism, not just those Communists who happened to be
in North Korea. His was an ideological struggle whose boundaries were
flexible, if not infinite. It was the ways in which these attitudes and assumptions interfaced with the situation as understood and defined in
Washington which eventually resulted in MacArthur's dismissal. Inchon
was the first step along that road.

The Situational Dimension

As Brockriede notes, "A rhetorical act occurs only within a situation, and the nature of that act is influenced profoundly by the nature of
the encompassing situation."[28] Situation, as he defines it, has six dimensions: format, channels, people, functions, method, and contexts.

The formats that dominate military decision making are the conference and the briefing. The meeting of 23 August was a hybrid of the two
formats, with eighty minutes of briefing, including discussion, and forty
minutes of MacArthur's oration. However, it is important to remember
that this was just one meeting out of a long line of exchanges, most of
which were conducted by telecon—the exchange of interlinked and secure teletype messages, which could be projected onto a screen for all
conference participants to see. Clearly, the format of the meeting of 23
August had rhetorical significance: the fact that the navy briefers were
limited to ten minutes apiece, that only one set of briefers was allowed
into the conference room at any one time, and the fact that none of the
briefers was present to hear, and potentially refute, MacArthur's oration on behalf of Inchon. All of these were rhetorically significant factors.
MacArthur spoke last and thus had the advantage of recency as well as
the positional power to end the conference at precisely the point at which
he wished it to end. By controlling the format, MacArthur could shape

both the type and amount of information conveyed and, more important, the opportunity or lack thereof to question and cross-examine participants, especially MacArthur himself. Indeed, there is no record of anyone questioning MacArthur after his oration. Substantively, the general had the last word on 23 August 1950.

While the dominant channels of communication on 23 August were direct, face-to-face oral discourse, many of the other conferences concerning Inchon were indirect, mediated, and conducted from a great distance. That these mediated channels were seen as problematic accounts, in large measure, for the repeated attempts to confront MacArthur face-to-face. The general was an expert, however, at using both direct and mediated channels to his own advantage. In face-to-face communication he was a consummate rhetor. As Ridgway notes: "General MacArthur was not merely a military genius. He was a brilliant advocate who could argue his point with so much persuasiveness that men determined to stand up against him were won to enthusiastic support."[29]

Although face-to-face channels were MacArthur's forte, he also knew how to use mediated channels to his own advantage. This he did by fixing on those aspects of the mediated message with which he agreed and ignoring those with which he did not. This practice appears to have been an intentional strategy on MacArthur's part, for it happened repeatedly—before, during, and after Inchon. Obviously, this penchant for selective interpretation was problematic, especially for Washington. Secretary of State Dean Acheson later wrote that the Truman administration had learned "to fear General MacArthur bearing explanations,"[30] for those explanations always seemed somehow to miss the main idea, whether on U.S. policy toward Formosa, planning for the rearguard assault, or the rules of engagement for pursuing the enemy across the 38th Parallel. MacArthur's interpretation and execution of official policy were often difficult to fathom, much less excuse. Ridgway eloquently understates the case by observing that "this wholly human failing of discounting or ignoring all unwelcome facts seemed developed beyond the average in MacArthur's nature."[31] Ultimately, the channels of communication made little difference simply because MacArthur had both the capacity and the will to subvert all communications to his predetermined ends.

While Carpenter's essay necessarily and rightfully focuses on the military decision makers, one must keep always in mind that in the U.S. system the military is always advisory to the civilian executive. It is the president, or in some cases Congress, who ultimately makes decisions, not the military leadership. Hence, even if MacArthur had convinced the Joint Chiefs in as thorough a manner as Carpenter seems to claim during the 23 August meeting, that persuasion *alone* could not have saved the Inchon operation. First, MacArthur spoke to only two of the four members of the JCS; second, the JCS were only advisory to the president and his cabinet. Because of these facts, the claim that the inventional topoi of courage and caution were central seems overstated, especially for the immediate audience. Carpenter points to MacArthur's remembrance of his father's warning about councils of war breeding timidity and adds to this Aristotle's observation about "elderly men" who have lived long and often been deceived. This is a marvelous quotation, but it hardly applies either to MacArthur's immediate audience or to his more distant one. In point of fact, the only "elderly" person at the 23 August meeting was MacArthur himself, who was closing in on his seventy-first birthday. The other participants were in the prime of life—General Collins was fifty-four, Admiral Sherman fifty-three, Chairman of the Joint Chiefs, Omar Bradley, was fifty-seven, and Air Force Chief Hoyt Vandenberg was fifty-one. The civilians in Washington were likewise in their prime years. Secretary of State Acheson was fifty-seven, Defense Secretary Louis Johnson was fifty-nine, Army Secretary Frank Pace was thirty-eight, and Deputy Under Secretary of State Dean Rusk was forty-one. A truly elderly decision maker was nowhere to be found, with the possible exception of Harry Truman, who was sixty-six. And, ultimately, that is what the battle over decision making came down to: MacArthur versus Truman—the oldest men involved in the conflict, neither lacking courage and neither all that cautious (although Truman, fortunately, had a palace guard composed of aides such as Clark Clifford and Charles Murphy to screen his more imprudent outbursts).

The plain fact was that MacArthur neither trusted nor agreed with the Truman administration. How else could one account for MacArthur's sporadic blasts, such as his statement on 10 August 1950, claiming that his recent trip to Formosa, a trip that had managed to send all the wrong signals to friends and foes alike, had been "maliciously misrepresented to the public by those who invariably in the past have propagandized a policy of defeatism and appeasement in the Pacific?"[32] That policy was, of course, the one being pursued by Truman's administration. For MacArthur Inchon was to be the first step in a massive movement away from defeatism and appeasement. The situation was such that, if

MacArthur could convince the JCS to approve his plan, the president would almost have to go along or risk giving the Republican Right even more ammunition, and this with elections looming in November.

MacArthur had good reason to believe that the JCS would be persuaded and that they, in turn, could secure Truman's approval. First, the JCS respected MacArthur's military acumen. Second, neither the JCS nor anyone else had a better plan. And perhaps most important, MacArthur was aware of the long-standing tradition that held that, all else being equal, the commander in the field was to be fully supported. As Blair notes, "the JCS was reluctant to overrule MacArthur and cancel Inchon for several reasons. One was the 'tradition,' born in the Civil War and religiously adhered to in World War II, of giving the theatre commander wide latitude in tactical operations."[33] MacArthur well knew the people he had to convince and the exigencies and constraints under which they were laboring. He understood that both the military and the political arms, each for its own reasons, needed positive news from the battlefront. As Manchester notes: "He believed the Chiefs would yield to him because he knew . . . that 'a victory is very essential at the moment.'"[34] Timing was a central factor in all deliberations over Inchon. MacArthur recognized the opportune moment, both tactically and politically, to forward his ideological agenda. So, too, did the JCS and the Truman administration, even though their agendas were, of course, quite different. Inchon served multiple lords, and MacArthur's speech of 23 August empowered them all.

From a functional perspective the importance of the 23 August meeting was that it allowed MacArthur to advocate on behalf of his plan, allowed the Joint Chiefs to hear about the dangers involved, and started a process of deliberation—mostly over the best place to land—which was not completed until 8 September, one week before the invasion. Hence, the meeting of 23 August served important functions for all involved. That MacArthur should later reconstruct the events of 23 August to conform to *his* functional needs should not be surprising. But the facts do not comport with MacArthur's reconstruction nor with Carpenter's valorization. What MacArthur succeeded in doing—and it was no small feat—was moving the Joint Chiefs from an attitude of rejection to a *latitude* of acceptance. He did *not* convince them that the landing must be made at Inchon, at least not on 23 August. He did persuade them that a landing at Inchon would not be impossible and that it could, if successful, reap many rewards. When the JCS sent MacArthur their cable of 28

August, it reflected a latitude of acceptance, embracing Inchon, Kunsan, or "a favorable beach south of Inchon if one can be located."[35] That this latitude persisted all the way until 8 September is demonstrated by the Joint Chiefs' query about the "feasibility and chance of success of projected operation,"[36] a query that seemed to indicate less than total conviction on their part. Nonetheless, MacArthur never wavered, replying that "there is no question in my mind as to the feasibility of the operation and I regard its chance of success as excellent."[37] Hence the meeting of 23 August served multiple, and important, functions. One need not valorize, essentialize, or mythologize MacArthur's address. It was powerful, thoughtful, and successful in keeping his plan alive as a viable option. One need not—and should not—attribute to the speech functions it did not serve.

MacArthur's methods were those of the deliberative orator, as Carpenter has argued. Since the only "text" of the speech is that reconstructed some fourteen years after the fact by MacArthur, the analysis of content, structure, and style is badly compromised. One can either accept, as I shall do, MacArthur's version as constitutive of the essential text or try to reconstruct a more accurate text from the memory fragments of those in attendance. This latter task is clearly beyond the scope of either Carpenter's essay or my own. Nevertheless, using MacArthur's version, one can still recognize several aspects of rhetorical method which are undisputed.

First, MacArthur used an argument from probability supported by the historical example of General James Wolfe at Quebec. He then followed the historical example by using causal reasoning to link known past effects to future anticipated effects. Second, he granted all the logistical difficulties that had been recited for the previous hour and twenty minutes but argued that they were not impossible to overcome. He thereupon launched into his encomium of the navy, carefully interlacing taunts and barbs with his sometimes ironic praise. The effect of this tactic was to arouse both the navy's pride and its ire, causing its representatives to rise to the bait—which they did. Third, MacArthur dealt specifically with the option of landing at Kunsan, the alternative site put forward by Collins and seconded by Sherman. Such a landing, MacArthur claimed, would be "an attempted envelopment which would not envelop."[38] In short, it would not accomplish the objectives of the assault.

To this point in the speech MacArthur had engaged almost exclusively in refutative proofs. Next, he turned to his confirmatory proofs, arguing that "seizure of Inchon and Seoul will cut the enemy's supply line and seal off the entire southern peninsula." Having laid out the numerous advantages of an Inchon landing, MacArthur then inserted the accusation about being "content to let our troops stay in that bloody perimeter like beef cattle in the slaughterhouse." The effect of this image was to force the Joint Chiefs to put forward a better plan if one existed or stand accused of letting their men be massacred like animals. MacArthur then turned to a long peroration in which he asserted that "the prestige of the Western world hangs in the balance." Now Korea is no longer viewed as an isolated instance of aggression in a land lying outside of America's defense perimeter; instead, it becomes the central battleground of a worldwide struggle that embraces all of Asia and implicates Europe, too. World historical significance is attached to the decision to counterattack at Inchon, as MacArthur prophesies: "I can almost hear the ticking of the second hand of destiny. We must act now or we will die." He ends by again asserting that Inchon will succeed and predicting that "it will save 100,000 lives."

As reconstructed by MacArthur, the oration artfully blends content, structure, and style into a unified whole. Add to this MacArthur's ability to speak extemporaneously and his well-known dramatic delivery, and one can easily understand why the address lingered in the minds of those who heard it, in some cases years after the event. But moving from the artistry of the speech to its practical effect on either military or government decision making requires more than testimonials. It is important to remember that most of the decision makers—Omar Bradley; Hoyt Vandenberg; Secretaries Acheson, Johnson, Pace, Finletter, Matthews; and Harry Truman himself—never heard the speech. Matters of structure, style, and delivery could not have influenced them, and MacArthur's ethos, as that term is understood by Aristotle, would also have played little or no part in their decision, since Aristotelian ethos operates through the medium of the speech. Hence, when Truman wrote in his *Memoirs* that he had "the greatest confidence that it [Inchon] would succeed,"[39] he must have been basing that confidence on the only part of the oration which Collins and Sherman could possibly have reported to him—the content or reasons for MacArthur's belief in the likely success of the operation.

Consideration of the speech's logos leads directly to the contexts that the act subsumed and of which it was a part. As Brockriede notes, "Each rhetorical act has some larger setting and fits into one or more ongoing processes."[40] Inchon was part of the Korean conflict. It was also part of several other foreign policy conundrums: the debate over who "lost" China, U.S. policy toward Chiang's regime on Formosa, and the negotiation and signing of a Japanese peace treaty. It was also part of the contest of ideologies known as the Cold War. Richard Whelan puts the matter succinctly when he writes:

> In retrospect, we may say that the rescue of South Korea was not an end in itself. It was a means to an end, or rather to several ends: (1) to convince the Soviets that they didn't dare to make any further aggressive moves and (2) thus to prevent World War III; (3) to uphold America's prestige in the eyes of the entire world; (4) as Truman later put it, "to demonstrate to the world that the friendship of the United States is of inestimable value in time of adversity"; and (5) to squelch domestic, and specifically Republican, criticism of the Truman administration. To these ends must be added one more . . . : to demonstrate the ability of the UN to *halt* aggression (not merely to denounce it) and thus to bolster the Western system of collective security.[41]

Just as MacArthur's speech of 23 August cannot be understood or appreciated apart from the interpersonal, attitudinal, and situational exigencies and constraints that gave it substance and form, so too the landing at Inchon and the whole of the Korean War were parts of a multiple-layered reality involving "public opinion, attitudes, images, expectations, and beliefs."[42] To attribute decisive significance to any one speech, action, person, or tactic is usually a mistake. MacArthur's speech of 23 August was important but not decisive in the selection of Inchon; the counteroffensive launched at Inchon on 15 September was crucial but not decisive in how the war would end; the three years stretching from 25 June 1950 to 26 July 1953, the period known as the Korean War, were formative in many ways but again not decisive, as Vietnam and Afghanistan were to prove.

Conclusion

Military decision makers clearly form a distinct discourse community. Even so, one must not assume that this community is fundamentally different than other discourse communities or that it stands alone, sui generis. Military decision makers, like all decision makers, are confronted with interpersonal, attitudinal, and situational factors that affect the decision-making process. Military decision makers, like others, work within a system of commonly recognized and widely practiced community norms. Some of these norms are based on history or tradition, some on law, and some on the unwritten code of the officer and gentleman (or woman). Some of these norms overlap with those operating in civilian communities, some do not. However, like all communities military decision makers are responsible for their persuasive efforts—responsible to themselves, to their colleagues, to their superiors, and, ultimately, to the nation at large, which they are constitutionally sworn to protect.

The story of MacArthur and Inchon can be told in many ways. One of those ways, that chosen by Professor Carpenter, is heroic. Another way, the way I have chosen, is less heroic but perhaps more instructive. It teaches several lessons about the interrelationships between rhetoric and community:

1. that rhetoric both operates within communities and by that very operation often forms new communities;

2. that community formation is a continuous process that is never over until the decision has been made or the action undertaken—and even then the contours of the community keep changing as members evaluate their earlier positions in light of subsequent events;

3. that certain kinds of rhetoric may be more persuasive within some communities than others. In the case of the military community, argument based on historical analogy from military history and special topoi of military decision making (e.g., strength of forces, terrain, lines of supply, etc.) may be more effective than would the same arguments directed toward civilian audiences; and

4. that rhetorical reality, like all symbolic creations, must continually be tested against the experiences, judgments, and interpretations of interlocutors both inside and outside of the discourse community. The myth of MacArthur's infallibility was partially created by, and totally sustained by, rhetoric. By allowing themselves to succumb to the power of that myth, both military and civilian communities allowed MacArthur to lead U.S. forces from the victorious battle of Inchon into the quagmire that was the Korean War.

Brockriede was right: "A rhetorical act will be perceived quite differently by each person who participates in it, and still differently by each person who observes and criticizes from 'the outside.'"[43] Carpenter and I are both outsiders. We seek to observe, examine, compare, analyze, and judge. That our lenses of observation, methods of examination, points of comparison, instruments of analysis, and processes of judgment differ should not be cause for alarm. Brockriede also argues that "the critic may profitably identify the single most compelling dimension of a rhetorical act under consideration and then investigate how that dimension interrelates with others which appear to be relevant."[44] Carpenter has identified several significant rhetorical acts and examined how ethos interacts with certain inventional topoi during the course of these acts. I have tried to expand the bases for interrelationships and to argue that in the case of MacArthur's 23 August 1950 oration that logos rather than ethos should be considered the crucial artistic dimension and that the decisive topoi are not the common topics of courage and caution—though they are certainly present—but, rather, the special topics of military cost-benefit analysis: securing the objective, inflicting maximum damage upon the enemy, gaining psychological as well as physical or material advantage, avoiding greater losses, and taking advantage of the enemy's expectations, among others. By widening the purview of analysis beyond the single speech and the immediate audience, the critic is able to see many more rhetorical dimensions in martial decision making, to increase the critical arsenal, and to delineate more fully the contours of a discourse community that has served the country from Lexington and Concord to Porkchop Hill, Heartbreak Ridge, and beyond.

Notes

1. Wayne E. Brockriede, "Dimensions of the Concept of Rhetoric," *Quarterly Journal of Speech* 54 (1968): 12.

2. Ibid., 1.

3. On the MacArthur/Eisenhower relationship see Martin J. Medhurst, "Commanding Presence: Eisenhower's Rhetorical Development" (paper presented to the annual meeting of the Speech Communication Association, 18–21 November 1993, Miami Beach, Fla.).

4. William Manchester, *American Caesar: Douglas MacArthur, 1880–1964* (Boston: Little, Brown, 1978), 4.

5. Matthew B. Ridgway, *The Korean War* (Garden City, N.Y.: Doubleday, 1967), 142.

6. Brockriede, "Dimensions," 2.

7. Richard Whelan, *Drawing the Line: The Korean War, 1950–1953* (Boston: Little, Brown, 1990), 189.

8. Clay Blair, *The Forgotten War: America in Korea, 1950–1953* (New York: Times Books, 1987), 232.

9. Robert Debs Heinl Jr., *Victory at High Tide: The Inchon-Seoul Campaign*, 3d ed. (Washington, D.C.: Nautical and Aviation Publishing Company of America, 1979), 41.

10. J. Lawton Collins, *War in Peacetime: The History and Lessons of Korea* (Boston: Houghton Mifflin, 1969), 125.

11. Blair, *Forgotten War*, 235–36.

12. Ibid., 236.

13. O. P. Smith, cited in Heinl, *Victory at High Tide*, 42.

14. MacArthur, cited in Ridgway, *Korean War*, 78.

15. Ibid., 78.

16. Ibid., 75.

17. Ibid., 42.

18. Collins, *War in Peacetime*, 141–42.

19. Manchester, *American Caesar*, 573.

20. Ibid., 574.

21. Ibid., 574.

22. Douglas MacArthur, *Reminiscences* (New York: McGraw-Hill, 1964), 350. All subsequent quotations from the speech of 23 August are from this source.

23. Collins, *War in Peacetime*, 120.

24. Ridgway, *Korean War*, 81.

25. Harry S. Truman, *Memoirs II* (Garden City, N.Y.: Doubleday, 1956), 345.

26. Whelan, *Drawing the Line*, 52.

27. Ridgway, *Korean War*, 145.

28. Brockriede, "Dimensions," 7.

29. Ridgway, *Korean War*, 33.

30. Dean Acheson, *Present at the Creation: My Years in the State Department* (New York: W. W. Norton, 1969), 412.

31. Ridgway, *Korean War*, 60.

32. MacArthur, cited in Acheson, *Present at the Creation*, 422.

33. Blair, *Forgotten War*, 235.

34. MacArthur, cited in Manchester, *American Caesar*, 573.

35. Cable from JCS to MacArthur, cited in Blair, *Forgotten War*, 236.

36. Cable from the JCS to MacArthur, cited in Manchester, *American Caesar*, 577.

37. Cable from MacArthur to the JCS, cited in ibid., 577.

38. MacArthur, *Reminiscences*, 350. All quotations from the speech are found on 349–50.

39. Truman, *Memoirs II*, 358.

40. Brockriede, "Dimensions," 11.

41. Whelan, *Drawing the Line*, 119–20.

42. Martin J. Medhurst, "Rhetoric and Cold War: A Strategic Approach," in Martin J. Medhurst, Robert L. Ivie, Philip Wander, and Robert L. Scott, *Cold War Rhetoric: Strategy, Metaphor, and Ideology* (Westport, Conn.: Greenwood Press, 1990), 19.

43. Brockriede, "Dimensions," 11.

44. Ibid., 12.

CHAPTER NINE

The Particular Aesthetics of Winston Churchill's "War Situation I"

Celeste M. Condit and April M. Greer

War constitutes the ultimate measure of the value of a community to its members because each war asks whether the survival of the community in its particular form is worth the sacrifice of all that each individual person owns, is, or can be. Over the past two decades scholars have done an excellent job of exploring the common strategies that communities use when calling for such sacrifices.[1] Such general understandings are important. Yet, if the battle for a community is about the particularity of that community, then it is also important to understand the particularities of war appeals within specific communities. At the least, such particularized study would provide general knowledge of a different kind by highlighting the breadth of the spectrum of human rhetorical resources.

Particularistic approaches to the rhetorical dynamics of war appeals have been discouraged by a set of broad assumptions that have permeated rhetorical criticism over the past two decades. Our approach to the discourse of war, in other words, is representative of our approach to most types of rhetorical events. Two assumptions pervade this approach: that aesthetics are universal and that ideology and aesthetics are separable. A particularistic study of the rhetoric of a community in the crisis of war therefore requires that we address these interrelated issues, in order to open up a different form of analysis and to stretch our understandings of the ways in which rhetoricians speak for their communities. Such a project requires first, however, the selection of a particular discourse.

For our own community World War II remains the most critical of formative events, because it tested the vision of Western democracy against the most perfected patriarchy the world has known. In the pivotal moments of this struggle it was Winston Churchill who defined the battle and articulated the value of defending the democratic community against the alternate way of life offered by the order of fascism. Churchill gave many speeches throughout the war, but, for a study of the aesthetics of the particular, the address he delivered in the House of Commons on 20 August 1940 offers the richest resource. This speech, most often called "The War Situation I," was judged by many of his contemporaries to be better than the other, more frequently anthologized speeches given in response to specific cataclysms such as the invasion of Poland, the fall of France, or the escape at Dunkirk.[2] The speech displays Churchill's particular eloquence and the means by which he preserved the broader community of democratic peoples.

An Aesthetics of the Particular

Before we can proceed to understand how a highly artful but highly particular set of utterances can do something so grand as preserve a society, however, we need a better grasp on the issues of aesthetics and epistemics than the discipline has yet provided. There is a long lineage of tension in the field between those who would see rhetoric as the servant of truth, judging the rhetorical product by its truthfulness (or ideology), and those who would make rhetoric into pure stylistics. Ramus, of course, made this separation most explicit and clear, but it has been fought out all along the way, even by those who repudiated the Ramistic split in order to reclaim "rationality" for rhetoric (usually at the cost of aesthetics). There have, all the same, been many who have urged against separating ideology and aesthetics, style and substance. With them we hold that oratory is an endeavor that demands the melding of all of what is excellent in being human. In practice this means that great oratory must not only encompass but also integrate both beauty and truth. Rhetoric must embody ideas artistically. Otherwise, it truly is "mere artifice" or "mere science." It has, however, been notably difficult, since Aristotle, to present such a combined view theoretically.

To move in that direction we need a concept that captures the sense in which knowledge or ideology is embodied in a particular form, what one might call an aesthetic. The term *aesthetic*, however, has connotations associating it with "art for art's sake," and we do not want that association. One might, instead, employ the word *emotion*, but emotion is both individual and unstructured. It is primal, biological, and responsive.[3] Aesthetics have emotional components, but these are structured by conscious cognitive effort as well as by a community's shared history of symbolic interaction. Hence, we turn to Raymond Williams, who has argued that there are systematic sets of responses to phenomena and conditions which are shared within communities of people. To appropriate the insights he developed we quote at length his definition of the construct "structures of feeling":

> "feeling" is chosen to emphasize a distinction from more formal concepts of "world-view" or "ideology." It is not only that we must go beyond formally held and systematic beliefs, though of course we have always to include them. It is that we are concerned with meanings and values as they are actively lived and felt, and the relations between these and formal or systematic beliefs are in practice variable. . . . We are talking about characteristic elements of impulse, restraint, and tone; specifically affective elements of consciousness and relationships: not feeling against thought, but thought as felt and feeling as thought: practical consciousness of a present kind, in a living and interrelating continuity. We are then defining these elements as a "structure": as a set, with specific internal relations, at once interlocking and in tension.[4]

We think Williams admirably gets at the sense in which our responses to a discourse are not responses to disembodied ideas but to ideas that are toned with specific and rich sounds, feelings, colors, and patterns. Others have addressed this sense of the full-bodiedness of human responses to ideas. From Kenneth Burke, especially, we have garnered the lesson that style and substance are always embodied together and that "meaningfulness" depends upon both.[5] Williams moves this analysis forward by situating these affective responses in community. Unfortunately, the scope of Williams's theoretical work is bounded by severe limitations.

Williams is concerned to show the ways in which different classes respond against a presumed "official" discourse, and to applaud the class fractures against the official discourse of homogeneity. For Williams separation and disidentification are valued. There can, therefore, be no theory about the desirable ways in which one might articulate the interests of different groups together. There is, moreover, no history. Class is eternal and stable in all significant respects, so there is no concern for particular acts and outcomes. The only moment in history to be taken seriously is the moment of revolution.

Williams writes within a tradition of oppositional theory, and the twin inherent failings of such a politics of opposition are that they have not offered a rhetoric of community which copes with heterogeneity, and they are insensitive to the varied events of history. Williams cannot, therefore, tell us about discourse as it is "addressed" in very particular historical conditions from one human being to others. To retrieve the concepts of identification, community, and history we turn back to the rhetorical tradition, in order to appropriate Williams rather than to adopt him. To the notion of "structures of feeling" we will add the rhetorical notions of contexts and community to produce a concept of "communal sensitivities."

Marie Hochmuth Nichols's analysis of Lincoln's First Inaugural Address provides the most fully developed, perhaps even overdeveloped, case of sensitivity to the nuances of context.[6] In her analysis Hochmuth Nichols was concerned with describing the particularity of the historical moment, that is, the very day on which Lincoln spoke. She depicted the weather, the crowds, and the trees in bloom as well as the architectural chaos of the venue at which the speech was given. In addition, she was concerned about the community to whom the address was presented, a community that was in the process of sundering itself. She recounted carefully the responses of different factions, preserving their tone and understandings.

Hochmuth Nichols also gave presumption to community and was distressed at the failure of "official" discourse to preserve the community by articulating successfully the needs, wishes, and interests of a variety of community members. For her there was the possibility that groups with different interests might accommodate those differences and produce a way of living together, or at least of living side by side, in concord rather than in war. History was the sequence of those attempts at various accommodations and their failures in war, and it was therefore important. Hochmuth Nichols's analysis thus started by outlining the events and issues about which various members of the community were sensitive; it then explored Lincoln's success or failure in articulating a vision that accommodated those issues.

Despite its many virtues, the view of community offered by Hochmuth Nichols is a bit too sanguine. Her account can only be surprised by failure. Success for great orators and good arguments is presumed. She does not have the tools to read the text for the sentiments that run counter to good arguments or to account for audiences who feel differently about the issues.

To understand the particular workings of oratory, therefore, we need to combine the traditions and talents of Williams and Hochmuth Nichols. From the tradition within which Williams writes we learn how to understand better the sometimes divided feelings of a community, not merely the issues that they face. From Hochmuth Nichols and her tradition we borrow a sensitivity to the historical context and situation and a respect for the historically tenuous community, even recognizing that such a community is necessarily a mythic construct summoned from the experiences of subcommunities that are otherwise in conflict with one another.[7] Together, these two lines of thought lead us to attend to a community's sensitivities.

In creating this merger, we are not ignoring the different politics involved in the projects of Williams and Hochmuth Nichols. We are, instead, calling attention to the site at which the universal (or, more accurately, the general) and the particular meet. We are trying to theorize and analyze the place where grand social trends and practices are sutured into being through particular performances and events. We are attending to what Anthony Giddens has called the "duality of structure."[8]

To understand this suture, this place where social theory meets rhetorical practice, consider the differences between the two scholarly views. First, notice that post-Marxists are primarily theorists and, therefore, have attended to the general—especially the struggle of the working class against the capitalist. In contrast, rhetoricians are, foremost, critics, disbelievers in the sufficiency of general rules, and, therefore, they have attended to the particular. In light of these different levels of abstraction post-Marxists have focused on the grand flow of texts, reading those texts as signs of a culture and asserting that the particular agents who create those texts and who decode them do not matter. Some have carried that assertion even to the foolish and unnecessary extreme that denies that agents exist in any meaningful or interesting sense.[9] The post-Marxist replaces the individual with the class, displaces the agent with the subject. The rhetorician, however, attends to precisely who has created the text and to whom they have addressed that text and asks about the relationship between the two agents. The rhetorician can be accused of ignoring the overdetermining factors that make agents who they are, that help agents to utter and decode particular words in particular ways. But the rhetorician strives to tell us who said what and why it was important on a different level.

One can, of course, choose sides in this dispute, claiming that one side or the other tells a sufficient story and that the other is flat wrong. For reasons far too extensive to elaborate here, we see the either-or approach as insufficiently sophisticated. Alternatively, instead of viewing the two approaches as in opposition, one can fuse the two components as parts of a dynamic social circle. The moment of the individual speaking has its own micro dynamics. Without those dynamics there is no broader flow of texts at the social level. Moreover, the micro dynamics influence the dynamics of the macro level. Simultaneously, however, the moment of the individual speaking is also embedded in the larger, more general flow of texts, and one cannot understand the micro dynamics fully without also understanding the macro dynamics of social discourse.

If one sees rhetoric and culture studies in this way, as micro and macro perspectives on the same social circle, then one has three options for one's own studies. The first is to perform classical rhetorical analyses. The second is to perform classical post-Marxist analyses. The last is to try to examine the site of the suture, where social flow and particular historical practice meet. It is the site of suture that we choose to examine in order to explore the interdependency of ideology and aesthetics and to understand the way in which an aesthetics can be particular. To determine how that might be done we explore first methodological issues and then the particular case.

Methodology

If we are trying to understand how a very particular utterance can shape the flow of human discourse on a macroanalytic level, we must, as we have indicated, employ methods that preserve the particularity of the utterance and yet link it to the broad course of human sentiments and actions. Viewing aesthetics as being particular to a historical situation, and viewing epistemics as being fully embedded in that aesthetics but also as a part of the larger flow of ideas, provides us such a link. Fortunately, to allow us to explore that link requires only relatively minor alterations in extant ways of approaching criticism which have been employed by rhetoricians and post-Marxists (especially as incarnated in culture studies).

The first step requires attention to the historical context. The traditional focus on events, political parties, and economics must, however, be joined to a careful and precise analysis of the feelings, values, and concerns of the community in the particular historical moment. This moment is more than a "rhetorical situation," for the rhetor has not yet constituted the situation in a particular form. Instead, it is a collection of events and speaking formations suffused by shared heritages. The second step is to study the text in question, attending both to the ways in which it fits or fails to fit the needs and desires of various members of the community and to the unique art with which the rhetor accomplishes the fitting together. Simultaneously, one explores how, in constituting this particular ideological/ aesthetic product out of this particular set of community sensitivities, in this particular situation, the rhetor reconstitutes the community or moves it in specific directions to future spaces. Finally, if the information is available, the critic might also seek to confirm the analysis with data about audience responses.

To highlight the difference between such an approach and the universalistic perspective now dominant, one need only compare the analysis that follows to the study of Churchill's speaking by William Rickert.[10] Rickert provides an archetypal analysis of a body of speeches given by Churchill during the war. He concludes that Churchill deployed three major metaphoric clusters: light-dark, ingestion-cleansing, and stormy weather. He further indicates that Churchill cast the war as a romantic quest.

Rickert's conclusions are, we think, broadly correct. They do not, however, tell us anything about the eloquence of Churchill's response to his situation. Are we to conclude that anyone who uses these metaphors and this myth is necessarily a great orator? We also learn nothing about the fittingness of Churchill's response to his audience. Are these appropriate metaphors for this community in its situation? If so, why? Finally, as we hope the following critical analysis will suggest, Rickert, though he describes Churchill's use of archetypes well, does not give us a sense of those many other particulars of Churchill's speaking which made him a great orator. Churchill's eloquence, we will indicate, drew much of its force from the creation of culture-typal metaphors for his people and from deploying highly specific metaphors tailored precisely to the immediate sensitivities of his community.

The War Situation

It took the passage of years, extraordinary eloquence, and a stagger-ing series of external events for the British people to decide that it was by the heroic vision of Winston Churchill that they wished to live and die. As late as 1938, nothing could seem less likely on the British scene than that Winston Churchill should soon be leading the nation in war. As John Lukacs argues, it was war hawk Churchill's worst year ever.[11] Throughout 1938 and most of 1939 Prime Minister Neville Chamberlain experienced nearly unanimous public support in his effort to ward off Continental war through peace treaties. The bloody destruction of the past world war rested heavily on the hearts of the citizens of England, and they wished to avoid falling into a pattern of increasingly destruc-tive Continental wars, with no clear gains at their ends. It was a period of serious concern and sanguine hopes.

Those widely held dreams of peace were pulverized by Hitler's partitioning of Czechoslovakia and the invasion of Poland on 1 Septem-ber 1939. Chamberlain, in an effort to preclude a German invasion of Poland, had committed Britain to Poland's defense, and, thereby, the former appeaser had boxed a reluctant British nation into war. Most of the British people accepted the necessity of fighting Hitler under these conditions.[12] For eight months, however, Chamberlain succeeded only in dragging his nation through the "reluctant war," also known as the "bore war" and the "phony" war.[13] The British people faced the enor-mous trials imposed by blackout conditions, the evacuation of children from London, and the issuance of rationing coupons. They watched minor bungled military efforts. There was, however, little real fighting and no clear statement of war aims. Finally, on 9 May 1940 Hitler in-vaded Holland and Belgium, and the pressing character of the war became more evident. Faced with this new trial, Chamberlain stepped down.

Winston Churchill had, for decades, warned of the danger of the path of peace and appeasement. When Hitler ungloved his iron fist, Churchill was transformed from outcast eccentric to prophet, and so he came to occupy the office of prime minister in May 1940. Churchill's broad rhetorical task was enormous. He had to rally an isolated island people to fight the most impressive military force the world had yet seen, one that had swept through the combined French and British army in days. By late August Churchill had demonstrated his ability to unify the nation. Nonetheless, the specific conditions he addressed for the speech on 20 August were difficult. Since 10 July the British citizens had experienced the first direct effects of the war—bombing from the air. The Battle of Britain had begun.[14] Additionally, Churchill had received substantial indications that the Germans planned to invade during late August or early September, and these threats had been published in the newspapers.

Churchill's speech came in the face of these threats, but it also came immediately after a substantial victory in this new war at home. On 15 August one of the early air battles over Britain had been fought, and the British had declared they had outfought the Germans three to one. The speech also came in the face of an offer by Hitler of a compromise peace, one that some British leaders saw as an attractive option.

In this context a successful defense of the island from invasion might be seen either as a platform from which to launch the Continental war or as a good chance to negotiate a favorable peace with Hitler, thereby forgoing Continental war. As a strong proponent of a Continental war, Churchill wanted to control the interpretation of the air victory as well as of the larger flow of the war. Churchill thus sought to contextualize the Battle of Britain as merely part of an extended and propitious effort to drive Hitler from power.

The Community's Sensitivities

Historians and British patriots alike have underestimated the difficulties of Churchill's task, portraying him as little more than a good rally speaker with a gift for a jazzy turn of phrase. To understand Churchill's rhetorical achievements we need to look closely at the community sentiments he was trying to direct toward fighting an extended and difficult war. In his first, vigorous speech as prime minister Churchill had offered the nation his "blood, toil, tears, and sweat," and from that point forward there had been virtually no *public* dissent from the commitment to war.[15] Although a few right-wing elements continued to find fascism an attractive, strong, and vigorous alternative to gridlocked parliaments, these voices became largely silent when war was declared.[16] On the Left there were others who disagreed with Churchill's wartime trajectory, and they were not silent, but they were largely ignored.[17] Hence, it has been the common conclusion among popular sources and historians writing before about 1980 that Churchill did not persuade his audience to fight but merely articulated their feelings. Churchill's modest version of this British nationalist hypothesis runs like this: "Vast numbers of people were resolved to conquer or die. There was no need to rouse their spirit by oratory. They were glad to hear me express their sentiment and give them good reasons for what they meant to do, or try to do."[18] In claiming this innate and inherent British unity, both Churchill and the nationalist historians failed to understand the extent to which the contingency of history is constructed through a rhetoric, which then comes to appear as though it were inevitable. Because Churchill and these historians have all wanted to believe that British enthusiasm for the defense of freedom was inevitable, they have dismissed the significance of the rhetoric that made it so.

This fallacy has been avoided in some of the more recent studies of the war.[19] These accounts stress the extent to which Hitler repeatedly offered Britain a negotiated peace and the realistic advantages of that peace for the island nation. They also describe the British political leaders who supported this "compromise peace." In his political biography of Churchill, John Charmley documents the active, behind-the-scenes maneuvering for negotiated peace by the likes of Lord Halifax and Lloyd George, which occurred during 1940. Of the more general British public attitude, Charmley concludes, "had they been told that all was hopeless, then they would have submitted, resignedly, to their fate; but when Churchill told them that if they all stood together they would win, when he told them that theirs was the cause of civilization against barbarism . . . they resolved that they would not be the first generation of Britons to live as slaves."[20] There is some evidence in the newspapers of the era to support this hypothesis. There were those among the "persons in the streets" who joined the lords in their opposition to the war.[21] On this account Churchill's rhetoric was a triumph of conversion, a mighty gale that convinced the reluctant to march into battle against their previous will.

While the more recent historical accounts such as Charmley's appeal to the self-aggrandizing instincts of rhetorical scholars, we must ultimately find them to be as inadequate as that of Churchill and the florid nationalists. A careful weighing and sifting of the opinion in the press in 1939 and 1940 suggests that the role of Churchill's oratory was more an outgrowth of popular spirit than Charmley's account suggests and yet also more active in guiding the nation than the British nationalist account would let on. We find, in these years, a nation that resisted war as long as a tenable peace was possible but one in which war became accepted as an unfortunate necessity once the scope and character of Hitler's ambitions became clear. We find, simultaneously, however, a nation that spent late 1939 and early 1940 in search of a leader who could articulate and execute this preference successfully. The relationship between Churchill and his nation was thus a reciprocal one. The diffuse sentiment of most of those who had a political voice supported the war and saw the need to eliminate Hitler, but this diffuse sentiment alone was ineffective. It was embedded in contrary concerns, it was unfocused and unamplified, and it was not unified and spoken in timely, and hence effective, response to specific situations. The people therefore sought a leader who could articulate their sensitivities, honing them into an effective community. Those leaders who sought other outcomes, such as Halifax and Lloyd George, were unlikely to be preferred, except upon the failure to find a leader like Churchill or the failure of this leader to bring about the desired results.

The progress of this reciprocal relationship is most evident in the pages of the *Economist* in the months from March through June 1940. In March, while Chamberlain was still prime minister but war had been declared, the article entitled "The War of Nerves" opined: "There is some sense of frustration. . . . It is not that the people do not care. They do— fervently. But they have been given little that is concrete to work for."[22] A week later the paper criticized Chamberlain's leadership directly, arguing, "It is not the excellence of our intentions that is in doubt, but our ability to carry them out" and "It should be shouted from the housetops that we have a Plan. . . . so that month by month, our own people may have some anchor for their hopes."[23] On 11 May 1940 the paper reported the debate in Commons on Chamberlain's leadership, saying that "the main theme of the debate was the need for vigour, for foresight in laying plans and ruthlessness in carrying them out, for imagination, for courage."[24] It urged further that "the choice of persons implies a choice of policies"—this after the paper had previously touted Churchill as the sole voice to "echo public feeling and speak the Government's mind."[25] Other voices were less consistent and less resolute in this campaign for leadership, but similar themes were echoed in papers as disparate as the *London Times* and the *New Statesman and Nation*.[26]

Thus, the politically active part of the nation sought out Winston Churchill as a mouthpiece who had demonstrated that he could articulate their views and make them effective. The activity of the populace does not, however, negate the importance of finding someone who had the necessary skills, that is, of finding someone who could take a diffuse sentiment, a national self-image, and an ancient heritage and turn them into something cogent, powerful, and effective in the specific situation. Churchill's rhetorical challenge was not to echo a sentiment that was already preformed, constant, and widely shared. It was to articulate a largely diffuse set of British sentiments in ways that appropriately accounted for the challenges that they faced and to do it on a public stage, where all might share the account and, hence, might effectively coordinate their action.

From such a perspective a great orator is not one who commands a people but, rather, one who serves a people by helping them to concretize what it is they would be and do, in ways that are consonant with major interests and understandings of those people. On this account Churchill's oratorical genius rested in his ability to crystallize a specific and compelling vision of an active and effective community from a diffuse set of heterogeneous sentiments. To understand this achievement we need to consider the British character and the problematic sentiments it faced in the moment.

Much has been written about the British character. The British have been portrayed both as a "cold" people and a "cheery" one.[27] They are generally thought of as pragmatic, reserved, and steady. Though "unemotional," they are said to be stubborn and imperialistic. In the face of Hitler's conquest in 1939 and 1940, however, two facets of the British character were of crucial importance. They were, first, an enormously proud people who believed themselves to be superior to all other peoples on the globe, having provided, through a special set of "geniuses," a uniquely admirable democratic government.

To find this self-interpretation one need only leaf through the newspapers of the era or listen to the speeches of government officials—one will hear the British trumpeting the "ancient courage of the race"[28] or congratulating themselves as "the most civilized" of governments,[29] "a proud people,"[30] with a "genius for the sea."[31] They claimed that "unity and courage are those qualities which in the past have made Britain Great Britain."[32] They also saw themselves as "decent," and, of course, in contrast to Hitler, they routinely congratulated themselves on being "the sole champions in Europe of freedom."[33]

There was, however, a second side to the British, and that was the pragmatic, "phlegmatic" sense of reasonableness and common sense.[34] The British were not about to tear off on a wild goose chase, expending lives and treasure to fight a war against all of Europe which they could not win. This side of the British character was also depicted in the papers and speeches of the era. Some of their favorite words of praise were "sane," "efficiency," or "cool, sensible and firm."[35] One wartime image advertisement for an aluminum manufacturer even offered, in bold print, a "Salute to Sanity."[36] British writers and speakers castigated "irresolution" and "hopelessly muddled thinking" and called for "hard thinking."[37] As John Charmley has related in unsurpassed detail, these sentiments were equally present in the deliberations of ministers in private and in their calculations about whether to "appease" Hitler in the name of peace and prosperity.[38]

The British response to Hitler's threat was thus, in 1939 and 1940, still indeterminate. The nation wanted to fight Hitler in order to preserve their independence and empire, but they were not interested in a war in which they were doomed to defeat. Churchill's primary task was therefore repeatedly to convince the British people that they could win a Continental war. At the time "The War Situation I" was delivered, three particular fears constituted the communal sensitivities that impeded that confidence. At some important level the British feared that they would be routed like the French. Further, they feared this because they respected Germany's power and even wondered if it were greater than their own. Finally, they knew that, though they might be able to stave off Hitler's attack on the island by themselves, evicting Hitler from the Continent was an altogether different matter. They, along with Churchill, knew that the broader war demanded the involvement of a highly reluctant United States.

Francophobia

The first of these concerns, the fear that they would suffer the surprising and humiliating defeat that the French had experienced, was expressed only indirectly. It is clear that the British had enough confidence in themselves to articulate the belief that they would triumph. A Gallup poll shortly after the fall of France indicated that only 3 percent of the population were willing to say that they would lose.[39] They also believed that they were not like the French, that they had a different character, a character that was more "resolute" and "tenacious." The British, however, were also reasonably self-critical and mildly realistic. They realized that the French had also appeared to be a substantial force opposing Hitler and that they had unexpectedly crumbled. They further often attributed this to Hitler's "Fifth Column" activities. They believed that the French had been "talked out of" substantial resistance. As A. J. P. Taylor put it, they "had their heads full of what was supposed to have happened in the Low Countries and in France, they foresaw German tanks rolling over the country, aided by fifth-columnists and parachutists."[40]

The British had good reason to fear that the French example would apply to them. Churchill in his memoirs recalls the reasons for this self-doubt: "Twice in two months we had been taken completely by surprise. . . . Would they suddenly pounce out of the blue with new weapons, perfect planning, and overwhelming force upon our almost totally unequipped and disarmed island . . . ? I was always sure we should win, but nevertheless I was highly geared up by the situation."[41] The British were particularly concerned about the effectiveness of Germany's use of propaganda.[42] Germans took every opportunity to give an outlet for those doubts. On 2 August the Germans made the propaganda threat seem real and present by dropping leaflets from the air to the British population below.[43] The pamphlets outlined Hitler's peace proposals. Any self-doubt had also been reinforced by a long series of defeats, not only in Poland, Belgium, and France but also in Scandinavia and very immediately in Somalia as well.

This combination of brave exterior and nagging doubt perpetuated the popular characterization of the battle as a "war of nerves," a phrase used by advertisers as well as parliamentary speakers.[44] The British public thus put up a brave front, but, they wondered, would they really stand firm when the time came? Churchill's task was to reassure the populace that they would. One strategy he used was to cut off "defeatist" talk by others, prohibiting government officials from speaking negatively and supporting, for a time, the Ministry of Information's hearty prosecution of those whose talk could be interpreted as abetting the enemy. Another strategy was his own positive enactment of confidence and resolution. Ultimately, however, the form of reassurance needed to be adapted to the British character, and that would mean "good reasons." After all, on 10 June the French minister had written that "the enemy is almost at the gates of Paris. We shall fight before Paris, fight behind Paris," and yet, no such fight had taken place.[45] The communiqué is sharply reminiscent of Churchill's speech averring that the British would "fight on the beaches, fight on the landing fields." To the Britons, therefore, reassurance required more than the emotional arousal from a repetitive set of clauses. It consisted of "facts" and "reasons."

A thousand French and Francophile critics have now reviled the British for their dependence upon the "rational world paradigm," so that one might expect that we need hardly establish further the British dependency on this mode of discourse, but all the same the high value put upon reasons and facts is evident throughout the British speeches and newspapers of the period. For example, the *Economist*, a most rational paper, proclaimed on 22 June that "Britain will fight on, and on Tuesday the Prime Minster told the people why. It is because cold calculation has decided that the defense of these islands is practicable."[46] The paper continued, "Not only should we fight on; we can do so with high hopes, soundly based, of ultimate success." In Parliament a similar privileging of reasoning and good reasons was expressed by the representative for Birmingham and Duddeston, who said, "Although we have always had confidence in victory, that confidence was not until very recently supported by much more than faith; but during the last seven or eight days it has been supported both by faith and by facts."[47] The British wanted proof that they were acting "sanely," and, as we will see, Churchill would give it to them.

Fear of German Superiority

The British were also at this moment highly sensitive to the prevailing image of German power in a different and more directly competitive manner. On the one hand, the propagators of the world's largest empire were a proud race, convinced of their own superiority, both moral and otherwise. They were not, however, romantics or idealists. They were not going to overlook the demonstrated power and efficiency of the Third Reich. As the *New Statesmen and Nation* conceded, "millions who hate the Nazis still admit in the secrecy of their hearts that if the Nazis are evil they are strong."[48] The British were especially impressed by the German machines. Repeatedly, journalists, parliamentary representatives, and letter writers referred to "Germany's overwhelming superiority in numbers and machines,"[49] or "'this advance whose spearhead has so far consisted of machines, not men."[50] In a powerful passage endowing the machines with only animal mentality, the *Economist* described "the Nazis' mechanised columns nosing their way along the enemy lines, thrusting here, thrusting there to find the weak spot in the defences, and once the weak spot has been discovered concentrating all their power and strength on that particular point, bursting through and spreading out behind the gap they have created."[51]

This respect for German power was obstructive to Churchill's efforts to rally the British people because it put in doubt the British ability to triumph. It was, however, perhaps more dangerous in another respect. British voices of the period were using the reduction of Germany's power to its machines to reassure themselves that they were superior as men (the nongeneric male nouns and pronouns were generally intended), though they were being defeated in war. This negotiation of hierarchy was captured in the comments of Minister of Parliament Lees-Smith, who claimed that the "great advantage which Herr Hitler has had has been in machines in the air and on the land" but also that "men who have come back from France all agree that if you take the modern German soldier out of his machine he is not as good a man as his father was in 1914."[52] The *Economist* likewise used Germany's mechanical triumph as a way of preserving the sense of British superiority without need for victory over Germany when it insisted that, "although our troops were never outclassed, they were outbuilt in almost every category."[53] Such a face-saving sentiment would allow Britain to rationalize a treaty with Germany while maintaining its self-respect, and, therefore, Churchill needed to reconfigure it if he were to make a truce with the führer unspeakable in the British public arena.

The United States' Isolation

The final community sensitivity that Churchill's speech addressed was the status of the United States. The British people might have been sanguine about their ability to defend the island fortress from Hitler's invasion by air and sea. It was quite another matter to imagine how they would fare in trying to drive Hitler out of Europe. The concern about the United States's willingness to participate in the vanquishing of Hitler is evident in the extensive attention all of the newspapers gave to American opinion throughout the year. The journalists carefully reported every uptake or downdraft in U.S. isolationism as well as every twist and turn in the U.S. presidential election. Letters from Americans avowing support for Britain were also routinely published. In June and July these concerns became explicit. The *Economist* admitted, "Our role here in Great Britain is to hold the bastion; for victory we shall need aid from overseas."[54] The *New Statesmen and Nation* agreed, stating: "Even more certainly, a public American decision unreservedly to come to the aid of Britain, whether it involved a declaration of war or not, would change the face of Europe overnight. Our island would no longer fight merely for survival. The liberation of the Continent, of which Mr. Churchill speaks, but which is still so imperfectly apprehended by our statesmen, would become a far swifter possibility."[55] To say the least, the British were very concerned to get the United States involved in the war and to reassure themselves that this would happen.

Due to a series of ancient sentiments and immediate events, on 20 August 1940 Churchill spoke to an audience that was severely challenged. The British people generally believed in the value of defeating Hitler but had serious concerns about their ability to achieve this task. They were worried that they might prove vulnerable to an invasion, which they were told was coming at any time within the month. They were impressed by German military power but able to rationalize that power with their own general superiority, and they watched a self-satisfied United States refuse to support the cause of democracy in the world. Churchill could merely have used brave and colorful words to urge his people on to victory, but he did much more than that. He artfully addressed and rearticulated these sentiments in ways that maintained the British fighting spirit.

America Rolls Along

Churchill's speech to the Parliament, the nation, and the world opened with an epideictic marker, as the prime minister reminded his audience, "Almost a year has passed since the war began, and it is natural for us, I think, to pause on our journey at this milestone and survey the dark, wide field." Rickert's archetypal analysis would here urge us to notice that Churchill set the stage by placing the British on a journey that began in a relatively low place, in the dark, and in a quiet mood. Contrary, however, to both Rickert's claims and our general expectations of archetypal metaphors, Churchill did not lead his audience forward on a journey to end the speech at a "broad, well-lit uplands," as he had done in other speeches. Instead, Churchill halted the journey in midstride, saying only, near the end of the speech, "We are still toiling up the hill; we have not yet reached the crest-line of it; we cannot survey the landscape or even imagine what its condition will be when that longed-for morning comes." Instead of completing the land journey he had started, Churchill shifted in his closing to the watery course of the Mississippi River. He described future U.S. involvement in the war in this peroration: "For my own part, looking out upon the future, I do not view the process with any misgivings. I could not stop it if I wished; no one can stop it. Like the Mississippi, it just keeps rolling along. Let it roll. Let it roll on full flood, inexorable, irresistible, benignant, to broader lands and better days."

Rickert's archetypal analysis of Churchill's speaking has claimed that Churchill usually "chose not to develop the river image," because, "while its natural flow would have pointed the way to a certain destination, its direction tends to be down (hence, toward the darkness of defeat) and its flow too determined."[56] Should we conclude, therefore, that, although its contemporaries thought otherwise, the 20 August address is a defective product, below the artistic standards of Churchill's other speeches?

If one imposed a universalistic template, one might see such a deficiency. We believe, however, that Churchill's mastery is a particularized one. The rhetorical art is not merely a matter of the rote placement of dark and low spaces at the beginning of a journey and high and light ones at the end of a speech. Churchill is more a master of the intertwined features of cultural sensitivities, situation, and metaphor than that.

To understand Churchill's mastery of the available rhetorical resources, we must consider several factors. First, recall that a major goal of the speech was to proclaim an extended offensive war against the Germans. Second, Churchill wished to do so in a war context that was ambiguous. On the one hand, the British had won the first battles of the air war over their territory. Yet there was still great uncertainty about Hitler's full power. Moreover, Britain had retreated from all of the land battles to date. Churchill knew that, if his people believed that the "Yanks were coming," they would be more likely to feel confident in this endeavor. Furthermore, in his secret correspondence with Roosevelt the prime minister had just struck a deal to trade the bases about which he speaks in the address for fifty used destroyers from the United States.[57] Churchill apparently believed (although incorrectly) that this was a serious turning point, even though the destroyers were mostly symbolic. As Martin Gilbert reports, "Once the destroyer deal went through, Churchill told the War Cabinet, the United States would have made 'a long step towards coming into the war upon our side.'"[58] The prime minister knew, however, that he might hurt Roosevelt's chances for reelection were he to argue explicitly that the United States would eventually be forced to involve themselves actively in the world war. Churchill did not want to lose Roosevelt, upon whose support he placed a great deal of hope (though this support was probably overestimated).[59]

Churchill thus sought to communicate more than that Britain was giving bases to the United States, without saying so directly.

Churchill resolved these several difficulties by resorting to the strategic ambiguity of a highly particular metaphor. It is clear to his audience that the flow of the Mississippi refers to the United States and its future course out to "broader lands." The metaphor, however, avoids proclaiming any specific actions on the part of the United States which might threaten FDR's electoral chances. All the same, it offered its audience the sense of access to enormous and impending power.

A variety of components constructed this sense of power. First, the brute physical force of the Mississippi itself, as one of the world's largest rivers, bestowed a sense of natural power. Second, for Churchill, as well as for some of his audience, the metaphor also drew impact from a cultural source—the forceful and sonorous bass-baritone delivery of the song "Ol' Man River," by Paul Robeson, which had played to packed houses in London.[60] These extrinsic factors were magnified by a variety of intrinsic factors peculiar to Churchill's deployment of the metaphor as well.

Most obviously, Churchill interwove the metaphor with words, such as *inexorable* and *irresistible,* which imparted a sense of destiny. He also employed alliteration, depicting a tide that was sweeping onto "broader lands and better days." Not only do these words make an alliteration on the strong sound of the *B* with the term *benignant,* but also *broader lands* was a mirror of the territorial conquests that were implied in Churchill's extended war. Further, Churchill built up the force of the torrent by repeating *roll* three times in different forms as well as through the complex structure of the last sentence, which piled up a series of adjectives, halted by commas and breathing, to extend the force of the sentence and the metaphor. In addition to all of this, Churchill placed himself, a powerful man, a speaker with the attention of listeners around the globe, as impotent before the flood, when he intoned, "I could not stop it if I wished." Then, extending the thought that "no one can stop it," he hinted that the force was larger than Hitler or perhaps than the current whims of the American people.

Finally, Churchill delivered these phrases with a set of emphases that further carried power. Here, again, we note the importance of particularity over universality. Churchill's voice, with its gruffness and muffled speech impediment, is hardly that resonant baritone that we idealize in universalistic notions of what is aesthetically appealing in speech delivery. But Churchill's gruff and resolute voice was highly familiar, and its steadfast flatness probably spoke to the majority of the British people of authenticity and sincerity in a way that a more lilting voice would not have achieved. It was, moreover, the particular pronunciation of the words, not the universal qualities of the voice, which carried the meaning. Churchill pronounced the first clause, "it just keeps rolling along," with a matter of fact, falling intonation, reinforcing the sense of inevitability. The *rolling* was rolled and played out, as was the *roll* in the next sentence, "Let it roll." Then, Churchill stepped up the pace on the third *roll,* creating a sense of the gathering momentum of the water's tide. He moved rapidly through the adjectives, carrying that sense of force but also pausing between each to emphasize their significance. Finally, he concluded the sentence, slowing, as the waters spilled out, easing their rush as they washed out upon the "broader lands and better days."

Churchill's use of the Mississippi metaphor thus constituted a tightly packed and carefully sculpted ideological and artistic whole. In spite of the brilliance of its construction and its delivery, an archetypal orientation might still lead to the objection that the metaphor was out of place. The "journey" and "light" metaphors, this line of analysis would suggest, set up the formal expectations that Kenneth Burke has called syllogistic progression, and with the Mississippi metaphor these expectations went unfulfilled or were even harshly daunted. As John Timmis has previously demonstrated, however, it was a unique characteristic of Churchill's style that he achieved maximum predictability with maximum novelty.[61] In this case Churchill achieved that special combination of novelty and comprehensibility not by the device of grammatical precision which Timmis identified but, rather, through figurative foreshadowing.

Earlier in the speech the United States had been introduced with a water verb, *flow.* Simultaneously, the flow from U.S. production of war goods was mingled with the flow of the British production, which gave "overflowing" reserves and a "stream" of production. Hence, Churchill prefigured the mixing of the British and American streams, before the last paragraph, in which the major metaphor was to be constructed. In this way he employed a qualitative form to set up an expectation that was then appropriately fulfilled by his peroration. The river metaphor thus carried through earlier expectations. Furthermore, Churchill subverted Rickert's claim that, because of their downward flow, river metaphors provide an inadequate archetypal ending for journey metaphors. Churchill's Mississippi did not flow down to defeat but out to the Delta, to broader lands. The appropriateness of this means of continuing the journey is etched in not only by artistic but by ideological factors, for the broader lands connoted the recapturing of the European Continent far more concretely than a more abstract high/low or light/dark archetype might have done.

Attending to the many particularities of the address, to the communal sensitivity of his audience toward the United States, as well as to the particular agenda Churchill was promoting, reveals that the Mississippi metaphor was not a failure but, rather, uniquely eloquent. Its appropriateness to its situation and community stand as a sign that Churchill was more than a poet; he was, in fact, a great person speaking well the hearts and goals of his community. Perhaps Churchill felt this too, for his administrative assistant, John Coville, reported that, riding home that evening, Churchill "sang 'Ole Man River' (out of tune) the whole way back to Downing Street."[62]

Machines of War

Churchill's use of the Mississippi metaphor provides one example of the value of a particularistic approach to aesthetics over the traditional universalistic approach. It indicates the way in which a particularistic perspective must take into account aesthetics and ideology simultaneously and also account for the audience's mixed sentiments and the speaker's goals. One cannot understand the art of the metaphor without understanding the community's ideological needs and the speaker's purposes. We turn now to a second example.

To the extent that "The War Situation I" attempted to shift British attention to the extended, offensive war and to articulate appropriate sentiments for the actions necessary for that war, Churchill needed to provide an extensive set of ramparts against British fears of their own weaknesses and German strengths. While appeal to the future aid to be provided by the United States fulfilled some of this function, there remained a need to face German power directly. Churchill addressed this sensitivity through a reason-giving aesthetic that provided places for humorous assaults on Hitler and which permitted the deployment of a refiguration of the relative power of Germany and Britain through subtle alterations in the machine metaphor.

Like most of Churchill's speeches, "The War Situation I" was a reason-giving address. As James Humes has indicated, Churchill's self-avowed major organizational and topical strategy was to choose a single argument and to support it in multiple ways. He made this argument early in an address and then developed appeals to emotion once the logical scaffolding was established.[63] Churchill's argument in this speech was that the British had reason to believe they could win the extended war. The reason giving was initiated through a systematic comparison of World War I and World War II. After portraying the differences between the two wars, Churchill concluded, "There seems to be *every reason* to believe that this new kind of war is well suited to the genius and the resources of the British nation and the British Empire" (emph. added). Churchill then proceeded to give rationales for immediate courses of action, including the blockade, and the need for Britain to refuse to provide food aid to the Continent. Churchill's third set of reasons to expect victory were constituted by a list of the immediate advantages that Britain held, including the fortification of the island, the strength of the navy, and "hope" of more supplies from "our friends across the ocean."

Throughout this accounting Churchill displayed an amazing ability to turn disadvantages into advantages. Did Britain have to evacuate at Dunkirk? Well, that was to its advantage, for its army was now at home. Had Britain faced horrors so great that "few would have believed that we could survive"? Well, then, that was the proof of her strength and ability to endure even longer trials. Churchill concluded that he had given "solid grounds for the confidence that we feel."

In this extensive first part of the speech Churchill thus answered the distinctively British concerns about its power with a distinctively British rhetorical strategy—explicit reason giving. He carefully justified and calculated, expending an extensive proportion of the speech in doing so. If one is looking for a contrast that illustrates the cultural specificity of this style, one need only examine the comparable discourse by Mussolini in the period to understand the extent to which the British were bound by a reason-giving aesthetic and the extent to which Churchill adhered to that aesthetic.[64]

Meanwhile, however, Churchill worked a second figurative front as well. Slowly, entwined with the logical scaffold, he reconfigured British weakness into British strength and German strength into German weakness. For example, Hitler was portrayed as "sprawled over Europe" rather than as dominating it. Through this careful word choice the führer was transformed from a mighty foe to an opponent who was overextended, lax, and vulnerable to attack. Moreover, in that simple word, *sprawled*, there may have lurked a hint of sexual lassitude which simultaneously depicted the evilness of the man. In contrast, Churchill transformed Britain's apparent inactivity on the offensive front from weakness to eventual strength with another metaphor, saying that "our offensive springs are coiled." Inactivity was thereby recast as an activity of storing power, employing a mechanical metaphor that implied a match to the special strength of the Germans.

As part of this subtle assault on the shared concern that the Germans might be invincible, Churchill also employed humor. It was, however, the most understated of humor, again appropriate to British social norms. He coyly announced, for example, early in the speech: "I read in the papers that Herr Hitler has also proclaimed a strict blockade of the British Islands. No one can complain of that. I remember the Kaiser doing it in the last war." Later, he cast doubt on Hitler's power by entwining it with the Nazi leader's perceived dishonesty in an extended cascade of wryly worded sarcasm: "If after all his boastings and blood-curdling threats and lurid accounts trumpeted round the world of the damage he has inflicted, of the vast numbers of our Air Force he has shot down, so he says, with so little loss to himself; if after tales of the panic-stricken British crushed in their holes cursing the plutocratic Parliament which has led them to such a plight—if after all this his whole air onslaught were forced after a while tamely to peter out, the Fuhrer's reputation for veracity of statement might be seriously impugned." Churchill thus used a logical scaffolding, tactical thrusts of humor, and calculated word choice to reassure the British of their ability to triumph over a deflated enemy. Each of these components, however, was subordinate to a larger developing metaphor that Churchill gradually unfolded to reshape the relationship between British and German power.

Recall that in the British public discourse the Germans had been synecdochally identified as a war machine and that, in the face of this mechanical superiority, the British had claimed only a superiority of their human character. The Battle of Britain had, however, given Churchill the resources to reconstruct these nationalistic human/machine relationships. Having spent the first third of the speech carefully tallying the British advantages in traditional warfare, Churchill moved in the heart of the speech, and in its most frequently quoted section, to the air battle.

He lauded the "British airmen who, undaunted by odds, unwearied in their constant challenge and mortal danger, are turning the tide of world war by their prowess and their devotion," and he memorialized them with the famous phrase, "Never in the field of human conflict was so much owed by so many to so few."[65]

Churchill spent the five central paragraphs of this speech detailing the air war, because he found here a place in which the British were the figurative match of the Germans. While the Germans had demonstrated their mastery of ground machines, Britain had shown signs of becoming the master of the airplane. Churchill supported these visions of superiority by claiming that the British had exceeded the ratio of three or four to one losses in the air against the Germans, although he later admitted in his memoirs that these figures were exaggerations.[66]

Notice what this highly particular metaphoric placement does for Churchill and the British people. First, in the most powerful image of the war—the machine war, that is—the British now can claim their own tool for superiority: airplanes over tanks. Churchill thus deftly effaces the prior grounds of German superiority. Second, notice also that the image fits beautifully into Churchill's light/dark, high/low, archetypal background set in the first part of the speech. The German tanks operate in the lowlands and in the past. The British airplanes operate in the bright skies of the present and the future. Third, one might even stretch things far enough to notice that the air metaphor is compatible with the water metaphor employed to describe the Americans. That is, the American tide will sweep away the grounded Germans, while the British fly above.

Finally, and perhaps most significant, the British pilots are separated from and in control of their planes, while the Germans are reduced to their tanks. The British have a "special genius" for air warfare. They are individuals, acting valorously, using their machines as tools for good. The Germans, in contrast, are reduced to their machines, having no mind beyond the enslavement offered by Nazi rule.

The first part of this relationship, the portrayal of British individualism and of Nazis as an unthinking mass, was foreshadowed in the beginning of the speech, in which Churchill declared Britain "the most united of all the nations, because we entered the war upon the national will and with our eyes open, and because we have been nurtured in freedom and individual responsibility and are the products, not of totalitarian uniformity, but of tolerance and variety." The second part of the relationship, the fusion of these national identities with air and ground machines, respectively, is finalized in the middle section of the speech, in which the individual exploits of the fighter pilots and the bombers are carefully recounted in contrast to a top-down, de-individuated Nazi "apparatus," as illustrated by this passage: "night after night, month after month our bomber squadrons travel far into Germany, find their targets in the darkness by the highest navigational skill, aim their attacks, often under the heaviest fire, often with serious loss, with deliberate careful discrimination, and inflict shattering blows upon the whole of the technical and war-making structure of the Nazi power." The brave symbolic individuals are depicted with thoughtful, rational, premeditated, and careful action, in contrast to the mindless apparatus they destroy. Throughout this speech the Germans are reduced to a single "he" or "Herr Hitler" or, at most, "Nazidom." They are never a collection of conscious individuals acting and choosing. Churchill preserves this effect even when it requires that he use a passive voice to describe the disasters that have befallen the European nations.

Within this construct ideology and aesthetics are completely intertwined. German de-individuation in favor of the *volk* or the commands of a dictator is precisely what the liberal individualist democracies disapprove of in Hitler. They see German Nazism literally and figuratively as the erasure of individual thought, deliberation, and will in a mindless state, or a state enthralled to the will to power of one (super)man. In contrast, the high-flying individualism that offers voluntary service to a community is the model of the British. The forced obedience of the unthinking German machine stands below and opposed to the individual British citizen bravely and sanely choosing unity, flying in formation in order to preserve individual freedom and autonomy of will as well as the possibility for "genius."

This complex metaphorical relationship clearly provides resources to help the British audience deal with the fear of German power, but it also addresses their fear of French-like collapse. Through their self-identification with airplanes the British escape France's fate. The French were defeated by armored tanks, on the ground, but they had no substantial air force and lacked the genius for it which is special to the British. This is why the British will triumph where others had failed. Therefore, it is immediately after the section defining Britain's genius in the air that Churchill is able to declare for the first time that the threat of Britain meeting France's fate is "a contingency now happily impossible."

Churchill thus offered in this speech a range of neatly integrated constructions to articulate the "good reasons" and "good images" why the British might face the extended war with confidence, rather than with fear or even false bravado. What we see speakers offer, however, is not necessarily what audiences hear, so it is desirable to look to see what articulations resonate with a community.

Reaction to the War Situation

Churchill's wartime speaking has been widely recognized as having captured the "British spirit" or having embodied the British persona. Although A. J. P. Taylor and others have belittled Churchill's style as "eccentric" and "romantic," and hence out of touch with the typical British character, they have also recognized that these qualities may have fit the special needs of the war situation. Taylor conceded that Churchill's eccentricities were "exactly suited to the mood of the British people."[67] War required both intensity and a greater reflection of the "whole people." As an editorial to the London Times commented, "The slow temper of the English is hot now."[68] At such a time the hotheaded Churchill was well suited to carry the British banner. The Economist likewise reflected awareness of these peculiar war needs when it warned that France's fall was due to "too many old men in high places." The moderate paper urged, "We must put a premium on youth and vigour and courage rather than on 'experience' and 'judgment.' . . . we may be thankful that we have a Prime Minister whose stoutness of heart none can question."[69]

The intensity of Churchill's speaking was probably matched by its broad appeal to people of varying classes. Taylor is right that Churchill's speaking included "Macaulay and contemporary slang mixed together."[70] Humes likewise observed that, "if his speeches had the earthy humour of a London pub, they also had the majesty of a coronation."[71] This colloquial style, however, was common in Parliament in the era, as a number of MP's adopted popular phrases such as "go to it" or "get a hustle on."[72] Moreover, Churchill's wry sense of humor, combined with his determination for total victory, seemed perfectly to capture the sense in which the British saw themselves as "cheerfully resolute" in the face of long odds.[73] In general Churchill's humor was well received by MP's and newspapers alike.[74]

Even putting the unique context aside, the newspapers and commentators of the era routinely employed classic British character descriptors to describe the prime minister's speeches, commending

Churchill as vigorous, resolute, and firm. The *London Times*, for example, noted after "The War Situation I" was delivered that "a crowded House was deeply impressed by the spirit of resolution and confidence which inspired the speech, and broke in upon it frequently with loud cheers."[75] Similarly, the *Economist* praised "the unconquerable spirit of Mr. Churchill and the people he speaks for" and urged upon the whole government "those qualities of faith, drive, ruthlessness, and courage the Prime Minister himself displays."[76]

Churchill, however, did more than personify an idealized British character. He also was successful in articulating a sentiment that the majority of British people could feel was their own. This general sentiment was widely repeated by MP's and journalists alike. Hore-Belisha responded to the 20 August speech by exclaiming, "He expressed our cause and our purpose in fitting language, and we may be proud to have a leader of that stamp at this time."[77]

In part Churchill's success with this speech can be attributed to the reason-giving style. As one member of the Commons put it, "The Prime Minister in his great speech this afternoon gave the House good sound reasons for confidence in the situation in which the country finds itself now."[78] The *London Times* likewise indicated that "The PRIME MINISTER'S fine survey of the war in the House of Commons yesterday was delivered with the authority of frank appraisal and balanced judgment, and encouraged the House to feel that secure confidence which comes only when all facts have been faced."[79] The *New Statesman and Nation* similarly noted that the speech "wisely offered" "welcome proof."[80]

This strategy, however, was not the sole successful factor. The respondents to the speech also enthusiastically adopted the metaphors Churchill had offered. The celebratory perspective on the United States constructed through the Mississippi metaphor may have received the greatest attention from the speech's respondents. In Parliament Lieutenant Colonel Moore-Brabazon declared: "The Prime Minister said some words to-day about America which, I must say, stirred my heart. They were significant, and they were moving."[81] Similarly, Cocks, although he was largely critical of Churchill, nonetheless agreed that "we all welcomed the words of the Prime Minister about America. We are glad to know that our relations with America are growing closer every day."[82] The newspapers were even more emphatic. Both the *New Statesman and Nation* and the *London Times* led their coverage of the speech with that passage, the *Times* referring to its "eloquent references to the irresistible process at work."[83] The *Economist* closed its coverage with this passage, making Churchill's peroration its own, calling it "all-important," and quoting the passage at length.[84]

Churchill's metaphorical placement of Britain in the air, against the ground machines of the Germans, was likewise successful. We must be careful, however, in the precise character of the claim made here. For, indeed, the newspaper headlines had trumpeted the triumph of the British airmen throughout the previous week. The day before Churchill's speech, for example, the *Times* headline screamed "Germany's Heaviest Air Defeat: 140 Machines Shot Down Out of 600," and similar announcements of triumph had filled the papers the week before.[85] Thus, Churchill did not invent attention to the fighter pilots. Instead, he concentrated and focused a praise that had been widely spread across newspapers during the previous week. More significant, however, Churchill took an additional step by fearlessly betokening these small successes as a certain sign of eventual victory. His interpretation (arguably overinterpretation) was enthusiastically adopted after the speech.

Not surprisingly, the papers picked up on Churchill's specific phrases, quoting especially the commendation "Never in the field." More than that, however, Churchill's specific interpretation of the fighter pilot image as a token of British character and as a symbol of future success was widely echoed. In Parliament Lees-Smith was not alone in echoing Churchill's interpretation, proclaiming that "one of the great lessons of the last week which, I think, is of vital significance, is that our young men, in this new element of warfare, have a genius for the air as strong as is our genius for the sea."[86] In keeping with this building mythos, Lieutenant Colonel Moore-Brabazon reminded his fellow parliamentarians that "we must remember that we were the first country to visualise the all importance of an Air Force *qua* Air Force."[87] Hore-Belisha took the additional step, interpreting the early air results as a sign of the end of German invincibility: "our fighter pilots have indeed placed us in their gratitude. They have definitely checked the unbroken sequence of Hitlerian victories, and have disproved the legend of Hitler's invincibility."[88] Simmonds joined the chorus: "I believe that if each one of us here, and for that matter every Englishman and every English woman, examines his or her feelings to-day we shall all admit that our whole outlook on life has been profoundly affected by the recent exploits of the Royal Air Force."[89]

The newspapers likewise adopted Churchill's interpretation of the fighter pilots' success as a sign of eventual victory. The *London Times* gloated that "the supremacy of our airmen's skill is now so triumphantly proved that, however violently they may be assailed by the still heavy odds against them, the enemy will spend his strength in vain." After once again recalling the "Never in the field" quotation, it further concluded, "The effect of the air battles is to reassure any doubters there may be that ultimate victory is certain."[90]

Churchill's reconfiguration of the British as superior by way of their individual genius for the flying machines, as opposed to the unthinking mass mind of the German war machine, was not completely unprecedented. It borrowed materials already active in the national conversation: British success in the air and prior portrayals of the Nazis. Churchill's intensification and refocusing of these materials, however, gave new grounds for optimism, and both that optimism and the new configuration were rapidly and eagerly adopted. As Britain won the air war across the next few months, there was no public discussion in Britain of negotiating a treaty with Hitler. Churchill helped the British to set their sights resolutely on a Continental war, and, eventually, the flow of irresistible events forced even the United States to abide by his vision.

Other Fronts

Churchill's Mississippi metaphor and his machine metaphors were obviously successful. Lest one think that this is merely a sign that anything the popular prime minister said would have been enthusiastically endorsed, we should give brief consideration to another facet of the address. Churchill's speech also sought to deal with the increasingly vehement demands that the nation announce specific war aims. Domestic critics, like the *New Statesman and Nation,* called for an enunciation of war aims in hopes of using the war to reform the national economy and political scene along more socialist lines.[91] Other critics focused on the international scene, hoping for a more effective League of Nations as well as for clarity about territorial issues and reparations. Churchill used this speech to reply to those challenges. He argued that no war aims could be "wisely" announced in the current conditions.

This argument was singularly unsuccessful. The *New Statesman and Nation,* for example, lamented that "on this point Mr. Churchill prefers to remain silent. But silence is in itself the tacit admission of a policy."[92] One might dismiss this rejection from a Left-leaning paper with a self-avowed "revolutionary" agenda for the war. Yet the *London Times* also disagreed with this dodge,[93] and the leftists opposing it in Parliament were joined by Labourites of more moderate hue.[94] This was an important issue, for, if war is fought to protect one's community, the definition of the community is a key factor in justifying that war. Churchill was able to sidestep this issue throughout the war only because the widespread agreement about what was wrong with Hitler's government provided sufficient desire for victory so that a delineation of what was right with Britain, beyond a few short platitudes, was not necessary to constitute a community willing to fight. Arguably, however, it was this failure to articulate an acceptable long-term vision for the community which led to Churchill's surprisingly rapid dismissal as soon as the threat of the Nazi alternative had been eliminated.

Even on important issues, therefore, Churchill did not receive knee-jerk approval from his British audience. Thus, where he did generate resounding approval, we have substantial evidence of his success in articulating British sentiment as he guided it. This successful war leadership was a consequence of his enormous ability to bind art and argument in an integrated whole that fit the particularities of situation and audience. Churchill did not merely wield the universal tropes and topoi of an orator with skill; he also devised specific ways to dissolve the insecurities of his audience with metaphors that might today sound less than ringing (as in the case of the Mississippi metaphor) or which might sound excessively jingoistic (as in the image of the British fighter pilots) but which were imminently artful as rhetorical appeals in their own situation. Due in some part to Churchill's extraordinary ability to perform that particularized art for and with his people, the Anglo-American community, with its cautious, individualistic, and rationalistic sensibilities, triumphed over the purified aesthetics of the will to power. The feminized face of patriarchy proved wiser, and in its own way stronger, than the purer father form.[95]

Conclusions

The ability to construct, adapt, revise, and maintain a sense of community is yet essential to human survival. Because human communities both share many similarities and yet are also particular entities facing particular events, relationships, and challenges, the rhetor who calls forth a community and sets its members into action is bound to deploy universals of art and ideology but to embed these universals in local discourses in highly particular ways. To understand our self-constitution, therefore, requires not only that we identify the universals of art or ideology but also the particular instantiations of art and ideology in distinct situations. It requires that we seek out the full range of human rhetorical resources as well as the commonalities that might be shared among different communities.

Because of his sensitivity to the particularities of his nation's feelings, his familiarity with the language of both the pub and the coronation, and his prowess at melding these forces, Winston Churchill was able to motivate his ambivalent island nation to stand at a crucial time against the most powerful military empire that had ever been sent forth to march across the boundaries of other lands. To achieve this task he employed metaphors and arguments that were not archetypal but, rather, culture-typal, and he employed them in ways that were carefully adapted to his immediate audience's needs. We, as readers or hearers of Churchill's rhetoric today, may not share the exact configuration of Churchill's audience. Nonetheless, we do better by ourselves if we understand the particular character of his accomplishment, rather than attributing our admiration of his oratory to his command of universals, not only because such adaptation to one's community is a special and important form of art but also because the consequences of that achievement surround us yet today.

Notes

1. Robert L. Ivie, "Presidential Motives for War," *Quarterly Journal of Speech* 60 (October 1974): 337–45.

2. Vernon Bartlett, *Parliamentary Debates*, 5th ser., vol. 364, House of Commons Official Report, 10th vol., sess. 1939–40 (London: His Majesty's Stationery Office, 1940), 1206–7. Hore-Belisha, *Parliamentary Debates*, 1184. All citations for 20 August 1940 are to this volume.

3. We are aware of the psychological experiments that demonstrate that emotion is actually a set of interpretations placed upon a biological condition. Here, however, we are moving the analysis to the social level. Although individual interpretations are socialized, that is a different level of analysis from that which looks at the way in which emotions, interpreted by individuals, are structured into aesthetic products by a specific, intentional act with communicative or at least expressive intent. Hence, while both emotions and aesthetics have subconscious interpretative components, only aesthetics have conscious dimensions that include a deliberate structuring of the emotional content for some additional social purpose.

4. Raymond Williams, *Marxism and Literature* (1977; rpt., New York: Oxford University Press, 1985), 132.

5. Kenneth Burke, *A Grammar of Motives* (1945; rpt., Berkeley: University of California Press, 1969). Another approach is provided by Janice Hocker Rushing and Thomas S. Frentz, "Integrating Ideology and Archetype in Rhetorical Criticism," *Quarterly Journal of Speech* 77 (November 1991): 385–407.

6. "Lincoln's First Inaugural," in *American Speeches,* ed. Wayland Maxfield Parrish and Marie Hochmuth Nichols (New York: David Mckay., 1954); reprinted in *Methods of Rhetorical Criticism: A Twentieth Century Perspective,* 2d ed., ed. Bernard L. Brock and Robert L. Scott (Detroit: Wayne State University Press, 1980), 73–113.

7. See Michael Calvin McGee, "In Search of 'the People': A Rhetorical Alternative," *Quarterly Journal of Speech* 61 (October 1975): 235–49. We use this framework in describing the character of Churchill's rhetorical skill in that which follows.

8. Anthony Giddens, *Central Problems in Social Theory: Action, Structure and Contradiction in Social Analysis* (Berkeley: University of California Press, 1979), 128.

9. This "extreme" is a "logical outcome" of the position in the sense in which a reductio ad absurdum is a logical outcome. It is a "pure case," but we believe all pure cases are excessively disinterested cases and that at best they serve useful marketing functions.

10. William E. Rickert, "Winston Churchill's Archetypal Metaphors: A Mythopoetic Translation of World War II," *Central States Speech Journal* 28 (Summer 1977): 106–12. A comparably "universal" focus on the content of his phrases is offered by Manfred Weidhorn, "Churchill the Phrase Forger," *Quarterly Journal of Speech* 58 (April 1972): 161–74.

11. John Lukacs, *The Duel* (New York: Ticknor and Fields, 1991), 23.

12. A. J. P. Taylor, *English History, 1914–1945* (1965; rpt., New York: Oxford University Press, 1984), 488. See also the newspapers of the era (e.g., "War of Nerves," *The Economist,* 16 March 1940, 454). Churchill routinely insisted this was the case as well. This acceptance is crucial, for it signaled a widely held belief of the members of an empire that they were better off as members of that empire than in its dissolution. While this acceptance was not uniform and complete, its breadth is important for understanding the ability of the empire to maintain itself in this period of extreme trial.

13. Lukacs, *Duel,* 19; Alfred F. Havighurst, *Britain in Transition: The Twentieth Century,* 4th ed. (Chicago: University of Chicago Press, 1985), 292; *New Statesman and Nation,* 27 July 1940, 79.

14. London was not yet the target of systematic bombings, but the outlying aerodromes and production facilities had come under regular attack. In June and July 526 British pilots were killed in action. On 13 August the Germans stepped up their attack on southeast England, sending a fleet of a thousand planes, including hundreds of bombers protected by fighters. Although the Brits

claimed far greater "kills" of German planes, 150 British fighter pilots were lost in the first engagement and almost 100 in the second. See Martin S. Gilbert, *Winston S. Churchill: Finest Hour, 1939–1941* (Boston: Houghton Mifflin, 1984), 734.

15. The *New Statesman and Nation,* a Left-leaning paper, proclaimed that "we are to fight on and that indubitably is the will of the country to-day" (6 July 1940, 6).

16. Lukacs, *Duel,* 11–13, 39–40.

17. Even, for example, after Churchill's "War Situation" speech a strong communist sympathizing voice could be heard in reply in the House of Commons. See Gallacher, *Parliamentary Debates,* 20 August 1940, 1250.

18. Winston S. Churchill, *Memoirs of the Second World War* (1959; rpt., Boston: Houghton Mifflin, 1987), 305.

19. See Richard Lamb, *Churchill as War Leader* (New York: Carroll and Graf Publishers, 1991), 48–51, 74–77; or David Day, "Churchill and His War Rivals," *History Today* 41 (April 1991): 15–21.

20. John Charmley, *Churchill, the End of Glory: A Political Biography* (New York: Harcourt Brace and Company, 1993), 412.

21. *New Statesman and Nation,* letters, 30 September 1939, 458; and editorial, 7 October 1939, 473; *London Times,* 3 November 1939, 6; and 10 November 1939, 9.

22. 16 March 1940, 455.

23. 26 March 1940, 1; and 30 March 1940, 556.

24. *Economist,* 11 May 1940, 847–48.

25. 18 May 1940, 889.

26. *New Statesman and Nation,* 9 September 1939, 364.

27. The most extreme of such characterizations is offered by Leonard Jeffries, who reportedly maintains that the British (and other northern Europeans) are "ice people." See "Professor's Theories on Race Stir Turmoil at City College," *New York Times,* 20 April 1990, B1. The view of "cheerfulness" is more a self-definition (see n. 73).

28. *Economist,* 4 May 1940, 1.

29. Lees-Smith, *Parliamentary Debates,* 20 August 1940, 1173; Cocks, in ibid., 1202.

30. *New Statesman and Nation,* 6 July 1940, 6.

31. Lees-Smith, *Parliamentary Debates,* 20 August 1940, 1178.

32. Profumo, *Parliamentary Debates,* 20 August 1940, 1182.

33. Cocks, *Parliamentary Debates,* 20 August 1940, 1203.

34. *New Statesman and Nation,* 20 July 1940, 57.

35. *New Statesman and Nation,* 9 September 1939, 6 July 1940, 36–37, 6; *London Times,* 22 August 1939, 11.

36. *London Times,* 2 January 1940, 50. Ron Carpenter (pers. comm.) has pointed out the way in which this manifested itself at Dunkirk, in long orderly lines of soldiers, waiting resolutely for their turn at evacuation among the shell-

ing and death. He points especially to photographs of the evacuation, as those printed in Norman Gelb, *Dunkirk: The Complete Story of the First Step in the Defeat of Hitler* (New York: Morrow, 1989).

37. *Economist*, 29 July 1939, 203.

38. Charmley, *Churchill*, 400–412.

39. Havighurst, *Britain in Transition*, 301.

40. Taylor, *English History*, 491. In the words of the *Economist*: "It was not the people, nor even the Army, but the generals whose morale cracked. . . . What was fundamentally at fault was the personal characters of the ruling men" (29 June 1940, 1100).

41. Churchill, *Memoirs*, 304.

42. As late as 27 July 1940, the *New Statesman and Nation's* "London Diarist" was warning that such precautions were not altogether successful and that Germans "will note with satisfaction that Britain has been recently behaving in one respect as France behaved. . . . I recall Hitler's remark that wars should not be begun until they have been won by a process of preliminary disintegration. The Fifth Column is the real secret weapon" (82). Churchill himself portrayed the threat as a serious one, recalling in an earlier speech (14 July 1940) that the people "may have feared for our survival when they saw so many States and kingdoms torn to pieces in a few weeks or even days by the monstrous force of the Nazi war machine" and that they were "poisoned by intrigue before they were struck down by violence" (see *Winston S. Churchill: His Complete Speeches, 1897–1963*, vol. 6: *1935–1942*, ed. Robert Rhodes James [New York and London: Chelsea House, 1974], 6248; see also 6257).

43. Gilbert, *Winston S. Churchill*, 710.

44. The phrase had originally been used to describe the "phony war" wherein waiting for a real engagement was the perceived problem, but its use shifted as it was extended into this period. See, for example, "Letter from Queenborough," *London Times*, 8 August 1940, 5. See also several advertisements of the period which utilized the theme of "nerves"—for example, the Ovaltine advertisments, "Children in Wartime," in *London Times*, 2 May 1940, 8, and 12 June 1940, 3; see also Vernon Bartlett, *Parliamentary Debates*, 20 August 1940, 1207. In the earlier period, see the Ovaltine ad, "Your First Line of Defense—Strong Nerves," *London Times*, 9 August 1939, 5; or in the same paper, "In a Time of Stress Guiness Is Good for Nerves," 20 September 1939; "How to Win Your 'War of Nerves,'" 10 March 1939, 5; and "In Times of Stress Wrigley's Quiets Your Nerves," 16 September 1939, 4.

45. Reported in *London Times*, 15 June 1940, 87.

46. 22 June 1940, 1067. See also terms such as *solid grounds* (*Economist*, 6 July 1940, 6).

47. Simmonds, *Parliamentary Debates*, 20 August 1940, 1210. See also *Economist*, 4 May 1940, 1; or *New Statesman and Nation*, 9 September 1939, 361.

48. 27 July 1940, 79.

49. *Economist,* 15 June 1940, 1031.

50. Ibid., 25 May 1940, 923; or 8 June 1940, 998.

51. 29 June 1940, 1101.

52. *Parliamentary Debates,* 20 August 1940, 1178.

53. 8 June 1940, 998.

54. 6 July 1940, 1. Also 15 June 1940, 1031.

55. 3 August 1940, 104.

56. Rickert, "Winston Churchill's Archetypal Metaphors," 110. Rickert might also be seen as ethnocentric in this analysis. The sense that water flows "down" is not only a physical fact in the United States, but also from our perspective it is a geographical fact—rivers flow down the map. The British, however, were experienced colonialists in the Southern Hemisphere, where major rivers flow "up" the map as well. This might have given them a different sense of the directionality of rivers.

57. Warren F. Kimball, ed., *Churchill and Roosevelt: The Complete Correspondence,* vol. 1: *Alliance Emerging* (Princeton: Princeton University Press, 1984), R-8x, 13 August 1940, and C-21x, 15 August 1940, 58–61.

58. War Cabinet NO. 227 of 1940, 14 August, 6:30 P.M., Cabinet Papers 65/8 cited in Gilbert, *Winston S. Churchill,* 733.

59. Charmley, *Churchill,* 413.

60. *Show Boat* opened at the Drury Lane Theatre to packed crowds on 3 May 1928. The Universal Studios film version was released in 1936. Both featured Paul Robeson (Stanley Green, *Encyclopaedia of the Musical Theatre* [New York: Dodd, Mead, 1976], 380–81). *The New Grove Dictionary of American Music* says of Robeson: "He packed Drury Lane, London, by his majestic presence and his singing (especially of "Ol' Man River") in *Show Boat.*" H. Wiley Hitchcock and Stanley Sadie, *The New Grove Dictionary of American Music* (New York: Macmillan, 1986), 54.

61. John H. Timmis III, "Textual and Information-Theoretic Indexes of Style as Discriminators between Message Sources," *Communication Monographs* 52 (June 1985): 136–55.

62. John P. Colville, *The Fringes of Power: 10 Downing Street Diaries, 1939–1955* (New York: W. W. Norton, 1985), 227.

63. James C. Humes, *Churchill: Speaker of the Century* (New York: Stein and Day, 1980), 48–49.

64. Elizabeth Jean Nelson, "To Ethiopia and Beyond: The Primacy of 'Struggle' in Mussolini's Public Discourse" (Ph.D. diss., University of Iowa, 1988).

65. The phrase had been germinated in the Operations Room of No. 11 Fighter Command as Churchill watched one of the fiercest battles played out with colored discs on maps. See Gilbert, *Winston S. Churchill,* 736.

66. Churchill, *Memoirs,* 365.

67. Taylor, *English History,* 488l; Halbert E. Gulley, "Churchill's Speech on the Munich Agreement," *Quarterly Journal of Speech* 33 (October 1947): 285; Jo-

seph W. Miller "Winston Churchill, Spokesman for Democracy," *Quarterly Journal of Speech* 28 (April 1942): 137.

68. 5 June 1940, 7.

69. 29 June 1940, 1100.

70. Taylor, *English History*, 488; Humes, *Churchill*, 190.

71. Ibid., 190.

72. Profumo and Lt. Col. Moore-Brabazon in *Parliamentary Debates*, 20 August 1940, 1182, 1194.

73. "Cheery tenacity" was the central slogan in a large advertisement that appeared in the newspapers during this period, and *cheerfulness* or *good-humoured* were terms also frequently applied to the citizen's attitude toward the war. See *New Statesman and Nation*, 20 July 1940, 57; *London Times*, 4 July 1940, 3, or *Economist*, 14 September 1940, 329.

74. *London Times*, 21 August 40, 4.

75. 21 August 1940, 4.

76. 24 August 1940, 236.

77. *Parliamentary Debates*, 20 August 1940, 1184. See also Sir Percy Harris, ibid., 1179; Braithwaite, ibid., 1254; and John Morgan, ibid., 1218.

78. Sinclair, ibid., 1268.

79. 21 August 1940, 5.

80. 24 August 1940, 173.

81. *Parliamentary Debates*, 20 August 1940, 1195.

82. Ibid., 20 August 1940, 1202. His endorsement was enthusiastically echoed by MPs Hore-Belisha, Braithwaite, and Hammersley (1186, 1195, 1254, 1258). The secretary of state for air began his response on behalf of the government noting the general agreement on this issue (1265–66).

83. 24 August 1940, 173; 21 August 1940, 4.

84. 24 August 1940, 236.

85. 19 August 1940, 4 . See also 20 August 1940, 4; 17 August 1940, 4; and 16 August 1940, 4.

86. *Parliamentary Debates*, 20 August 1940, 1178.

87. Ibid., 1193.

88. Ibid., 1183–84.

89. Ibid., 1210.

90. *London Times*, 21 August 1940, 4; see also 5. On 24 August it proclaimed, "The first phase of the Battle of Britain has ended" (4) and cited Churchill's "never" phrase again.

91. See, for example, 6 July 1940, 3; or 27 July 1940, 79.

92. 24 August 1940, 176.

93. 21 August 1940, 5.

94. Mr. Gallacher, *Parliamentary Debates*, 20 August 1940, 1251. See also Stokes,

ibid., 1126–27; and Rathbone, ibid., 1231–36. More ambiguously, see Bartlett, ibid., 1209.

95. We borrow here Michael Calvin McGee's insight that British government was feminized by the rule of Elizabeth I. See "The Origins of 'Liberty': A Feminization of Power," *Communication Monographs* 47 (March 1980): 23–45. In a comparative essay we would note further that the art of the British is a more pastoral art. Churchill's metaphors are of light and loft and dignity, whereas those of Hitler are of power and force and struggle.

CHAPTER TEN

Churchill's
"Machiavellian Moment"
The Negotiation of Anxiety in
"The War Situation I"

James Jasinski

A central element in Condit and Greer's essay "The Particular Aesthetics of Winston Churchill's 'War Situation I'" is the relationship between the text and its context. They maintain that one of the unique features of the discipline of rhetorical studies is its conceptualization of "texts as situated historical events." But they acknowledge a tendency in disciplinary critical practices to neglect the particular. In response to this perceived problem in disciplinary practice, they propose a model for investigating the situatedness of text in context. The model instantiates, in the words of literary historian Louis Montrose, "a refiguring of the socio-cultural field."[1] In constructing their model, Condit and Greer draw from the disciplinary tradition of rhetorical studies, which is supplemented by work in the sociology of literature. Their refiguring of the sociocultural field culminates in the concept of "communal sensitivities" as a way of negotiating the text/context relationship. They conclude that the rhetorical critic's task is "to understand the feelings, values, and concerns of the community in the particular historical moment" in order to investigate "the ways in which [a text] fits or fails to fit the needs and desires of the community." Based on a detailed reconstruction of British "sensitivities" in the late 1930s, Condit and Greer conclude that "Churchill's eloquence . . . drew much of its force from the creation of culture-typal metaphors for his people and from deploying highly specific metaphors tailored precisely to the immediate sensitivities of his community."[2]

Postmodern thought, in and through its various conceptual and methodological guises, challenges the presumed identity and stability of context which is at the core of Condit and Greer's project. If poststructuralism, for example, has taught us anything, it is that all representations are based on exclusions. Even an exhaustive account of communal sensitivities—and I think Condit and Greer certainly approach that standard—remains plagued by the possibility of alternative renderings of a community's sentiments. LaCapra's observations on the "rhetoric of contextualization" address this issue. He writes: "An appeal to the context does not *eo ipso* answer all the questions in reading and interpretation. And an appeal to *the* context is deceptive: one never has—at least in the case of complex texts—*the* context. The assumption that one does relies on a hypostatization of 'context,' often in the service of misleading organic or other overly reductive analogies. For complex texts, one has a set of interacting contexts whose relations to one another are variable and problematic and whose relation to the text being investigated raises difficult issues in interpretation."[3] Historical evidence can be adduced to help adjudicate competing reconstructions of the past to a certain degree. But, if contexts are, as LaCapra suggests, fragmentary and multipliable, no amount of evidence is sufficient to establish a singular, unitary context. Neither the critic, the historical audience, or, for that matter, the advocate has access to a unified, fully present context. Texts inevitably negotiate, both explicitly and implicitly, multiple contexts through an advocate's orchestration of diverse traditions, linguistic idioms, and rhetorical resources. Critics, in turn, while remaining committed to the idea of the rhetorical text as a "situated historical event," need to be sensitive to the way contextual dynamics problematize their effort to ground textual analysis in a situated historical context.

To illustrate the significance of the issue of multiple contexts and their impact on interpretative practice, I want to propose a relatively minor modification to Condit and Greer's reconstruction of British communal sensitivities in 1940. What I hope to show is that even a relatively minor modification in the mode of contextualization can lead to some fairly significant alterations in the way we analytically reconstruct the Churchill address. The contextual modification I propose foregrounds the experience of anxiety which is the result of a community's confrontation with its own fragility and mortality, or, in Pocock's terms, a "Machiavellian moment."

In his monumental study of the classical republican heritage in Anglo-American political thought, J. G. A. Pocock introduces the concept of the Machiavellian moment to describe a recurrent problem that all modern republics must at some point confront (and, in some cases, confront repeatedly). The Machiavellian moment, according to Pocock, "is a name for the moment in conceptualized time in which the republic was seen as confronting its own temporal finitude, as attempting to remain morally and politically stable in a stream of irrational events conceived as essentially destructive of all systems of secular stability."[4] In the language of Florentine political theory *corruption* and *fortune* are the terms used to represent the forces threatening the political community's capacity to survive. *Corruption* could be used to signify a variety of social forces that made the exercise of virtue problematic. *Fortune* signifies "the irrationality of history" and the inherent insecurity of human existence. While the terms *corruption, fortune,* and *virtue* do not play an explicit role in Churchill's address, nor are they clearly present in the community's sensitivities, the pattern of republican thought that these terms embody, as Pocock suggests, functions as an inherited tradition, a kind of deep structure, which continues to shape twentieth-century Anglo-American political thought and perception.[5] We might say, then, that in 1940 Great Britain faced the threat of what seemed to be absolute human corruption—Nazi fascism—which magnified the irrationality and insecurity of human existence. In a way unlike any in its long history the British nation confronted its temporal finitude, the possibility of its imminent demise. Churchill, and the nation, faced a modern variation of the Machiavellian moment.

Among the resources Florentine political thought made available to human agents is the possibility of prudential action. Pocock and Eugene Garver, in different ways, discuss the way the practical enactment of prudence functions in the Renaissance political world as an antidote to irrational events and temporal anxiety. In Garver's view prudential action negotiates the "problem of flexibility and continuity" by creating a means of stable innovation which allows "active flexibility in the light of changing circumstances."[6] Prudence makes it possible to adapt old solutions to new problems, thereby achieving normative and practical stability. Recontextualizing Churchill's address helps reveal its prudential gestures. Condit and Greer discuss Churchill's comparison of the two wars against German aggression as part of his reason-giving logical scaffolding. They emphasize an early passage in the address: "there seems to be every reason to believe that this new kind of war is well suited to the genius and the resources of the British nation." But Churchill's reason giving assumes a particular form that I would describe as prudential. Churchill's challenge in the opening section is the common prudential problem of adapting the old to the new, of discovering elements of the past which allow one to respond effectively, rather than habitually, to new circumstances. Churchill's guarded optimism is the result of his ability to fashion a response to the new circumstances introduced by the war (e.g., the fact that "the fronts are everywhere") out of traditional cultural resources, thereby crafting a form of stable innovation. The key prudential gesture in the opening section of the address is the conditional sentence: "If all these qualities are turned, as they are being turned, to the arts of war, we may be able to show the enemy quite a lot of things that they have not thought of yet." In this passage Churchill invokes traditional British "qualities" (e.g., traditions of "freedom and individual responsibility," "tolerance and variety") in order to adapt them, to "turn" them, to the new conditions (the war) which threaten the nation's existence.

A similar pattern of adapting tradition to new circumstances reappears later in the address. As Condit and Greer note, Churchill discusses one specific innovation that he believes works to Great Britain's advantage: the introduction of the airplane. But Churchill does not portray Britain's air power as a pure innovation that is unrelated to its traditional resources. The innovative potential of the airplane can be harnessed because it is combined with the "prowess" and "devotion" of the British military (invoking the tradition of the citizen-soldier which dates back to Harrington's anglicizing of Florentine doctrine) and because it is combined with traditional British military doctrine. In his discussion of defense preparations Churchill notes how "all this is classical and venerable doctrine. As in Nelson's day, the maxim holds, 'Our first line of defense is the enemy's ports.' Now air reconnaissance and photography have brought to an old principle a new and potent aid." Churchill's prudential gesture here follows the pattern established in the opening section of the address: innovation is made possible by the adaptation of tradition.

Recontextualizing Churchill's situation as a Machiavellian moment forces the critic to investigate the discursive negotiation of anxiety. In the Heideggerian phenomenological tradition, anxiety arises when individuals confront the indefiniteness, the multiple possibilities, of the future.[7] Extending this account of the emergence of anxiety to a communal level is consistent with Pocock's discussion of a polity's confrontation with finitude. We can say that when a community's future is marked by extreme indefiniteness, when the commonly taken-for-granted continuation of the community is rendered problematic, there exists an at least potential problem of communal anxiety. How does Churchill negotiate this aspect of the Machiavellian moment? How does he respond to the indefiniteness of the future, to the possibility that Britain lacks the resources and capacity to survive as a nation?

One of the notable aspects of the address which Condit and Greer fail to appreciate fully is Churchill's supreme self-control, or self-discipline. What Condit and Greer refer to as British self-doubt and the more fundamental problem of anxiety which I want to consider cannot be found literally present in the text. British anxiety, even more than a possible negotiated truce with Hitler, is ultimately "unspeakable." Even such common stylized expressions of anxiety such as aporia are completely absent from the speech. The address exudes restrained confidence. But the absence might hint at a part of the text's dynamic which Condit and Greer overlook.

They argue that Churchill's "reason-giving aesthetic" is the discursive mechanism for negotiating British self-doubt and, by extension, the communal problem of anxiety. This assumes that the problem of anxiety is amenable to a rational or reasonable cure. But the literature on individual anxiety suggests that "talking cures" are frequently ineffective, so it is quite possible that Churchill's reason giving did not respond fully—was in fact incapable of completely resolving—the complexities of his situation. In that case what rhetorical function does reason giving fulfill? Black's observations on the "sentimental style" provide a way of addressing this question. Black describes the sentimental style as "an aesthetic anesthetic" that strove for "a total control over the consciousness" of the audience.[8] I suggest Churchill's reason giving might function similarly.

Churchill's reason giving works as a kind of rhetorical double gesture, a discursive force moving in two different directions. On the one hand, as Condit and Greer suggest, reason giving functions as a reflection of British character and works to convince the public that there were "solid grounds" for confidence. But reason giving also works indirectly to displace or sublimate anxiety by structuring the form in which the experience of anxiety could be expressed. Public fears or anxieties, however warranted or unwarranted they might be, are not so much directly confronted or addressed by Churchill as they are diverted or deflected through import tonnage reports and details about the salvage operations of the Ministry of Aircraft Production. "Fact," and not inchoate fear, becomes the only acceptable discursive form for structuring and articulating public experience. Public anxiety is not brought out in the open but buried beneath a structure of amplified data.

The problem of anxiety can also inform our reading of the metaphors in the address. Condit and Greer argue that a universalist and/or archetypal reading might conclude that the opening and closing framing metaphors (of a journey, of the Mississippi) were incompatible and mistakenly judge the speech defective. A "particularized" reading of the speech, they maintain, reveals Churchill to be "a master of the intertwined features of cultural sensitivities, situation, and metaphor." I also want to attempt a particularized reading of these metaphors. I want to try to show that a metaphorical tension remains (a tension between the journey metaphor and the metaphors drawn from elemental forces of nature, including the Mississippi River) which functions as a kind of textual trace of Churchill's ongoing struggle with the problem of anxiety.

Let me start by reviewing Condit and Greer's reading of the metaphors, in particular their reading of the final image of the Mississippi. First, they suggest that the Mississippi image refers to the United States and "its future course." This particularized reading is problematic in that the river image seems more directly related to Churchill's just completed discussion of the "mixing" of U.S. and British resources. Second, they argue that earlier "water" images referring to the United States "prefigured" the Mississippi metaphor and established a "qualitative form" that is fulfilled in the peroration. The point is also problematic; the first figurative reference to the United States which I detect is as a "bridge," an image that is not exclusively connected to water. Third, they maintain that the river metaphor works as an "appropriate means of continuing the journey" figuratively established in the exordium because of its "ideological" entailments. While there may be a degree of ideological reinforcement between the opening and closing images, there is also a significant difference between an agency-based metaphor such as "journey" and metaphors drawn from natural forces which require no human action or intervention. This is the metaphorical tension I want to explore.

Churchill employs metaphorical images drawn from two elemental forces of nature, fire and water, on ten occasions in the address (e.g., "cataract of disaster," conviction is "burning," "spark of hope," "cleansing and devouring flame," turning the "tide" of war, etc.). Further, on two occasions Churchill supplements the fire/water family with images

of morning or daybreak. Collectively, these natural metaphors constitute a significant rhetorical form in the address. Metaphors that rely on
some form of human agency are present in the speech, but, interest-
ingly, they cluster in the opening four paragraphs. In the introduction
the journey and game metaphors figure prominently, but they are largely
absent from the remainder of the address. Journey images only occur
twice outside the introduction.

There are moments in the address when nature and human agency
work to complement each other—British airmen, for example, turn the
"tide" of war. But, in general, nature and human agency are disjointed.
Water moves, fire devours, morning comes, no matter what any individual or community might do. Churchill acknowledges the incapacity
of human agency in the face of the force of nature, as Condit and Greer
note, in the peroration when he admits that he could do nothing to stop
the course of the river even if he wanted to; "no one," Churchill reminds his audience, "can stop it." What interpretative possibilities
does this disjointed metaphorical structure present? We can, as
Condit and Greer urge, read the "broader lands" covered by the rushing Mississippi as a gesture back to "the dark, wide field" of the
opening metaphorical journey. But does the river aesthetically and
ideologically complete the opening journey? Does the concluding image overcome the gulf separating human agency from the forces of
nature? This gulf, in my view, remains. To appreciate the interpretative
possibilities of this figurative and ideological tension, we need to return
briefly to the idea of the Machiavellian moment and the classically inspired Florentine language of politics.

As Pocock and others have shown, Florentine political thinkers understood politics as a struggle between three critical forces: virtue,
corruption, and fortune. Like the good republican that he is, Churchill
calls forth British virtue to defeat fascist corruption; the qualities that he
speaks of being turned to war in the opening section of the speech are
the central civic virtues of the republic. These virtues—freedom, individual responsibility, tolerance, among others—are not the same as the
virtues of the Florentine republic, but they nevertheless constitute
Britain's source of strength and function as an antidote capable of ward-
ing off the forces of corruption. But Churchill's disjointed metaphorical
structure exhibits traces of doubt which call into question the sufficiency
and capacity of civic virtue. The metaphors of elemental forces paint a
different picture: of Hitler being devoured by fire or washed away by a

raging torrent of water. A virtuous citizenry, united and actively involved in its own defense (captured in Churchill's image of the "workmen" as "soldiers" in the opening section of the speech), is absent in these metaphors; agent and virtue have been metaphorically marginalized. Instead, nature emerges as the actor.

It will be useful at this point to recall the images of fortune in Florentine political thought. Among the common ones are fortune as a wheel, as a woman, and as a river. In chapter 25 of *The Prince* Machiavelli writes: "I compare fortune to one of those torrential rivers which, when enraged, inundates the lowlands, tears down trees and buildings, and washes out the land on one bank to deposit it on the other. Everyone flees before it; everyone yields to its assaults without being able to offer it any resistance."[9] By invoking the image of the raging Mississippi, Churchill seems to be turning to the realm of fortune, conceptualized within Florentine thought as both a source of instability which threatens the republic as well as an opportunity for exercising *virtu*, and recasting it in the role of potential savior. But in Churchill's case the appeal to fortune does not amplify his call for action; rather, it appears both to conceal and to reveal Churchill's own doubts and anxiety about the virtue of the British public and their capacity to thwart Hitler's corrupt ambition. The power of the metaphorical pattern in the address, I would argue, stems not so much from any aesthetic or ideological coherence between journey and river but in the artful blurring, a discursive finessing, of the relationship between virtue and fortune. The river metaphor not only prefigures an alliance with the United States; it seeks to forge an alliance with fortune. But it is not fortune, pure and simple, which Churchill's imagery and final words solicit. In his final sentence—"Let it roll on full flood, inexorable, irresistible, benignant, to broader lands and better days"—Churchill assumes a rather prophetic voice as he predicts ultimate victory.[10] A turn to prophecy is, Pocock notes, part of a specific tradition in Florentine political thought. More important, the prophetic mode introduced in the closing line of the speech completes, as it transforms, Churchill's appeal to fortune. For, as Pocock observes, in what we might label as the prophetic republic tradition, fortune is convertible into divine providence through the "public action" of "prophecy."[11] Fortune and providence, then, emerge as the resources Churchill draws upon to negotiate the anxieties of his Machiavellian moment.

Notes

1. Louis A. Montrose, "Professing the Renaissance: The Poetics and Politics of Culture," in *The New Historicism*, ed. H. A. Veeser (New York: Routledge, 1989), 17.

2. The "communal sensitivities" model that Condit and Greer propose remains firmly grounded in the disciplinary tradition of rhetorical studies. The dominant paradigm of critical practice, according to Black's 1965 reconstruction, is grounded in

> the effort to reconstruct the popular attitudes and prevailing sentiments of the time in history when the rhetorical discourse appeared. This reconstruction involves the critic's thinking and feeling himself [*sic*] into the thoughts and feelings of the rhetor's immediate audience, so that he can empathize with that audience and attempt to gauge their reactions to the discourse. In this procedure, the critic's own reactions to the discourse play a decidedly subordinate role. He apprehends the discourse, insofar as he is able, via the minds of others. . . . [The] critic is preoccupied with the immediate audience of the discourse; in a sense, his eye is where that audience's eyes are: on the issues of the discourse, on its doctrines, on the ideas to which the audience is asked to assent. And insofar as his focus is thus, then his own responses to the discourse will have no place in the critical performance." (Edwin Black, *Rhetorical Criticism: A Study in Method* [1965; rpt., Madison: University of Wisconsin Press, 1978], 56–57)

3. Dominick LaCapra, *Rethinking Intellectual History: Texts, Contexts, Language* (Ithaca: Cornell University Press, 1983), 14, 35.

4. J. G. A. Pocock, *The Machiavellian Moment: Florentine Political Thought and the Atlantic Republican Tradition* (Princeton: Princeton University Press, 1975), viii.

5. In highlighting the possible influence of the performative tradition of Florentine republicanism, I do not mean to imply that it was the only political tradition that Churchill, and the British public, could draw upon.

6. Eugene Garver, *Machiavelli and the History of Prudence* (Madison: University of Wisconsin Press, 1987), 10.

7. See, for example, Michael J. Hyde, "The Experience of Anxiety: A Phenomenological Investigation" *Quarterly Journal of Speech* 66 (1980): 140–54.

8. Edwin Black, "The Sentimental Style as Escapism, or the Devil with Dan'l Webster," in *Form and Genre: Shaping Rhetorical Action*, ed. K. K. Campbell and K. H. Jamieson (Falls Church, Va.: Speech Communication Association, n.d.), 81, 78.

9. Niccolò Machiavelli, *The Prince*, trans. Daniel Donno (New York: Bantam Books, 1966). I want to thank Bob Hariman for calling my attention to this passage.

10. On the idea of prophetic voice or ethos, see James Darsey, "The Legend of Eugene Debs: Prophetic *Ethos* as Radical Argument," *Quarterly Journal of Speech* 74 (1988): 434–52; and Margaret D. Zulick, "The Agon of Jeremiah: On the Dialogic Invention of Prophetic Ethos," *Quarterly Journal of Speech* 78 (1992): 125–48.

11. Pocock, *Machiavellian Moment*, 43–44. For Pocock the key figure in this tradition is Savonarola.

Part Three:

Artistic and Scientific Community

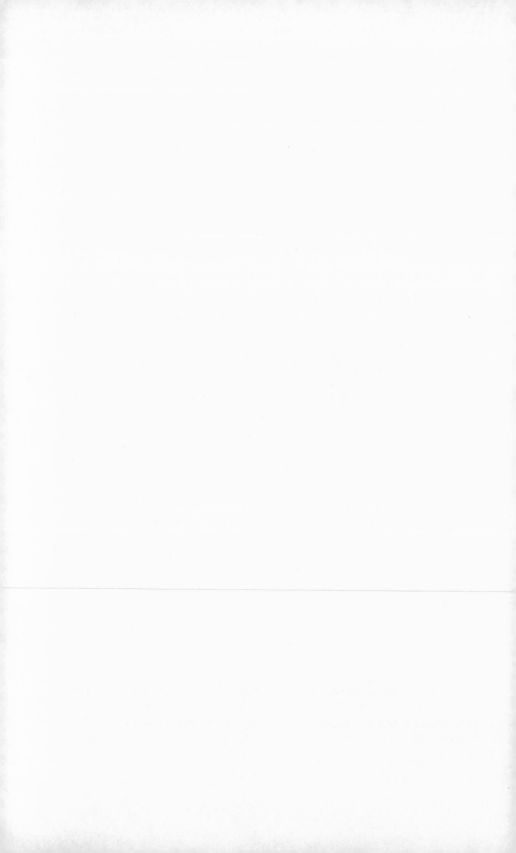

CHAPTER ELEVEN

Thinking through Film
Hollywood Remembers the Blacklist

Thomas W. Benson

In 1990 Robert De Niro starred as a blacklisted Hollywood director in Irwin Winkler's film *Guilty by Suspicion*. I propose to use the film as the focal point for a critical speculation on the rhetorical recreation of public moral memory.[1] *Guilty by Suspicion* is another retelling of the story of the blacklist.[2] It is also an explicitly political film directed to contemporary viewers, using a resonant historical tale to calculate the prospects for public life and civic community. I propose a reading of the film and its reception that attempts to take into account the text, the times, and the tradition. Using the film itself as the focal point of analysis, I will attempt to reconstruct a reading of the text that takes into account the historical period of its setting in the time of the Hollywood blacklist and the time of its intended reception in the immediate post-Reagan 1990s. Further, I will attempt to locate the film's use of traditional, deeply embedded rhetorical forms and practices that give form to the text. One aim of such a reading is to make accessible to the world of explicitly political discourse the figural underpinnings of thought that are otherwise unnoticed, depoliticized, naturalized, and whose effects are achieved precisely because they are taken for granted.

I offer this experiment in rhetorical reconstruction under the heading of a general question of long-standing concern to rhetorical theorists: When we employ the rhetorical instruments of our cultural tradition to shape our symbolic appeals, how are we to understand the ways in which those instruments and traditions, and the material practices used to employ them, shape our thoughts?

Rhetorical critics are curious about how the tropes and commonplaces of our discourse, reinforced by the modes of cultural production and distribution, embed deeply held but mostly unexamined patterns of thought. We use these taken-for-granted patterns to shape our thought and our social world, even our physical world. One of the tasks of the cultural critic is to bring these mostly implicit patterns into the realm of the explicit, so that we may all reflect more self-consciously about what is guiding our choices.

I do not propose to address these questions at the level of purely theoretical argument but, rather, to observe and attempt to describe them—admittedly only partially—in the living action of a rhetorical text. Irwin Winkler's film *Guilty by Suspicion* appears to be a promising site for such a reconstruction. It is a well-made but by no means classic film, widely reviewed on its release, attempting both to achieve success as a star vehicle for Robert De Niro and to reshape our memory about a recent and contested political event in American life. The film puts into play both the tension between public and private life and the tension between political rhetoric and depoliticized narrative, resulting, as I hope to show, in a political content strongly shaped by its rhetorical form. The film shows us something of the ways in which it makes sense to argue that our political consciousness is prefigured by traditional forms.

In 1947 the House Un-American Activities Committee (HUAC) held a series of hearings on alleged Communist infiltration of the Hollywood motion picture industry. These hearings, under the chairmanship of J. Parnell Thomas of New Jersey, helped to give birth to a new domestic rhetoric for the Cold War—friendly witnesses (who testified that Hollywood was infested with Communists and who were willing to name names); unfriendly witnesses (suspected of "subversion" and unwilling to disclose information about their own political activities or those of associates); the Hollywood Ten, the most adamant unfriendlies, who refused to testify on the grounds that the First Amendment to the Constitution prohibited Congress from requiring them to testify about their political beliefs and activities. And the blacklist.

The Hollywood Ten eventually spent time in prison for contempt of Congress for their refusal to testify; in prison at the same time was J. Parnell Thomas, the recent chair of HUAC, convicted of corruption in office.

The Hollywood blacklist, which quickly spread to the entertainment industries on both coasts, was a loosely organized but widespread and pervasive operation begun by a group of Hollywood executives in 1947 with the famous Waldorf declaration, in which they committed the motion picture industry to blacklisting: "We will not knowingly employ a Communist or a member of any party or group which advocates the overthrow of the Government of the United States by force, or by any illegal or unconstitutional method."[3]

In June 1950 the blacklist took on a new scope with the publication by Vincent Hartnett of *Red Channels*, a listing of entertainment workers with allegedly subversive associations.[4] Hartnett began to work with an organization calling itself American Business Consultants and went into the business of publishing a periodical called *Counterattack*, warning against Communist subversion in U.S. corporations, to which the media were bullied into subscribing. American Business Consultants (ABC) began to collaborate with Vincent Hartnett in an ongoing listing of alleged subversives and was soon in the business of peddling accusations and clearances. In the resulting blacklist hundreds of people lost their jobs and their careers, not for advocating the overthrow of the government, and in many cases not for being Communists or former Communists, but simply for coming under suspicion. Some lost their lives.

The House Un-American Activities Committee held an additional series of hearings on Hollywood in the period 1951–53. *Guilty by Suspicion* is set at the time of this second round of hearings. The film tells the story of Hollywood director David Merrill (Robert De Niro), a nonpolitical liberal who is named as a Communist by a committee witness and who finds himself subject to the blacklist. Most of the film is devoted to Merrill's tribulations as he is hounded from one end of the country to the other, meanwhile becoming reconciled to his former wife. Offered a chance to clear himself by testifying before the committee, Merrill agrees to appear, but, in the final scene of the film, at the hearing itself, Merrill angrily refuses to play the game of clearing himself by implicating others and leaves the committee chamber in moral triumph, his wife on his arm, as an old friend, called as the next witness, also refuses to testify. The committee has won this round, but History and Hollywood (the Hollywood of 1991) clear Merrill of all charges and condemn the committee and the blacklist as a hysterical witch-hunt.

In its dual focus on the public actions of the House Un-American Activities Committee and the effects of those actions on the private lives of its victims, the film promises to offer us a rich and creative way to think and feel about this ugly period of our past. Reliance solely on the personal or the political seems to many critics as a sure way to miss much of our cultural and historical situation. And, to be sure, *Guilty by Suspicion* affirms traditional family values of loyalty and intimacy, celebrates hard work and professional success, and strongly criticizes the

bullying interference of government officials into the legitimate political lives of private citizens. But, despite these achievements, the film,
when examined from a rhetorical perspective, appears to evade both
the personal and the political by relying on shallow formulas that
render both politics and personal life as Hollywood stereotypes. In
offering this reading, I do not mean to suggest that there is only one
possible interpretation of the film or that its effect on its audiences
can be determined by one critical reading. Nor do I wish to engage
in the critical game of Hollywood bashing; it is always too easy to
say that a popular film is insufficiently political or that it simplifies
its subject matter. Rather, I propose a dialogical reading of the film—
that is, a reading that does not privilege the act of critical interpretation
over the text but, rather, regards both as incomplete and open-ended
elements in an ongoing cultural conversation.

At the center of *Guilty by Suspicion* as a political story is the experience of David Merrill. The film opens in a dimly lit hearing room,
identified in a caption as an executive session of the House
Un-American Activities Committee, Los Angeles, California, September 1951. A man, Larry Nolan, is being bullied by the committee
to "demonstrate his loyalty" by informing on his friends as a condition for "purging" him of his former membership in the Communist
Party. His choices are clear: having himself been named by others
and having confessed to attending a few meetings of the Communist Party, Nolan can refuse to inform, thus risking a jail sentence
for contempt of Congress and ensuring that he will never work again,
or, as a condition of further employment in the industry, he can give
the committee names that it obviously already knows.

In the next two scenes of the film David Merrill arrives by train in
Los Angeles and is picked up by his lifelong friend Bunny, a screen-
writer, who takes him home to a surprise birthday party, where, in a
corner, Larry Nolan confesses to his wife that he has informed to the
committee. For the remainder of the film we follow David Merrill as a
sort of Hollywood Everyman, who embarks on a series of parallel
quests—to regain his family and to find a way of responding to the fact
that he, too, has been named to the committee as a Communist. This
narrative structure is one of the strengths of the film, as it permits Merrill
(and us) to experience and observe the political and personal effects of
the hearings and the blacklist on himself and his colleagues, friends,
and family.

Soon David Merrill is offered a script to direct by his studio boss, Darryl Zanuck, but is told that, because he has been named as a Communist sympathizer and is therefore under suspicion, he must first clear himself with the committee. David now begins his education in the clearance process and begins to think through his own response to the committee, which climaxes only in the final scenes of the film. David's confrontation with the clearance process, and especially his own ultimate actions in responding to the committee, form the core of the manifestly political thread in *Guilty by Suspicion*. Strikingly, when the film's political mysteries—HUAC's investigation and David's response—are revealed, we discover they are not political after all.

Zanuck refers David to a clearance lawyer named Felix Graff, and David, mystified, arrives at a seedy, dim apartment in downtown Los Angeles, where Graff introduces him to a committee staff member, Ray Karlin, for a conversation preliminary to David's testimony before the committee. Karlin explains that David has been named as a Communist sympathizer. Karlin makes it clear that David is not actually under suspicion but that it will be necessary for him to "purge" himself by testifying about his actions "and those of others." They want him to testify about Sterling Hayden, Howard Da Silva, Lionel Stander, Elizabeth Cummings, and his old (and fictional) friend Bunny Baxter.

DAVID: Well, I don't know about the others, but Bunny Baxter is not a Communist. He's not a Communist.

KARLIN: That's the committee's responsibility to determine, not yours, Mr. Merrill.

DAVID: No, no, but I'm telling you. Bunny Baxter is not a Communist, I've known him all my life. He's not a Communist and I'm not going to say he's one.

KARLIN: You really want to be associated with these people, you a decorated naval officer, dropped behind enemy lines. I'm very disappointed.

DAVID: I don't care. I don't give a shit if you're disappointed or not. I inform on these people and they lose their jobs, they lose their—everything. . . .

DAVID: [to Graff]: Did you tell them I would do this, that I'd be a fucking stool pigeon?

David, unprepared by his lawyer for what the committee wants, refuses to be a stool pigeon and stalks out of the room as Karlin tells
him that he will be subpoenaed at the committee's next public hearing in Washington. Because David has clearly not been prepared by
his lawyer, his response is established as an unpremeditated revela-
tion of his character.

David's response at this early point in the film is absolutely characteristic of the American movie hero. Confronted with a problem in a
community gone wrong, his response is individualistic, instinctive, and
governed by a code of personal honor. It is important, I think, for us to
notice how David's honorable refusal is situated in the sequence of the
film: it comes immediately before a verbal exposition of the depoliticized
politics of the situation. Having summoned his refusal to turn informer
from his American manhood, his already established character as a
friend, a father, a former and perhaps future husband, a naval hero —
and, not incidentally, Robert De Niro — David Merrill walks out of the
room. He is followed by the lawyer, Graff, who provides instruction for
David and, through an ironic screen, us, but only after David's instinctive response has been evoked in his face-off with the powers of darkness.

> GRAFF: David, listen. I'm on your side. But make no mistake
> about these guys. They are some of the most unethical bas-
> tards. Parnell Thomas, their recent chairman, is serving time
> in a federal prison for fraud.
>
> DAVID: Why are they after me then?
>
> GRAFF: They're looking to get their picture in the paper and
> Hollywood gets it there. Look, this is not about national
> security, it is not about loyalty, it is about power, it is about
> publicity. Already they sent ten men to jail. You want to be the
> next? Everybody said you were a team player. [David drives
> off, leaving Graff on the sidewalk].

We do not know at this point in the narrative the answers to several
questions that we are hereby alerted to ask. What exactly is the lawyer
telling David? Is Graff complaining that the committee is not political
because, properly speaking, it is their business to engage in politics and
government? Or is he complaining because they are hypocrites, and that
politics is irrelevant? Does he speak for the filmmaker? If he does, is the
filmmaker stating an observation only about the politics of the blacklist

or about politics in general—including politics now? We do not know the answers to these questions, but we have been put on notice that in order to make sense of the film as a narrative we need to make sense of its politics. Only gradually will we become aware that the film does have a political agenda—an agenda that is a conventional, paradoxical, and disabling denial of the politics of politics.

This sequence at the hotel does much to establish David's isolation and the atmosphere of menace that surrounds the committee. As in many of the scenes that directly involve the committee, the sequence with Karlin and Graff in the hotel room stretches the surface visual realism of *Guilty by Suspicion* toward irony and expressionism. As the sequence opens, the camera pans down from a rooftop neon sign advertising the Hotel Rosslyn in a valentine frame to a huge revolver hanging on a pair of chains, advertising Cowan's Gun Shop. Underneath the sign an injured person is lifted onto a stretcher by two ambulance attendants, as David drives up in his open sports car. As he walks up the shadowy stairs, David encounters a small girl, sitting on the steps, who drops her ball. It bounces down the steps. David retrieves the ball and continues up the stairs.[5] Graff and Karlin are already in the hotel suite, and as the three of them talk, it appears that Graff has already told Karlin that David would cooperate. Then, in a gesture seemingly devised to cast doubt on Graff's loyalty to his client, the film departs from its usual rule of showing us only the world visible to David. After David has left the hotel suite, Karlin says to Graff, "Go talk to him, Graff," indicating the committee's power to influence or perhaps control Graff in a relationship that is not revealed to David. The moment also has the effect of reinforcing and sharing with the audience the privileged position of the narrating agency—a narrating agency that in *Guilty by Suspicion* is insistently didactic. Graff immediately complies, but, when he catches up to David, he speaks of the committee with contempt, indicating that he is playing a complicated double game.

Throughout the film it is difficult for the characters to know who to trust, a situation attributed directly to the committee. The cinematic move of allowing us to observe a bit of conversation David has not heard establishes that, in addition to the subjective experience of isolation and distrust the film conveys, we may believe that there are "objective" reasons to endorse those subjective concerns of the characters.

From this point until the end of the movie one of David's tasks will be to prepare himself for the ultimate gunfight with the committee, as he is subjected to the ordeal of losing his work, losing the ability to support his family, losing his friends, and being hounded by FBI agents. On the few occasions when he reflects directly on how he will respond to the committee when the showdown arrives, his reflections emphasize the personal rather than the political. Let us follow this thread through the film and begin our consideration of it as a way of thinking about the politics of the blacklist.

On a visit to an old friend David reveals that he is under suspicion. She tells him to leave.

> FELICIA: Look, why don't you just give them what they want, David? I really am surprised at you.
>
> DAVID: Well, don't be. Maybe they just asked me the wrong way, or maybe I'm just stubborn and I don't like to be pushed around. Or maybe, to hell with it, I'll just give them what they want, cause I'm sure as hell tired of this shit.

In a later scene, near the end of the film, having suffered the indignity and deprivations of the blacklist, David wanders into a Christmas party at the law offices of Felix Graff. He is still wondering if there is not some way out short of testifying against his friends. Graff explains to him how the system of the investigation, blacklist, and clearance closes off his options. At the beginning of the scene Graff assumes David has decided to testify.

> GRAFF: . . . you've made the right decision.
>
> DAVID: I haven't made any decision yet.
>
> GRAFF: No?
>
> DAVID: Isn't there anything I can do? What about the American Civil Liberties Union, someone? I mean, what if I take the Fifth? They can't do anything to me if I take the Fifth Amendment, right?
>
> GRAFF: It's not really much of an alternative. It sends a message that you're hiding something. The only thing to hide as far as they're concerned is membership in the Communist Party. Sure you protect yourself against self incrimination, but you end up guilty by suspicion, and where does that get you?

DAVID: You asked me how I'm doing. You want to know how I'm doing? I can't get a job. Can't get a job. All my friends— gone. I'm being followed by the FBI everywhere I go. I lost my house. I can't even buy my son a bike for Christmas.

GRAFF: Is it worth all this pain, David? Is it worth all this pain to your little boy, for example?

DAVID: What about my friend's little boy? What about Dorothy's little boy? What about that six-year-old little boy who lost his mother?

GRAFF: Well, that's exactly what I'm saying. Is it worth all this? I mean, what are they really asking you to do? Just say, I'm sorry, I was young, I was foolish, I made a mistake. I was immature. I mean, that isn't much.

DAVID: No, I'm being asked to do a lot more than that.

If I am reading this scene properly, both David's reluctance to testify and his lawyer's appeal to testify are based on appeals to personal rather than public matters. Not only, as we were told in an earlier scene, is the committee not engaged in a legitimate public enterprise, but any appeal that David might make at the public, constitutional, or legal levels will fail to restore him to the community. David's attempts to appeal either to constitutional rights or to community feeling ("What about my friend's little boy?") are systematically refuted by Graff. Hence, the issue, according to the logic of the film, must be decided at the personal level and not at the political level—either by serving one's self-interest or by remaining loyal to one's friends and a code of personal honor. Either way the committee has so poisoned the public sphere that public and private life, irretrievably intermingled, cannot be restored to harmony.

When David finally confronts the committee, in the last scene in the film, he clearly establishes not only his "innocence," but his innocence of any sort of politics whatever.

TAVENNER: . . . Mr. Merrill, are you now a member of the Communist Party?

DAVID: No.

TAVENNER: Were you ever a member of the Communist Party?

DAVID: No.

TAVENNER: Did you attend Communist Party meetings in the fall of 1939?

DAVID: Twelve years ago, in an organization as perfectly legal as the Republican or Democratic Party, where I heard they were getting together to talk about new ideas, yes, I attended a few Communist Party meetings.

TAVENNER: Will you tell the committee the circumstances under which you attended these few meetings, that is, when, where.

DAVID: Well, I only attended two or three, at the most, I think, and it was over a period of two or three weeks.

TAVENNER: And what were the circumstances under which you stopped attending these meetings?

DAVID: Well, they threw me out. I think I just argued too much.

This passage is remarkable, it seems to me, for its assertion and denial of the political. After parenthetically noting that the Communist Party was as legal (in 1939) as the Republican or Democratic Parties, David clearly asserts his own innocence of politics and implies the conspiratorial dogmatism of the Communists: "Well, they threw me out. I think I just argued too much." Like any other red-blooded American movie hero, David is just too plain independent, ornery, and individualistic to last long in a political party, especially the Communist Party.

In an important sense *Guilty by Suspicion* is a bravely political film in its condemnation of the blacklist and the Un-American Activities Committee. But in an equally important sense the film loads the dice against its own politics by depicting a world in which neither the committee nor its victims were actually doing politics: the committee was only seeking headlines in a malevolent carnival of inquisition and purgation; the victims were either innocent, nonpolitical American liberals drawn temporarily into the Communist orbit by naive idealism or, in some cases, by love and lust or, in a few cases, they *were* actually Communists who fled the country, informed on their friends, or, originally drawn to communism by their psychological marginality, collapsed under the pressures of the time. In other words, the best politics (David's) and the worst politics (the committee's) are no politics at all.

I do not mean, by offering this reading of the film, to lampoon it. Indeed, in important ways the film depicts understandings of the blacklist that are true to understandings of it at the time and consistent with later historical reconstructions. The historical record supports a narrative that shows the committee as headline-hunting dunces and Hollywood liberals as running for nonpolitical cover as soon as the Hollywood Ten made a directly political attack on the committee and paid with a year in prison—and as soon as the blacklist began in earnest. On the other hand, the historical record also supports the view that the committee and its supporters employed time-worn red scare tactics both as a way of attacking the New Deal and as a way of frightening Hollywood and the nation into a passive acceptance of Cold War politics and conservative resistance to a long list of progressive causes. Nevertheless, the nonpolitical politics of the film seem so natural to us partly because they are a dominant theme both in our films and in our political culture, and it is in this sense that it may be useful to see the politics of *Guilty by Suspicion* as naturalized by prefiguration.

The core figure expressing the politics of *Guilty by Suspicion* is the character of David Merrill, who has much in common with the stereotypical reluctant hero in American film and literature. The reluctant hero, according to Robert Ray, performs an ideological function in American culture by suggesting that it is possible to face the demands of community life without having to sacrifice our individuality. This ideology, argues Ray, falsely teaches us that we can avoid having to make real choices and prevents the development of a popular art that envisions a workable community. Ray describes the reluctant hero tale as, in "its most typical incarnation . . . the story of a private man attempting to keep from being drawn into action on any but his own terms. In this story, the reluctant hero's ultimate willingness to help the community satisfied the official values. But by portraying this aid as demanding only a temporary involvement, the story itself preserved the values of individualism as well."[6]

Although we can recognize David Merrill, with his insistence on making his response to the committee on his own individualistic terms, as a reluctant hero, part of the pathos of *Guilty by Suspicion* and part of its paradoxical appeal as a political tale is that, although David can walk away from the committee with his honor intact, the situation is rigged so that he cannot, in fact, win. Our analysis suggests that part of the film's rhetorical case against the committee is not so much that it violates the principles of our civic life but that it prevents a resolution in David's favor and on David's terms as an individualist hero.

Our analysis of the text of *Guilty by Suspicion* suggests the extent to which the film effaces politics in making its political appeal against the committee and the blacklist. But it would be a mistake to suggest that *Guilty by Suspicion*, though shaped in terms of Hollywood's invisible but dominant formulas, is driven entirely by antecedent textual strategies. Rhetorical calculations and the climate fostered by the blacklist also seem to have contributed to the design of the film. An inspection of the available history of the production and reception of the film reinforces, though sometimes with considerable differences in emphasis, the textual analysis so far developed.

Irwin Winkler (b. 1931), who wrote and directed *Guilty by Suspicion*, intended at first to be its producer. Winkler, who had not previously written or directed, had a long and successful career as a producer, starting in 1967, including the first five *Rocky* films; several Martin Scorsese films (*New York, New York* [1977], *Raging Bull* [1980]; *Goodfellas* [1990]); and *They Shoot Horses, Don't They?*; *Point Blank*; *The Right Stuff*; and *Round Midnight* (1986).[7] While he was producing *Round Midnight*, Winkler met John Berry. "Berry, who played the part of the nightclub owner in that film, was forced to move to Europe to continue his career after fellow director Edward Dmytryk accused him of being a communist in 1951."[8] Winkler decided to build a film around Berry's experience, employing Bertrand Tavernier, who was directing *Round Midnight*, as the director and commissioning a screenplay from Abraham Polonsky, another blacklisted writer and director. A subsequent falling out between Winkler and Polonsky prompted both men to put their versions on the record in interviews, providing us with considerable insight into the evolution of the rhetorical intentions and methods driving the film that emerged from this process.

According to Polonsky's account of the process, as reported by Victor Navasky, Polonsky's first script described the life of an American former Communist, opening the film with an appearance before HUAC and then following the director into exile in Europe. Both Tavernier and Winkler said that they preferred to have that climactic scene at the end of the film. "In that case," said Polonsky, "it's no longer a survival-in-Europe story. It should be a picture about Hollywood. And if it's a picture about Hollywood, it will have to be a picture about the political controversy."[9]

Polonsky then wrote a version of the script in which the principal character engages with his associates in a series of discussions about how to handle the assault by HUAC, weighing the merits of various forms of resistance, including the appeal to the First and Fifth Amendments to the Constitution. As the project developed, Tavernier dropped out to work on another film, and Winkler took over as director. Then he surprised Polonsky by producing a script of his own, based on Polonsky's but with crucial changes. In Winkler's script David Merrill became a nonpolitical liberal instead of a former Communist, and Merrill's wife was downgraded from being a successful microbiologist "confronted with a loyalty-oath dilemma" of her own to being a former schoolteacher who divorced Merrill because he worked too hard.[10]

Critics were divided in assessing the politics of *Guilty by Suspicion*. Some, such as Roger Ebert, praised the film as a "powerful statement against the blacklist."[11] Other critics regarded the film's message as potentially important but said that its treatment by Winkler was overly didactic and heavy-handed.[12] But the crucial critical debate over *Guilty by Suspicion* centered on the depiction of its hero as nonpolitical. Objections of this sort came from both the Right and the Left, a point made by Victor Navasky. Writing in the conservative *National Review*, George Szamuely quotes Navasky, whom he identifies as a "stalwart . . . defender of the Hollywood Communists," as writing that HUAC "went after Party members exclusively, and subpoenaed nobody who had not already been identified as a Communist by at least two sources."[13] Szamuely suggests that the Communists got what they deserved from the committee, though he assigns responsibility for the blacklist itself not to the committee but to public opinion and Hollywood moguls. Winkler's conversion of the De Niro character into a nonpolitical liberal, writes Szamuely, "encapsulated Hollywood's predicament: It likes to strike heroic postures of liberal defiance. But since the culture is a liberal one largely shaped by Hollywood, it has to invent a fearsome right-wing oppressive America against which to hurl its paranoid fulminations."[14]

Ronald Radosh, writing in the *American Spectator*, argues that Winkler distorts his depiction of the HUAC period in numerous small and large ways, especially by failing to reflect accurately the long struggle between Communists and liberals in Hollywood from the 1930s into the 1950s. Radosh would have preferred a film that could condemn HUAC, whose "hearings were clearly punitive—their 1951 investigations turned up nothing," and at the same time recognize the sins of the Stalinists, who hid their views behind the First Amendment while slavishly following the Soviet line.[15]

David Denby, writing in *New York* magazine, asks: "But what if Merrill weren't so innocent? What if he *had* been a party member for a while or had some genuine political passions? He might not be as immediately sympathetic to the audience, but dramatically he might have come to life, and the civil-liberties issues would be clearer. After all, it is not only the purely innocent who need protection against blacklists. Few people interested in the period get past the drama of victimization and righteousness. The Hollywood Ten, for instance, who went to prison for contempt of Congress, were victims but far from heroes. They were Communists with no particular commitment to free speech."[16]

But, whatever the political or rhetorical merits of their objections, Denby, Radosh, and Szamuely may themselves be remembering history selectively. It is true that in his book on the period, *Naming Names*, Victor Navasky claims that, "by the 1950s, [HUAC] went after Party members and former Party members exclusively," though it made some "mistakes." On the other hand, Navasky makes it abundantly clear that "the free-lance vigilantes made no such distinctions. Between HUAC's errors and this network's wider definition of the red menace, the blacklist extended well beyond those with direct links—past or present—to the Communist Party."[17] Later in his book, in a chapter on the victims of the blacklist, Navasky says that the "red hunt" brought "misery to the lives of hundreds of thousands of Communists, former Communists, fellow travelers, and unlucky liberals."[18]

Several key characters in *Guilty by Suspicion* appear to be based on, or are designed to echo, actual participants in the Hollywood of the 1950s. David Merrill (Robert De Niro) is allegedly based on directors John Berry and Elia Kazan. The project was originally to have been loosely based on John Berry, a director who chose European exile to escape the blacklist. Winkler says that David Merrill is also based partly on Elia Kazan, though Kazan was a friendly witness, who named names.[19] The David Merrill character also resembles Sterling Hayden (a war hero and former Communist who informed in the 1951 hearings) and Lillian Hellman (who refused to name names, on moral grounds).[20] Joe Lesser (Martin Scorsese) is based on Joseph Losey; though his character in the film is a Communist, Losey is usually described as a non-Communist radical or liberal. Losey went into exile in England rather than testify.[21] Darryl F.

Zanuck (Ben Piazza) 1902–79, was a producer and head of Twentieth-Century Fox. Larry Nolan (Chris Cooper) is based on Larry Parks, originally a member of the "Unfriendly 19" of 1947, who became the first witness at the 1951 hearings and whose breakdown and naming of names became infamous. The character Felix Graff (Sam Wanamaker, who was blacklisted) is based on lawyer Martin Gang. Ray Karlin (Tom Sizemore) is based on Roy Cohn, who was an aide to Senator Joe McCarthy and not associated with the House committee. The character of Abe Barron (Stuart Margolin) is based on Abe Burrows. Dorothy Nolan (Patricia Wettig) "is loosely based on Dorothy Comingore, who played Orson Welles' opera-singer wife in *Citizen Kane* and who lost custody of her child after she was blacklisted and ended up a drunkard."[22]

Textual evidence seems to indicate that the David Merrill character is based partly on Lillian Hellman, who was called before HUAC in May 1952. Hellman was widely admired for her stand, defended on grounds of personal morality, that she would willingly testify about her own activities but would refuse to testify about others. Her letter to the committee seems to have been borrowed by Winkler in composing David Merrill's testimony before HUAC, though the film simplifies some of the complexities of the legal issues involved.

Hellman wrote to the committee shortly before her appearance to negotiate an arrangement whereby she would be willing to waive her Fifth Amendment rights against self-incrimination if the committee would agree not to ask her about other people. Her letter says, in part:

> I am ready and willing to testify before the representatives of our Government as to my own opinions and my own actions, regardless of any risks or consequences to myself.

> But I am advised by counsel that if I answer the Committee's questions about myself, I must also answer questions about other people and that if I refuse to do so, I can be cited for contempt. My counsel tells me that if I answer questions about myself, I will have waived my rights under the Fifth Amendment and could be forced legally to answer questions about others. This is very difficult for a layman to understand. But there is one principle that I do understand: I am not willing, now or in the future, to bring bad trouble to people who, in my past association with them, were completely innocent

of any talk or action that was disloyal or subversive. I do not like subversion or disloyalty in any form and if I had ever seen any I would have considered it my duty to have reported it to the proper authorities. But to hurt innocent people whom I knew many years ago in order to save myself is, to me, inhuman and indecent and dishonorable. I cannot and will not cut my conscience to fit this year's fashions, even though I long ago came to the conclusion that I was not a political person and could have no comfortable place in any political group.[23]

The committee declined Hellman's offer to testify about herself so long as she would not be asked to implicate others. Hence, she took the Fifth Amendment and became another victim of the blacklist.

In his *New York Times* review Navasky quotes extensively from interviews with Polonsky and Winkler, using Polonsky, in part, as a spokesman for the voice of former American Communists, largely denied a role in the history of the period by Winkler's script. Polonsky argues that his version of the script dealt "with the consequences of political beliefs, the way in which people invoked the Fifth Amendment to protect First Amendment values. It was about the importance to society of standing up for what you believe."[24] From Polonsky's own testimony his script would seem to have been a reiteration of the claim that the Communist Party was just another American political party, loyal to and deserving the protection of the Constitution—claims that have been variously disputed since the 1930s. But because we do not have access to Polonsky's script, of which there appear to have been at least two very different versions, one leading up to and one beginning with the committee hearing, it is not possible to tell whether that script would have provided the political and historical complexity that Navasky, Szamuely, Radosh, and Denby find missing in *Guilty by Suspicion*. What we do have is *Guilty by Suspicion* and the commentary it has provoked, all of which invite further dialogue and debate.

Irwin Winkler's defense of his choice of a nonpolitical hero, iterated in a series of interviews, appears somewhat cautious and inconsistent, though that impression may be partly an effect of the inevitable fragmentation and distortion of the interview process. At times Winkler said he wanted to find a hero he could identify with—as he could not do with a former Communist. Winkler sometimes defended his choice by, in effect, calculating the politics of his audience, arguing that, if he had chosen a Communist hero, then the film would be perceived as a defense of communism rather than a liberal condemnation of the blacklist. Winkler defended his choice to Nina Easton: "Abe [Polonsky] wanted the character to be a die-hard communist," [Winkler] recalls. "He wanted to do a political story. I thought it was more interesting if the guy wasn't even a communist. That was something you can relate to. If he was a communist, it's too easy for the audience to understand why [HUAC] called him up and attacked him. I never wanted this to be a defense of communism. I wanted it to be a defense of liberty."[25]

Winkler's defense and his film raise the question of whether, if the only liberty we defend is the liberty of the nonpolitical, we are in fact defending liberty. Just this consideration prompts Navasky to remark, "Perhaps *Guilty by Suspicion* is an appropriate metaphor not only for just how far Hollywood has come after all these years, but also for how far it and the political culture at large still have to go."[26]

A credible case can be made out either for or against the historical legitimacy of *Guilty by Suspicion*. Those objecting to the film can point to its general avoidance of the presence of Communists among the Hollywood victims of the early Cold War red scare. Those defending it can point to the film's generally convincing depiction of the atmosphere of the times and can reasonably claim that many of the characters were based on actual living persons. These are legitimate issues for debate, and, whatever one's case against the film's simplifications, even distortions, of history, it must be admitted that no film trying to make a claim for a wide audience would escape the charge of simplification. It seems to me that, if we take a rhetorical perspective on the film, its production, and its reception, regarding the filmmaker as presumptively in good faith, we are likely to find out a lot about what it appeared possible to accomplish with narrative on the issue of the blacklist. Any film, even a heavily didactic film, relies upon evoking a large zone of taken-for-granted, commonsense understandings with its audience as the basis for accepting a theme, a character, or a story. Without disregarding the possibility that any particular rhetorical move may be a historical distortion, and should be identified as such, we may also use the filmmaker's process of adaptation as a blueprint of the filmmaker's take on the artistic and political sensibilities of the public. And so, when we find Winkler borrowing from John Berry his victimage; from Elia Kazan his wiry hair and status as a leading director; from Lillian Hellman her appeal to nonpolitical, old-fashioned American decency as the basis for resisting the committee; and when, at the same time, we see Winkler rejecting

John Berry's politics, Elia Kazan's naming of names, and Lillian Hellman's gender, we have before us a dynamic portrait of what it might be appropriate to call the motivations of a rhetorical text. If, using the tools of rhetorical analysis, we are able to go beyond the text in this way, we may be able to come back to the text with greater understanding, and we may be able to use the text to advance the discourse that it invites us to enter.

In response to the critical observation that the politics of *Guilty by Suspicion* is an escape from politics, the film might be defended by an appeal to one version of the historical record, since there certainly were many "innocent" victims of the blacklist. But the film's escape from politics might also be defended by the argument that the film is not about the politics of the blacklist but about the intersection of the blacklist with the personal lives of its victims. Winkler himself defended his depoliticization of the story partly on the grounds that he was interested in finding a personal story that he could identify with, as the basis for investing himself artistically. "I chose to do a story about a nonpolitical person because I find that much more interesting. . . . I wanted to do it about a moral man who got too caught up in his career—the glitter, the fancy car, the lavish apartment. . . . What's interesting about David Merrill's character is that, as his success and the symbols of his success start to slip away, the values of friendship and being with his family and those he loves begin to reassert themselves. He regains his morality."[27] There is considerable support for this view in the text of the film itself. On the other hand, when we look closely at the "personal" side of the narrative, it appears that the characters are not only victimized by the blacklist but also manipulated by the politics of the film and by the formulaic conventions of the narrative itself.

The historical record of the blacklist is full of evidence of the ways in which the blacklist destroyed personal lives, breaking up families and friendships, destroying careers, driving its victims into alcoholism, broken health, and suicide.

The central thread of the personal side of *Guilty by Suspicion* traces David Merrill's relations with his friends and family from the time he first comes under suspicion until he defies the committee in the final scene of the film. Central to the film as a personal narrative is David's reconciliation with his former wife, Ruth (played by Annette Bening). Early in the film we learn from a conversation between David and Ruth that their marriage dissolved because he allowed his work to come before his family. At this early stage in the film, just before he learns that he is under suspicion, David still seems to put family obligations after his work. That soon changes. But even from the first David and Ruth seem to be on good terms and to give every sign that they are capable of acting as a couple. And from the first David and Ruth are contrasted to another couple, Larry Nolan and his wife, Dorothy. It was Larry Nolan who broke down and named names in the first scene of the film and whose confession to his wife at David's surprise homecoming party in the next scene caused her to get drunk and throw Nolan out of their apartment. Larry and Dorothy are a highly symmetrical pair of foils for David and Ruth. But, while Larry and Dorothy serve to condemn the committee, they fall into Hollywood cinematic formulas that undermine the historical point they have been created to establish in the film.

Larry Nolan, the Hollywood writer turned informer, is depicted as a weakling and a disloyal coward who buckles under committee intimidation, naming his friends and possibly even his wife as Communists. When his wife throws him out, he invades the house with the FBI to snatch away his son, on the grounds that, as a former Communist, his wife is an unfit mother. The character of Nolan, based loosely on the historical figure Larry Parks, is rendered as a stereotype, however. This lessens his complexity as a foil to the David Merrill character or even as an example of the destruction wrought by the Un-American Activities Committee, since his weakness and cowardice are so unrelieved that he seems an accident waiting to happen—if the committee had not brought this about, something else would have.

An early scene in the film demonstrates the fairly traditional use to which the Larry Nolan character is put. The scene occurs immediately after the surprise party at David Merrill's home and is set in the courtyard of Larry and Dorothy Nolan's apartment building. As David and Dorothy arrive at the courtyard, they discover Larry making a bonfire of his books. He is ripping his books apart and throwing them on the fire. Dorothy rushes upstairs to the apartment as David approaches Larry.

DAVID: Larry, what the hell are you doing?

LARRY: Reorganizing my library. . . .

DAVID: These are all good books—*The Catcher in the Rye, Tom Sawyer*. What the fuck's the matter with you? . . . [Dorothy appears at a second-story window, with her young son].

DOROTHY: Ask him who he named today, David. Ask him.

LARRY: Don't listen to her, she's cracked.

DOROTHY: I mean, how many of your friends did you sell out? Did you name me? Did you name your son?

[At this point, Larry throws a book at Dorothy; it crashes through a window next to her; she responds by throwing Larry's typewriter into the courtyard. David turns to Larry and asks]:

DAVID: What did you do?

Everything in this scene, and the earlier and later scenes in which Larry appears, establish his contrast to David Merrill. Both are the fathers of small boys—who are, in fact, apparently classmates. Larry might have been positioned to illustrate what would have happened if David had decided to give in to the committee. But, instead of constructing Larry as a test case of the good man who decides to follow the path of the friendly witness, the scene shows that Larry is a classic weakling and coward. His book burning is a grotesque self-dramatization; his throwing a book at a window in which is wife and son are standing is the dangerous, irresponsible act of a hysterical bully.

Dorothy, Larry's wife, is another victim of the committee, but she, too, is a classic weakling, prone to hysteria and alcoholism. At David's homecoming party Dorothy makes such a scene that David does not trust her to drive home alone. In a later scene David and Ruth rush to the studio, where Dorothy has locked herself in her trailer on the set of a new film. Dorothy sits huddled in a corner, sobbing, drunk, and out of control, as she tells David and Ruth that Larry and an FBI agent took away her son, after Larry claimed she was a Communist and an unfit mother.

Dorothy's suicide prompts considerable pathos, but its leverage at the personal and political level is undermined by the way Dorothy's character is established as part of the Hollywood narrative tradition. Dorothy meets Ruth and David at a seaside restaurant after David has returned from a failed trip to New York to look for work. Dorothy, her formerly red hair now dyed blonde, in her pathetic and unsuccessful attempt to cash in on the fervor created by Marilyn Monroe, and obviously lying when she says she has given up drinking, assumes that David has been to New York to start work on a new play. When he tells her he has no new play, and hence no part for her, she does not believe him and rushes out of the restaurant. David and Ruth follow her out to her car and stand next to it as Dorothy deliberately shifts the car into reverse and accelerates over the cliff edge to her death. The scene of the suicide marks another moment when the film narration shares with us knowledge that it obscures from the characters. As Dorothy sits in her car, David and Ruth stand next to it, trying to offer their support. A series of close-ups shows us that Dorothy is deliberately shifting the automatic transmission into reverse but that David and Ruth cannot see this. Hence, when Dorothy has killed herself, David and Ruth cannot know for certain—as the audience does—that she did it on purpose. Either way her distress is caused by the committee, but David is given the opportunity—which he takes, when he answers the committee investigator who asks him about Dorothy—of refusing to enter into speculation about whether she killed herself on purpose. His tact on this point is in contrast to the brutal casualness of the committee toward Dorothy and her reputation.

Was Dorothy's death the fault of the House Un-American Activities Committee? Well, yes, in a way. But Dorothy's death is as much a case of death-by-Hollywood formula as death-by-blacklist. Such deaths are a common plot device in epics of Hollywood heroics, used partly to condemn the unfeeling victimizers who prompt it but also, and equally important, to underscore the strength of the protagonist in standing up to similar ordeals. Consider the self-killings, for example, in such familiar films as *The Searchers, An Officer and a Gentleman, Dead Poets Society,* and *The Deerhunter* or in films about the anticommunist 1950s such as *The Front, Fellow Traveler,* and *Daniel.* In each of these films, as in *Guilty by Suspicion,* a suicide is the act of despair of a person who lacks the psychological strength to pick up after a series of defeats and get on with life, and so, in a sense, the victimizer is let off the hook. Hence, the Hollywood narrative tradition, used as a resource to condemn the committee for victimizing the helpless, undermines its own rhetoric by suggesting that it was not so much the committee as Dorothy's own psychological weakness that led to her death—and, in any case, our attention is focused on admiration of David and Ruth, who do summon the strength to survive.

The key personal relationships are those among David and his wife and son. This personal story in one sense underscores the antipolitics of the film's public themes, in that it shows us a David who becomes reconciled with his wife when he realizes, in the midst of his suffering, that he needs his family and that they matter more to him than work or success. Similarly, the film uses the victimization of David and his family as a way of demonstrating that the chief effects of the blacklist were to devastate personal lives.

Guilty by Suspicion seems to be teaching us that, in the world of the blacklist, the public world offered no satisfactory choices but that there is satisfaction to be found in personal life. But the reconciliation of David and Ruth has a politics all its own. We are invited, it seems to me, to read the relationship of David and Ruth Merrill through the gender politics of the 1990s. If I am right in this reading, then the film is twisting history and politics in a characteristic way. *Guilty by Suspicion* may be read as one of a small genre of recent films that we might call melodramas of remarriage (the notion of these films as a genre is borrowed from Stanley Cavell's generic analysis of Hollywood comedies of remarriage).[28] In each of these films we see a couple who, still married or recently divorced, are no longer close because the husband has been devoting too much time to a successful career. A remarriage is made possible when an event in the husband's world subjects him to trauma and mortification. When he realizes his former mistake, recovers his humility, and acknowledges the strength and autonomy of his wife, the reconciliation follows. The metaphors of mortification in these films are not subtle. Let us look at just two examples, *The Doctor* (1991) and *Regarding Henry* (1991) .

In *The Doctor* William Hurt plays Jack, a big-time San Francisco surgeon, a high-pressure technical doctor, full of jokes but with a hard shell. His relationship with his wife and family has suffered from years of neglect. What does it take to shock him into rearranging his life? Jack has a hoarse throat, which turns out to be laryngeal cancer. It does not respond to radiation therapy. Jack, voiceless, dependent on his wife, and perhaps terminal, is transformed as a doctor and as a husband. He survives the cancer. He tells his wife, "I need you." All is forgiven.

In *Regarding Henry* Mike Nichols directs Harrison Ford and Annette Bening in the story of Henry, an unsympathetic man, a successful personal injury lawyer who defends the bad guys against malpractice suits. His family life is cold (in fact, both he and his wife are having affairs, we eventually discover). What mortification will redeem Henry and restore his marriage to harmony? Henry's transformation begins when he goes out for a pack of cigarettes and is shot in the head and chest by a hold-up

man. He suffers severe brain damage and only slowly recovers the ability to speak and function. Henry's mental retardation makes him nice,
which unfits him for further practice of the law (the fact that he has
slowed down intellectually is relevant but apparently not decisive). Henry
leaves the law after setting right a case he had cheated to win before his
own life was turned upside down, then reconciles with his wife and, with
her and their dog, Buddy, in tow, rescues his daughter from boarding school
in the middle of a chapel service. "I missed her first eleven years," he tells
the headmistress, "and I don't want to miss any more."

I think it might be a mistake to see *Guilty by Suspicion* as precisely
parallel to these two other husband mortification films, since *Regarding
Henry* and *The Doctor* do not also commit themselves to the sort of public political thematics of *Guilty by Suspicion*. Nevertheless, in dealing with
the politics of family life, the films are nearly identical. The parallels are
so striking as to constitute a coherent intertextual frame that seems un-
deniable, a 1990s politics of remarriage in which the union can be restored
only by an extraordinary mortification visited upon the husband through
some force external to the family. In each case the husband, spectacu-
larly successful at work but neglectful of his family, is forced to work his
way through a pattern of mortification: he adjusts his relation to his
work and family, heroically survives his trauma, and, significantly, acknowledges the strength and autonomy of his wife, and his dependence
upon her, at which point he reassumes a fairly traditional role as the
patriarch of the rebalanced family.

If we attend closely to what *Guilty by Suspicion* is dramatizing for us
and what dance of thoughts and feelings it is inviting us to dance with
it, it appears that public politics is dismissed as in fact motivated, for
good or ill, by personal considerations—and yet, when we look at the
personal elements of the story, we find that they are dominated entirely
by the film's formulaic, didactic version of the blacklist, refracted through
the gender politics of the 1990s.[29]

Tracking David Merrill's mortification and remarriage through the
film in more detail may allow us to see what counts as mortification, as
the grounds for redemption, and as the state to which remarriage aspires. On his first night back in Hollywood, David Merrill's agent tells
him that he has an appointment at nine o'clock the next morning with
Zanuck. David at first hesitates, saying he is supposed to see his son at
that time, then agrees. Next morning he sees his son only briefly, because he does not want to miss his meeting with Zanuck. Ruth scolds

him for neglecting his son: "The David Merrill express rides again, eh, David?" A few days later David arrives late to join his former wife to watch their son Paul perform in a school production of *Peter Pan*. Although Ruth firmly reminds David of his habitual avoidance of family obligations in favor of work, there appears to be no particular bitterness between them. Indeed, in the scene in which David and Ruth rush to the studio to comfort the hysterical Dorothy, it is clear that they are a couple and that they really belong together. When they are comforting Dorothy, they do so as a couple. David says to Dorothy, as the three embrace tearfully, "It's okay, you're with us now." Ruth adds, "We love you."

Ruth's declaration of independence comes after it is clear that David is in trouble, but it is not an abandonment of David so much as her way of contributing to the family economy—even though the family is broken. David arrives at Ruth's house too late to take Paulie to school, as he had promised. He is confused about the new situation he finds himself in and people's changing perceptions of him. Ruth tells him, "Maybe everybody thought that making movies means more to you than anything else." Ruth then tells David that she is going to go back to teaching and will move into an apartment. It soon becomes clear that David will be unable to support himself. He cannot find work. He loses his house and tries without success to work in New York. When he returns to Los Angeles, broke and unemployable, his rehabilitation in the family begins, but it will not be complete until he has suffered further and passed a series of tests. Hounded by the FBI from a job repairing cameras in a New York shop, David calls Ruth, collect, to say he is coming back to Los Angeles. In his first arrival in Los Angeles, at the opening of the film, David appears in the bustling train station, full of energy and success, where he is met by his friend Bunny Baxter and taken off to a surprise party. In this second arrival David comes to town by Greyhound bus, rumpled and unshaven, and waits, apparently for hours, from day into night, on a bench. Eventually, Ruth arrives in her car, apologizing for being late. She was held up at work—his old excuse. He tells her it's okay.

RUTH: Do you want to drive?
DAVID: No. . . .
RUTH: . . . Come on, you always want to drive.
DAVID: No, you better drive.

David sleeps on the sofa in Ruth's apartment and awakens the next morning to see Ruth, in a bra and half-slip, getting ready for work. She asks him to fasten the clip on her necklace but tells him to stop when he touches her shoulder. She invites him to dinner with her and Dorothy. After asking her if she can afford it, and apologizing for asking, he agrees that he can come if she is paying.[30] Having lost his career, having waited without complaint at the bus station, having declined the prerogative of driving his wife's car, having accepted his wife's invitation to take him to dinner, having established that neither he nor Ruth has ever been romantically disloyal to the other, and having with a touch on the shoulder expressed his continued desire for Ruth, David seems to have set the stage for a remarriage. But Ruth, though she is willing to indulge in a little banter about their suspended sex life together, and ready to offer him her sympathy, is not ready to be reconciled. David's mortification is not yet complete.

Soon David is offered work directing a quickie western, from which he is soon fired in his own turn as the blacklist catches up to him again. In a scene set in Ruth's home we see David, Ruth, and Paulie working— Ruth correcting school papers, Paulie doing his homework, and David working on the storyboard for his new movie. When Paulie has trouble with his fractions, David immediately drops his own work to help out. Ruth tries to deflect Paulie, out of old habit, but David insists on helping. As Paulie walks past his father, David looks up from his work:

DAVID: What's up?

PAULIE: Fractions.

DAVID: Let me see. [Takes Paulie's paper, as Paulie sits next to him on sofa.] Okay, one over two—

RUTH: Paulie, Daddy's working.

DAVID: I sure am. Boy, I hated fractions. I got a D.

PAULIE: You never told me you got any D's.

DAVID: I sure did. Only one or two, though. Okay, one over two is less than or greater than one over one? What do you think?

David has now proven to us, and to Ruth, that he no longer places his work before his family. One more step remains, and it occurs without much delay. David arrives at Ruth's apartment to find his old friend

Bunny waiting for him. David had earlier told a committee investigator that Bunny, his oldest friend, was no Communist, and he warned Bunny that he had better get a lawyer, since the committee had his name. Bunny's response was to deny he had anything to worry about, but in his fear he blurted out a suspicion that David might have given the committee his name. Now, in Ruth's kitchen Bunny tells David that the committee has subpoenaed him and that once, long ago, he briefly joined a group to send canned goods to the Russian defenders of Stalingrad because of a girl he was pursuing. The committee says the group was a subversive organization. Now he asks David's permission to betray him. With Ruth looking on, Bunny breaks down and begs David to accept this betrayal.

> BUNNY: So they, uh, they got me for perjury. And the only thing I can do, really, is just cooperate a little bit.
>
> DAVID: A little bit.
>
> BUNNY: Ten years from now, who's gonna care? David, I need your help. I would like permission, I need your permission to use your name, David.
>
> DAVID: You want my permission to inform on me.
>
> BUNNY: I have to give them some names, David. It's not enough to eat shit here, you have to give them names.
>
> RUTH: They already have David's name.
>
> BUNNY: But they don't have it from me, Ruth, and that's the whole point of this fucking hearing, isn't it? Screw your best friends. Please. This is your fault, David. You're the one who told them we were friends. You came back and then I was called, David. Now you've got to help me out.
>
> DAVID: Why don't you just give them my name, Bunny; it doesn't matter.
>
> BUNNY: I couldn't do that to you. Let me use your name. Please.
>
> RUTH: Get out of my house, Bunny. You get out of my house, please.
>
> BUNNY: What's the difference, please, please. You're dead already. Please.
>
> DAVID: Get out. Get out.

[BUNNY leaves; RUTH begins to weep; DAVID gets up to embrace and comfort her].

DAVID: Don't cry. Why are you crying?
RUTH: So you won't.
DAVID: I love you.

Cut; it is the next morning; David and Ruth are in bed together. The reconciliation is complete. The terms of that reconciliation, which, as we shall see, apparently mean restoration of a fairly conservative version of the nuclear family defended by the man as head of the household, have required that Ruth establish an independent personhood that she can relinquish to David only after he has undergone not only a conversion to traditional family values but a mortification that he is able to survive with his dignity and manhood intact.

The reconstructed family forms the personal side of *Guilty by Suspicion*. As I have tried to show, that personal story is itself deeply political, in that it recreates the conservative nuclear family dream of the 1950s and 1980s through the mechanism of a Hollywood version of feminism that requires mortification of the male and a passage through dependence upon the wife in order to restore the family to its patriarchal stability. Further, the personal story is so streamlined, so much in the service of making sentimental points that serve the film's didactic needs, that the characters often lack real texture and substance. This is true even of those closest to David—Ruth and Paulie, who serve the film only insofar as they establish our relation to David.[31] I have argued that the public side of *Guilty by Suspicion* encourages us to imagine an effacement of the public realm by reducing it to a contest of personal character and private motives. Conversely, the personal half of the story is itself a formulaic narrative dominated by the politics of the Hollywood family. But the family drama, though it is in a sense political, is political in much the same limited sense that the film's public side is political; it is political in that it appeals to power arrangements, but it is nonpolitical in that it does not envision a world of choice, debate, or pluralism in arriving at those arrangements. In both politics and personal life, says *Guilty by Suspicion*, action flows from character and personality, along channels that are invisible, naturalized, and intertextually foreordained.

I seem to be arguing that, as a political film, *Guilty by Suspicion* is, on the one hand, historically defensible and sentimentally convincing but, on the other hand, self-contradictory and self-defeating. If that is so, and I think it is, the fault, if any, lies not merely with the filmmakers, it seems to me, but also with the cultural and historical material they have to work with—that is, with the culture that in fact gave rise to and in turn is the product of Hollywood and the House Un-American Activities Committee. Why self-contradictory and self-defeating? Because what it complains of at one level it advocates at another.

Let us look, for example, at the film's complaint about the House Un-American Activities Committee. At the core of the case against the committee is that it accuses loyal Americans of betraying their country, using a standard of loyalty that is historically out of context. Having made the accusation of betrayal, the committee offers to rehabilitate its victims through the infamous clearance process, by which the victim may purge him- or herself of guilt and suspicion by enduring mortification, confession, and a purification gained by betraying all former loyalties in naming the names of former friends as possible subversives. This system deprives people of their constitutional freedoms and takes away all choices that might offer alternative salvations, forcing people to choose self-destruction whichever choice they make.

The film depicts this process admirably and condemns it convincingly. But, on reflection, a remarkably similar pattern plays itself out on the personal level in *Guilty by Suspicion*. Just as the political story in the film is about the cycle of guilt, mortification, and redemption, so is the personal story. David Merrill, though sexually loyal to his wife, has betrayed her by putting his work before his family. He is guilty of disloyalty, and he can be restored to his family after undergoing not only sincere change and renunciation of his former ways but also a mortification that purges his guilt and ensures that he will forsake other loyalties to preserve honor and family. The cycle of betrayal, guilt, mortification, and purification, which we resent so much when it is enacted by the committee, is exactly repeated for our admiration in the remarriage of David and Ruth Merrill.

Virtually every other human relationship in the film is tested on the issues of loyalty and betrayal. Zanuck professes his loyalty to David but says that the money men in New York force him to honor the blacklist. Larry Nolan betrays his family. Bunny Baxter suspects David of betraying him then asks for permission to give David's name to the committee. When David goes to New York to look for work, he revisits his old friends

Abe and Felicia. Felicia invites him to their apartment. When he arrives it turns out that Abe is out of town, and it is clear that Felicia is prepared to betray Abe if David is interested—which he is not. But, when David tells Felicia about his troubles, she immediately sends him out the door (offering him some money, in cash, rather than in a check, which might be traced back to her). In the final scene of the film, as David enters the hearing room to testify, we learn that Abe has just appeared as a friendly witness, betraying his old friends to prove his loyalty to the committee. At the thematic level the personal and the political are united in the mirrored cycles of loyalty, betrayal, victimage, mortification, and purgation. At the narrative level the themes are further united in the focus on the figure of David Merrill.

As we have seen, the climax of the film is reached when David finds a solution to his problem that reconciles his political with his personal problem, when he finally decides how to answer the committee. He does it by collapsing the political into the personal, so that the two lines of action finally converge in a satisfying narrative conclusion.

Let us return for a moment to the climactic scene of the film, David Merrill's testimony before the House Un-American Activities Committee. David has tried and failed to explain to the committee the political innocence of his past life. Now they press him to name names — who else was at those meetings he attended years before? David responds, "I will be happy to answer any question about myself, but I will not answer questions about anyone else."

The committee presses David about having attended an anti-bomb rally years before, telling him that the sponsors of the rally were a subversive organization and asking him for the names of others in attendance. He is threatened with a charge of contempt of Congress. Then the committee asks about his wife, who is seated in the chamber. Was she a Communist? No, says David. Nevertheless, she is identified by the committee as having been at the ban-the-bomb rally, and therefore, they say, she is a subversive who ought not to be allowed to teach in the public schools. In one of his few statements that has anything to do with politics David replies that his wife and her students have a constitutional right to discuss public policy in school or anywhere else.

Ideologically, historically, and politically, the film thus reaches its climax on the solid ground of defending the Constitution from its enemies on the committee. David's lesson in civics may amount to little more than a brief gesture, a whiff of *Mr. Smith Goes to Washington*.[32] Nevertheless, in this brief scene, at last, David is able to resolve his defiance of the committee in a gesture that also unites loyalty to his family and his friends. But even here politics and the personal are driven apart as much as they are driven together.

When asked about Dorothy Nolan, who committed suicide early in the film, David throws back at the committee the famous response of Joe Welch to Joe McCarthy at the Army-McCarthy hearings:

CHAIRMAN: What about Dorothy Nolan? Was she ever a Communist Party member?

DAVID: She's dead.

CHAIRMAN: That's not what I asked you, Mr. Merrill. Now all you have to do is sit there and answer these questions. Was Dorothy Nolan a member of the Communist Party? Yes or no?

DAVID: Don't you have an ounce of decency?

CHAIRMAN: Mr. Merrill, as unfortunate as it may be, Dorothy Nolan was a known drunk, an unfit parent, and on several occasions had been named to be a member of the Communist Party.

DAVID: She was a good wife, a good mother, and you're responsible for her death.

CHAIRMAN: She was named on several occasions as being a member of the Communist Party.

DAVID: She was falsely accused. She couldn't get work, her son was taken away from her, all because of this committee.

CHAIRMAN: Dorothy Nolan killed herself, and the Communist Party twisted her mind.

DAVID: In the name of ridding the world of Communists, you destroyed her life. Don't you have any shame? She's dead! . . . [As the committee accuses David of being a Communist and threatens him with contempt of Congress, David continues, amidst a rising tide of shouting and a pounding gavel]:

DAVID: I might not be the best citizen in this country, but I was raised to stand up for what I believe in, and I'm going to raise my son in the same way. And as hard as that is sometimes, I'm going to try to live it. And if that isn't what a real American is, then we've failed, God damn it. Shame on you!

The film ends with David and Ruth walking out of the hearing room. They notice their old friend Bunny Baxter walking in to take his place as the next witness, and they overhear Bunny as he tells the committee that they have no constitutional right to inquire into his political beliefs. And so a wife is protected and a friend is redeemed.

In defying the committee, David has recaptured his ideologically traditional role in the family. It is remarkable how clearly the film establishes this. David's personal redemption and remarriage can occur only when Ruth, established as independent, accepts him back to the marriage bed. But we never see Ruth in the film when David is not present: she exists for us in terms of David's redemption. And once she has accepted David she is immediately put back into her place. When Bunny leaves the apartment and Ruth embraces David, we cut to David and Ruth in bed. David is lying awake; Ruth is asleep. At the committee hearing, we often cut to reaction shots of Ruth, but she has no further role except to react and to support David and, most important, to be protected by him.

Part of the satisfaction we may feel in this ending stems from its familiarity. It follows a well-worn groove, as the outlaw hero, bloodied but (in a sense) victorious, rides from the scene. The scene itself has been rehearsed for us earlier in the film, in fact. When David picks up an off-the-books job on a Hollywood back lot, he briefly takes over the direction of a B western movie, which itself is evidently a plagiarism of Fred Zinneman's *High Noon*. At the climax of the film the sheriff, having rid the town of the bad guys, takes off his star and throws it in the dust at the feet of the cowardly townspeople, then climbs on the buckboard next to his wife and rides out of town. He has discharged his duty to the civil community (which hardly deserves it), but not at the cost of his own independence. So it is with David Merrill, who understands that the best politics is to stand up for what you believe in, to exercise personal nobility in the face of the perversions of civil society.

There are many forces pushing an American film about the blacklist in this direction. Narrative, especially film narrative—and most especially mainstream American film narrative—not only condenses its material to provide a clear line of action, but also organizes itself around a strong central character who is surrounded with villains and dependents and who prefers personal action to public discussion as a way of resolving conflict. In *Guilty by Suspicion* this turns a political film into a traditional antipolitical story. Among those who argue that the House

Un-American Activities Committee was looking for more than personal publicity are those who argue that it was attempting to frighten Hollywood away from the political sphere. It is perhaps paradoxical that, in making a film that condemns HUAC, the film seems to deny the viability of a public sphere just as it denies that there were more than a few self-consciously political people in Hollywood (the rest merely attended a few meetings and rallies out of curiosity or sent canned goods to Stalingrad or tried to stay in the good graces of pretty girls named Magda).

Hollywood has a strange career as a political force in American life, which may be partly understood by noticing that film politics is part of a system of political economy. The case of *Guilty by Suspicion* provides a small case in point. Irwin Winkler himself alleges that part of his motive in making the film was political, that he wanted to make a film that was "a defense of liberty." The economy of communication in the American marketplace means that Winkler, supported by the resources of Time-Warner, one of the largest conglomerates in the economy, has an access to the American audience that is simply unmatched. The positive resources that confer access to the public forum for giant media corporations dangerously unbalance the capacity of the system to sustain community formation through democratic discourse.[33]

I have tried to suggest that, when we use film to teach ourselves about politics, we may be dealing with a medium, a narrative tradition, a political economy, and a political history that tend to overdetermine the outcome of any such enterprise in the direction of antipolitical melodrama. The rhetoric of film has often appealed to good causes in the public realm, but it has typically done so in a way that disparages the political and warns of the community as an entrapment.

On the other hand, we might remind ourselves from what point of view such a criticism is offered. If we can claim that Hollywood film prefigures the politics of its treatment of virtually any subject, might not the same suspicion be employed to reflect on the tradition of rhetorical criticism, which might itself be accused of prefiguring the outcomes of its own investigations? As a craft and an academic practice, rhetoric is in the business of demonstrating the ways in which our various modes of knowledge are shaped by myth and the figures of rhetoric and by taken-for-granted practices of production and distribution. At the same time, rhetorical criticism, especially as practiced by critics in speech communication in the twentieth century, carries with it a strong practice of idealizing the public sphere, in terms of which rhetorical acts are judged. We are inclined to accept the distinction between public and private and to assume that an issue that involves politics in virtually any sense is properly understood, discussed, and resolved by public debate. The authors of *Guilty by Suspicion* could make out a good case, it seems to me, that a rhetorical criticism of the film is itself prefigured by its own theoretical assumptions to describe the film as prefigured.[34]

Melodrama prefigures our desires for independent, nonpolitical heroes and for happy endings. Rhetorical theory prefigures the desire of rhetorical critics for an idealized public sphere.

On pragmatic grounds, too, defenders of *Guilty by Suspicion* against the critique I have developed here could point to the historical record. The film not only borrows richly from actual events of the blacklist period, but its suspicions of public debate as an alternative to personal action are supported in the public documents. A reading of the record— the congressional debates on the House Un-American Activities Committee from 1938 through the 1960s as well as the many volumes of hearings and reports released by the committee—reveals that the debate over the committee, such as it was, was static, undeveloped, ineffectual, and in many ways impeded by the practices of the Congress itself. Despite almost universal condemnation by the few scholars who took up the question, the public sphere in the widest sense, including the courts, the Congress, and the press, not only did not reach what I think would now be regarded as the sensible decision to resist or abolish the committee, but they provided virtually no space in which a fair discussion of such a contingency would be possible. Opposition to the committee was marginalized or, worse, was itself vigorously attacked as disloyalty. In Hollywood itself the committee seems to have pushed films in a more conservative direction and to have had a chilling effect on any attempts to sustain a civic community.[35]

In the era of the blacklist public rhetoric largely failed to meet reasonable standards of the public sphere, nor did it adequately portray the interpenetration of public and private worlds. With some notable exceptions intimidation, fear, and hysteria effaced the private reality of actual persons, reduced public rhetoric to slogans, and encouraged a decorum of nonpolitical disinterestedness and "objectivity" in academic debate. For this reason it is all the more unfortunate, but perhaps more understandable, that after all these years an antiblacklist film such as *Guilty by Suspicion,* resurrecting the old Hollywood craft at its best, creates so insistently an antipolitical rhetoric, in which it pits the formula hero against the demonic bad guys. We have come far enough to be able to condemn the blacklist in mainstream popular arts, but a close inspection of the rhetoric of that condemnation reveals, on the one hand, an academic rhetorical criticism that is itself groping uncertainly for a just balance of the private with an idealized public sphere and, on the other hand, a popular art that is unable to move the personal beyond formulaic melodrama and whose politics is no politics. Perhaps it would not be too exaggerated to say that part of the satisfaction we take in a film such as *Guilty by Suspicion* is that it allows us as viewers to purge our American conscience of our mortifying, reflexive suspicions of our own incomplete citizenship. We have learned to condemn the blacklist. It is not so clear that we have learned to understand it.

Notes

1. An earlier version of this essay was presented as the G. P. Mohrmann Lecture at the University of California, Davis, in May 1994. Anne Gravel worked as a research assistant on the project, summer 1992.

2. The themes of "public memory" and "popular memory" as rhetorical concerns have been addressed recently in such works as Stephen H. Browne, "Reading Public Memory in Daniel Webster's *Plymouth Rock Oration*," *Western Journal of Communication* 57 (1993): 464–77; Carole Blair, Marsha S. Jeppeson, and Enrico Pucci Jr., "Public Memorializing in Postmodernity: The Vietnam Veterans Memorial as Prototype," *Quarterly Journal of Speech* 77 (1991): 263–88; and Stephen H. Browne and David Henry, ed., *Rhetoric and Public Memory* (Beverly Hills, Cal.: Sage, forthcoming). For rhetorical analyses of film and public memory, see, for example, Martin J. Medhurst and Thomas W. Benson, "*The City*: The Rhetoric of Rhythm," *Communication Monographs* 48 (1981), rpt. *Rhetorical Dimensions in Media*, 2d ed. (Dubuque, Iowa: Kendall/Hunt, 1991), ed. Martin J. Medhurst and Thomas W. Benson, 446–467; Martin J. Medhurst, "The Rhetorical Structure of Oliver Stone's *JFK*," *Critical Studies in Mass Communication* 10 (1993): 128–43; Elizabeth Jenkins, "Film at the Service of Revolution: Bertolucci's Use of the Rhetoric of the Italian Communist Party in *1900*" (Ph.D. diss., Pennsylvania State University, 1994). John Bodnar, *Remaking America: Public Memory, Commemoration, and Patriotism in the Twentieth Century* (Princeton: Princeton University Press, 1992), is a comprehensive recent treatment of public memory; Bodnar uses the term *public memory* to refer to use of "official" or "vernacular" discourses and ceremonies to promote patriotism. My appropriation of the term in this essay does some violence to Bodnar's conceptual apparatus, in two ways: (1) it is not clear that film and the popular arts may be rightly categorized as either official or vernacular discourse; (2) although patriotism is clearly a rel-

evant theme in historical reconstructions of the memory of the blacklist, and indeed is a central issue of contestation, and although the events whose commemoration Bodnar describes have also been the subject of motion pictures, the blacklist seems unlikely to be the sort of event that could be properly commemorated by parades or public monuments. Imagining a matrix of the commemorative decorum of such disparate events as the Vietnam War, the Kennedy assassination, a Pilgrim arrival, and the blacklist suggests intriguing differences in the rhetorical codes of our collective memory. Despite their differences, these historical remakings have much in common: they are often the result of intense contestation and employ the methods of rhetoric to create symbols that attempt to place a subject beyond argument; though (and because) they are remembering a history from an anxious present, these remakings of history typically attempt to step outside the exigencies of time into a zone of permanent and stable memory. For variations on this theme, see also Henry A. Giroux, "Beyond the Politics of Innocence: Memory and Pedagogy in 'The Wonderful World of Disney,'" *Socialist Review* 23 (1993): 79–107; Roger I. Simon, "Forms of Insurgency in the Production of Popular Memories: The Columbus Quincentenary and the Pedagogy of Counter-Commemoration," *Cultural Studies* 7 (1993): 73–88; and James E. Young, *The Texture of Memory: Holocaust Memorials and Meaning* (New Haven: Yale University Press, 1993), for citations to which I am indebted to Brian Ott.

3. Quoted in Stefan Kanfer, *A Journal of the Plague Years* (New York: Atheneum, 1973), 76.

4. Ibid., 99–101.

5. This moment of the girl with the ball appears to be a gratuitous quotation of Fritz Lang's *M* (1931). In the opening sequence of M, the story of a manhunt for a child murderer in Berlin, a mother waits in her apartment for her young daughter's arrival home for lunch. The daughter, Elsie, leaves her school and walks along the street bouncing a ball, then stops to bounce it against a kiosk, which displays a poster announcing a reward for the capture of the murderer. The shadow of the murderer (Peter Lorre) falls in profile across the poster. The mother looks down a labyrinth of empty staircases, calling for Elsie. The child's ball rolls across a bit of ground; her balloon is stuck in overhead wires. She is dead. The girl with the ball in *Guilty by Suspicion* may or may not be an allusion to *M*. The scene may certainly be read as a moment of simple narrative realism, reinforcing, in passing, David's automatic gesture of help when he catches and returns the ball. Reading the moment as a quotation from *M* would deepen the sense of menace on the staircase as David ascends to meet the committee, and it would deepen the contrast between David's innocence and the taint that is assigned to him by the committee, justifying his pursuit throughout the film, which is thereby compared to the pitiless and relentless search for M. On the other hand, reading the moment as an allusion to *M*, for those who get it, might backfire, since it may also be read, if an allusion, as a gratuitous and un-

earned claim to profundity. There are several other allusions in *Guilty by Suspicion*. When he finally lands an off-the-books job directing a B western, David finds himself on the set of what looks very much like *High Noon* (1952). When David is tracked down in New York to the small camera repair shop where he has found work, the FBI questions his employer menacingly. David responds to the concern by thanking his employer for his help and quitting before the apologetic man is forced to fire him. The scene appears to be a clear quotation from *Godfather II* (1974), in which De Niro, as Vito Corleone, is forced out of his job as a grocery clerk by the local boss, who wants the place for a relative. In each of these films—*M, High Noon, Godfather II,* and *Guilty by Suspicion*—whatever their other considerable differences, the central character is forsaken and endangered by friends and enemies and/or by the community and its official representatives.

6. Robert B. Ray, *A Certain Tendency of the Hollywood Cinema, 1930–1980* (Princeton: Princeton University Press, 1985), 65. See also Thomas W. Benson, "Respecting the Reader," *Quarterly Journal of Speech* 72 (1986): 198–200; Thomas W. Benson and Carolyn Anderson, "The Ultimate Technology: Frederick Wiseman's *Missile*," in *Communication and the Culture of Technology,* ed. Martin J. Medhurst, Alberto Gonzalez, and Tarla Rai Peterson (Pullman: Washington State University Press, 1990), 257–83.

7. For a rhetorical analysis of the first *Rocky* film, see Janice Hocker Rushing and Thomas S. Frentz, "The Rhetoric of *Rocky*: A Social Value Model of Criticism," *Western Journal of Speech Communication* 41 (1978): 63–72; Thomas S. Frentz and Janice Hocker Rushing, "The Rhetoric of *Rocky*: Part Two," *Western Journal of Speech Communication* 42 (1978): 231–40.

8. Nina Easton, "Back to the Dark Days," *Los Angeles Times,* 10 March 1991, sec. CAL, 23.

9. Polonsky, quoted in Victor Navasky, "Has *Guilty by Suspicion* Missed the Point?" *New York Times,* 31 March 1991, 2:16.

10. Ibid.

11. Roger Ebert, review of *Guilty by Suspicion* in *Video Companion 1994,* in *Microsoft Cinemania '94* (Microsoft Corporation, 1993), CD-ROM edition. See also Dave Kehr, "Blacklist Blues," *Chicago Tribune,* 15 March 1991, sect. 7, C37. Both Kehr and Ebert praised the film for its realistic portrayal of Hollywood atmosphere and culture.

12. For variations on this theme by critics who seemed sympathetic to the anti-HUAC sentiments of the film but had some reservations about its realization as drama, see, for example, "Guilty by Suspicion," *Variety,* 11 March 1991, 62; Eleanor Ringel, "De Niro Drama Guilty of Overstating Case," *Atlanta Journal/Atlanta Constitution,* 15 March 1991, D3; Charles Sawyer, "Guilty by Suspicion," *Films in Review* 42 (1991): 267–68; Julie Salamon, "Film: The Hollywood Blacklist," *Wall Street Journal,* 28 March 1991, section A12; Ralph Novak, "Guilty by Suspicion," *People Weekly,* 1 April 1991, 12–13.

13. George Szamuely, "The Way They Are," *National Review* 43 (15 April 1991): 48. Szamuely's quotation from Navasky comes from Victor S. Navasky, *Naming Names* (New York: Viking Press, 1980), 85.

14. Szamuely, "The Way They Are," 61.

15. Ronald Radosh, "Soundrel *Times*," *American Spectator* 24 (June 1991): 31. Radosh's essay was originally commissioned for the *New York Times*, which then declined to run it; Radosh recounts his conflict with the *Times*, and with Victor Navasky, an essay by whom did make it into the *Times*, in a long headnote to his *American Spectator* review.

16. David Denby, "The Usual Suspects," *New York*, 1 April 1991, 59.

17. Navasky, *Naming Names*, 85–86. In his *Times* story Navasky says that "all but a handful of witnesses called by the committee" were former Communists" (Navasky, "Has *Guilty by Suspicion*" Missed the Point?" 9).

18. Navasky, *Naming Names*, 333. There is a large and controversial literature on the blacklist and related subjects. In addition to Navasky's book, a list of books considering the history of the blacklist and its effects on American culture would include, but not be limited to: Larry Ceplair and Steven Englund, *The Inquisition in Hollywood: Politics in the Film Community, 1930–1960* (Garden City, N.Y.: Anchor, 1980); Nancy Lynn Schwartz, *The Hollywood Writers' Wars* (New York: Alfred A. Knopf, 1982); Gordon Kahn, *Hollywood on Trial: The Story of the Ten Who Were Indicted* (New York: Boni and Gaer, 1948); Stephen J. Whitfield, *The Culture of the Cold War* (Baltimore: Johns Hopkins University Press, 1991); Stefan Kanfer, *A Journal of the Plague Years* (New York: Atheneum, 1973); Lary May, "Movie Star Politics: The Screen Actors' Guild, Cultural Conversion, and the Hollywood Red Scare," in *Recasting America: Culture and Politics in the Age of Cold War*, ed. Lary May (Chicago: University of Chicago Press, 1989); David Caute, *The Great Fear: The Anti-Communist Purge under Truman and Eisenhower* (New York: Simon and Schuster, 1978); most of these lead to other useful sources. For a defense of the committee from the Right, see William F. Buckley, ed., *The Committee and Its Critics* (Chicago: Henry Regnery, 1962). For personal recollections of the blacklist period, written from a number of positions, see, for example, John Henry Faulk, *Fear on Trial* (New York: Simon and Schuster, 1964); Philip Dunne, *Take Two* (New York: McGraw-Hill, 1980); Lillian Hellman, *Scoundrel Time* (Boston: Little, Brown, 1976); Dalton Trumbo, *The Time of the Toad* (New York: Harper and Row, 1972); Alvah Bessie, *Inquisition in Eden* (New York: Macmillan, 1965); Edward Dmytryk, *It's a Hell of a Life but Not a Bad Living* (New York: Times Books, 1978); Sterling Hayden, *Wanderer* (New York: W. W. Norton, 1977); Herbert Biberman, *Salt of the Earth* (Boston: Beacon Press, 1965). On the theme of mistaken accusations and the difficulty of combating them, see Thomas Rosteck's account of Edward R. Murrow's "The Case of Milo Radulovich" and "Annie Lee Moss Before the McCarthy Committee," in Rosteck, *"See It Now" Confronts McCarthyism: Television Documentary and the Politics of Representation* (Tuscaloosa: University of Alabama Press, 1994).

19. Clifford Terry, "Producer Takes a Direct Approach," *Chicago Tribune,* 10 March 1991, 13:8.

20. In the final sequence of *Guilty by Suspicion,* David and Ruth wait outside the hearing room. David's lawyer, Felix Graff, joins them and says to David, under the impression that David is going to name names: "Mark my words, David. You're gonna come out of this thing bigger than ever before." Compare this to Sterling Hayden's account in *Wanderer,* in which he describes leaving the hearing room in 1951 after naming names. Hayden and his lawyer, Martin Gang, are threading their way through the crowd. "'Hear 'em, hear 'em?' laughs Gang. "Mark my words, boy, you are going to emerge from this thing bigger than ever before. I wouldn't be at all surprised if you became a kind of a hero overnight. Wait till they hear about your testimony out on the Coast tonight. . . . Why, you're going to end up smelling like a rose'" (Hayden, *Wanderer,* 390).

21. Peter Travers, "Guilty by Suspicion," *Rolling Stone,* 4 April 1991, 60.

22. Irwin Winkler, quoted by Terry, "Producer Takes a Direct Approach," 8.

23. Hellman, *Scoundrel Time,* 93.

24. Polonsky, quoted in Navasky, "Has *Guilty by Suspicion* Missed the Point?" 16.

25. Winkler, quoted in Easton, "Back to the Dark Days," 23.

26. Navasky, "Has *Guilty by Suspicion* Missed the Point?" 16.

27. Winkler, quoted in Navasky, "Has *Guilty by Suspicion* Missed the Point?" 16.

28. Stanley Cavell, *Pursuits of Happiness: The Hollywood Comedy of Remarriage* (Cambridge: Harvard University Press, 1981).

29. In this and the next paragraph I am drawing on Kenneth Burke's notions of dramatism, dancing of an attitude, and the dramatic cycle of guilt-victimage-redemption. (Burke, *A Rhetoric of Motives* [Englewood Cliffs, N.J.: Prentice-Hall, 1950]).

30. This is the dinner at which Dorothy commits suicide. When they leave the restaurant it is David who puts money on the table.

31. *Guilty by Suspicion* does not provide much space to get to know Paulie or to speculate about the effects of the blacklist on a child. A feature film is likely to make such simplifications. For a contrasting way of telling such a story, see Sally Belfrage, *Un-American Activities: A Memoir of the Fifties* (New York: HarperCollins, 1994). Belfrage was the daughter of Cedric Belfrage, an Englishman living in America who founded the *National Guardian* newspaper, was hounded by Joseph McCarthy, HUAC, and the FBI, and was eventually deported, in 1954. Unlike David Merrill, Cedric Belfrage actually was for three months a Communist Party member in 1937 and devoted many years to politically progressive causes in the face of the political repression that followed World War II. Like David Merrill, Belfrage was too "argumentative" and "couldn't take the discipline" (129). Sally Belfrage's nuanced and ambivalent memoir helps to demonstrate how simplified is Winkler's treatment of Paulie. For another treatment

that casts doubt on Winkler's depiction of the isolation of blacklisted families, see Deborah A. Gerson, "'Is Family Devotion Now Subversive?' Familialism against McCarthyism," in *Not June Cleaver: Women and Gender in Postwar America, 1945–1960*, ed. Joanne Meyerowitz (Philadelphia: Temple University Press, 1994), 151–76. Other memories of family solidarity under the blacklist are recalled in Griffin Fariello, *Red Scare: Memories of the American Inquisition, An Oral History* (New York: W. W. Norton, 1995). See also Patricia Bosworth, *Anything Your Little Heart Desires* (New York: Simon & Schuster, 1997).

32. Peter Rainer titles his review of the film "Mr. De Niro Goes to Washington," *Los Angeles Times*, 15 March 1991, F1.

33. Only as this essay was going to press did I discover Ronald V. Bettig, *Copyrighting Culture: The Political Economy of Intellectual Property* (Boulder, CO: Westview, 1996), which has an excellent discussion of some of the issues involved in corporate ownership of the culture industries. On corporate domination of the public sphere and its distortion of First Amendment issues, see also Thomas W. Benson, "Killer Media," in Medhurst and Benson, *Rhetorical Dimensions*, 378–97.

34. We also, to a large degree, accept as a field a distinction between "public" rhetoric, on the one hand, and "interpersonal," "small group," and "organizational" communication, on the other, and organize our departments, degrees, and journals in such a way that rhetoric is studied as a branch of the humanities and the others as branches of the social sciences. "Media studies" in its various forms is riven by similar distinctions, sometimes bitterly contested but often simply taken for granted.

35. Victor Navasky counts the community as a victim of the blacklist; see chap. 12: "The Community as Victim," *Naming Names*, 347–70.

CHAPTER TWELVE

The Social-Political Dimensions of Film

A Response to Benson's Analysis of *Guilty by Suspicion*

Bruce E. Gronbeck

Tom Benson's analysis of *Guilty by Suspicion* is an intricate, nuanced reading of that 1990 film.[1] He not only plumbs the relationships between past and present but also nicely plays the political and the personal off against each other in his study of Irwin Winkler's depiction of the blacklist era. In probing rhetoric's relationship with history, social or collective memory, the past understood as people and events, and mass-mediated discourses, Benson draws on aspects of traditional rhetorical criticism even while driving more deeply into what he calls "the commonplace sphere of public discourse and the popular arts."

I find little to fault in Benson's effort. Rather, I take his essay as an opening, an excuse to comment on topics he has introduced, and I will attempt to press his ideas beyond the edges of the aesthetic universe he investigated. This commentary is offered in the spirit of inquiry celebrated by Wander and Jenkins over twenty years ago, when they talked about criticism as informed talk on matters of importance.[2] I will tackle three matters of importance isolated in Benson's essay: the discursive construction of history and collective memory, questions of how the personal and the political exist in individual lives, and the status of the rhetorical analysis of mass-mediated discourse, which is to say, how we are to understand the idea of "public address" in the wake of such films as *Guilty by Suspicion.*

Rhetoric, History, and the Collective Memory

Let me begin with some thoughts on *Guilty by Suspicion*'s status as an item of history and the collective memory. Recent works by Janas, Nerone, Cox, Berkhofer, Kammen, and Kellner supplement some of my own writing on questions of the discursive constructions of the past and, in particular, compel us to explore more fully than have most rhetoricians notions of collective memory.[3]

To begin, I take history to be a discursive practice. History is not to be confused with the past. The past is a collection of happenings from previous times, happenings to which we have no direct access; we can access only documentary, iconic, and recollected traces of that past and its events. Rather, history is a collection of stories and arguments about those events.[4] Also, history is a disciplined discourse, for the most part consisting of the writing of trained professionals who have little to do with chroniclers or writers of popular histories.[5] As is true in most disciplines, the professionalization of history has put gaps between the academically elite *auteurs* and the rest of us and between their discourses and public readers's versions of the past.[6] Third, as a discursive practice, history is an argumentatively formed narrative—simultaneously a story and an interpretive or realistic argument about the past. To be both an argument and a narrative simultaneously is to give history what Hexter called the rank-and-file problem:[7] how can such a dual genred discourse be composed? We know that it can be managed by the well-trained *auteur*, the professional historian. Additionally, others—say, filmmakers—can learn to construct narratives that provide homes for interpretive arguments.

One last orienting notion should be mentioned: the past is more than merely of historical interest; its importance to social, political, moral, and economic analyses of problems and their presumed solution is crucial to the life world. That is, the past is not in the possession of historians, to be fondled and formed only by such professionals for their amusement and our instruction. Just as the past should not be confused with history, so should it be understood broadly as a resource for human beings of many different stripes and with multiple purposes. The past makes its way into a great variety of discursive worlds: political deliberation over public policy, economic interpretations of tax proposals and market activity, myths of origin which form individuals into a people, psychoanalytic analyses of mental illnesses and their treatments.

As for collective or social memory, it, too, is a discursive practice but one not to be confused with history writing proper. It is a practice that assembles a society's moral stories—social and political myths, fables, fairy tales, and what Aristotle called reminiscences,[8] that is, special events that are imbued with socially charged significance. The social memory is a collectivized discourse; it is the construction of no *auteur* but, rather, as Lévi-Strauss remarked about myth, it is built by everyone who recounts a socially relevant story from the past.[9] It is less argumentatively than exhortatively formed; the moral of the story is its raison d'être. The collective memory is recalled so as to let the past guide the present, even if that means that the past occasionally must be in Cox's word "re-membered,"[10] remade to be a better guide. The collective memory is shaped into easily recognizable scripts, or formulas,[11] which can be overlaid on today's or tomorrow's world to provide understanding and moral guidance. The United States' collective memories of the Holocaust are powerful forces in how we construct our Middle East policies; stories of Lincoln and Robert E. Lee become model discourses about moral action; slave narratives become originary myths even for today's urban African Americans.

These distinctions between history and collective memories understood as types of speech and writing, of course, should not be drawn too sharply, for kinds of social and critical history often function for their readers in the same ways as collective memories do. Yet the distinctions are useful when analyzing event texts such as the film *Guilty by Suspicion*. While Benson identifies it as a historical study, I would argue that this film is more accurately viewed as a textualization of collective memory. Benson's effort to tally its factual inaccuracies seems to me a misplaced effort. So what if the characters are composites of people from the past? What if the factual account is distorted? If we, instead, understand *Guilty by Suspicion* as an exploration of collective memory, a reminiscence of the past offered in exhortative rather than argumentative terms, then we approach the film in quite different ways: (1) its story about the redemption of flawed artists, of artists who have lost their social-political souls because of their aesthetic excesses, then is a story adaptable to our own time; (2) if viewed as a collective memory, *Guilty by Suspicion* is a commentary on the red scare of the 1980s—the era of the Evil Empire, of the downfall of Western communism, of the time when we finally experienced the therapeutic purging of the paranoia so much a theme of the film; the attacks on art are made relevant to the attacks on the National Endowment of Art and notorious artists in the Reagan-Bush years; (3) viewed as a collective memory, *Guilty by Suspicion* is also an articulation of positive, not negative, relationships between the personal and the political; both the personal and the political are made relevant to the social in this film—that is, to our understanding of community.

Asking what the film inscribes on our own time, what exhortations it offers us in the 1990s, seems to me much preferred to examining its reconstruction of the past and its historical discourses. If viewed as an exhortative construction *in* 1990 *for* 1990, for its times, then *Guilty by Suspicion* is freed from its deep setting in a past, from its historicity. The film becomes explicitly rhetorical—a fable about artists in society, about the consequences of shutting down pluralist politics, and about the importance of healing the breach between the personal and the political. The film gains more power, or at least more interest, when understood as a discourse of social memory rather than a faulty reconstruction of a historical record.

If considered a rhetorically sensitive film for the early 1990s, then *Guilty by Suspicion*'s moral force is released from a bondage to the past. The story of broken and troubled marriages, of the disintegration of film (and potentially other) communities, and of the institutional repression of personal political inquiry and social loyalty becomes relevant to our interpretations of the 1980s family values discussions, concern over the loss of community,[12] and interrogation of federal support of the arts. *Guilty by Suspicion* becomes not flawed history but, rather, a sociodrama reconstructing the past so that its moral visions can frame its own context, our context, in useful ways.

The Personal and the Political

One of the great strengths of Benson's analysis is his superb exploration of the personal in *Guilty by Suspicion*—of the defilement and reconstruction of personal lives and personal relationships, especially marital relationships. The life of David Merrill is clearly detailed. The marital reunion theme and its ties both to other films and to social relationships in the 1990s are sketched in convincing ways. Benson's rhetorical analysis of personal relationships is deft.

Yet the nature of the political and its relationship to the personal in this movie merits further study. Contrary to Benson, I believe that the political context, a political problem, is not only asserted in this film but is still a framing context by the end of the picture. The personal and the political rather precisely parallel each other throughout the film. David Merrill is flawed not only as a political actor but also as a social actor; his art has deprived him of both the political and the personal, and both need to be recouped. The recouping of family and of friends (in particular, his friend Bunny) drives the plot, yes, but David's acquisition of social consciousness and skills is in lockstep with his acquisition of a political memory and temperament. His anti-institutional political sensibilities pervade the movie; every time we are tempted to make *Guilty by Suspicion* into a myth of self-discovery, we see a G-man in the background, watch David surrender his career to his unfocused but unmistakable political principles, weep with him over the momentary loss of his friend Bunny, and cheer with him and Bunny in the final, triumphant scenes.

Granted, neither the personal relationships nor the political ideology is complex. Undoubtedly, Irwin Winkler could have made his dramatic challenges more daunting. Yet that should not detract from the film's articulation of one of the great slogans of our time: the political is personal *and* the personal is political. In the film politics demands individual commitment and action, and personal relationships demand the give-and-take, the exchange of values for identifiable costs and rewards, which characterize politics. In *Guilty by Suspicion* it is very easy, and I think profitable, to read the political *through* the personal, and vice versa. If personal relationships can become politicized, as they certainly were in the film, and if political acts such as attending Communist lectures are depicted as personal exploration rather than ideological exercises, as David Merrill says was his motivation, then we are asked to collapse the political and the personal. They become indistinguishable facets of character. And, thus, the audience is exhorted to live out a contemporary theme—the wholeness or integration of life principles—which has been inscribed on the past so as to urge continued vigilance today.

The Rhetoric of Mass-Mediated Discursivity

My third consideration is framed by the following statement from the opening page of Benson's essay: "When we employ the rhetorical instruments of our cultural tradition to shape our symbolic appeals, how are we to understand the ways in which those instruments and traditions and the material practices used to employ them, shape our thoughts?" Two questions, actually, are being asked. Benson wants to explore the limitations of traditional rhetoric's focus on the political understood as public, ideologically driven or sensitive discourse as well as the actual limitations of that kind of discourse. That is, he views rhetorical criticism as limited by its traditional focus on talk in the public sphere, on the oral and literate discourses of traditional politics. And, thus, he also believes that the public sphere itself seems limited to explicitly political sorts of talking and writing. In particular, what has been taken traditionally to be public matters are those written and spoken about in traditional places by people who understand the political to circumscribe a discrete set of rhetorical behaviors. In *Guilty by Suspicion* David Merrill's disengagement from such politics is what causes Benson to label this an antipolitical film. The public sphere of life, therefore, is but one arena among the many that constitute human life and is separable from the private, personal, or interpersonal spheres of sociality and self-identity.

If I, in fact, have understood Benson's argument, I would offer the following counterarguments. The easiest way to proceed would be to use Benson to critique Benson. Not only has he used a rhetorical perspective here to illumine a portrait of the personal in *Guilty by Suspicion*, but he has devoted his scholarly career to investigating the rhetoric of the image.[13] He has been able to examine the public sphere as though from the outside, demonstrating that the rhetorical perspective can be enlarged beyond the traditional realm of practical, institutional politics (congressional witch-hunts) so as to be an instrument of broad ideological critique.

A better response to Benson's argument, however, is to note that most of the contemporary understandings of rhetoric, in fact, are sensitive to discursification in multiple forms—not just traditional political talk engaged in by people with the word *politician* emblazoned on their foreheads but in the discourses of personal relationships and in the manifold forms of mass-mediated discourses, which we know to possess significant political potency.[14]

A third line of analysis would emphasize the fact that *Guilty by Suspicion* is not a slice of life—chronicled events in the lives of single and married people. It is, of course, a filmic representation or construction of the so-called private, or personal, sphere. It is mass-mediated discourse that positions its spectators in particular ways; in controlling our subject positions, our specularity,[15] via its verbal, visual, and acoustic codes, the film asserts its power over our sense even of the personal. That power is inevitably a kind of politics in its own regard, in part, certainly, the gendered politics that Benson intimates lies at the base of Hollywood's films of remarriage. More than that, in its unrelenting focus on the male world (the character of Dorothy Nolan notwithstanding) *Guilty by Suspicion* explores almost exclusively the psychic and social-political worlds of males. David Merrill's wife Ruth's motivations, hopes, fears, and sense of her places in the world are left on the cutting room floor. She is as much a political victim of social hierarchy as she and her husband are victims of red scare ideological hierarchies.

In other words, the notion of politics is a contested concept for at least some spectators of the 1990s. The socially situated viewer can read *Guilty by Suspicion* allegorically, as a story about ideologically driven attacks on art and artists, as well as culturally, as a story about the silencing of the personal and the gendered in our time. Politics is depicted as institutional, and yet, if we are sensitive to the absent present, politics in a film such as this one is socially powerful as well. A well-crafted collective memory can give us perspective on multiple aspects of our lives.

Rhetorical analysis, I am suggesting, is composed of a congregation of highly flexible methods and, more important, ways of seeing human lives which can be put to work in the study of manifold forms of discourse and multiple discursive codes. The time is past when we must either retreat to a nineteenth-century, Bairdian understanding of "public address" as students of political speech[16] or berate our lack of effort to understand film, radio, television, and computer bulletin boards as fields of discourse as much a part of the public deliberation as was Isocrates' *Panegyricus* or Burke's "On American Taxation." In our time public address is hot-wired interaction, and Benson's career in analyzing especially celluloid discourse is testimony to rhetoric's service to democracy in the electronic age. Electric rhetoric is here, and by now Benson is surrounded by other practitioners, many of whom use his work as foundation, of a new rhetorical criticism of a new public address. Benson himself has opened rhetorical analysis to new subjects and argued, at least implicitly, that the public sphere encompasses far more than governmental politics.

Another notion is worth exploring: given the personal and social dynamics within which the political is explored in *Guilty by Suspicion,* and in our own time, politics itself is depicted as bivalued. Not only is politics to be understood as a matter of *policy,* as courses of institutionally sanctioned thought and action, but also as a matter of *polity,* as relationships between people. As we collapse in our present-day thinking the polis into the demos, the political into the social, then the operation of the public sphere becomes understood as the ways we collectivize ourselves. The public sphere is animated as an arena not only for political deliberation but also for communal identification. Through our public talk we make community. The inhumanity of congressional witch-hunting is less in its political assessment and control than in its destruction of community. Insofar as *Guilty by Suspicion* plays out the disintegration and then (potentially) reintegration of community, it is fertile ground for the rhetorical critic wishing to explore in verbal and visual discourses all manifestations of public ethics.

I do not mean to suggest, of course, that the time to analyze the instrumental or representational powers of oral discourses is past. Speech still is the center of personalized moral commitment; speech still must be understood as the most thoroughly human communicative mode for asserting desire and destiny. Yet I would reaffirm the importance, the critical importance, for rhetoricians of studying the electronic public spheres. Radio, television, film, and the rest are not mere conduits for talk. They are, rather, interpersonal, symbolic mediations in their own right, with their own modes of invention, disposition, style, and delivery, their own mechanisms of discursification, and their own constructions of social-political worlds. They are the public address of our time, the realms in which we make both policy and polity, and must be treated as such if we are to serve our communities in constructive ways.

Notes

1. I wish to thank Iowa's Project on the Rhetoric of Inquiry for providing me with the office, equipment, and coffee needed for writing essays such as this one. I appreciate the project's attention and contribution to my scholarly well-being and productivity.

2. Philip Wander and Steven Jenkins, "Rhetoric, Society, and the Critical Response," *Quarterly Journal of Speech* 58 (1972): 441–50.

3. Michael J. Janas, "Rhetoric, History, and the Collective Memory: The Civil War in Contemporary America" (Ph.D. diss., University of Iowa, 1994); John C. Nerone, "Professional History and Social Memory," *Communication* 11 (1989): 92–101; J. Robert Cox, "Memory, Critical Theory, and the Argument from History," *Argumentation and Advocacy* 27 (1990): 1–13; Robert Berkhofer Jr., "The Challenge of Poetics to (Normal) Historical Practice," in *The Rhetoric of Interpretation and the Interpretation of Rhetoric*, ed. Paul Hernadi (Durham, N.C.: Duke University Press, 1989), 183–200; Michael Kammen, *Mystic Chords of Memory: The Transformation of Tradition in American Culture* (New York: Alfred A. Knopf, 1991); Hans Kellner, *Language and Historical Representation: Getting the Story Crooked* (Madison: University of Wisconsin Press, 1989); Bruce E. Gronbeck, "Ar-

gument from History₁ and Argument from History₂ Uses of the Past in Public Deliberation," in *Argument in Controversy: Proceedings of the Seventh SCA/AFA Conference on Argumentation,* ed. Donn W. Parson (Annandale, Va.: Speech Communication Association, 1991), 96–99; and Bruce E. Gronbeck, "The Rhetorics of the Past: History, Argument, and Collective Memory" (paper presented at the Conference on Rhetorical History, University of Nevada–Las Vegas, 1995).

4. See Berkhofer, "Challenge of Poetics."

5. On chronicling, see Hayden White, "The Value of Narrativity in the Representation of Reality," *Critical Inquiry* 7 (1980): 5–27; on popular history, see Allen Megill, "Disciplinary History and Other Kinds," in *Argument and Critical Practice: Proceedings of the Fifth SCA/AFA Conference on Argumentation,* ed. Joseph W. Wenzel (Annandale, Va.: Speech Communication Association, 1987), 557–64.

6. See the argument in Janas, "Rhetoric, History, and the Collective Memory," chap. 1.

7. John H. Hexter, *Reappraisals in History: New Views on History and Society in Early Modern Europe,* (New York: Academic Library, 1961).

8. In his treatise *De memoria et reminiscentia,* in *The Basic Works of Aristotle,* ed. Richard McKeon (New York: Random House, 1941).

9. Claude Lévi-Strauss, "The Structural Study of Myth," *Structural Anthropology,* trans. C. Jacobson and B. G. Schoepf (New York: Basic Press, 1963), 1:206–32.

10. See Cox, "Memory."

11. See Nerone, "Professional History."

12. See Robert M. Bellah et al., *Habits of the Heart: Individualism and Commitment in American Life* (Berkeley: University of California Press, 1985), for a discussion of the loss of community in the 1980s.

13. For example, Thomas W. Benson, "*Joe:* An Essay in the Rhetorical Criticism of Film," *Journal of Popular Culture* 8 (1974): 608–18; Thomas W. Benson, "Another Shooting in Cowtown," *Quarterly Journal of Speech* 67 (1981): 347–406; Thomas W. Benson and Carolyn Anderson, *Reality Fictions: The Films of Frederick Wiseman* (Carbondale: Southern Illinois University Press, 1989).

14. On the rhetoric of relationships, see Steven W. Duck and Kristine Pond, "Friends, Romans, Countrymen, Lend Me Your Retrospections: Rhetoric and Reality in Personal Relationships," in *Close Relationships,* ed. C. Henrick (Newbury Park, Calif.: Sage, 1989), 17–38. On the rhetoric of media, see Martin J. Medhurst and Thoms W. Benson, ed., *Rhetorical Dimensions in Media: A Critical Casebook,* 2d ed. (Dubuque, Iowa: Kendall/Hunt, 1991).

15. For a summary of the literature on specularity, see John Fiske, *Television Culture* (London: Methuen, 1987), especially chap. 4.

16. I address this matter in "Electric Rhetoric: The Changing Forms of American Political Discourse," *Vichiana,* 1st yr., 3d ser. (Napoli: Lofreddo Editore, 1990), 141–61.

CHAPTER THIRTEEN

Rhetoric and Scientific Communities

John Lyne

The Discovery Channel recently aired a program called "The Human Brain: The Universe Within." From watching it, I learned a great deal, a feeling produced in no small part because of the spectacular computer-generated graphics depicting brain processes. Among the celebrity scientists and philosophers interviewed in the series was Patricia Churchland, a philosopher of mind who is looking closely at recent discoveries in neuroscience and brain studies. In capsulizing what one could hope to learn by these studies, Professor Churchland said that, by studying how the brain actually functions, we may be able to discover why people sometimes make bad decisions. I puzzled at the assumptions behind this observation. As a student of rhetoric, I thought how the statement of this surely admirable and seemingly plausible goal was in fact occluding most of the considerations that I know weigh on the decision-making process.

As a student of public discourse, I think of decisions as occurring within the frame of social pressure, symbolic interchange, and rhetorical influence. Thus, it seems rather reductive to suggest that exploring the mechanisms of the brain would lead us to "better" decisions. Am I to suppose that if the members of the Federal Reserve paid more attention to their own brains than to economics, they might have a clearer sense of when they should raise interest rates? Notice, too, that the notion of what constitutes a better decision is implicitly held above the fray, in the realm of some sort of objective rationality. The arbiters of what is the better jury decision, the better choice of a mate, the better foreign policy move might presumably, someday, be the experts on the human brain. Now I am not suggesting that Professor Churchland would regard these inferences as anything but caricature. But does her rhetoric not invite them? Does it not, by hinting at this ideality, give away a bit too much about what Burke would call the occupational psychosis of the brain scientist? Should the speaker be surprised if the general public took her to be suggesting just the sort of future that I've sketched?

I was attracted to rhetorical studies because I was interested in studying how people can use language and persuasion to influence thought, action, and culture. As a voracious consumer of political and cultural discourse, I enjoy playing the armchair rhetorical critic of what I see on television and in the newspapers. I especially love seeing those very specific turning points, in which someone's intervention seems to shift the whole direction of talk in the public arena. I investigate scientific arguments because the discourses of science have substantial impact on thought, action, and culture in our time—and that influence will be all the stronger if we accept the opinion that they have little to do with persuasion in the public space. Mark a space as being empty of rhetoric, as writers sometimes do with respect to science, and you invite rhetorical abuse. Mark a place as "not public," and you discourage scrutiny. And mark any discourse as not addressed to some community, and you lose any claim such discourse would have on that community.

I see work from scientific journals entered as evidence in debates of importance between academics and sometimes in forums outside the academy. When people take an interest in a scientific issue because it affects them personally (as, say, when a chemical plant may be locating near them, when their health or employment are affected, or when they just get fixated on a celebrity trial), they can get surprisingly sophisticated surprisingly quickly. One television talk show provided viewers of the O. J. Simpson trial an 800 number, through which they could order a special book on the use of DNA testing in the courts. And, from reading a lot in, around, and about scientific discourse, I believe that, for whatever disagreements gets played out on CNN, radio talk shows, and other popular sites, the roots of disagreement are very often in the scientific literature right from the start. But the arguments play out in different ways depending on the nature of the audience. And I am convinced that, even among rigorous practicing scientists, the basis for persuasion has more to do with rhetoric, in a conventional sense, than is generally realized.

I've tried to show that rhetorical-based meaning effects in the rhetoric of sociobiology and paleobiology are factors in producing various, often distorting, effects on various audiences.[1] What I call "bio-rhetorics" have been used to organize discourses about human nature and social institutions. As a way of handling nature/nurture issues, this can be good or bad, but it is particularly misleading and dangerous when such rhetorics draw upon supposed findings in genetics to provide argumentative warrants for social policy arguments. I had become convinced that social scientists were picking up the implied authority of genetics and grossly distorting the matter, and this was seeping into the general culture. By analyzing their rhetoric on its own terms, I could enter the fray to some extent but would always be vulnerable to the charge that I was not a scientist, not even a social scientist, and hence had simply misunderstood the issues. So I made an effort to dig deeper, and, working with Henry Howe, a biologist, I was led to what appear to be three distinct strands of what we call genetic rhetorics which have been fitted in Procrustean fashion to a single rhetoric in sociobiology, the study of the biological bases of behavior. This force fitting has in turn enabled theorists to posit theoretical and empirical evidence of a number of "genetic strategies" supposedly exhibited in members of our species. It is one thing to posit a gene for a heredity disease, quite another to begin speculating on the genetic bases of social behaviors, such as criminality. As I continue this work—and I am beginning to track issues in neuroscience and even theoretical physics—I do not expect that everyone wants to take the journey with me. But I want to maintain that it represents no diminution of the commitment to study "public" discourse.

Rhetorical scholars have traditionally taken as their founding image, if I may use that term, that of the single speaker, standing before an audience in the civic area, speaking about things political, where *political* is understood as encompassing questions of value and policy as applied in particular circumstances. Late-twentieth-century realities force some attenuations of this image. Most political speakers these days are seen on television, for instance, and their appearances before immediate audiences are usually staged for the purposes of television coverage. A second attenuation of the image is the reality of complex, multiple, and scattered audiences. Broadcasting of speeches problematizes the notion of public discourse, in that it throws into the same pool of listeners a great many people who have shown only the minimal commitment needed to turn on the TV, plus whatever inertia was required to prevent switching the channels.

And, as it turns out, moreover, a "target audience" very often cannot be conveniently isolated from those who are not a part of the target audience. That nonisolation can itself inspire rhetorical strategy, of course, as witness the "Daniel in the lion's den" approach that is crafted around a visit to a hostile audience, which is in turn overseen by another audience. Want to signal "courage and integrity"? Tell off some group that will respond icily or, better yet, with boos and hisses, then broadcast the experience to a more important audience. The strategy was used by John Anderson in 1980 and, recently, by Senator Arlen Specter of Pennsylvania in lecturing a group of very conservative and largely religious Republicans that it needed to lighten up a bit. Carried by C-Span, the speech reached just the right audience of pundits and opinion leaders who could potentially lift him from the pack. Maybe, just maybe, I'm sure Senator Specter hoped, this would single him out from a group of otherwise pandering would-be presidential candidates. In any case, audiences are more complicated than ever, given the accessibility made possible by the media.

Finally, the notion of the "text" has itself become problematized in new ways, whether we want to call the complications "postmodern" or simply call them "facing reality." Contemporary habits of reading and listening are interventions into the flow of information and image, often idiosyncratic interventions at that. It is hard to know when anyone is listening or what they are paying attention to, apart from mega-events in the culture, such as the O. J. Simpson Event, when literally everyone seems to be tuned in.

Given the new media practices, and in the context of new theories, the notion of how the public should be conceived has been much problematized. So, too, has been the question of the relationship of the discourses of science to their various publics. To my way of thinking, debates about the public sphere—whether and how it may exist—are not dispository in considering this issue. There are ways that scientific discourse can be described as going public at virtually every minute of its production and dissemination. The notion that scientific discourse is not from the start discourse at least on its way to becoming public is perpetuated in large part because of some mythic images of science widely shared not only among the public but among many communication scholars as well. Here are five of them:

First, science is a physical and intellectual practice that only later becomes an object of communication. Science is a collective enterprise that is sustained only within a highly specialized network of communication. Participation in that network is the very sine qua non of scientific practice. In that sense it is even more dependent on carefully honed systems of discourse and communication than are the practices in the humanities. Add to this the presence of interpersonal competition, inflated egos, and the constant need to justify expenditures, and one has an area rife not only with communication but with rhetorical practice. The Human Genome Project is a multibillion dollar project, the importance of which is only beginning to be addressed in our society. Its potential to change our lives and social practices is vast. Are we well served by keeping it under wraps as science, a no-man's-land for rhetoricians, assuming that our mandate to do socially responsible rhetorical analysis can wait until all the important implications have already been spun out? I believe that the answer is no.

Second, whereas rhetoric has always been seen to operate upon the contingent, science supposes itself to be an engagement with timeless, changeless Truth and trading in certainties. This is an oddly antiquarian view of what the sciences have been for the last few hundred years. Yes, Aristotle did use the distinction between the contingent and the certain as a way of demarcating rhetoric from science. He was, of course, right in his time but clearly wrong in ours. I do not want to be glib, and I don't want to violate my usual rule that deference to Aristotle in most cases is justified, but this is one case in which to stick with Aristotle would be akin to sticking to the flat earth theory.

Correlatively, science is not generally the study of that which is timeless and changeless. Many of the modern sciences are explicitly historical in character—think of geology, paleontology, or astronomy, for instance. Even physics, which comes as close as any science to aspirations of timeless, unified truth, is now working within a paradigm that is explicitly historical. Just glance at your coffee-table copy of Stephen Hawking's book *A Brief History of Time.*[2] The keyword *time* is right there in the title. Not withstanding Hawking's public relations rhetoric concerning at attempt to "read the mind of God," he is exploring a dynamic, changing universe. Like all other physicists who make the Big Bang a point of reference, he is positing remote historical situations that, far from being changeless, are explosively dynamic.

Third, there is rhetoric about science but not rhetoric within science. When I hear this, I have to wonder what would have to be ruled out of that vast and multifaceted set of activities called "science" to make that true. Every university has large buildings dedicated to science. Do we suppose for a moment that acts of verbal persuasion are not occurring in those building? Well, not at the "core," you say? What is that core, I counter? Should we idealize only one part of science—the image of the solo researcher hunched over the microscope or computer—and leave out the context in which these activities are advocated, defended, explained, justified? And what about the phase at which findings are incorporated into technologies? Are the wise uses of technology not, as Richard McKeon suggested decades ago,[3] legitimately within the purview of rhetorical inquiry?

I must confess to occasional flights of fancy in which I peruse arcane journals, with titles such as *Evolution, Behavioral Psychology,* and *Sociobiology.* It is sort of like an anthropological expedition, and I am weakly socialized in the folkways of the relevant communities. Why do I do that? And does it have any relationship whatever to the motive just discussed? Perhaps not. Perhaps my fragmented psyche admits of no unifying narrative, and I should just accept the fact that I'm interested in a lot of unrelated things. But I would prefer to give a different account. I would prefer to observe that scientific journal articles are, as Charles Bazerman has shown us,[4] highly subject to the generic rhetorical constraints of their respective disciplines. They are targeted to intended audiences, which meets the criterion for one sense of "community"—that is, the criterion of disciplinarity. Where I think rhetorical scholars need to raise consciousness is in showing just how permeable the boundaries of such communities are and how the discourse not only draws from but feeds back into the shared values, assumptions, and preferences of the larger community.

Fourth, there are essentially two contexts of scientific rhetoric—the internal and the external. Dilip Gaonkar is correct in observing that this assumption operates in much of the literature,[5] but the assumption is an oversimplification, which at least some of us have tried to critique. The problem with this sort of duality is that it subtly overstresses the internal-external distinction in analyzing the contexts of science. Mind you, I believe that this distinction is not without merit. My critique is not to say that one must somehow figure out how to reduce the two contexts to one. This is what the philosophers of science have attempted on the side of the internalist account—that is, to explain science strictly in terms of its internal logic. And it is what many sociologists of science, and some rhetoricians, have attempted on the externalist side—that is, in terms of social or ideological processes.

In my view it is mistaken and wrongheaded to attempt the reduction on either side. When Michael McGee and I first responded to the new talk of rhetoric of inquiry some ten years ago,[6] we argued that this reduction could be dangerous, and I have not changed my mind since. Externalist critiques of science which would, in effect, perform a reduction of science to ideology simply boil away what is distinctive and powerful about science; moreover, they overlook the way in which discourses of science can effectively shield themselves from the ideological commitments of the political culture, in effect interfering, blocking, or rerouting them. But this incomplete absorption of science by the ideology of the general culture is not simply "unfinished business" for the theorists and critics, not simply a lump of undigested material waiting to be processed. Rather, the difference between scientific inquiry, practice, and discourse must be appreciated if one is to understand the special tension that occurs between the essentially antirhetorical stance of science and the avowedly rhetorical character of general public discourse.

Rather than pursue reduction of internalist accounts to externalist interpretations—or the reverse—I argue for the opposite strategy of moderately pluralizing our account of the contexts of address. At a minimum, I believe, one needs the three contexts of intradisciplinary, interdisciplinary, and extradisciplinary frames just in order to pull out the dynamics of some important rhetoric-audience relationships. This immediately blurs the too-sharp distinction between technical and popularized contexts and is in fact premised on the notion that the "popularizing" of technical claims is implicitly there from the start, insofar as those with technical expertise must connect with those whose knowledge is centered elsewhere. Yet this more triangulated account continues to acknowledge the real discursive constraints on scientific discourse demanded by the pertinent disciplines. I have no interest in debunking science—that vast, abstract foil for some scholars. Leave that to the English Department. I would much rather work at finding ways to bring science to the table when matters of civic interest are discussed.

Fifth, understanding scientific discourse as public rhetoric requires different tools and assumptions than have been applied by rhetorical scholars traditionally. Let me be quick to acknowledge that there is no single paradigm at work in the rhetorical tradition. Still, the conversation about theory has in this century been framed largely by the figures of Aristotle and Burke. Between them, I believe, one has ample theoretical resources to go about the study of scientific discourse as rhetoric. When I say "as rhetoric," I do not mean to suggest that scientific practice is constituted just by rhetoric. I depart from Alan Gross in respect to this claim that, once the rhetorical account of science is rendered complete, there is no remainder.[7] Instead, I see scientific discourse as operating within the context of numerous practices—verbal, mathematical, physical, economic, and institutional.

Consider the public passion for the O. J. Simpson trial. The intertwining of technical discourse with the discourse of praise and blame, justice, public values, fairness, policy, prudence, and decorum is quite thorough. Woe to the advocate who cannot add some proofs of the special sciences to his or her arsenal of general proofs. And woe to the technical expert who cannot make his or her conclusions felt persuasively. Even given the widely repeated claim that DNA testing of blood samples would reduce the chances of a mismatch to one in millions at least, we would be unwise to rule out the possibility of some slick-tongued lawyer making that seem less than a convincing level of proof: "After all, one in a hundred million could still leave two or three people in America alone who might have committed this crime! Ask yourselves, ladies and gentlemen, are you prepared to take away this man's life without having even considered those other two or three people—not to mention others around the globe who might have been brought in for this dirty work?"

Students of rhetoric should not think of science as something that occurs within the space of a laboratory. Part of it does, of course. But science is also a part of the very fabric of our public discourse as well. Rush Limbaugh gets hoots of approval by quoting nuclear scientist Dixie Lee Ray (who never met a technology—or technological by-product—she didn't like). Ray used her scientific savvy to puncture the loose claims in the press about global warming or the ozone layer. I have seen the famous, late "Dr. Socks" herself reduce rhetorically sophisticated opponents to jelly by undercutting their case on apparently scientific grounds. This is not science contra popularization; it is science as popular tool of persuasion. Trot out charts and statistics against the mushier popular rhetoric, and it's red meat for the very audience of yahoos who are not supposed to use science in their thought processes. So, one cannot even do a thorough rhetorical critique of Rush Limbaugh without opening up technical knowledge.

This is not really new, of course. Arguers and sophists of every generation have figured out how to deploy the appearance of technical knowledge to support their case. What has changed, in degree sufficient to make it almost a change in kind, is that the information flow in our society is such that very specific scientific information can be called up by almost anyone. The potency of public discourse is very much hostage to the discourses of science and information which may be mobilized to check it, challenge, deflate it.

I am comfortable with Aristotle's general formulation of rhetoric as concerning the available means of persuasion in the particular case. In the late twentieth century, if one goes into the very civic forums, mutatis mutandis, which Aristotle spoke of—the courtroom, the city councils and other places of deliberation, commencement ceremonies, news conferences, and other settings where praise and blame are dispensed—one usually finds modern science deployed as a resource of persuasion. How impoverished would be the environmentalist opponent of a new development if he or she were unable to muster scientific proofs! How feeble the work of the defense attorney if he or she were unable to deal persuasively with ballistics, blood tests, DNA tests, and what not. The notion that the civic forums of our time are not contexts for the discourses of technical knowledge is strangely archaic. And note: these are not discourses merely about science. Rather, they are contexts in which scientific inquiry is itself proceeding.

Once having cleared away these myths, we are in a position to consider how discourses in, of, around, and about science induce that final product of the rhetorician's interest: judgment, judgment by relevant audiences. I share the interest of fellow rhetoricians such as Leff, Farrell, and others who call attention back to the importance of situated judgment as an appropriate upshot of the rhetorical art. But I believe we must also not neglect another faculty, without which judgment is impoverished and retrograde. That is the faculty of *imagination*, or, more specifically, moral imagination. Moral imagination is the capacity to envision how a situation can admit of other descriptions and perspectives, how others may be affected, how attributes may be claimed or rejected as part of "us," how we understand who is part of our community, how the course of language we unleash may do its work over time. Richard Rorty hails the "strong poet" whose imaginative work produces new ways of social being, new bases of community.[8] But we are all lesser poets and thus always in need of such moral imagination that is required to play a robust role in the civic life of our time. We need to ponder more often the sort of powers that are unleashed in the very language of science. When "gene talk" is used loosely, especially by a scientist, it can have significant consequences for audiences somewhere down the line—somewhere, that is to say, outside the discipline in which figurative language will be understood as figurative language.

I recognize that this puts a strain on the rhetorical critic. For starters the notion of meanings being changed, or shifted as claims move before different audiences, complicates the notion of intentionality, but that has become complicated in any case. We are aware that some contemporary methods of rhetorical analysis and critique do not rely on any presuppositions about the intention of the speaker or writer, and, indeed, some even find such a notion counterproductive. Moves to excise intentionality from the interpretation of rhetorical texts have sometimes come from what are essentially technical difficulties. As it is notoriously difficult to locate and define with any high degree of confidence the intention of others when they speak, critics have often sought to locate the most important determinants of meaning elsewhere. Sometimes the claim has been made that intentions, as psychological entities of questionable status, are in principle unascertainable and, hence, not appropriate objects for scholarly investigation.

More recently rhetorical scholarship has been coming face to face with a more radical critique, one that not only problematizes intentionality but also undercuts the very notion of individual agency. The wave of Continental theory and reading practices that have swept our universities over the last fifteen years has upset nearly every apple cart that was ever lovingly tended by rhetorical scholars, including assumptions about the capacities of individuals to act efficaciously. Rhetoric will continue to struggle with this challenge, perhaps emerging with more reflective and richer accounts of what is studied. For the time being, however, it seems that the very things that the public address tradition has taken as defining assumptions are themselves under assault from every angle. The very notion that a person can strategically and intentionally plan a speech that can have an effect in the world and that this very strategy, intentionality, and efficacy can be studied, even made object lessons for speakers and audiences alike—this has been called into question in the most fundamental ways.

Yet the fact that it can be very difficult to ascertain intentions does not mean that we cannot routinely make fairly reliable and well-evidenced judgments about intentions. The fact that the notion of the individual is disdained by those whose politics or metaphysics so instruct them does not reduce the weight of possibility and attendant anxiety felt by every speaker who has to step into the moment and invent rhetoric. Those moments are not about to disappear from our society. I may not have a good answer to Zeno's proof that motion is impossible, but I am required to go on moving, just the same. So, let the critique, the theory, the excitement of the new, continue. Maybe every instance of speech analysis might be preceded with a moment of silence, in which the analyst says to him- or herself something like this:

The notion of autonomous and self-directing individuals is at best a half-truth, owing to the social construction of meaning, the weight of the unconscious, and the incompleteness with which the liberal mythology illuminates the fundamental sources of experience; the notion of clear and discernible meanings that align with intended meaning effects of a speaker is largely illusory, given the inevitably indeterminate and discontinuous nature of meaning, the fact that discourse controls people more than people control discourse, and the indiscernibleness of intentions; moreover, the notion that human agency is the result of persons "acting" is highly problematic. . . . NEVERTHELESS:

So, nevertheless: Famous neuroscientist Antonio Damasio has written a book about the brain called *Descartes' Mistake*.[9] That's a bold title for a nonphilosopher. He's daring to correct Descartes—not just pick on the pro forma slam at "the Cartesian cogito" coming out of the English departments but actually writing a book offered up as a correction. Interesting, though, that a work of late-twentieth-century neuroscience would take a seventeenth-century philosopher as its foil. A battle of mythic proportions? His observations and experiments with brain-damaged patients, assisted by remarkable new imaging techniques, *show* us that Descartes was wrong. Philosophy has succumbed to science at last. Philosopher Patricia Churchland is quoted on the book cover. Professor Damasio conveys a wealth of scientific knowledge to the general reader and conveys a sense of the cutting-edge importance of his work. He makes a powerful argument for why cognition and the emotions need to be understood together. He aligns himself with some thinkers and criticizes others. He seems to be onto something big. I wonder how the work might be different if there had been any rhetoric in his book?

We who take an interest in public discourse must be concerned with how the discourses of scientific knowledge may mesh with the discourses of value and action, because, one way or another, they will. Science will affect policy and values, willy-nilly.

New techniques for detecting a gene causally responsible for breast cancer—along with a growing list of other genes that have been linked to specific hereditary diseases—might very soon, some believe, produce new practices of eugenics. Unlike the eugenics of the past, this eugenics will be powered by private patents and private decisions. A woman who carries the disposing breast cancer gene can now have several of her eggs fertilized in vitro, have each tested for the presence of the offending gene, and have placed back in her womb one that is free of the gene. As breast cancer is one of the leading causes of death among women, this is no marginal matter. A company named Myriad Genetics holds a patent on the BRCA1 gene, which causes a major class of breast cancers. Similarly, a gene for colon cancer, one of the leading causes of death among males, has been isolated, and presumably embryos carrying that gene could be artificially selected out.

Whatever restrictions governments may wind up placing on procedures such as these, it seems clear that the expense of the procedures will for some time at least make this type of genetic intervention available only to those who can afford it, raising the specter of whether only the well-to-do should be able to avoid passing on a deadly gene to their offspring. In addition to having access to face lifts and other expensive forms of body maintenance, the wealthy might also be able to protect their own "stock" from disease in ways unavailable to the general public.

So, what rhetorical practices will this produce? For starters there will be various disputes about the ethics of this sort of experimentation on embryos and about the increased use of genetic testing as a prelude to abortion. Beyond that I am not sure if we have any reliable guidance from the past about how we should conduct prudent public discourse about matters such as these. What is required is moral imagination in dealing with these new powers only dreamt of before in science fiction. This leads me to think that the qualities of moral imagination and judgment necessary to speaking persuasively about such things could come increasingly from works of fiction, especially science fiction. Moral imagination can be stimulated by science fiction—even the average viewer of "Star Trek" winds up considering possibilities that have never been considered before. My colleague John Nelson seems right on track when he uses science fiction texts to explore issues in political and ethical theory. So is my recent colleague, Kate Hayles, in exploring imaginative literature to increase the repertoire for talking about science.

I want to return now to the issue of scientific discourse being embedded in a variety of sociocultural frames, because I think this is key to understanding how science may serve or disserve us. If one thinks of science as a project authorized by the broader community because it is expected to benefit that community, then one is pressed to think of how a scientific mode of understanding becomes absorbed by more general modes of understanding. The question that Peirce pressed when entertaining the notion of a Speculative Rhetoric that would embrace the sciences was a broader, community-oriented question.[10] How do scientific theories and practices become embedded in the thoughts and habits of a scientific community? How are they communicated and appreciated? These are not merely sociological issues, if one takes Peirce seriously, but part of the broader purview of scientific rationality. That larger project of communication, and indeed persuasion, is as much an interest of "the scientific intelligence" as is the laboratory experiment. Scientific rationality requires syntactic rigors, semantic ingenuity and accuracy, and rhetorical efficacy. Otherwise, it dies on the vine. Being persuaded, so often the benchmark of rhetorical success, is the very quest of the curious but skeptical mind—that is, of the scientific intelligence. Being *falsely persuaded* is its bane, the very danger Plato feared.

And what are the criteria for distinguishing and isolating false persuasion? The answer, all attempts to the contrary, is that there is no general answer. That which "justifies" persuasion is as complex and nuanced as the content and circumstances of any given domain of investigation. And it is even more so, because the ways and means of persuasion are not just the domain-specific ones. There are different audiences who are persuaded by different evidence and arguments. This is not to embrace a wide-open populism that would make the opinions of the average person the equal of the expert. For those questions that are domain specific the person best positioned to be persuaded is the person who knows the most about the given subject—knows the false leads that have tripped up others as well as the fuller story behind any snippet that the novice might pick up. So, up to a point, anyway, what persuades those best in a position to know is what we should value, even if it is necessary continually to debate the question of who, in any given matter, is in the best position to know.

One must respect the suspicions that arise whenever expert testimony is introduced to sway public opinion. When experts speak in a public forum—the courts, before Congress, on television—the very fact that they are in such a forum usually indicates that the matters they are addressing have more than a technical dimension. During the summer 1994 Supreme Court confirmation hearings of Judge Stephen G. Breyer before the Senate Judiciary Committee, the judge ventured a strongly held opinion that the federal government should calculate the number of human lives saved by any regulatory policy and be forced to justify any shifts in spending in terms of how many lives would be saved. This was the voice of a man accustomed to thinking and writing of such matters in merely technical terms. He was quickly and effectively taken to task by Senator Joseph Biden, who pointed out that the matter of when and how lives were to be protected was not just a technical question but in the profoundest sense a political one. Our society has decided to spend vast sums on health care for the elderly, for instance, but balks at spending far lesser sums on preventative health measures that would surely save more lives. Expertise does not settle issues such as these.

General audiences accustomed to seeing experts testifying on opposite sides of a question have learned to be savvy about such things. They know that few questions that come before them, in which their own assent is being called for, are likely to be purely technical questions.[11] Expertise is often, perhaps one should say usually, in the service of money or some other external motivation. The expert must therefore be viewed with a critical eye. In fact, it can be argued, a part of the necessary preparation for receiving expertise is to apply a touch of rhetorical criticism: "Why is this person in this situation trying to get me to believe just this?" Knowledge is disseminated by testimony and comes to reside in the larger community primarily by that means. Such testimony needs to be viewed and evaluated not just as an epistemic but also as a rhetorical performance. A scientific rhetoric, like any other, must be persuasive to succeed. And the burden inherent in making a scientific theory persuasive is that it has to be more than appealing on its own terms but regarded as consistent with other things known. The audiences of scientists and nonscientists who receive scientific discourse are, from a rhetoric perspective, users of meaning who place models and theories into various relationships, using various strategies.

We know that the practice of science does not occur within a vacuum. Practicing scientists get a sense of what is important and worth pursuing from broader social values, and, conversely, we expect scientists, whether supported by public or private funding, to bring something of value back to the broader society. This mutual implication of values alone would prevent scientific rationality from being a closed system. And one might also say that there is a mutual implication of ends, which makes the proper conduct of science a legitimate concern to the entire society. Ethical violations within the conduct of science are therefore violations against the broader society that supports and depends upon scientific work. So much seems generally appreciated. Yet the notion persists that scientific rationality somehow governs a separate province, untainted, ideally, at least, by the reasoning and folkways of everyday experience. Yes, one hears it acknowledged: the ethical, the aesthetic, and even the rhetorical dimensions of science hold an interest all their own—but these do not touch the core cognitive values of science.

The picture that I would want to paint of science is one of a cognitive continuum, no less than one of a practical, rhetorical, aesthetic, or ethical continuum—in which knowledge and techniques learned in general life transfer to the more specific contexts of science. It seems obvious that puzzle-solving and pattern recognition skills learned from amateur sleuthing, playing computer games, figuring out what caused one's favorite houseplant to die, are patterns that recur in scientific investigation. And, I would suggest, tropes and figures applicable in broader life seem just as obviously—once we take off the doctrinal blinders—to operate within science as well. Obviously, scientists attempt to discipline these more general habits as well as to eliminate the bad ones. That discipline, thankfully, is imperfect.

Let's consider just one general pattern that infuses discourses of evolutionary biology. The notion of natural "selection" carries residues of the everyday usage—that is, connotations of choice in selecting, which is closely associated with purposive action. Darwin embellished these connotations with overtones of an all-wise Nature, culling as necessary for the greater good. Social Darwinists elided the job of nature and the job of social institutions in selecting the fittest. And now sociobiologists have the genes colluding with cultural practices to select the most promising behaviors—promising, that is, from the viewpoint of the genes, who (one feels almost a grammatical necessity in this context to make genes *who*s rather than *which*s) struggle to ensure their own survival. On display here is a pattern of reason which was invented in the nineteenth century, accommodated to recent assumptions about the stuff of life. The reasoning about how genes operate did not originate full blown when we learned the mechanics of the double helix. Rather, existing patterns moved in around the new knowledge to give it a context and efficacy in evolutionary explanation. Terms deeply embedded both in science and in culture—terms such as *selection, fitness, adaptation*—continued to carry the weight of accumulated meaning and association. No technical specification can really cleanse these terms of those associations. When biometric geneticists apply finely honed equations to specify the meaning of fitness, their arguments about fitness cross into other domains in which those equations are all but unknown. The terminological configuration of *selection/adaptation/fitness* traits goes galloping across a range of different disciplinary and nondisciplinary contexts, carrying what I think can meaningfully be called rhetorical force, independent of precision and controls.

Theoretically, each level of biological science should have its place in a grand reduction, in which every level of explanation is consistent with every other. In practice such a consistency is not required. Molecular geneticists can and sometimes do doubt the prevailing theories of evolution, for instance. The undigested parts of the collective scientific enterprise sustain their own activity, consistent or not with the next level up or down the chain of reduction. Practitioners who know their jobs quite well may know nothing about what other practitioners do, still less about what others see them as doing. Viewed in terms of meanings, this suggests a great deal of nontransparency. It also suggests a great deal of de facto inconsistency. To understand science as discourse requires some sense of the macro and micro levels of discursive practice in which any given discourse is embedded, because these levels interanimate one another. Sometimes this is a lively conceptual interchange. At other times it can be only an apparent interanimation that is really more a matter of terminological residues. If one looks at the way the notion of "fitness" is used across the discourses of genetics, evolution theory, and sociobiology, for instance, it appears that the suggestive power of the terminology is part of what connects the different levels and regions of discourse.

The highly specialized nature of organized science produces regions of discourse which can be isolated from one another even if carried out in close geographical proximity. One writes to fellow specialists who read the same journals, not necessarily for the colleague down the hall. But this breaking up into specialties, or into regions of discourse, is in many ways made possible because of the presupposed possibility of reduction. This is what makes each separate activity part of a single enterprise and additively consistent, at least as a regulative ideal.

Rhetoricians who make claims about scientific discourse being rhetorical are apt to provoke a fight from those who believe this means some sort of slander on science. Rhetoricians, of course, usually mean it as a compliment. Being rhetorical does not have to come at the expense of being other things. Indeed, it can be disastrous for rhetoric as well for science if scientific rhetoric grows into something independent and isolable from scientific practices. Henry Howe and I have attempted to show how a simplified and streamlined rhetoric can create the illusion of a synthesis from among several distinct traditions in genetic research. The rhetoric floats, so to speak, above the practices and thus drifts somewhat too freely into new territories.

One of the classical episodes of science gone awry is that of Soviet agriculturist T. D. Lysenko, who used an ideological framed political rhetoric to push his program into the forefront of established science under the protection of Joseph Stalin. The case has been examined as a study in the dangers of making science subservient to politics or to bossism of any sort. What I believe the case also shows is the way that a scientific rhetoric can latch onto ingrained discursive practices and be carried along by them. Lysenko managed to get press and Party approval by connecting his reports of spectacular improvements in crop yields to a pre-sold rhetoric about the superiority of materialism over idealism, of Russian over Western science, of the people over elites. Moreover, he managed to stigmatize research in genetics as a means of venerating his own experimental methods and to help move forward a bandwagon that would set back genetic research in the Soviet Union a generation.

One might say that Lysenko tapped into and amplified preexisting affective habits on his way to creating an all-too-easy method of explanation. This, coupled with reports of vitally important improvements in grain yields, made his program politically appealing indeed. As state institutions and journals dedicated to the program spread, and as shielding from outside critique increased, Lysenko's positive story had a fertile field in which to grow. The agreeableness of the story being told by Lysenko, and by those sycophants who enlisted in his program, was a key to its rhetorical efficacy. Something needed to puncture this rhetoric before it could run roughshod over sound scientific practice, not to mention common sense. That nothing did is testament to the dangers of a good story and a politically savvy rhetoric when they are in the service of poorly reviewed science.

Those of us who wish to celebrate rhetoric need to assemble reminders of rhetoric gone bad, and especially so when we become advocates of a rhetorically sophisticated science. At the same time, we need to think about the possibilities of rhetorical cures for the diseases most incident to rhetorical processes. And what are these cures? The brief answer, as best as I could imagine it, is "rhetorical engagement." Rather than dismissing the rhetorical forces that combine to make a scientific story persuasive, one needs to take them seriously and engage them in critique. This would entail examination of rhetorical figures to see not just if they work but also where they may draw their rhetorical efficacy. This would be part of a general critical consideration of language and imagery. Those metaphors introduced for purposes of convenience or ease of explanation would not so easily be relegated to the bin of incidental features of the discourse. Aspects of "gene talk" used to excite the imaginations of others would be accounted serious components of a discourse which also aspires to a high quality of scientific rationality. Indeed, the rhetoric of figuration would be accounted a part of its rationality.

Notes

1. John Lyne and Henry Howe, "'Punctuated Equilibria': Rhetorical Dynamics of a Scientific Controversy," *Quarterly Journal of Speech* 72 (1986): 132–47; John Lyne and Henry Howe, "Rhetorics of Expertise: The Marketing of Sociobiology," *Quarterly Journal of Speech* 76 (1990): 134–51; Henry Howe and John Lyne, "Gene Talk in Sociobiology," *Social Epistemology* 6, no. 2 (1992): 1–54.

2. Stephen Hawking, *A Brief History of Time* (London: Bantam, 1988).

3. Richard McKeon, "The Uses of Rhetoric in a Technological Age: Architectonic Productive Arts," in *The Prospect of Rhetoric*, ed. Lloyd F. Bitzer and Edwin Black (Englewood Cliffs, N.J.: Prentice-Hall, 1971), 44–63.

4. Charles Bazerman, *Shaping Written Knowledge: The Genre and Activity of the Experimental Article in Science* (Madison: University of Wisconsin Press, 1988).

5. Dilip Gaonkar, "The Idea of Rhetoric in the Rhetoric of Science," *Southern Communication Journal* 58 (1993): 258–95.

6. Michael C. McGee and John Lyne, "What Are Nice Folks like You Doing in a Place Like This? Some Entailments of Treating Knowledge Claims Rhetorically," in *The Rhetoric of the Human Sciences: Language and Argument in Scholarship and Public Affairs*, ed. John S. Nelson, Allan Megill, and Donald N. McCloskey (Madison: University of Wisconsin Press, 1987), 381–406.

7. Alan Gross, *The Rhetoric of Science* (Cambridge: Harvard University Press, 1990).

8. Richard Rorty, *Contingency, Irony, and Solidarity* (New York: Cambridge University Press, 1989).

9. Antonio Damasio, *Descartes' Mistake* (New York: G. P. Putnam's Sons, 1994).

10. John Lyne, "Rhetoric and Semiotic in C. S. Peirce," *Quarterly Journal of Speech* 66 (1980): 156–68.

11. McGee and Lyne, "What Are Nice Folks like You Doing in a Place Like This?"

CHAPTER FOURTEEN

Feuding Communities and the Feudalism of Science
Democratizing the Community and / of Science

Charles Alan Taylor

In recent years the various "rhetorical turns" reconfiguring the intellectual geometry of recent decades promised to bring "rhetorical studies" if not to the center at least a bit further from its accustomed position at the institutional margins. Such might still be the case, though our own well-honed hand-wringing has as well ushered in a necessary and valuable but still damnably deflating reflexive moment. In this moment Dilip Gaonkar has argued that, "in its current form, rhetoric, as a language of criticism is so thin . . . that it commands little sustained attention."[1] Even Alan Gross, although presumably as a hostile witness, "left open the possibility that, as a discipline, rhetoric of science is intellectually superfluous."[2] In their broadest terms these observations suggest more or less directly that, in our rush to cash in the interpretive currency of rhetoric, we have so artificially inflated its value that our globalized rhetoric threatens to become the funny money of the hermeneutic enterprise.

I do not intend to take up this claim directly here but, rather, to suggest alternatively that this internal critique of the rhetoric of science presumes a different disciplinary psychosis—a thoroughgoing ambivalence regarding just how far into the pristine inner sanctum of science we are *really* willing to go. Even as our critical practices exorcise the intellectual demons of the Vienna Circle by insisting loudly with Alan Gross that "science is rhetorical, without remainder,"[3] we simultaneously pull our punches, conceding that we are apt to be dismissed by those scholars who, again in Gross's terms, "willingly pay the high opportunity cost of mastering 'real' science."[4]

This tension, I think, stems less from globalizing *rhetoric* than from a far less reflexively monitored impulse—globalizing science. Even as we trumpet the failure of the multiple *isms* vying to characterize the *scien-*

tific method, our reading strategies consistently avoid anything resembling an oppositional characterization, even to the point of premising critique on formulations of "real science." Perhaps the most compelling evidence of this dualism are the remarkably frequent allusions to the global *institutional* voice of science. Since confession is alleged to be good for the soul, consider the homoglossia implicit in my own claim to have discovered "*the* scientific community's response to creationism."[5] Or consider Howe and Lyne's claim that, "as in the creationism case, scientific rhetoric here plays differently to different audiences, who can become unwitting purveyors of conceptual distortions."[6] This claim of distortion is all the more striking because it follows from an analysis of quite disparate subcommunities.

In this essay I want to think aloud about the implications of this globalization because they too may bode ill for rhetoric of science's intellectual and institutional exchange rate. This thinking takes the form of an alternative perspective for reading science and Lyne's version of its rhetorics, with an eye toward reshaping the relationship of science and society in our community.

We have devoted much time, attention, and ink to the connections between rhetoric, science, and community. I want to extend these critiques by pointing toward the possibility of constructive interfaces between them. It is this characteristic that I think might prefigure more democratic discourses of and about science in our postmodern polis.

This view of "interdependent co-operation" (not always *cooperative;* indeed, usually agonistic) takes science to be a series of social and technical practices that stabilize in particular configurations at particular times, as a function of the symbolic mediation of multiple and competing constraints. This orientation gives presence to discourses conventionally considered nonscientific or, at best, peripheral to the conduct of science, such as those concerned with enrolling allies and funds, sustaining cultural authority, and the like. Science here is a motile, cultural category, one that, to borrow Professor Leff's description of rhetoric, "finds its habitations in the particular."[7]

Metaphorically, this interdependent co-operation is enacted as a complex cultural "ecosystem." The multiple species that constitute an ecosystem have primacy within their own distinguishable ecological niches, but none is isolated from others, who maintain similar primacy in their own niches. How the activities of any single species affects myriad others is the outcome of contextual interactions, emphasizing the profound interconnectedness of the whole. For example, the recent identification of the "breast cancer gene" might be read as one outcome of an especially fortuitous interaction between scientists, federal funding agencies, the pharmaceutical industry, and women's health advocates, constrained as well by individual rivalries and institutional alliances within the biomedical research community. A rhetorical analysis of that case would be well positioned to map the discursive means by which those intersections were constructed as well as the arguments around which the individual and institutional alliances were created and upon which the ecosystem achieved its local, and hardly inevitable, closure in the gene's identification.

Consider, additionally, the configuration of sociotechnical practices that led to the demise of the Superconducting Supercollider. The SSC began its public life as something of a scientific panacea, enabling the pursuit and potential capture of the fundamental building blocks of matter—the elusive "top quark"—and, in so doing, reinforcing the prestige of American "big science." As the project ran into inevitable cost overruns, construction delays, and partisan bickering, however, this "monument to the scientific mind" became to many a "shameless boondoggle," designed to reward influential members of Congress or the "pampered elites" of high-energy physics. When Congress voted ultimately to end funding for construction on the facility in (more precisely, under) Waxahachie, Texas, this public symbolic metamorphosis or mutation was complete.

A rhetorical analysis would not be concerned explicitly with the ontological status of the top quark but, rather, with the rhetorical stabilization of this cultural ecosystem and its implications for understanding the shifting nature and authority of science—issues that themselves constrain ontological judgments, if not ontologies.

At this point I want to turn to an alternative reading on Lyne's rhetoric of science which views the shifting authority of gene talk as a contextual stabilization of multiple "species" as a precursor to reconfiguring these formations, in which biorhetorics will no doubt continue to circulate. In so doing, I want to suggest that the ironic globalization of science which proceeds from Lyne's characterization of scientific audiences leads us away from the democratic community with which rhetorics, on their better days, are identified and toward a sort of postmodern feudalism.

The Feudal Community of Gene Talk

In their large and still growing body of work on the rhetorics of sociobiology, Professor Lyne and his coauthor, biologist Henry Howe, have emphasized two central themes: "(1) genetic metaphor is often used *as a legitimating principle* in sociobiology with little or no genetic reasoning or evidence; and (2) genetic terminology used as metaphor often leads to misunderstanding of projected expertise, and consequently to miscommunication of evidence and authority."[8] As the discourses of sociobiology circulate among and between various audiences, freed from the rhetorical encumbrances of genetics, it "takes the form of an oversimplified and misleading arch-determinism."[9]

Central to this critique are the tacit boundaries that mark the contexts in which the language of genetics is used *appropriately,* serving *via negativa* as the standard against which the "gene talk" of Wilson, Dawkins, and others should be measured and, inevitably, found wanting. This grounds their critique upon a global conception of science enacted through transcendence of its constituent communities. This lack of reflexivity makes problematic the potential of their critical practice to enhance the communal discussion of the bases of appropriate human behavior.

As I see it, a primary limitation of this "interpretive vocabulary" is that, while rightly problematizing the gene talk of sociobiologists, it fails to recognize that *genetics* talk is equally a product of the stabilization of particular ecosystems, itself a locally, albeit professionally, validated configuration of practices. By deproblematizing these evaluative rhetorics, they, in effect, lodge agency for judgment in nature, which we must assume speaks clearly, with only minor dialect shifts, to "real" scientists. Consider, for example, the strategy of delineating "the genetic rhetorics that perfuse texts of prominent sociobiologists, and compar[ing] them with their authorizing *principles* in genetics" (emph. added).[10] Remarkably, we are told, gene talk's apparent inadequacy is attested to not by rhetors but by "the facts," represented as the necessary products of a globalized science. Viewing those facts as products of local judgments, on the other hand, would allow us to conclude (with equal empirical justification) that authorizing and authorized *principals* have evaluated and delegitimated the discourses of sociobiology. Principles do not close down debates; principals, via selection and application of competing principles, do.

Of course, one might reasonably respond that, sure, there are lots of genetics labs, but they do have a great deal more in common than I suggest. Perhaps. That which they presumably share, however, would be the empirical data, interpretations of which might differ. Indeed, what counts as the "relevant" probative context is a rhetorical accomplishment, not an inherent property of a given context, less yet of the claims circulating within it. Indeed, the availability of that empirical data is itself the outcome of stabilized configurations that extend well beyond the antiseptic walls of laboratories. As they note, "the pragmatics of funding patterns have conspired with demands of experimental rigor to produce dramatically uneven progress in subdisciplines of genetics." As a result, "the uneven progress within subdisciplines . . . has produced rather different vocabularies of . . . critical terms."[11] If such is the case, then, while members of professional communities are perhaps the best interpreters of the "empirical data," the generation of that data is connected inextricably to the funds to support certain research programs rather than their competitors. This sort of judgment implicates rhetorical processes we traditionally have considered nonscientific.[12]

Hence, it would seem that the empirical foundation upon which Howe and Lyne so painstakingly premise their very reasonable critique is itself pragmatically contingent on wider configurations of practices—many of which require judgments from those who have never set foot in a genetics laboratory. My point is not at all that Howe and Lyne are wrong; on the contrary, a more practical consideration of the empirical basis of their critique might well allow closer scrutiny of the genetic evidence, perhaps leading to a more rigorous critique of sociobiologists' assumption of genetic authority.

There might well be (and, I think, is) compelling reason to challenge the discourses of sociobiology on political, philosophical, and empirical grounds. Nonetheless, I am concerned that globalized scientific communities declaring epistemic victory over the dilettantes of sociobiology on empirical grounds in the way suggested by Lyne and Howe misconstrues, or at least, underestimates their interpenetrability.

Despite their explicit claims to the contrary, this reading strategy entails that wider circulation of empirical discourses necessarily involves processes of "popularization" which enact more or less sophisticated (and condescending) processes of "dumbing down." Of course, "to the discerning eye, the mismatch between the gene talk used by sociobiologists and the seemingly identical rhetorics employed by geneticists was at least baffling."[13] The appropriate visual acuity stems presumably from the "facts" that appear to illuminate only those within particular right-thinking scientific subcommunities. Indeed, Howe and Lyne suggest that these discourses of nature are paired *by their natures* with appropriately discerning interpreters through the "rhetorics indigenous to the three modern paradigms of heredity."[14]

My point here is not that all interpretations of the facts are of equal legitimacy. This sort of vicious relativism is as discredited as its positivist alter ego. My point is that to claim that the relative legitimacy of a given interpretation is a natural condition of the material to be interpreted, rather than a function of an audience's evaluations of the evidence adduced on its behalf before contextually authorized audiences, vests the privileged few with literal "ownership" of knowledge claims. The rest of us are expected to toil without need of understanding, less yet an opportunity for meaningful critique on this epistemological manor—an intellectual and communal feudalism. This, it seems to me, borders perilously close to the scenario against which Professor Leff warned us in 1987: "lacking a model that provides entry into the world of civic action, the rhetoric of the human sciences would leave human scientists isolated in the web of their own technical practices."[15]

If, on the other hand, we adopt a reading strategy that characterizes the rhetorical transformations that (dis)empower contextual configurations of the multiple species, we at least leave open the potential for this meaningful "entry into the world of civic action."

Where does this leave us? Perhaps in a muddle. Or, perhaps, confronting the very strong possibility that these carefully tended boundaries break down even in so-called technical disputes such as this and thus, in principle, break down in other such cases. Such collapses should be welcomed for in their wake we can consider where future walls (or, better yet, future checkpoints) might be built, perhaps empowering previously silenced voices but also proving useful for practicing scientists. To suggest that all hierachical configurations of practices are rhetorical constructions is equally to suggest that they are subject to, may even cry out for, alternative constructions—a task to which rhetorical critics should set themselves.

While more inclusive rhetorics of science would encourage a more critical evaluation of what science can and *cannot* tell or do for (or to) us, this should not be viewed as somehow anti-intellectual, or antiscience, in particular. On the contrary, perhaps it is the artificially inflated conception of scientific expertise and its accompanying disillusionment that disempowers informed public debate—a technical discourse's own "worst enemy."

This disillusionment, an inevitable outcome of grandiose expectations, is especially problematic in an age when many of the compelling social issues demanding our attention draw, at some level, on technical discourses. From judgments regarding where (if anywhere) to locate toxic waste sites to the demands placed on jurors to make sense of increasingly technical testimony in legal proceedings, it is imperative that a meaningful "balance of trade" in discursive commerce be sought by privileging intellectual humility over hubris.

Understood in these terms, science is an active, important constituent of the ecosystem but one that, like any other, must justify its share of the resources to those who make allocation decisions and to those who might, in one way or another, be affected by the potential reallocations and/or the productions funded by them.

This seems especially compelling in an age marked by increasing scarcity of material resources and an exponential growth in demands for them, especially for "megaprojects" such as the Human Genome Project or the ill-fated Superconducting Supercollider. In retrospect it now seems apparent that the empirical "fate" of the top quark was more dependent on what happened in Washington, D.C., than Waxahachie. One disgruntled (now unemployed) former SSC technician seemed to sense this requirement, lamenting that "the work is so far removed from everyday experience, it's hard to see the connection. . . . We don't use a language people can understand."[16]

Inadequate understanding is but part of the problem, and enhancing admittedly unacceptable levels of scientific literacy is but part of the solution. Perhaps a larger part of the problem is the taken-for-granted assumption that "people," given improved understanding, would be compelled naturally to concede the funds for such projects. Perhaps we would be. Maybe we should be. Justifying such judgments in our postmodern community, however, requires crafting more realistic, inclusive, and constructive rhetorics of science by the interdependent co-operative (and, I hope, cooperative) communities of practitioners, consumers, and critics alike.

Notes

1. Dilip Gaonkar, "The Idea of Rhetoric in the Rhetoric of Science," *Southern Communication Journal* 58 (1993): 263.

2. Alan Gross, "Guest Editor's Column," *Technical Communication Quarterly* 3 (1994): 6.

3. Alan Gross, *The Rhetoric of Science* (Cambridge: Harvard University Press, 1990), 213.

4. Gross, "Guest Editor's Column," 5.

5. Charles Taylor, "Of Audience, Expertise, and Authority: The Evolving Creationism Debate," *Quarterly Journal of Speech* 78 (1992): 277–95.

6. Henry Howe and John Lyne, "Gene Talk in Sociobiology," *Social Epistemology* 6, no. 2 (1992): 2.

7. Of course, this is the "flash point" for those troubled by the potential epistemological anarchy of recent themes in the otherwise heterogeneous science studies literature. It is a reasonable unease—if science is a local, indeed mundane, production, how is it that it "travels" so widely and with an admittedly remarkable degree of credibility? After all, few of us are likely to bank on the physics of rhetorical criticism as we choose to fly to and from scholarly conferences. While this exceeds my goals for this essay, the general SS account suggests that the authority of science proceeds from its ability to interpolate particular knowledge claims into the interests of more and more disparate communities of technical actors. For example, so many communities have interpolated the physical behavior of mercury in the presence of changing temperature gradients that it would be profoundly disruptive, indeed rather silly, to attempt to "pry open" its empirical black box—or even to give a thought about it.

8. Henry Howe and John Lyne, "Howe and Lyne Bully the Critics," *Social Epistemology* 6 (1992): 231.

9. Howe and Lyne, "Gene Talk," 3.

10. Ibid., 4.

11. Ibid., 6.

12. An additional instance of this nonreflexive discussion of the basis of empirical critique can be seen in their critique of extrapolations from animal to human—hence, socially shaped—populations: "The direct application of molecular genetic discoveries to the behavioral ecology of compex organisms is severely limited. Convenient experimental organisms . . . for inherently *expensive* research allow few intriguing inferences relevant to bird or mammal, much less human social behavior. The financial strictures on molecular genetics of birds and mammals are prohibitive" (ibid., 22).

13. Ibid., 27.

14. Ibid., 4.

15. Michael Leff, "Modern Sophistic and the Unity of Rhetoric," in *The Rhetoric of the Human Sciences: Language and Scholarship in Politics and Public Affairs,* ed. John Nelson, Allan Megill, and Donald McCloskey (Madison: University of Wisconsin Press, 1987), 30.

16. Quoted in Earl Lane, "Top Scientists Hit the Unemployment Line," *Indianapolis Star,* 31 October 1993, A15.

Conclusion
Rhetoric and the
Restoration of Community

J. Michael Hogan

Communities are living creatures, nurtured and nourished by rhetorical discourse. As the studies in this volume illustrate, communities may unite around common life experiences or shared visions of the future—commonalities manifested in their rhetorical discourse. Unfortunately, so too may communities be defined by a common enemy, as Rod Hart reminds us, constituted by the rhetoric of demonization and hate.

In contemporary culture the rhetoric of hate has escalated. The result is a culture at war with itself, a culture fragmented into subcommunities polarized and alienated from one another. This fragmentation, in turn, subverts deliberation and problem solving, for, while hatred may promote in-group solidarity, it discourages constructive engagement. If we hope to sustain healthy communities, we must learn more not only about the rhetoric of hate, as Hart urges, but also about the alternatives to hate in community relations.

By examining a diverse array of political and professional communities, the essays in this volume contribute to a broader understanding of the rhetoric of community. They illustrate how communities may be understood not just in terms of common prejudices or hatreds but also in terms of political or social topoi, patterns of metaphors, stylistic signatures, special vocabularies, and a variety of other rhetorical conventions and tendencies. The rhetoric of each community investigated in this volume reflects a specific historical context, shared memories, and common life experiences; each community is, in some ways, unique. Yet all teach larger lessons about how communities constitute themselves and relate to other communities. As such, they illustrate a range of rhetorical possibilities for negotiating the tension common to all communities: between defining their own, distinctive identities and relating productively to those outside the group.

Historically, feminists and African Americans have provided perhaps the most instructive examples of the difficulty of negotiating this tension. As the essays by Osborn and Watson suggest, early feminists shared a noble vision, manifested in what Osborn characterizes as the "constructive" and "creative" dimensions of their metaphorical patterns. At the same time, however, they never totally divorced themselves from the antagonistic, even warlike, modes of thinking characteristic of the patriarchal culture, nor did most early feminists, as Watson reminds us, completely surrender their individual identities and ambitions to the cause. In some ways innovative yet also reflecting metaphorically the dominant culture and their individual identities, the early feminists began but did not complete the process of forging a distinctively feminist language.

Similarly, Mary Church Terrell, as the voice of African Americans in the turn-of-the-century debate over lynching, displayed a unique moral eloquence exposing the hypocrisy of the dominant culture. At the same time, however, she remained trapped in an economic and cultural milieu that precluded her from fully and forcefully articulating the outrage of African Americans. Whether because of the economics of the media, as Campbell suggests, or because of more subtle and diverse mechanisms of control, as Aune describes them, the voice of African Americans remained deferential, almost apologetic, even in response to an unspeakable horror. The dilemma of African Americans was clear: if they were to be heard at all, they had to abide by the rhetorical conventions of the dominant culture, attempting to persuade without threatening.

W. E. B. Du Bois, of course, rarely deferred to white society, and, as Stephen Browne skillfully illustrates, he eloquently articulated what it meant to be black in America, specifically in the city. Yet, as Darsey points out, Du Bois never really resolved the tension between his own community and the larger culture, not even in his own mind, much less for the nation. At "home" neither in the black community of his day nor in the larger culture, Du Bois died in mental as well as physical exile— a leader whose followers were yet to be born. As a black intellectual who was ahead of his time, Du Bois defined the black experience for many who came later, but in his own day he remained an outsider, uncomfortable even within his own ethnic community.

Like racial and ethnic tensions, the tension between military and civilian communities has persisted for centuries. In American history this tension has manifested itself in everything from the Founders' hostility toward standing armies to the chilly reception that greeted returning Vietnam veterans. As the essays by Carpenter and Medhurst suggest, this tension may be rooted in the rhetorical processes of the military culture itself—processes at odds with the larger culture's ideals of democratic deliberation. The military culture is no less "rhetorical" than any other community, as both essays emphasize, since persuasion remains the essential tool of leadership. Yet privileging secrecy over scrutiny, consensus over debate, the rhetoric of the military community is a far cry from a free "marketplace of ideas."

Different rhetorical dynamics come into play as political leaders seek to rally whole nations to war. A leader does not just "call" a democratic community to arms; the community must be *persuaded* to accept the sacrifice of blood and treasure, and that requires *interaction* between leaders and the led. Thus, Winston Churchill in his "War Situation I" speech did not merely articulate existing war sentiment, as Condit and Greer argue, nor did he radically transform the British public's attitudes toward war. Rather, he developed a "reciprocal" relationship with the public, articulating their concerns yet also forging a new community will. Indeed, Churchill's relationship with the British public may have been more complicated still, as Jasinski suggests, involving a sort of therapeutic function: the management of the community's "anxiety" when confronted with its own "fragility and mortality." However one interprets the speech, it illustrates the complexity of war rhetoric and its importance in defining the character of a national community.

If war is an exceptional and ultimate test of community, the routine test is how artists, scientists, and others with special talents or training impact the intellectual and cultural life of a nation. Artists, in particular, often seem to speak out boldly, but, as Tom Benson's study of one apparently "political" film illustrates, established rhetorical conventions may serve to depoliticize their work. Thus, while Irwin Winkler's 1990 film *Guilty by Suspicion* condemned the reactionary politics of the "blacklist" era, according to Benson, its reliance upon "shallow formulas" ultimately rendered it politically impotent. Bruce Gronbeck discerns a bit more "politics" in the film—a political statement not about history but about Reagan's America. Yet even that reading affirms the central implication of Benson's study: that artists typically cross the line between society as it *is* and as it *ought* to be cautiously, taking refuge in the safety of established conventions or political allusion.

Scientists, like artists, live in two different worlds; they are citizens both of their professional communities—communities with special training, privileges, and powers—and of the larger culture. Like artists, they are dependent upon the confidence and goodwill of the larger society to sustain their endeavors, and those endeavors, in turn, shape the larger culture's quality of life. As a result, as John Lyne argues, the rhetoric of science should be viewed as "public" from the start, inviting, indeed necessitating, rhetorical critique. For Lyne that not only means critiquing the truth claims of scientists but also calling upon them to exercise "moral imagination." For Charles Taylor it means even more: that no claim to scientific "truth" should go unexamined or be privileged over others—that the epistemology of empiricism itself invites rhetorical critique and public scrutiny.

These studies do not solve the problem of community. If anything, they remind us how difficult it can be for communities to negotiate the tension between defining and sustaining themselves and relating constructively to those outside the group. Beyond that they illustrate the diversity and complexity of the rhetorical forms that create, sustain, and sometimes fragment or destroy communities. In short, they do not solve the problem of fragmented communities, but they do point to *where* we might look for answers: to the public talk that constitutes communities and defines their relationships with others. By showing how the problem of community is, in significant measure, a rhetorical problem, they focus our attention upon rhetorical solutions.

Restoring Community

While most of the studies in this book take us back in history, the questions they raise persist. Can feminist or ethnic and racial communities successfully sustain and celebrate their own identities without alienating themselves from the larger community? How can the demands of military efficiency be reconciled with the democratic ethos, and by what rhetorical means do political leaders rally communities to war? What role do artistic communities play in defining the larger culture's response to important political and social issues, and how can scientific communities exercise what Lyne calls "moral imagination"—considering the ethical and social as well as the technical implications of their discoveries?

These questions persist because the problem of community is rooted in enduring moral conflicts. At bottom, communities are defined not just by demographics and common experiences and interests but also by differing moral codes, and those codes resist understanding in purely intellectual terms. As James Davison Hunter has argued, "wars" within and between communities typically are wars "of moral visions," and it is naive to think that a settlement to such conflicts can be "rationally negotiated." According to Hunter, we cannot expect to achieve a "consensus of values and beliefs" in our diverse culture, for "divisions, at this level, are firm and unyielding." We can, however, work toward a new consensus about *"how* to contend over the moral differences that divide," and Hunter offers four practical steps toward such a "public agreement over *how* to publicly disagree."[1]

The first step, according to Hunter, would be to change "the environment of public discourse." As Hunter observes, the new communicative technologies constitute "the chief environment" for contemporary public discussion, and they are not at all "conducive to rational deliberation." According to Hunter, "the reason is plain":

> Genuine debate . . . is always a dialectic; always a direct and immediate exchange. Positions taken and accusations made can be challenged directly by rebuttal, counterpropositions, cross-examination, and, inevitably, the presentation of evidence. . . . But it is impossible to generate these dynamics in television commercials, in political print advertisements and proclamations, and issue-oriented direct mail. . . . Because there is no dialectic, because there is no mechanism for ensuring accountability, the newer communications technologies provide an environment that predisposes actors to rhetorical excess.

Hunter concludes with a warning about the consequences of failing to develop alternatives: "Without a change in the environments of public discourse, . . . demagoguery and rhetorical intolerance will prevail."[2]

Second, Hunter urges a "rejection by all factions of the impulse of public quiescence." Democracy, as Hunter suggests, "depends upon the contribution of many voices." Without a common belief that "public standards do exist and without a commitment to determine what they are," there is "no basis for making public compromises, there is not even the will to make the effort." Thus, Hunter concludes, we must "avoid the temptation . . . to be 'idiots'—a word, which in one of its original meanings, described the totally private person who is oblivious to the importance of and need for public-minded civility." In other words, a new consensus over *how* to debate requires, at the most basic level, a commitment *to* debate.[3]

Third, productive public discussion requires that we learn about, and respect, "the sacred" within "different moral communities." The sacred, according to Hunter, is that which "communities love and revere as nothing else," that which is "nonnegotiable and defines the limits of what they will tolerate." If genuine debate is to occur, all parties involved need to understand what, "from the perspective of the opposition's moral tradition," is and is not "reasonably tolerable." A "common recognition of what constitutes a 'vital threat' for the opposition," Hunter concludes, "predisposes all factions to pursue their respective agendas in the public realm with a measure of prudence and caution."[4]

Finally, a new consensus on how to debate requires that public advocates recognize "the inherent weaknesses, even dangers, in their own moral commitments." For those on the "progressivist" side of the cultural divide this means overcoming their "reticence to talk about the limits or boundaries of the acceptable and the unacceptable," while those on the "orthodox side" have been guilty of the opposite tendency: they have been too eager to "set limits," to "establish and maintain laws that reflect the good." Both attitudes, Hunter argues, are fundamentally contrary to the very concept of community. Both reflect "an implicit yet imperious disregard for the goal of a *common life.*"[5]

Hunter concedes that his "practical steps" actually might be a "bit fanciful." The first involves, in effect, disowning the new technologies, while the other three involve significant changes in public psychology: a restoration of the public's sense of civic obligation, a new empathy for those who disagree, and a new critical self-awareness about one's own moral commitments. Nevertheless, such changes remain a "vital possibility," according to Hunter, for pluralism with toleration represents the essence of the American legacy. "As historians have made very clear," Hunter writes, "our founders faced similarly imposing historical odds in forging the public philosophy that established the American experiment in democracy in the first place. Not to endeavor again would betray that legacy."[6]

Yet any new consensus about how to debate must be accompanied by *structural* or *institutional* changes. If public discussion is to be guided by a new community spirit, as Hunter suggests, we must change not only the attitudes of advocates but also the contexts, or "environments," of public discourse. Hunter offers no blueprints for building new communication environments, but other writers have proposed a wide variety of reforms. In closing, we shall reflect briefly upon three arenas of reform that have generated substantial literatures: the political process, the media of mass communications, and the educational system.

Proposals for reforming the political system are legion, of course, both in the electoral and policy-making arenas. In the electoral arena the problem of maintaining community is addressed most directly by proposals designed to increase voter turnout and to otherwise encourage more political participation. These range from ideas for making it easier to register and vote to a host of proposals for shortening campaigns, improving political advertising and debates, and modifying or even eliminating the electoral college. Campaign reforms enacted since the late 1960s have had some positive effects, involving more citizens in the nominating process and reducing the political influence of wealthy contributors. At the same time, however, many of these reforms have had unforeseen and, to many, undesirable effects: the weakening of the party system, for example, and the increased influence of political consultants and political action committees (PACs).[7]

Likewise, proposals for reforming the institutions and processes of government are numerous, ranging from comprehensive plans for "reinventing government" to specific proposals for limiting the powers or terms of elected officials. All are offered as ways to restore the citizenry's sense of civic involvement and political efficacy. All are touted as at least partial solutions to the problems of political alienation and nonparticipation. Institutional reforms, however, inevitably meet political resistance and typically evolve incrementally. Moreover, they often backfire, not only failing to solve the problems they were designed to solve but also causing new and unforeseen problems. As a result, institutional reforms cannot be counted on as a quick fix to the problem of community. Increasing the efficiency and accountability of government undoubtedly would enhance the sense of political community, but institutional reforms must be undertaken cautiously and monitored for unintended effects.[8]

The mass media's effects on community likewise have attracted considerable scholarly attention, and again there have been countless proposals for reform. All seem to agree that the new communicative technologies—not only television but also direct mail, computer networks, and other advances in mass communication—have contributed significantly to the fragmentation of community. Yet there remains considerable disagreement over the nature and causes of problems with the new communicative technologies.

Some blame the new technologies themselves for the degradation of public discourse, arguing that today's multiple media, and especially television, have "dramatically and irreversibly shifted the content and meaning of public discourse," fragmenting our public discourse and reducing much of it to "dangerous nonsense."[9] Others blame the economics of the media, attributing most of their failures on the structures and concentration of media ownership.[10] Short of utopian schemes for dismantling the communications industry or even banning the new technologies,[11] however, few offer concrete solutions. That leaves us to consider not the technologies themselves but the conventions governing their *use*. Electronic technologies no doubt constrain public discourse, but, as Ben Bagdikian once summarized their potential for good or ill, "Electrons have no morals."[12]

Kathleen Jamieson has been among those suggesting ways in which the conventions of political advocacy and reporting must be changed if something of the "old eloquence"—the eloquence of reasoned public discourse and constructive political engagement—is to be recaptured in the televisual age. In *Eloquence in an Electronic Age* Jamieson invites readers to "conspire" with her in imagining a new political world, a world made "safe for deliberation":

In this utopia, the political process would conspire . . . to invite elaborated thought rather than stock phrases and slogans. . . . Candidates for office would not necessarily be expected to speak often. They would be expected to speak thoughtfully, knowledgeably, and well. . . . Reporters and candidates would return to the model of the 1950s when "the highlight of a typical day was a formal speech to an important audience. These speeches," recalls David Broder, "distributed to the press in advance, provided the copy for most of that day's news coverage, as well as raw material for second-day stories analyzing policy shifts or comparing one candidate's positions with his opponents." . . . To the prosecutorial function the press has adopted since Watergate would be added the obligation to educate the electorate. . . . Thoughtful, reasoned discourse would be as likely to be covered by reporters as leaks, scandals, hyperbolic accusations, and confessions.[13]

Jamieson's "utopia," of course, presumes an electorate interested in, and equipped to process and evaluate, substantive discourse on complex political issues. Toward this end Jamieson joins with virtually all who have written about the problem of community in proposing reforms in one last arena: the educational system.

In the final analysis the restoration of community requires politically literate citizens who embrace their responsibility to participate in the various communities that constitute their political and social worlds. Recognizing this fact, Jamieson would construct her new political world "from the classroom up," with students studying more history and philosophy, more rhetoric and literature, with a view toward increasing the "visual and verbal literacy" of the citizenry. If we hope for more "enlightened" public discourse, Jamieson argues, students must be educated "to recognize and reject faulty premises, data, and claims, whether visual or verbal."[14] Likewise, Neil Postman offers education as the "desperate answer" to the otherwise insoluble problem of a citizenry "amused" rather than enlightened and empowered by public discourse. Such a view, Postman concedes, may be "based on a naive and mystical faith in the efficacy of education," yet there is at least some "reason to suppose that the situation is not hopeless":

Educators are not unaware of the effects of television on their students. Stimulated by the arrival of the computer, they discuss it a great deal—which is to say, they have become somewhat "media conscious." . . . Besides, it is an acknowledged task of the schools to assist the young in learning how to interpret the symbols of their culture. That this task should now require that they learn how to distance themselves from their forms of information is not so bizarre an enterprise that we cannot hope for its inclusion in the curriculum; even hope that it will be placed at the center of education.[15]

If education is to reinvigorate community, however, it must extend beyond media awareness—and well beyond the classroom. It must address the meaning of community itself, and not only schools but also families, community groups, churches, and a variety of other social institutions, indeed all of the institutions of civil society, must be involved in the process. This broader sense of education is the hallmark of the one intellectual/cultural movement dedicated explicitly to the restoration of community: the Communitarian Movement. In the Communitarian Platform, most recently published in Amitai Etzioni's book *The Spirit of Community*, this broader sense of education is offered as the key to rebuilding "active communities that seek to reinvigorate the moral and social order": "A Communitarian perspective recognizes that the preservation of individual liberty depends on the active maintenance of the institutions of civil society where citizens learn respect for others as well as self-respect; where we acquire a lively sense of our personal and civic responsibilities, along with an appreciation of our own rights and the rights of others; where we develop the skills of self-government as well as the habit of governing ourselves and learn to serve others—not just self."[16]

Proposals for restoring community invariably provoke controversy. Some propose reforms in the electoral and policy-making processes; others blame the problem of community on past reforms. Some blame the new communicative technologies for the fragmentation of communities; others envision solutions made possible by the "information age." Some credit progressive or multicultural education with fostering community; others view such programs as the root of the problem. Hence arises a dilemma that seemingly defies resolution: the very fragmentation that concerns us precludes consensus about solutions.

Studying the rhetoric of community does not resolve the dilemma, but it does at least map some of the discursive routes toward rebuilding community. If the problem of fragmented communities is to be solved, we must first understand how communities are unified or fragmented by rhetorical discourse. Only then can we begin to suggest new, more constructive methods of conflict resolution, public deliberation, and problem solving. Only then can we begin to forge a new public agreement about *how* to disagree.

Notes

1. James Davison Hunter, *Culture Wars: The Struggle to Define America* (New York: Basic Books, 1991), 296, 318.

2. Ibid., 320–21. Hunter identifies the courtroom as the "other chief environment" of contemporary public discourse, and it likewise is structurally not conducive to deliberation and problem solving. It is unfortunate that so many Americans turn to the courts as a "first step" in attempting to resolve conflicts, according to Hunter, since "attorneys . . . are paid to win, not to do what is right."

3. Ibid., 321–22.

4. Ibid., 322.

5. Ibid., 322–25.

6. Ibid., 325.

7. For a summary of electoral reform proposals, see Stephen J. Wayne, *The Road to the White House: The Politics of Presidential Elections*, 3d ed. (New York: St. Martin's Press, 1988), 275–97. See also W. Lance Bennett, *The Governing Crisis: Media, Money, and Marketing in American Elections* (New York: St. Martin's Press, 1992), 201–18.

8. See William Crotty, *Political Reform and the American Experiment* (New York: Thomas Y. Crowell, 1977).

9. Neil Postman, *Amusing Ourselves to Death: Public Discourse in the Age of Show Business* (New York: Penguin Books, 1986), 9, 16.

10. See, for example, Timothy W. Luke, *Screens of Power: Ideology, Domination, and Resistance in Informational Society* (Urbana: University of Illinois Press, 1989).

11. See, for example, Jerry Mander, *Four Arguments for the Elimination of Television* (New York: William Morrow, 1978).

12. Ben H. Bagdikian, *The Information Machines: Their Impact on Men and the Media* (New York: Harper Colophon, 1971), 303.

13. Kathleen Hall Jamieson, *Eloquence in an Electronic Age: The Transformation of Political Speechmaking* (New York: Oxford University Press, 1988), 250–53.

14. Ibid., 250, 253.

15. Postman, *Amusing Ourselves to Death*, 162–63.

16. "The Responsive Communitarian Platform: Rights and Responsibilities," in *The Spirit of Community: Rights, Responsibilities, and the Communitarian Agenda*, ed. Amitai Etzioni (New York: Crown Publishers, 1993), 253–54.

Contributors

James Arnt Aune is associate professor of speech communication at Texas A&M University. His research focuses on rhetorical theory, legal rhetoric, and the philosophy of communication. He is the author of *Rhetoric and Marxism*, and his essays have appeared in *Hasting's Constitutional Law Quarterly, Quarterly Journal of Speech, Communication Studies,* and *Argumentation and Advocacy.*

Thomas W. Benson is the Edwin Erle Sparks Professor of rhetoric at the Pennsylvania State University. He is former editor of the *Quarterly Journal of Speech* and *Communication Quarterly* and author or editor of *Readings in Classical Rhetoric, Rhetorical Dimensions in Media, Speech Communication in the Twentieth Century, Reality Fictions: The Films of Frederick Wiseman, American Rhetoric: Context and Criticism, Landmark Essays on Rhetorical Criticism, Rhetoric and Political Culture in Nineteenth-Century America,* and other works.

Stephen H. Browne is associate professor of speech communication at the Pennsylvania State University. His areas of teaching and research include American reform rhetoric, rhetorical theory, and textual interpretation. He is coeditor of *Philosophy and Rhetoric* and author of *Edmund Burke and the Discourse of Virtue.*

Karlyn Kohrs Campbell is professor of speech communication at the University of Minnesota. She is the author or editor of many books, including the two-volume *Man Cannot Speak for Her,* two volumes of *Women Public Speakers in the United States,* and *Shadowboxing with Stereotypes: The President, the Press, and the Candidates' Wives.* She is coauthor (with Kathleen Hall Jamieson) of *Form and Genre: Shaping Rhetorical Action* and *Deeds Done in Words: Presidential Rhetoric and the Genre of Governance.* She has won many awards for her work, including the Speech Communication Association's Distinguished Scholar Award and the Winans-Wichelns Award.

Ronald H. Carpenter is professor of English at the University of Florida. His publications include *The Eloquence of Frederick Jackson Turner, History as Rhetoric: Style, Narrative, and Persuasion,* and numerous book chapters and essays in journals such as *Communication Monographs, Quarterly Journal of Speech,* and *Presidential Studies Quarterly.* He has been recognized by *Communication Education* as among the most prolific scholars in communication studies, and he has won the Speech Communication Association's Golden Anniversary Monograph Award.

Celeste M. Condit is professor of speech communication at the University of Georgia. Her work focuses on the role of rhetoric in social change. She is the author of *Decoding Abortion Rhetoric,* which received the University of Georgia's Creative Research Medal, and coauthor (with John Louis Lucaites) of *Crafting Equality.* She also coedited (with Roxanne Parrott) *Evaluating Women's Health Messages,* and she has published approximately fifty scholarly essays.

James Darsey is assistant professor of communication at Northern Illinois University. His analyses of American public address focus on the rhetoric of marginalized groups. He is the author of *The Prophetic Tradition and Radical Rhetoric in America.*

April M. Greer is a graduate student in the Department of Speech Communication at the University of Georgia.

Bruce E. Gronbeck is the A. Craig Baird Distinguished Professor of public address, Department of Communication Studies, University of Iowa. He specializes in rhetorical and media studies, with particular interest in American politics in the electronic age. His edited books include *Media, Consciousness, and Culture: Explorations of Walter Ong's Thought; Presidential Campaigns and American Self-Images;* and *Critical Approaches to Television.* He has been a Fulbright lecturer in Sweden, Finland, Italy, and Slovenia.

Roderick P. Hart is the F. A. Liddell Professor of communication and professor of government at the University of Texas at Austin. He is the author of *Public Communication, The Political Pulpit, Verbal Style and the Presidency, the Sound of Leadership, Modern Rhetorical Criticism,* and *Seducing America: How Television Charms the Modern Voter.* A former Woodrow Wilson fellow, Hart recently has been named a research fellow of the International Communication Association and a Distinguished Scholar by the Speech Communication Association.

J. Michael Hogan is professor of speech communication at the Pennsylvania State University. He is the author of *The Panama Canal in American Politics* and *The Nuclear Freeze Campaign.* His essays have appeared in many journals, including the *Quarterly Journal of Speech, Communication Monographs, Presidential Studies Quarterly,* and *Public Opinion Quarterly.* He has received both the Winans-Wichelns Award and the Golden Anniversary Prize Book Award from the Speech Communication Association.

James Jasinski is assistant professor of communication and theatre arts at the University of Puget Sound. His work on early American public address and rhetorical criticism has appeared in the *Quarterly Journal of Speech* and other scholarly journals.

John Lyne is professor of communication at the University of Pittsburgh. He is the former chair of the Department of Communication Studies at the University of Iowa and general editor of the University of Wisconsin Press series "The Rhetoric of the Human Sciences." He is a former R. K. Mellon Visiting Fellow at the Center for Philosophy of Science, University of Pittsburgh. His work focuses on the relationships among rhetoric, philosophy, and science.

Martin J. Medhurst is professor and associate head of speech communication at Texas A&M University, where he also coordinates the Program in Presidential Rhetoric in the George Bush School of Government and Public Service. He is the author or editor of seven books, including *Beyond the Rhetorical Presidency, Eisenhower's War of Words: Rhetoric and Leadership,* and *Dwight D. Eisenhower: Strategic Communicator.* His work has appeared in many journals, including *Quarterly Journal of Speech, Communication Monographs,* and *Armed Forces Society.*

Michael Osborn is professor emeritus at the University of Memphis. He has received both the Golden Anniversary Prize Monograph Award and the Douglas Ehninger Distinguished Rhetorical Scholar Award from the Speech Communication Association, and in 1990 he received the Distinguished Research Award from the University of Memphis. A former president of the Speech Communication Association and of the Southern States Communication Association, he presently serves on the Tennessee Humanities Council and the Decatur County Economic Development Board.

Charles Alan Taylor is associate professor in the Department of Communications, Drury College. His research on the rhetorics of science and inquiry has appeared in the *Quarterly Journal of Speech, Communication Monographs, Critical Studies in Mass Communication,* and *Technical Communication Quarterly.* He is the author of *Defending Science: A Rhetoric of Demarcation.*

Martha Watson is professor of communications and dean of the Greenspan College of Urban Affairs at the University of Nevada, Las Vegas. She is former editor of the *Southern States Communication Journal* and the *Quarterly Journal of Speech.* Her publications include critical biographies of Emma Goldman and Anna Howard Shaw (with Wil Linkugel). She is the editor of *A Voice of Their Own: The Woman Suffrage Press, 1840–1910* and the author of *Lives of Their Own: Rhetorical Dimensions in the Autobiographies of Women Activists.*

David Zarefsky is professor of communication studies and dean of the School of Speech at Northwestern University. He is the author of *President Johnson's War on Poverty: Rhetoric and History* and *Lincoln, Douglas, and Slavery: In the Crucible of Public Debate.* A past president of the Speech Communication Association, he also received the organization's Winans-Wichelns and Distinguished Scholar Awards.

Index